A
PATTERN
FOR
HISTORY

A
PATTERN
FOR
HISTORY

Arthur R. M. Lower

McClelland and Stewart

ISBN: 0-7710-5374-6

McClelland and Stewart Limited,
The Canadian Publishers,
25 Hollinger Road,
Toronto, Ontario.
M4B 3G2

Printed and bound in Canada.

Canadian Cataloguing in Publication Data

Lower, Arthur R.M., 1889-
  A pattern for history

Includes index.
ISBN 0-7710-5374-6

1. History - Philosophy. I. Title.

D16.8.L62   901   C78-001272-0

By very nature it is a labyrinth and chaos, this that we call human history; an abatis of trees and brushwood, a world-wide jungle at once growing and dying. Under the green foliage and blossoming fruit trees of Today, there lie, rotting slower or faster, the forests of all other Years and Days. Some have rotten fast, plants of annual growth, and are long since quite gone to inorganic mould; others are like the aloe, growths that last a thousand or three thousand years. You will find them in all stages of decay and preservation; deep down to the beginnings of the History of Man. Think where our Alphabetical Letters came from, where our speech itself came from; the Cookeries we live by, the Masonries we lodge under! . . . The tap roots of them are with Father Adam himself and the cinders of Eve's first fire! At bottom, there is no perfect History; there is none such conceivable.[1]

1. Thomas Carlyle, *Oliver Cromwell's Letters and Speeches,* Vol. 1 (New York Edition of 1885,) p. 20.

Acknowledgements

I express my appreciation to colleagues with whom I have discussed various topics pertinent to this book and in particular to W. E. C. Harrison, with whom I used to talk over the subjects on which I built the seminars in Queen's University that expanded and systematized them. The historical thinking of my colleague James Leith and of Alan Gowans of the University of Victoria also parallels my own. I wish especially to thank Mr. S. R. Blair, President of the Alberta Gas Trunk Line and his company for the subvention which has made publication possible. My deep appreciation goes to my former student, Marshall Crowe, at present Chairman of the National Energy Board, for his continuing interest in my book and for having brought Mr. Blair and myself together. The officers of McClelland and Stewart have been courteous and helpful.

And I would like to voice publicly here the feelings that friends have often told me should have been reflected in my Autobiography and say how much I have owed throughout life both by way of direct assistance and indirect inspiration to the dearest and sweetest little companion man could ever have had, my late wife Evelyn.

Arthur R. M. Lower
June, 1978.

Contents

Introduction

"We live in a period of revolutionary change." The *cliché* confronts us everywhere. Revolutionary change is necessarily of pressing concern to each and every member of society. In such periods, familiar landmarks are swept away, new situations must be confronted, old habits of life discarded. Personal fortunes may melt away. New people with new and unfamiliar ideas and strange appearance are seen in the streets. Even the old familiar objects of life found customarily in the shops, may no longer be obtainable. Styles in dress and personal appearance change. The language changes, with new and unfamiliar terms being heard on many lips and seen in the printed word. The manners of social intercourse change. Deepest of all, the minds of men change: old beliefs and allegiances are discarded, new ones, to which a prerevolutionary generation accustoms itself with extreme difficulty, make their appearance and their propagators press for, often demand, allegiance to them. Happy the land that can come through a revolutionary period with its institutions more or less intact and without blood.

Since we are living in a revolutionary age we shall meet its challenges more easily if we understand it, and to understand it, a certain amount of historical perspective is necessary. These pages essay the task of portraying a valid historical perspective. They are not a close history of a particular period or of a given sequence of events. Rather, they are an attempt to scrutinize a considerable section of history, nothing less than "Western civilization" during two millennia or more, with a view to determining whether long trends are to be found in it. This is not to proffer

13

a cure for our ills. The course of man's affairs is far too complex, the human situation too immense, for any kind of patent "cure."

Why then write about things that cannot be much influenced by the writing? Why write about anything? Why try to do anything about anything? Thinking that only calls for immediate action is short-sighted, and the way in which long-term thinking has "paid off" has often been demonstrated. This has happened most conspicuously in the area of science, but the historian and student of man and affairs has also contributed his share. To give an example: in 1947 the British withdrew peaceably fom India, abandoning an empire they had held for nearly two centuries. There was a time, not so long ago, when almost certainly they would have fought to retain their hold on India, with consequences only too easy to imagine. Some results of withdrawal were that British trade with India increased, the number of Britishers living in India increased and relationships ensued of an amicable nature. Humanity may not learn much from its experience but it occasionally learns something and this British decision to withdraw was one thing, and a big thing, that was learned. It was not a decision suddenly arrived at: it had been debated over the years, and in the course of the debate, the history of British-India relationships had been intensively explored. The study of history had proved practical and useful. Surely no greater commendation need be sought.

If I have established a justification for writing about a lengthy period of history, let me tell what such an examination could be expected to produce. I use a simile that I have often used in other places.

The human race may be likened to a ship with its crew and passengers. The ship is well on its way and accurate accounts have been kept of its course by dead reckoning, that is, a compass course which calculates direction and speed to determine the position on the chart. But the ship's officers can never get what sailors call a "fix": that is a landfall or an astronomical reckoning of the ship's exact position. Unfortunately, too, they know only the course she has followed, not what course she should follow. They go on blindly, reckoning that it will be best to keep the same course as before, altering it, naturally if an iceberg appears in the way.

The study of history is the ship's course. The decision to maintain the course already followed, with only necessary alterations, will do for the conduct of human affairs. We can see an iceberg ahead, but we cannot see the end of the voyage. Surely, however, it is the wise assumption that the course ahead will be more or less like the one already followed. In this simile, we have history and its bearing on the future. My claim is that a wise inspection of history gives a certain vision of the future. Is this turning the historian into a seer or a soothsayer? I do not think so. Attempts to foretell the future are made every day: a breed, indeed, has grown up which claims to be scientific and which calls itself "futurologists." I would claim the right of the careful historian also to make some cautious extrapolations on the graph of human affairs, and that is the purpose of this writing.

Extrapolation, reasonable forecasting, is not much in favour with the gild of historians, who go in for the minute examination of short periods and armour their studies with prodigious arrays of footnotes. "Academic historians are liable to look askance at writing based more upon a general grasp of the evolution of European attitudes of mind than upon familiarity with the minutiae of research . . ."[1] I did much of this detailed close-up investigation myself in my younger days, but it seems to me that as a historian grows old his tasks of minute exploration should be finished and he should be able to take wider views. This will not increase his popularity with his junior colleagues, who, as the above quotation indicates, may remind him that his approach is "out of date." If so, so be it. My conviction is that if, by carefully restricting himself, one historian is not prepared to allow himself to be shot at, then he should not object to another putting himself in that position. I cannot shake off the belief that a historian must be something of a prophet. Hence these pages. I must leave it to others to decide how successful I have been in the role and how correctly I have used the historical material at my command.

In the generation after the First World War, there was much concern with getting a view of mankind as a whole, one that would transcend local differences and reveal the more general aspects of man. The political reflection of this concern lay in the first world institution, the League of Nations. In the realm of letters, writers such as H.G. Wells wrote histories of the world, and the historical-encyclopaedic giants Oswald Spengler and Arnold Toynbee expounded their ideas of what mankind's history had been about and of the "laws" under which it operated. Persons who wrote history in those days of dawning universalism perhaps were not under the same temptation to confine themselves to the local and the specific as was the generation that was to succeed them.

The writers who flourished between the two wars were rapidly passing off the stage in the 1960s, and by the 1970s, they had virtually disappeared. Those who succeeded them were more caught up in the specific. Since their world was in a revolutionary situation and the essence of revolution lies in the attempt to build anew, attention to the task was hardly surprising. Moreover, apart from the circumstances of the day in any age, when it comes to looking at what has gone by, everyone who has faced youth knows how difficult it is to interest young people in much beyond the moment. Not only young people, but nearly everyone. "Let the dead past bury its dead" is a line of verse whose validity lies in the nature of existence.

In the New World, it is especially hard to arouse interest in our distant past, for little of it is visible. The contrast with Europe needs no elaboration. Sheer space accentuates the problem.

Yet modern communications bring everyone closer and closer to-gether, so that, whether we like it or not, the consciousness of "one world" increases, and interest in other worlds that once existed perhaps must diminish. Such a situation by no means indicates the approaching end to concern with history, for man can never wholly forget his past. Paradoxically, as the past of the local area, nation, city, even continent, lessens in importance and the view of the world as a unit strengthens, the more both the local area and its past seem to be cherished. This is possibly nostalgia but it may also reflect the dry-as-dust material served up today by the average professional historian. As a correspondent, an instructor of youth, puts it

> The present generation of historians have chosen to turn their backs on the question whether history has any meaning and to occupy them-selves with the techniques of their craft, with the result that while the profession has never been more efficient, it has never had less to say . . . As the business model has come to dominate society, so the scientific model has come to dominate the academic community. To judge from the complaints of my students what it adds up to is an experience of particulars without an over-view. There is as I see it, a generation gap between the historian's guild and youth . . .

If this last sentence reflects the situation, then history as a living art and not a dead discipline has some prospect of a future.

The current interest in popular anthropology, much of which specu-lates on the origins of man, his nature and character, indicates what in any case is obvious, that man will always be interested in man and the trail he has left behind him.

Of late years, the concept *one world* may have crowded attention to the historic divisions in the human race to the back of the stage. Former generations divided man up simply, seizing on the visible differences between groups. This easy method of classification is no longer much employed. Rather, differences of a less purely biological nature have replaced it and we tend to speak of *cultures* – the culture of the Western world, the culture of the Orient, and so on. A *culture* corresponds, with some irregularity, to the similar conception of "way of life."

Contemplating the rise and also the decline of those great anthropologi-cal artifacts, cultures, many a man has tried to find some key that would unlock their secret. At the close of his *Decline and Fall of the Roman Empire,* Edward Gibbon, as all his readers know, announced that he had found *the key* to the history of the classical world and its Byzantine successor: "I have narrated," he said, "the triumph of barbarism and religion." Georg Hegel, the nineteenth century German philosopher, went still farther. He supplied *the key* to all history. Time rolled by in an orderly succession from thesis to antithesis to synthesis, and there you had it! A formula for ordering time! Karl Marx, propounded his formula and rewrote history in accordance with it. Feudalism gave way to bourgeoism, or capitalism, and bourgeoism to proletarianism. At that point the state "withered away" and the reign of equality, justice and truth set in, apparently to last forever. Oswald Spengler, another German not unduly modest, announced that he, too, had found *the key* to the whole historical process. In his book *The Decline of the West* (1918), he maintains that *cultures* arise, develop their own unique approach to things, exhaust their possibilities, then slowly decline. No sooner was Spengler more or less out of the way than, in an even more monumental effort, Arnold Toynbee produced his "key." In thirteen volumes he showed that history was all a matter of "challenge and response": a culture of some magnitude arises when the degree of challenge thrown out to those affected by it prompts an adequate response. Each of the distinct civilizations that history has known is an entity itself, has beginning, development and end. If others come in the future, they will run similar courses.

But man, the most complex of mammals, puts everyone off the trail. Many scholars and writers simply throw up their hands and proclaim that no *key* can be found to the totality of history. They come close to the Shakespearean verdict – Life's "but a tale told by an idiot, full of sound and fury, signifying nothing." It is hard to accept that. Man's story, people struggle to believe, is more than blind chance.

We live in the media of time and space. In our relations with time and space, chance plays its part. But so does order. Order represents human will and human foresight. History is both chaotic and orderly. Such a statement made, there walks on to the stage the leader. His stage may be small or it may be huge, but whichever it is, he has a great part in determining the nature of the play. We do not need to go all the way with Thomas Carlyle and see in history little else but the "hero" but we can go a considerable way and still bear in mind that there are great areas of life and action in which we seem the helpless pawns of fate.

World cultures provide plenty of illustrations for both elements, chance and order. It was surely chance which, on two celebrated occasions, a century apart, 1588 and 1688, caused the wind to blow in exactly the right direction to enable England to triumph over Spain and William of Orange to land his army at Torbay. Some people would say it was "the hand of Providence," which is what Arabs must be saying about the chance that put lakes of oil under their otherwise useless desert sands. For order, illustrations are equally easy to find: that beautifully symmetrical structure, the American Constitution, which has served the United States so well, was not put together by hit and miss but by thoughtful, well informed men quite conscious that there were engaged on a job of construction that could order the future. History is a mixture of chance and will, of chaos and order.

In the mixture, it is impossible to fail to observe the huge place of certain individuals. We may, if we please, along with Carlyle call such men "heroes." Some world cultures seem, indeed, to rest on the shoulders of a single man, as Chinese culture formerly on the shoulders of Confucius and the Buddhist way of life on those of Gautama Buddha. In like manner, Christianity is the way of life ascribed to Jesus of Nazareth, Mohammedanism that of Mohammed, Protestantism that of Martin Luther and Communism that of its founder, Karl Marx.

All these men founded religions or new versions of old religions. There is nothing strange about that, for leadership however manifested, necessarily gives rise to a cult. If the cult be shallow, it probably dies with its leader: what is left of Bonapartism or of Hitlerism today? But shallow or deep, men *believe* in their leader and readily ascribe to him powers and allow him privileges which ordinary mortals may not share. Each founder becomes a kind of god. The range of rank in *godship* is enormous. In the largest examples, such as those given above, the great religions, the leaders are elevated beyond the heaven-storming heights of Everest. Naturally they remain in men's minds as founders, prophets, gods.

> Every human structure has its source in and is energized by a theology or religion. Therefore, political and social orders are largely shaped by man's basic beliefs . . . It makes no sense to deny that we have a theology or a religion, as the Communists do. Everybody has a religion, something that he believes in, even if it is only himself . . .

Who is to assess the dimensions of the great world religions in the human scheme of things? The great men who rest at their bases gave rise to ways of life that endure over the centuries and shape the nature and fate of untold millions of men. No doubt if they are looked at closely, the examiner's eroding eye reduces their rank and stature. Only the semi-historical figure Jesus seems safe, and he, we take as we find him in the only authority to come down to us, the New Testament. Mohammed we know much about. He has long been humanized, with all of man's short-comings, but his prestige remains. Luther is no hero in St. Peter's. Karl Marx exists in his writings: as a man, except to the initiates, he is of no great consequence. As a founder it may well be that Lenin will bulk larger than Marx, just as in founding Christianity, St. Paul, that other interloper, probably bulked larger than Jesus.

I call the present effort *A Pattern for History* and the title requires me first of all to take brief glances at the great world cultures that lie close to our own, Judaism, the classical world and that one which has cradled our own, Christianity. Next, it requires some scrutiny of European history as a whole during the last two millennia. It seems to me that such a scrutiny will establish "a pattern for history." It will be a partial and irregular pattern and hard to trace and it will leave much historical material not woven in. Such an attempt will require the reader to beware of the microscope and get used to looking at the panoramic scene. Many a professional historian may have little regard for such an attempt. *But may I ask such persons if their microscopic studies do not add up to a general intelligible view, do they add up to anything at all?*

My suggestion is, and it finds some support in man's psychology, that an historical cycle originates in an impulse that begins in emotion and conviction, that both emotion and conviction come to be toned down by intellectual processes to ratiocination, to "ages of reason" and that when men are sufficiently intellectualized, their society, becoming freer and freer, begins to edge into anarchy (That seems to be the point at which we stand today). Then, after a period of anarchy, perhaps chaos, order asserts itself, sometimes sternly, and a new cycle begins.

What follows, along with the preliminary inspections of world cultures, is intended to illustrate my thesis. Logically it should include an examination of all the great cultures, but practical considerations and the limitations of my personal knowledge confine the examination to the West.

The magnitude of the revolutionary changes of our times calls for all the careful thought that can be bestowed upon it. The disappearance of old empires and the rise of new, the upheaval in our deepest beliefs caused by the scientific view of the world and its supersession of the old, semi-mystical attitudes embodied in traditional lifestyles, the resulting abandonment of the oldest and most cherished types of behaviour – the list could be extended indefinitely. It all, it may be argued, began long ago. Of course. History has no beginning and no end. But if we can get even a small hint of "the course of the ship," will it not be helpful?

Notes

1. From review by M. J. Sydenham of Christopher Dawson, *The Gods of Revolution* in *Canadian Historical Review*, Dec. 1973, p. 434.

CHAPTER ONE

"The Spirit of
the Age"

I

"The Spirit of the Age"

Writing history is something like describing the weather. The world is large, the winds blow, the clouds drift. Putting it all together into an ordered picture, even if he gets reports from outer space, is often too much for the meteorologist. He tabulates the data that come in to him and he is able to give a reasonable account of what has happened over fairly large areas. He can also predict what will likely happen, but only for short periods ahead. He can, however, always describe and predict in a general way the major phases of the weather, the seasons and to a limited degree, the months.

Today the meteorologist can write the history of climate fairly accurately, though he could not tell us anything about February 1, in 10,000 B.C. The historian is in much the same position: the farther he goes back into the past, the more he is confined to the big general points; the closer he comes to his own day, the more heavily do all the infinite details press in upon him. Like the weatherman, the historian is chary of prediction, though prediction it is that the general public wants from both of them.

The historian is not so much interested in the history of climate as in the climate of history, and this is an interest he shares with most of mankind. Everybody knows that "times change." Nothing attracts attention more readily than pictures of yesterday. Everybody likes to dress up in the clothes of former days.

The large historical "seasons" are conventionally dubbed "ancient," "mediaeval," "modern." There are also many smaller divisions more or less plainly marked out. Little is more conspicuous in history than the differences in "ages," "epochs," "periods," or, (as we get closer to ourselves) "the times." What commoner phrases are there than "olden times," "modern times," and "the future"?

Some trends in history, especially those arising out of geographical situations, are of great length. The ground swells, in some cases, may run on for centuries. Two good examples come readily to mind: (1) The idea that refuses to die, of European unity, which can be traced from Roman days to our own, Charlemagne, the Holy Roman Empire, the Mediaeval Papacy, Napoleon, the Concert of Europe, "the Powers," the League of Nations, the United Nations, NATO, the Common Market, all these terms turn on the same idea, the dream of unity, compounded of yearnings for peace and love of power. (2) The attempts, traceable from the twelfth century, to determine the outcome of the struggle between the French and the English monarchies by securing alliance with the countries along the courses of the lower Rhine and the Scheldt – the "Low Countries." This three-cornered situation is plain at every point: Henry II *versus* Louis VII, John *versus* Philip Augustus, Edward I *versus* Philip the Fair, Edward III *versus* Charles V, the Rise of Burgundy, the Tudor idea of "Keeping the French out of Flanders," the Peace of Utrecht, the Declaration of War in 1793, the creation of the Kingdom of Holland, 1815, the neutrality of Belgium, 1830. With Germany substituted for France, the First World War and the invasion of Belgium, the Second War and the Channel ports, became an altered version of the older rivalry.[1]

In shorter or lesser sequences, the same transcendence of the individual human experience may be found – for example, the canalization of the St. Lawrence, dreams about which began in the late eighteenth century but were only realized in the late 1950s. The union of England and Scotland, culmination of centuries of effort *pro* and *con,* gives another example.

These continuities are naturally most visible in geographical situations. But they come up even in the most non-material. The unremitting submerged warfare of the Middle Ages against clerical and papal pretensions, taking the forms of somewhat blind heretical movements, merge with the Reformation. After much the same underground courses, ideas of equality wind up in modern socialistic doctrines. The idea of responsible ministers, naturally very vaguely put, appears in English history from the thirteenth century on. The longest-range situation of all is the Near East: the struggle over Palestine, though often dormant for centuries, has rested on much the same underpinning since the days of ancient Egypt.

It is invariably possible to direct a penetrating ray into this particular time sequence or that. By such a method it is that most of our exact, detailed knowledge of the past has been built up. The lifetimes of patient effort that have gone into establishing what today is taken for granted, an exact chronology, illustrate this "coral island" factor in building history. A good many years ago, elaborate research established that the usually accepted date for the accession of Richard I was three days out. The discovery aroused a mild degree of excitement among mediaevalists.

Of the various "ages," there are innumerable descriptions. There are literally libraries of books on *feudalism* in one or other of its aspects. There is an equal number on the *Renaissance* and on *Victorianism*. We have little difficulty in describing, more or less adequately, these many subdivisions of the traditional primary division, "ancient, mediaeval and modern." But how does it come about that one such age passes into another? The fact of change is inescapable and comes under everyone's observation. Things – and people – become "old fashioned." They are cast aside, both things and people, as worn out, no longer of use or interest. As Alan Gowans' questions so clearly frame it:

> What is the origin of the successive waves of ideas and attitudes that seem to dominate thought and shape institutions universally one after another, age through age? Why has a given set of assumptions seemed self-evidently right and unquestionable to one generation of men all over the world but foolish and reprehensible to the next, time after time, throughout history? If this pattern is universal, does it have a universal cause?[2]

"Everything moves at once." Every phase of life affects every other phase, no matter how dissimilar. It is, for example, misleading to survey "Victorian literature" without surveying Victorian politics, science, art, manners, economics, and so on. This gets recognition in a general way. But there is always peril in concentrating too intensely on one thread in human affairs when it is the whole cable of many strands that has to be accounted for.

The *ages* may be long or short, decidedly or lightly marked. Nothing was more marked than nineteenth century Puritanism, more especially, but not exclusively, in the English-speaking world – what was commonly called *Victorianism*. It penetrated every nook and cranny of life. While traces of it still remain, for practical purposes it is gone, along with the "frills and furbelows," the crinolines of its women, the "stove pipe" hats of its men. In like manner, perhaps right from the beginning of history, certainly from the beginning of European history, one age gives way to the next, sometimes "leaving not a wrack behind." How explain *change?*

A record of, let us say, Beethoven's Fourth Symphony is being played. As the beautiful music goes on, the thought comes, "How extraordinary it is that in the last quarter of the twentieth century, sitting surrounded by all the advantages of an advanced technical society, one may yet almost turn time backward and hear the early nineteenth century speaking to him through one of the greatest of its masters." Beethoven spoke early in the last age. But his predecessors from an age previous to his could have been heard, too. And books could have been pulled down from library shelves and through the printed page, still earlier voices have been heard: earlier and earlier voices back into the remote depths, all of them summoned and speaking to us, if we wished it, right in our own living rooms.

The experience and the opportunity is so common that few think twice about it. But try to go back through the centuries imagining what men have had at their command in this way. The farther we go back, the less and less bountifully the table is spread. How could even a Beethoven have given us any light on the music of Brahms? It is one among the greatest of human delights and privileges to be able vicariously to live in the different ages of man. It is a privilege of which only the few can avail themselves, and all of them, however they describe themselves, must be, in a measure, historians, for this supreme experience, this never-ending, never-exhausted table of delight, the panorama of the successive changing ages of man, is reserved for those who by application and imagination are competent to take a place at it.

II
Change

One approach to explaining change, lies through evolutionary concepts. In human affairs, it is surely possible to trace logical lines of sequence. Human affairs in the large, and to a considerable extent, in the small, seem to go through a threefold stage, evolutionary in nature and with considerable logic about them. The first stage is marked by the build-up of energy or emotion that generates zeal. This may well derive from a sense of physical well-being, thus giving support for those who believe in economic determinism. Ages of zeal are ages of conviction. When men bend all their energies to accomplishing the task in hand, whether it is small or large, other considerations go by the board. The conquest of North America by the pioneer affords apt illustration. The great ages of accomplishment, which are also the great ages of faith, religious or otherwise, are not noted for their urbanity. They tend to be crude in manners, crude in thought, crude in behaviour. They are masculine ages, and if women are prominent in them, they are the type that has many masculine traits about it; able to take care of themselves in the hurly-burly along with the men – an Eleanor of Aquitaine, a Catherine of Russia, an Elizabeth of England, none of them shrinking violets. Add to the queens the pioneer women of North America, still plainly visible in the Amazons of the American Middle West, deep-voiced, sturdy women, women of massive physique who in pioneer days could handle a rifle with any man.

North America, indeed, affords a good, clear example of the way in which "civilization" creeps upon the young, vigorous society-in-the-making. Quickly, once the axe of the pioneer has provided shelter and his plough food, the voice of the schoolmaster becomes heard in the land. The pioneer preacher does his large share. Technical contrivances of all sorts find their way into every prairie sod hut. The pioneer woman persuades her husband to buy a sewing machine or a new house with inside toilet. Good manners are slowly accepted as not mere effeminacy. Pioneer energy does not disappear but it is curbed.

This evolution of a code of manners might do as an index of the growth of a culture. From the informalities of the early stages of social existence to the guarded approaches to a president or, still more, to the rigidly mannered conduct of royalty and its peripherals in the great days of royalty, the route lies unbroken, as the etymology of words strongly illustrates – from *heathen,* people who live on "the heath," from *pagani,* country dwellers, to the people who dwell together in the *civitas,* the city, who are *polite, civilized, urbane, in urbe,* in a city.[3]

When mannered habits of life break down, it may be a sign that a particular civilization is drawing to a close. It is tempting to point to the disorder of our times. But we must constantly remember how hard it is to decide what is the main current and what is merely an eddy. To many a Florentine the gloomy days of Savonarola must have seemed the end of his city's glory, but Florence survived to mother many a famous son. So, too, the fires in the burning American cities of the early 1970s were put out and possibly not even Detroit, with its two murders a day, was doomed. It is always wise to remember Adam Smith's cautious Scottish saying that "there is a great deal of ruin in a nation." However it may be viewed, the period between the disintegration of one culture and the formation of another – in one of which period we are at present – is trying and unpleasant. Old dreams end, new ones do not yet have form and substance. It is comparable to youth facing life for the first time "on its own."

In the evolving society, energy or emotion or zeal – perhaps the term applied to this deep-down experience does not need to be too exact (the word faith would also fit in) – gradually cools. Like the individual, the sequence ages. The drive of the Crusades lessens. The Russian Revolution passes its best days.

As enthusiasm cools, intellectual forces begin to operate. Rationalism overrides raw energy or emotion and erodes the original thrust. Few today would be silly enough to shout out Calvin Coolidge's ringing Philistine declaration of 1924 – itself drawn from the currents of the previous century – that "The United States' business is business." "Systems" of philosophy and theology dissect and codify faith.[4] Issues that had once seemed simple become complex. Matters of right and wrong become "questions for discussion." Uncertainty arises where certainty once prevailed. Action becomes more restrained and eventually enfeebled. It becomes "sicklied o'er with the pale cast of thought."

"Thought" has many aspects, but the contrast between the behaviour of the man of thought as a type and the simpler person of direct action is plain. It is the pale cast of thought which disintegrates empires, as the British Empire was disintegrated in the middle of the twentieth century: General Dyer at Amritsar in 1924 was the last Englishman who shot first and thought afterward. In 1947, the British thought first: there was no shooting and India received its independence.

Accompanying the shift into intellectualism, there arises aesthetic concern. The shift predicates increasing leisure and specialized groups concerning themselves with what man can do in his spare time, notably, with the arts. The artistic sense is such an old story, in human affairs that it is necessary to avoid dogmatism in respect to its appearance in society. After all, prehistoric European caves are full of excellent art. In the art of historic times, the relationship between aesthetic interest and the stage or state of society is close. In a society close to the pioneer stage, a society puritan and rigorous, because of the drive of accomplishment, as millions of New World people can testify, far away from the average man's concern were matters of aesthetic interest. They were not absent, but they were elementary and usually looked upon with contempt: they were "all right for the women." Aesthetic concern arrives when a certain degree of self-consciousness has been reached, when people feel that they are here to stay, so to speak: when the fury of construction has died down a little, but before society becomes *blasé*.

The intellectualizing and aestheticizing (to use barbarous words) of situations, impulses and modes of thought sooner or later allows the *laissez-faire* concept to become, first, acceptable and, later, prevalent. A good illustration is afforded by the way in which that tight, God-ordered community, the Puritan colony of Massachusetts gradually opened up to individualism (in both religion and business). "Let everybody make up his own mind" becomes easily enough, "let everyone do as he likes." The relationship of a free society to anarchy is direct. Whether we should abandon our devotion to a free society in order to escape anarchy introduces another factor, that of free will. It may be that an age can influence its destiny and avoid abysses by its collective intelligence. Since genuinely free societies are rare in history, that is still something to be proved. It is, however, consoling to point to the long history of free, or more or less free, institutions which it has been the privilege of the English-speaking world to inherit. The age-old striving for freedom which registered itself in institutions has not yet lost all its virtue. A society may go a long distance on the road to anarchy without actually becoming anarchic if it does not lose its institutions.

A few fortunate situations in history have permitted of the possibility of many people "doing just as they liked," but the condition for such freedom is spacious environment. The outstanding examples are of course from the New World, more particularly, the United States. Yet the United States never lost its historic heritage of institutions and consequently its society, however disorderly at times, has never been anarchic.

Self-will, however, can go so far that an anarchic society may result. Then, as Thomas Hobbes said "clubs become trumps." If actual anarchic conditions appear, as in England during the Wars of the Roses, the wheel may turn full circle, and order be restored at the price of freedom, at which point the cycle can begin again. When a collectivity is struggling for coherence, the situation is necessarily charged with emotion and calls not for debate, but for a rally, a falling-in-line.

III
The Threefold Evolution

The three-stage evolution from zeal to intellect to disorder can be followed through various periods of history, though with some difficulty. It is never neat. There are always loose ends, much overlapping and also failures in chronological precision. But that is what we must expect in human affairs. The sequence helps greatly in looking at long periods. It is closely related to the idea of logical evolution. Logical evolution is a notion that has always been near the surface of human mentality. Beginnings, middles, ends. Youth, maturity, age. Sunrise, noon, sunset. Creation, existence, day of judgement. History and thought are full of such contrasting phrases. They each contain a distinctly evolutionary concept.

Many of the simple processes of daily life portray the idea. Technical development affords the clearest illustration. It is especially plain in the field of communications. Within about a generation (1820-1855), the older types of ship were pushed aside by the clipper ship as hulls got larger and finer, masts taller, sails larger. *Cutty Sarks* and *Flying Clouds* made the voyage from distant Australia, or "rounded the Horn," in shorter and shorter periods, drawing the two coasts of America almost into one. Then along came the steamship and away went the clipper. The internal combustion engine put on the roads "the horseless carriage." The "horseless carriage" quickly evolved into the modern automobile. It would seem in both cases, and there are countless other examples, that a peak of perfection is reached and from that point maintained more or less on a level plateau, until, as in the case of the clipper, superseded. Of course, since we have already reached the moon, there is no telling how far the evolution of communication may get.

It is not so easy to trace out evolutionary sequences in matters more closely concerned with human behaviour but several illustrations, one or two minor, others major, may be offered.

The first comes from the minor sphere of table manners. British people and most of those stemming from the nineteenth century empire, keep their forks in their left hands, their knives in the right. Americans cut off a piece of meat with knife and fork and then keep the fork in the right hand to convey food to their mouths. The logic of the situation has impelled considerable numbers of Americans to keep their knives in their left hands for cutting, using their right hand for lifting their food. The employment of the two hands has thus been reversed.

Everybody is more or less interested in the evolution of clothing. Take the wig, for example. It appears in the seventeenth century, apparently, to replace the flowing locks of ageing Cavaliers, grows to portentous size by the end of the century, when ''full-bottomed wigs'' gave the most gorgeous heads of (somebody else's) hair to the baldest man.   There is a comical passage in *The Beggar's Opera* (John Gay, 1685-1732) in which two elderly gentlemen, getting into an altercation, end up by pulling off each other's wig, leaving two completely bald heads confronting the audience. In the eighteenth century, the wig, having reached a zenith, declined into more moderate proportions, to end up shrunk to a queue at the back of the head. It hangs on in England in that most conservative of callings, the law, and has lately been given a new lease of life by the women. Women's clothing, of course, is in a perpetual state of short-term evolution. The ground-sweeping skirts of the early century rose to reveal ankles, theretofore almost as mysterious as ''limbs.'' The two World Wars made the skirt rise. By mid-century, it has been elevated so far that little remained to hide the focus of male imaginations. The ''come on'' value of skirts is in proportion to their height. It reaches its peak, then comes down.

The arts are standing examples of evolution. Perhaps the plainest lies in the field of music. Modern ''serious'' music began its spectacular development in the sixteenth-seventeenth centuries. It reached its pinnacle in the century stretching from about 1740 to 1840, a pinnacle marked by Handel's *Messiah* (1742) and by Beethoven's *Fidelio*, 1805. The crowning glory of the nineteenth century was its music. One listens, charmed and delighted, to almost anything composed in that period. From the apex the vast achievements slowly run down as the end of the century approaches. Puccini's (1858-1924) beautiful operas are all written before 1910. After about that year, at latest after Ravel (1875-1937) the great age in music is over.

The name Sibelius will at once be brought forward in dissent. But Sibelius, 1865-1957, could be said to be a remnant, in the hinterland, Finland, still echoing the great century. But clearly, this does not deny him his own individual genius. What follows is at best ''intellectual'' music, music written from the head, not the heart. The old evolution dramatically ends and those who never hear what has been written since will not miss a great deal.

No doubt the First World War had to bear a considerable load of guilt in this connection.

A third illustration takes us into the intricate world of religious ritualism. It concerns the evolution that has occurred in such prominent Protestant denominations as the Methodists. Methodists were originally simple lower-middle class people whose religion contained a great deal of frothy emotionalism. There was little order or ceremony in their services. Everything was done under emotional stimulus, with little regard to decorum. But Methodists, as time went on, improved their fortunes. The effect on Methodist services was to put restraint on mere emotionalism. Enthusiastic members ceased to call out from their pews "Amen" or "Praise the Lord." The minister who, in the nineteenth century, had never gone farther towards clerical dress than a white tie and frock-coat began in the twentieth century (after the First World War) to wear a gown. A clerical collar followed. Old fashioned people called this garb "papistical," but it persisted. Choirs put on gowns and women in them began to cover their heads (as St. Paul had bade women to do).

The evolution parallels the physical changes in church buildings. The Methodist "chapels" at first were just "meeting houses," in which seats faced a platform. In the course of the nineteenth century, "preaching" changed into a "service." Decorum was sought in the introduction of a pulpit and a choir. Stained glass windows frequently followed, and other forms of church adornment. These, however, were never carried as far as was traditional in Roman Catholic or Anglican churches, nor did they often reach the same heights of aesthetic quality. The central point of the Methodist service never ceased to be the sermon, the effectiveness of which depended on the calibre of the man delivering it. It was natural for gifted preachers to "hold the spotlight" and the reflection of this, dating from about the 1890s, was the appearance, at least in North America, of church buildings in which the seats were arranged in semi-circles, as in theatres.

As emotional fervour cooled off, other conventional aspects of a religious service tended to receive emphasis. Probably the influence of ritualistic Anglicans made some imitation easy. Thus after the Second World War the "processional" appeared – the choir marched to its place down the centre aisle of the church, followed by the minister. Ministers themselves became more thoroughly professional. In the nineteenth century, theological colleges, which at first had been regarded with some suspicion, were not only accepted but began their steady climb into "halls of learning." In the twentieth century ministers were expected, then required, to have degrees in Arts. An educated ministry could not supply the heady emotionalism of a previous generation. Instead of the old *extemporare* prayers, "direct from the heart," prayers that had been previously composed came to be offered. In one great denomination deriving in part from Methodism, printed prayers were eventually supplied which were read in unison. The sermons preached seldom retained more than traces of the old-fashioned exhortations. They could be expositions of scriptural texts, ethical inculcation or intellectual discourses at levels varying with the congregation. The minister had ceased to have as his major objective "salvation" in ecstatic, semi-mystical sense and in his non-pulpit work at least, he had become a parish priest, looking after the personal cares of his people in the time-honoured way.

Another physical change in the church buildings followed the slackening of former zeal and the adoption of a measure of ritualistic formality. New churches, as they were built – and in America hundreds were built after the Second World War – went back to the more conventional, the ancient, arrangement of interiors. The church became rectangular and sometimes had transepts. The seating was in straight rows. The minister might be removed a little farther from the congregation in a pulpit placed to one side of the "chancel." Something very much like an altar appeared at the rear. On or above the "altar," there might be a cross, of all symbols that most directly identified by militant Protestants with "popishness."

Within less than two centuries, this important Protestant denomination, the Methodist, had abandoned its old emotional spontaneity and had become, not rigidly formal, but formal to a considerable degree. And more important, the ideas of both ministers and people had become liberalized, so that sectarian narrowness had disappeared and a broad tolerance taken its place. One necessary result of this had been that a vacuum of conviction had appeared. Why people went to church or what they thought of when they got there remained their own secret. Few of them could have been afraid of hell-fire. Few could have taken much stock in the old doctrines of conversion and salvation. Few could have believed with any conviction or intelligence in "eternal life." The decline in church attendance during the 1970s was probably a direct result of previous intellectualizing processes.

Would ethical practices decay along with doctrine? As prosperous middle and upper-middle class people, few Methodists or ex-Methodists would be found in criminal courts. Few would retain the taboos against alcohol, cards and dancing. But would their family life go to pieces, with parents divorced and children irresponsible, as had that of so many who, or whose forebears, had already drifted away from the church? Did the very width of its own liberalism condemn this strong denomination to something like disintegration? Could there be another chapter, recovery?

The various stages through which Methodism (and possibly Anglicanism too) had proceeded, emotionalism giving way to intellectualism, intellectualism passing into formalism and thence loss of vitality, illustrates the logic of social evolution. The Christian church of the first few centuries seems to have run through a similar gamut. One can find in the gospels no evidence for formalization and the minimum of evidence for a priesthood. But these quickly came in. The *overseer, episcopus, bishop,* rose to higher and higher levels of respect and authority and in a mere three centuries the Christian church had evolved the full panoply of formality, with its ritual and its hierarchy.

IV
Education and Equality

Another major illustration of logical evolution may be drawn from the field of education. Prior to the nineteenth century, "schooling" was severely limited in reach, save for peculiar places like Scotland and New England. Popular or "democratic" education in the Western world as a whole is a nineteenth century phenomenon based on the notions of equality that were widespread in speech and sometimes achieved in practice, more especially in the United States, but which also powerfully affected Great Britain and also, in varying ways, the continent. Every boy must have his chance. The notion of efficiency, both as workman and citizen, was also strong. "Gentlemen, we must educate our matters," said Hon. Robert Lowe in 1870, when compulsory primary schooling was being introduced in England after the Second Reform Bill (1867) had greatly extended the franchise. From these sources and others (particularly undemocratic Prussia) the idea of schooling for everyone took strong hold of all the great societies and the end is not yet. At first the common school was a humble institution – the "three r's" was its curriculum – but it picked up prestige and weight with the passage of time, until today most of our tax money goes into it.

By the end of the nineteenth century, secondary schooling was coming within the reach of nearly every qualified child. In the early twentieth century, the democratic atmosphere and great wealth of the United States began to extend into higher education the idea of free, or almost free, education to all qualified persons. Since the Second World War, the idea has been pushed almost as far as would seem possible, so that in the 1970s the doors of universities were opening wider and wider, with strong opposition manifested to the very idea of exclusion. It is impossible to adjudge the effects, for the field is huge and involves millions of people, of whom some must be good, many indifferent and a great number (in the academic sense) hopeless.

It is, however, relatively easy to trace the consequences of universalizing what is in itself a good thing, schooling, when the processes involved have to be handled in a mass way and given the numbers concerned, for the most part by second-rate people. The original half-emotional, half-rational drive for universal schooling becomes increasingly focused on the material aspects of schooling and the pressure mounts for better buildings and better equipment. A vague faith arises in the unlimited efficacy of "education." The material aspects of schooling most intelligent men of goodwill can readily achieve. But material objectives shade into non-material and at that point they give opportunity for the enthusiasts, the charlatans and the sentimentalists. This seems to be the stage reached by, say, about 1930 in modern mass education. Its direction often slipped into the hands of the sentimentalists and the charlatans, and the result was sometimes anarchy. Today, the 1970s, many children can no longer, in any real sense, read. From illiteracy to illiteracy in a little more than a century! Salvation may come from the conscientious people who actually have to face pupils in the classroom and from the tax-conscious citizen, but not from those who sit in offices and tell the teachers how to teach.

An example of this stage in education comes from a personal experience. On a certain occasion, two educational "experts" were brought in to tell teachers about the latest accomplishments in common, or grade, school education. The two brought with them two motion picture projectors and screens, and a huge box of miscellaneous objects, mostly newspaper clippings, which they called a "kit." The projectors whirred, and a succession of disjointed images appeared on the screens. It was explained that "the kit" contained material from which the pupil could construct his understanding of the depression of the 1930s. This "kit" was all dumped out on the table and pupils were supposed to come and pick out what interested them. The experts were asked if any sense of chronological sequence in history could be extracted from their material. They answered that they did not attach importance to chronological sequence in history. Meanwhile, the disjointed images kept flashing across the screens. The two "experts" could not express themselves except in English that was as disjointed as their pictures.

If this was not anarchy, what was it? Yet it was plausibly put forward as "education." What could the next stage be? Sooner or later, the particular Department of Education that was thus wasting the public's money and trying to make the children's schooling into a farce might get a capable, strong administrator who would "crack down" on such nonsense and return the official system to a semblance of sanity. Then things might begin over again.

. . .

The above illustrations from various aspects of life are given to bear out the idea that everything has its cycle of evolution. The idea receives support from Teilhard de Chardin in his *The Phenomenon of Man:*

> One after another, all fields of human knowledge have been shaken and carried away by the same underwater current in the direction of the study of some development. Is *evolution* a theory, a system or a hypothesis? It is much more: it is a general condition to which all

theories, all hypotheses, all systems, must bow and which they must satisfy henceforth and if they are to be thinkable and true. Evolution is a light illuminating all facts, a curve that all lines must follow . . . [5]

The pages that follow apply this idea, not to minor sequences, such as those given in illustration, but to the wide field of Western history itself. This involves pursuing over the centuries an elusive phantom, "the spirit of the age."

Notes

1. With air and missile power, this long example of continuity will take on quite different forms – an era may have ended.
2. Alan Gowans, *On Parallels in Universal History Discoverable in Arts and Artifacts* (University of Victoria, Victoria B.C., 1972). The suggestion underlying the words *all over the world* is open to debate.
3. Meaning of "pagan" in classical times ("Hellenism").
4. As modern economic science, for example, has codified the old faith as free enterprise.
5. Pierre Teilhard de Chardin, *The Phenomenon of Man*, Fontana Religious Books, (Collins, London, 1965). See pp. 241 *et al.*

CHAPTER TWO

Judaism – I

In looking at the history of the West with the hope of casting some light on how its various ages or eras change and pass into their successors, the wisdom of taking an overview of Judaism before embarking on some inspection of Christianity is obvious. Christianity, it is now thought, grew out of Judaism more gradually than hitherto supposed. For nearly two centuries, it has been recently stated, "Christianity was a discussion within Judaism, not a religion apart from it."[1] Christianity bears on it at every point the marks of the predecessor religion.

Individuals could be held to be the founders of some of the great cultures. But who was the founder of Judaism? General Montgomery, the victor of El Alamein, could talk confidently of Moses as one of the world's greatest generals[2] and presumably as such the founder of the people whom he led out of Egypt. General Montgomery was not handicapped by the limitations of scholarship. For the Semitic culture that preceded the Babylonian Exile of 586 B.C. usually known as Hebraism, Moses as the founder will do as well as another. In the specific sense, it cannot be said that the post-Exilic culture has a founder. But no one doubts its ability to endure and its pervasive influence. Two pieces of "luck" have immensely accentuated its survival qualities. One of them has been that the Jew has managed to maintain himself separately enough from his host countries to secure the benefits of persecution. The other is that for many centuries he has been carried down through history on the shoulders of those who have built stronger or at least more widely adopted cultures than his own.

Thanks mainly to its successor religion, Christianity, we know a great deal about the origins of Judaism, its nature and its world view.[3] In contrast with neighbouring peoples the Hebrews of Old Testament days well before the Exile of 586 B.C. had a specific view of the meaning of history and of the meaning of "God." History was not the endless cyclical repetition reflected in the literature, if not in the formal historical works, of Greece and Rome, but an ordered succession of events, with beginning, unfolding and, less clearly, end. Authorities seem agreed that this unique view of time arose as a result of the peculiarly hard conditions the Hebrews experienced in their early centuries. The folk tales of their captivity in Egypt and their deliverance eventually were recorded. The writings, coupled with the constant battle for existence in the land of Canaan, came to make them see themselves as a chosen people. Here was a foundation stone for them, the idea of the Chosen People who naturally, since they had survived and were chosen, had a mission to accomplish.

Closely related to this idea of *choice* was the view that evolved of the Godhead. Yahway, their god, came to be more than another of the innumerable deities of "the peoples." Above all, he had, so it came to be believed (and it is still believed) made a covenant with his people. "Ye shall be my people and I will be your God." He had given them "the promised land." Here was the rock upon which Hebraism was built, the idea of the covenant, the promised land and the sense of mission. The covenant imposed a heavy duty. From these conceptions stemmed all the future.

After many generations, the Hebrews succeeded in building up a secular state. It gave some centuries of relief from their historical position of suffering, caught between the hammer and the anvils of the great neighbouring kingdoms. Its history is written in the two Books of Kings,[4] and these reflect from another angle this peculiar consciousness of history. The apparent permanence of the secular kingdom gave hope and it is only when hope comes to lend significance to the future that interest in the past mounts high enough to bring about the past as an evidence of hope for the future. That is, when sufficient self-knowledge and self-awareness have accumulated within a community, that community passes over from being a collection of mere bands of individuals into an entity to which a collective term may be applied, a term such as tribe, people, even nation and at long last, nation-state.

By the period of the Books of Kings, the Hebrews had apparently escaped from the most drastic divisions of tribalism and could think of themselves as a nation. Religiously, although their lapses had been many, they were on the way to the formulation of their magnificent conception, monotheism. But Yahway had not moved out of Canaan: he was still the god of the land living in his temple in Jerusalem. Much of the structure so arduously built up was to be knocked over by the Babylonians. The temple was destroyed and nearly everyone was carried off to the banks of the Euphrates. There, they were to remain for half a century and more. The Exile was apparently cataclysmic and out of it came what was to become a new culture, one more detailed and which was to become the basis for subsequent Judaism. The framework of the old religion would endure, but it was to receive many an addition not known to preceding generations.

In Babylon, some of the exiled Jews intermarried and were assimilated. Others, filled with the ancient determination to preserve their identity and disgusted with many features of Babylonian polytheism, stuck together and used every means of reinforcing their Jewishness. One of these clearly was writing and reading, and in common. Here, possibly, was the origin of the synagogue – a meeting where the ancient writings could be read and expounded.

A most important result flowed from the very removal from the land of Canaan. The temple had gone. Had its occupant, Yahway gone with it, or was he at best wandering vagrantly upon the hills of Judaea? It would have been in accordance with the ancient view of gods to have believed so. This view was dramatically presented when some of the people who had been sent to Palestine to replace the Hebrews complained to the king that "the nations which thou hast removed and placed in the cities of Samaria, know not the manner of the God of the land: therefore he hath sent lions among them, and behold, they slay them, because they know not the manner of the God of the land." The king replied, saying "carry thither one of the priests whom ye have brought from thence and let him go and dwell there, and let him teach them the manner of the God of the land."[5]

The Exiles on their part were certain that the God back in Palestine and the God whose worship they were trying to keep up on the Euphrates, several hundreds of miles away, was one and the same God. A God who could move about like that and continue to protect his people could be no ordinary god. Moreover, was he not keeping the Exiles together as a separate group among aliens and, what was more, did he not eventually bring them back to the promised land? There must have been many similar circumstances combining to further that idea which even before the Exile had made substantial progress, the universality of the Godhead.

The Exile, with its associated calamities, especially the destruction of the historic temple, must have caused not only deep heart-searching but have stimulated thought about both past and future. Was the destruction of the nation the destruction of history? That is, had Yahway's concern ceased? The record of the past was available. Did it afford any vision of the future? It seemed clear that no great secular state would be possible, perhaps no state at all. Israel would always be ground between the upper and the nether millstones.[6] Yet the Exile must have enlarged the view of those who had so journeyed in strange lands. The result apparently was to throw concern to religion, and to thought which shaped along the lines of the ideal society, with lofty conceptions of justice, such as those of the prophet Micah: "What doth the Lord require of thee but to do justice, and to love mercy, and to walk humbly with thy God?" (Micah, VI, 8).

This was the road to Messianism (the word simply means "the Anointed") so beautifully expressed in the eleventh chapter of Isaiah, which begins prophetically: "And there shall come forth a rod out of the stem of Jesse, and a Branch shall grow out of his roots." The coming of "the Messiah" "will bring equity for the meek of the earth" and "with righteousness shall he judge the poor" (Isaiah, XI, 4). The dramatic picture follows of peace among the animals – "The wolf shall lie down with the lamb." These, presumably are, in their loftiest range, symbolic for the behaviour of man, though we are told that "the Messiah" or deliverer, more directly in mind was Cyrus, the Persian,[7] who, it was hoped, would deliver the oppressed Jews from the tyranny of Babylon. However that may be, the splendid poetic effect is unfortunately spoiled by what follows, the usual boring Old Testament maledictions on the evil-doers, by whom, no doubt, is meant the Babylonian masters.

Such visions are repeated again and again. Perhaps the most familiar statement they receive is in the famous passage from Isaiah LIII ("Who hath believed our report?"). This passage contains the immortal words, made twice immortal by their employment in Handel's great oratorio, *The Messiah*, "He is despised and rejected of man . . . Surely he hath born our griefs." And "But he was wounded for our transgressions, he was bruised for our iniquities, the chastisement of our peace was upon him and with his stripes we are healed." These chapters are usually studied under the rubric of "the Suffering Servant." But the ideals set out for the perfect servant are evidently universal images of ethical perfection. It was no ordinary heathen god who stood for ethical perfection. Thus the road to deistic universality was reached by this route, too. The conclusion is that the Exile advanced in some Jewish minds the grand conception of monotheism.

Unfortunately, it was only in some Jewish minds. The grand ideal had been discerned, it had been presented, but the Jewish people were not able to reach the heights it demanded. Their God expanded, took on the attributes of universality, but they refused to share him (except under impossible conditions mainly perhaps circumcision) with others. A turn to ritualistic formalism naturally occurred. But centuries later, in Jesus of Nazareth and especially Paul of Tarsus the same choice was presented and the same decision was made. This second decision was to be the point of no return in Jewish history. It consigned the Jew to a compartment of history, never to its full amplitude. He retreated to tribalism, kept apart from the rest of mankind and so remains to this day (insofar as he remains true to his Judaism) a separate man, a man who does not have a message for all men, a man who must go it alone apart from the rest of his fellows, to whom, nevertheless, he bequeathed a formal code of ethics (as in the Ten Commandments) and many of the most enduring of the Western world's institutions (as for example the weekly day of rest).

At least, that would be the logic of his decision if the universal hope of "salvation" that Christianity offered continued to hold its former high place in the hierarchy of values. Now that so many assume that life, probably begins and ends here on earth and have decided that the spark of immortality is not in man, then perhaps it does not matter much what a specific group of people believe or do not believe about this question of God's universality. Christians, that Jewish sect, embraced the universality of God, God for everyone, and founded a world religion. A few centuries later Mohammedans did the same. The Jew satisfied himself with the maintenance of his own identity.

Nevertheless it was in the period of the Babylonian captivity and in the centuries that succeeded it that many of the aspects of Judaism were added which have passed with little change into Christianity. The tendency of many histories of Western civilization to put their emphasis on Greece and Rome as the predecessors of the West is therefore to some extent regrettable, for since the history of the West has been largely the history of Christianity, the predecessor religion, Judaism should receive more attention than it usually does.

During the Exile, there could be none of the ancient observances associated with the temple. There was no temple. Fasting, prayer, the institution of the Sabbath (probably Babylonian) and the synagogue had to take its place. These greatly changed the nature of Hebrewism, in fact made it over into Judaism. A deep sense of sin, something conspicuous by its absence in the classical world, seems to have arisen, growing out of the exiles' very misfortunes. The determination to preserve at all costs their identity came to mark them *exiles,* and when at last they got back to their more or less barren hills, their sense of being a chosen people, already emphatic, heightened.

The place that fasting and prayer and the sense of sin came to occupy in Judaism was large, and no one needs to be told how prominent it was later to become in Christianity. The same is to be said of the conception of the *Sabbath,* changed though it was to become into the Christian Sunday. The synagogue is especially interesting. At first it was not a place of worship, but a place of instruction, where *The Law* could be expounded. It can surely be regarded as the forerunner of the *ecclesia,* the Christian church (as the Book of Acts clearly indicates) and thus as the progenitor of that most characteristic and powerful of Christian institutions, the sermon.

Out of the synagogue were to come the persons known to us as the scribes. Clearly they were destined to become the intellectuals of Judaism (see Chapter 3, p. 43) and as could be predicted, there was to be begotten from them that legitimate but difficult child of intellectualism, scepticism. The scribes seem to have numbered among themselves those to whom the Bible here and there refers as "the Scorners." Such men found their fullest expression in the author of Ecclesiastes ("Vanity of Vanities . . ."). Synagogue and scribe seem to parallel in interesting fashion the much later development found in mediaeval Europe, where in the twelfth century, intellectualism pushed into the earlier zeal and eventually found its home in that characteristic mediaeval institution, the university (which has been assailed ever since as the nest of heterodoxy, heresy, doubt). In both cases some sixteen or seventeen centuries apart, do we not have examples of that progression from emotion to intellect which seems to mark out a pattern for history?

Many of the Jews of the Exile are said to have done very well in Babylon – it was during the Exile that the proclivities of the Jewish people for trade are said to have become pronounced. Later on, after the Greek founding of Alexandria, many Jews were drawn to the new rich city, and the same talent appeared among them. Yet the determination not to allow themselves to lose their Jewishness was as strong in one situation as in the other, or in any of the situations into which they were scattered, or had scattered voluntarily. No other small group in history (except that minor group, the Gypsies), surely, shows this same phenomenal and really inexplicable ability to keep itself separate from the peoples among which it finds itself. No other group makes anything like as much of its homesickness for the region which with almost complete irrationality it considers "home," the spare hills of the land of Canaan.

The struggle to preserve their identity has endowed the Jews with a sense of racialism equalled probably nowhere else on earth. Of this, the notion of the chosen people was another aspect. Most peoples who have met with some success in their history have come to see themselves as a chosen people, a people with a mission, and this has been a prominent factor in history. It has also at times been one of the most dreadful. The little Jewish people have held it persistently. This sense of mission must always be under the surface in any organized group of humans. Nowhere has it received more frequent or more forceful expression than in Christianity, both directly, as in missions for the propagation of the faith and indirectly in the convictions of destiny possessing various nations. The history of nearly every nation in Christendom testifies to the compelling force of a sense of mission.

From the sojourn in Babylon came important practices and spiritual concepts that have greatly influenced subsequent history. The group of Exiles was very active in a literary way. Although their singers proclaimed that they could not "sing the Lord's song in a strange land," many of them apparently did, with the result that some important books of the Old Testament are supposed to have been written in Exile. And then there was the discovery by Nehemiah on the return to Canaan of the so-called "new book of the Law," which revivified the place of the collections of folk rules that had hitherto governed Hebrew conduct and which gave to the Jewish people a code for all time. It is hard to overestimate the place in their life of *The Law*. Apart from specific points, there was the constant influence of the existence of *The Law,* a code giving rules for life, something so different from anything possessed by classical Paganism. In the New Testament, St. Paul makes frequent reference to it and through apostolic channels, portions of the Code (theoretically the entire Code, since it is contained in the accepted scripture, the Old Testament) passed over into Christianity, as notably the Ten Commandments and the Tables of Prohibited Degrees in marriage.

During and perhaps after the Exile, various basic doctrines found their way in from Persia. It apparently was a Persian or Mazdaist doctrine that the dead would live again, with rewards for the righteous. During and after the Exile this doctrine came gradually into Judaism and apparently by the Maccabean period or about 165 B.C. was with some exceptions, generally accepted.

By about the same time another Persian notion had come in, the belief in angels, good and bad. And last but not least, the idea that there must be a representative for both of the fundamental states, good and evil, God naturally for good, but with some sort of opponent to keep him up to the mark. This opponent, "the Adversary," is taken over as Satan, who is first mentioned in the Book of Zechariah (III), "And he showed me Joshua, the High Priest standing before the angel of the Lord, and Satan, standing at his right hand to resist him." Zechariah proclaims that he began to prophesy in the second year of Darius, who began to reign in 521 B.C. There had been suggestions of the doctrine before, but it was in the years after 521 B.C. that it got its formal expression. The real place it has had in *Christianity* needs no elaboration.

Upon a subject than which none has been more thoroughly or frequently discussed, a few pages such as those above can hardly be expected to cast a new flood of light. That has not been the intention. Rather it has been to indicate some of the major heritages the antecedent culture, Judaism, has left to its successors, predominantly to Christianity.

Of these, everyone would name at once as the chief, monotheism. It may be noted in passing, however, how unstable this concept has always been. To the Hebrews, the graven image was always just around the corner. Later on, when Satan made his appearance it was not long before a whole host of lesser devils came to keep him company. All these were "gods" of a sort. They provoked their righteous counterparts, the angels, and the great archangels. Never, however, did the Jew admit into his pantheon, a woman. There never was in Judaism an Aphrodite or a Mary. Later on, in Christian times, monotheism formally gave way to the tritheism of the trinity and later still to the astounding roster of saints and devils that blessed and tortured the mediaeval mind. It was only the strong commands of Mohammed, ("there is no god but Allah") and the prohibition of making images of any sort for religious purposes that kept such things out of Mohammedanism.

The idea of the chosen people was another heritage almost as potent. But far more lofty from every point of view, surely, was the ethic of Judaism, an ethic that needed little addition to allow it to take its place in that formulation upon which we have not yet improved and which we are accustomed to regard as the perfect and ultimate expression of good behaviour, the ethic of Jesus of Nazareth. This too, of course, was Jewish.

One can hardly begin to write on these subjects without finding himself carried away by their profundity, their reach into the ultimates of human existence. It is necessary for him to remind himself that his primary concern is with the bearing of Jewish culture upon "a pattern for history." That bearing will be found embedded in Jewish convictions. Here was a group of people chosen of God. The choice had been explicitly made in the past, it had been demonstrated over the centuries and it would go on indefinitely in its manifestations of the will of God. It has been often said that Jewish culture was primarily historical, governed by the sanctions of the hallowed past, enduring the calamities of numerous presents, looking forward to the indefinite future when with the triumph of God's will, a "sun of righteousness would arise with healing in his wings." Such an outlook could hardly be otherwise than historical and provide a pattern for history.

That pattern was to be handed on to the still greater culture to which it gave rise, Christianity.

Notes

1. This quotation is taken from a press report (*St. Petersburgh* (Florida) *Times,* January 20, 1974), commenting on the issue of the first volume of Compendia of the Jewish Background of the New Testament. The author of the quotation is Rev. M. de Jonge, general editor. The title of the first volume of the new series is *The Jewish People in the First Century.*

2. B. L. Montgomery, *The Memoirs of Field Marshall B. L. Montgomery* (New York, 1958).

3. A fairly recent survey of the institutions of ancient Israel is that by Father Bernard de Vaux, Director, École Biblique, Jerusalem, published in French in 1957, Tr. 1961, (McGraw-Hill, New York, 2 vols.), under the title *Ancient Israel, Its Social and Religious Institutions.* It is a work of

meticulous scholarship, but has no comment on the inner nature of ancient Israelite society and life.

4.   The Hebrew monarchy was to furnish much ammunition for mediaeval debates on the nature of kingship.

5.   II Kings, XVII, v. 26.

6.   See George Adam Smith, *Historical Geography of the Holy Land* (Fount Religious, Paperbacks Series, 1976).

7.   We find this explicitly stated in Isaiah LXV: "Thus saith the Lord to his anointed, to Cyrus, whose right hand I have holden, to subdue the nations before him . . .")

CHAPTER THREE

Judaism – II

In Jewish history, the *scribes* gradually emerged from among the *wise*, to become a class by themselves. They corresponded to the *litterati* who make their appearance in nearly all societies at a given stage of development and to whom the command of the written word – or the preliterate ritualism – gives importance. Even before the Exile, the term seems to have been applied to those who devoted themselves to studying and editing the early writings, especially *The Law*. By the close of the Persian period, about 330 B.C. the *scribes* were becoming the dominant intellectual leaders. Editing quickly led to interpreting and expounding, and the new institution, the synagogue, gave a splendid forum. The *scribes* assumed the education of the masses in *The Law*. The place of a body of able men so situated could not have failed to be large. "The wise man shall inherit confidence among his people and his name shall live forever." The *scribes* became councillors of state, judges, literary men. "The wisdom of the scribe comes by opportunity of leisure," says the author of the Book of Ecclesiasticus, painting an accurate picture of the gifted, well-placed man in any society.

Unfortunately, the intellectually gifted man has his own disabilities. In fair weather he may be guide, philosopher and friend to society and society will give him respect, honour and place. But, like that of other peoples, the course of Jewish history never did run smooth. Ambition, prosperity and success brought their usual consequences of the loss of colour and warmth in the old institutions. The nemesis of formalism was lurking just round that corner, and the sharp intellectual was waiting there

43

to attack formalism and the hypocrisy that usually goes with it. Something of the sort seems to have occurred among the Jews left in Palestine during the period of the Exile. The prophet Jeremiah could burst out that "the false pen of the scribes hath made the Law a falsehood" (Jeremiah VIII, 8), thus bringing into sharp contrast the old and the new. It is not hard to recognize the intellectual at his usual eroding work and the old fashioned lashing-out against him. One can cast forward there to Abelard and St. Bernard, some 1600 or 1700 years in the future.

After the return from the Exile, with the work of Nehemiah and Ezra the Jewish people apparently got into their stride once more, but there was to be another outbreak of scepticism and pessimism later on, which gave rise to some striking documentation. During the Greek period, that is, the period following the conquests of Alexander and his successors in the fourth and third centuries B.C., when much of the Middle Eastern world was Hellenized, Greek intellectualism impinged on the Jewish people and apparently cut a wide swath among their intellectuals. Its mark is plain for all to see upon the Book of Proverbs and the apocryphal Book of Ecclesiasticus. This latter book can be dated with some precision between 200 and 170 B.C. The Greek period is usually considered to have ended with the revolt of the Maccabeans 165 B.C., against Antiochus IV of Syria, leading to a strong national revival and a cycle that lasted until the Roman conquest destroyed the Jewish nation. The mark is plainest of all in the book of Ecclesiastes which might be called a Judaized version of the philosophy of Epicurus, who lived about a century (342-270 B.C.) before the writing of Ecclesiastes. That philosophy, a century later still was to find its lofty exposition in the long Latin poem *De rerum natura* whose author was Titus Lucretius Carus, or, more simply, just Lucretius, a Roman who lived approximately from 100 B.C. to 55 B.C.

This second period of scepticism in Jewish history had come after the miseries of the Greek conquests. It represented one of the hollows in Jewish fortunes, not only materially but spiritually, for the influence of the dynamic culture coming out of Athens – think of names like Zeno the Stoic, Diogenes the Cynic and above all, Epicurus the Rationalist – drew many Jews away from their traditions and caused them to immerse themselves in Greek thought, so different and so upsetting to their own. The writer of Ecclesiastes was one of these. To read him is to make readily apparent in what a dissolving way intellectualism impinges on traditional belief. Ecclesiastes represents the last stage in scepticism before "things as they are" dissolve into anarchy. No community could live by the pessimistic creed enunciated by this writer. Such a creed could only lead to a despair that would make little effort to prevent things going from bad to worse. One is reminded sharply of the lack of purpose, prominent though not dominant, in American and British life in the 1970s. The question there is "how bad do things have to get before they become worse"? And that is a question that can never be answered precisely because we never know our position on the voyage across the ocean of history.

Intellectual erosion sooner or later affects the most solid of traditional structures, sometimes tumbling them. Again, our modern world gives ready examples: the dissolution of empires, the weakened position of the papacy, at once come to mind.

Eroding impingement, intellectual or other, does not necessarily come from without, but that is how Greek philosophy came to the Jews – an alien culture treading upon their own. It must have made a serious impression on Judaism, but it did not submerge it. Judaism lived to fight another day and thenceforth was able, with the exception of exceptions, to confine its difficulties to within. The exception of exceptions was, of course, Christianity, which temporarily broke the unity of the Jewish world and carried off many of its members.

Epicurus preached the doctrine of complete rationalism. To him that meant complete materialism. Everything came out of nature and must return to nature. It was absurd to believe that there would be anything "supernatural." The doctrine left no room for the old gods (who by Epicurus's time, had not much life left in them anyway), for heaven or hell, for miracles or anything else of the sort, down to the most humble of popular superstitions. We moderns with educations bearing the heavy marks of scientific findings, would have found him an understandable man.[1]

At a range of over two centuries and in the Latin world, rather than the Greek, Epicurus found his outstanding disciple, interpreter and transmitter in the Roman poet named above, Lucretius, a few quotes from whom will make his philosophy stand out clearly. The quotations are taken from R. E. Latham's Penguin Books translation:

> The next step now is evidently to elucidate . . . the nature of mind and of life. In so doing I shall drive out . . . the fear of Hell which blasts the life of man . . . (97)

> *The mind* . . . the seat of the guidance and control of life, *is part of man* no less than hand or foot or eyes are parts of a whole living creature. (99)

> Water flows out in all directions from a broken vessel and the moisture is dissipated, and mist and smoke vanish into thin air. Be assured, therefore, that spirit is similarly dispelled and vanished far more speedily. (109)

> Mind and body are born together, grow up together and together decay. (109)

> Body and mind are effects of the same cause. (113)

Mind cannot exist apart from body and from the man himself who is, as it were, a vessel for it. (112)

If the spirit is by nature immortal and can remain sentient when divorced from our body, we must credit it, I presume, with the possession of five senses. In no other way can we picture to ourselves departed spirits wandering through the Infernal Regions. So it is that painters and bygone generations of writers have portrayed spirits in possession of their senses. But eyes or nostrils or hand or tongue or ears cannot be attached to a disembodied spirit. Such a spirit cannot therefore be sentient or so much as exist. (115)

From all this (the preceding argument) it follows that *death is nothing to us* and no concern of ours, since our tenure of the mind is mortal . . . If any feeling remains in mind or spirit after it has been torn from our body, that is nothing to us, who are brought into being by the wedlock of the body and spirit, . . . Or even if the matter that composes us should be reassembled by time after our death and brought back into its present state – if the light of life were given to us anew – even that . . . would still be no concern of ours once the chain of our identity had been snapped. (121)

As for all those torments that are said to take place in the depths of Hell, they are actually present here and now, in our own lives. (126)[2]

The reader may ask, "what has all this material about a Greek philosophy as put into Latin verse two centuries after his death, by a Roman, to do with a Jewish intellectual writing in Palestine a generation or so after the death of the Greek philosopher?" The relationship is direct. The author of Ecclesiastes, as I have said, is evidently a Jew who has been deeply influenced by Epicurus. His whole book is Epicurus in Jewish dress, a sombre costume. The author, therefore, anticipates Lucretius, his successor after two centuries, and gives us the Hebrew version of what Lucretius was to say in Latin. The parallel is not hard to substantiate, for one has only to turn to the book of Ecclesiastes itself, where almost every verse carries the Epicurean imprint, but in characteristic Jewish literary expression.

Everyone knows the words with which the book opens – "Vanity of vanities saith the Preacher; all is vanity." From this plunge into pessimism, the book never recovers. Everything is indeed, vanity. The writer pictures a lucky man who accomplished everything that man can accomplish – "gardens and orchards, servants and maidens, men singers and women singers," "whatever his eyes saw, he kept not from them, he withheld not his heart from any joy." But "all was vanity and vexation of spirit." So he goes on, finding nothing in life to commend, through some

6,000 words of writing. Good writing, too, though for that we must, at least in part, thank the translators of the Authorized Version. Better prose by far than the prose translations of Lucretius, better by far than Dryden's verse translation of Lucretius. But how different: the Latin classic is of the mind, the Hebrew book of the heart, the one intellectual, the other emotional.

But what an inferior quality of emotion: a detestation of life as life, a belittlement of life, in Ecclesiastes. A calm and courageous acceptance of life, whatever it has had to offer, on the part of the pagan Roman poet and his Greek predecessor.

A few random quotations from Ecclesiastes, to match those already given from Lucretius:

> There is a vanity which is done upon the earth: that there be just men unto whom it happeneth according to the work of the wicked: again, there be wicked men, to whom it happeneth according to the work of the righteous: I said that this also is a vanity.

Lucretius also sees this situation, but he does not repine: somehow or other it comes out of "things as they are," that is, *nature*.

To continue from Ecclesiastes:

> For the living know that they shall die: but the dead know not anything
> . . .

> As (the rich man) came forth out of his mother's womb, naked shall he return to go as he came, and shall take nothing of his labour . . . And this also is a sore evil . . . and what profit hath he that hath laboured for the wind?

Where Ecclesiastes writes about death, in the last chapter of the book, the tone makes a strong contrast with the splendid injunction to those facing death which Lucretius puts into the mouth of "nature," which is quoted below. Lucretius's words are full of calm, courage, acceptance. They receive a nineteenth century re-expression in the lines of William Cullen Bryant's poem *Thanatopsis* ("A View of Death"), lines that cannot fail to make a strong appeal to thoughtful courage:

> So live that when thy summons comes to join
> The innumerable caravan, that moves
> To that mysterious realm, where each shall take
> His chamber in the silent halls of death,
> Thou go not, like the quarry slave at night,
> Scurged to his dungeon, but, sustained and soothed
> By an unfaltering trust, approach thy grave,
> Like one who wraps the drapery of his couch
> About him, and lieth down to pleasant dreams.[3]

It is impossible to disguise partiality for the many attitudes of Lucretius, his absence of complaint, his calm acceptance of life as an aspect of nature (though there might be added to his creed some of the major heritages bestowed by Christianity). The attitude enshrines rationality and courage with not a little of what we often call Stoicism. It banishes all the cobwebs of superstition, all the ghosts of supernaturalism. It is a creed by which men could live in today's chaotic, perilous world – if they had courage enough and intelligence enough to face up to it. Few can. Those who can, need no Billy Grahamesque "conversion." Like Lucretius, they may be able to see into the centre of things and understand the *natura rerum*.

Ecclesiastes, the Hebrew writer, "the Preacher," as he calls himself, whines. He is dried up and hopeless, though flickers of the old Jewish faith come through: "though a sinner do evil an hundred times and his days he prolonged, yet surely I know that it shall be well with them which fear God. But it shall not be well with the wicked, neither shall he prolong his days, which are as a shadow, because he feareth not before God" (Ecclesiastes, VIII, vv. 12-13). Despite a few such more or less conventional utterances, the prevailing tone runs to the extremes of pessimism, self-pity and cynicism. There is comfort neither for living or for dying in this extraordinary book. How decidedly the balance is in favour of the pagan Epicurus and his disciple, the pagan Lucretius!

Ecclesiastes evidently lived in troublous times. To his mind there could have been little ahead for men. But Lucretius also lived in troublous times.

The remarkable contrast and parallel between the two writers comes out strongly in the words Lucretius puts into the mouth of Nature, splendid words of courage and realism:

> Suppose that nature herself were to find a voice . . . 'What is your grievance, mortal, that you give yourself up to this whining and repining? Why do you weep and wail over death? If the life you have lived until now has been a pleasant thing . . . Why, you silly creature, do you not retire as a guest who has had his fill and take your care-free rest with a quiet mind? Or if all your gains have been poured profitless away and life has grown distasteful, why do you seek to swell the total? The new can turn out as badly as the old and perish as unprofitably . . . Do you expect me to invent some new contrivance for your pleasure? I tell you, there is none. All things are always the same . . . There is nothing new to look forward to – not though you should outlive all living creatures . . .' What are we to answer, except that Nature's rebuttal is justified and the plea she puts forward is a true one?

Unfortunately most mortals require the carrot of hope stretched out in front of them if they are to carry on, so Lucretius's doctrine must remain a doctrine for the few. For the elderly, who can have little hope, he may reach far:

> (As to the elderly:)
> Away with your tears, old reprobate. Have done with your grumbling. You are withering now, after tasting all the joys of life. But because you are also pining for what is not and unappreciative of the things at hand, your life has slipped away unfulfilled and unprized. Death has stolen on you unawares before you are ready to retire from life's banquet filled and satisfied. Come now, put away all that is unbecoming to your years and compose your mind to make way for others. You have no choice.

The poet adds, very sensibly, ''The old is always thrust aside to make way for the new and one thing must be built out of the wreck of another'' (Lucretius, *de rerum natura,* III).

Then we turn back to ''the Preacher'' and ''hear, then, the conclusion of the matter.'' What follows (in his last chapter) is a kind of funeral march, sad, selfish, repining, hopeless and – magnificent. It may well end this attempt to build a parallelling contrast between two writers who each lived in the descending cycle of their country's history, these lines of a poetic quality so far beyond anything one finds in Lucretius, ethically so far below the pagan Roman:

> Remember now thy Creator in the days of thy youth, while the evil days come not, nor the years draw nigh when thou shalt say 'I have no pleasure in them.' While the sun, or the light, or the moon, or the stars, be not darkened, nor the clouds return after the rain: in the day when the keepers of the house shall tremble, and the strong men shall bow themselves, and the grinders cease because they are few and those that look out of the windows be darkened. And the doors shall be shut in the streets, when the sound of the grinding is low and he shall rise up at the voice of the bird, and all the daughters of music shall be brought low. Also when they shall be afraid of that which is high, and fear shall be in the way and the almond trees shall flourish, and the grasshopper shall be a burden, and desire shall fail: because man goeth to his long home, and the mourners go about the streets. Or ever the silver cord be loosed or the golden bowl be broken or the pitcher be broken at the fountain, or the wheel broken at the cistern. Then shall the dust return to the earth as it was and the spirit shall return unto God who gave it. Vanity of vanities, saith the Preacher, all is vanity.

Notes

1.   It is of course shallow to condemn Epicurus as standing for "pleasure" and mere "avoidance of pain."

2.   *Lucretius: On the Nature of the Universe,* translated by R. E. Latham, (Penguin Classics, 1951) pp. 97, 99, 109, 113, 112, 115, 121, 126. Copyright© R. E. Latham, 1951. Reprinted by permission of Penguin Books Ltd.

3.   Bryant was nineteen when he wrote the poem. He may have been familiar with Lucretius.

CHAPTER FOUR

The Classical World

The search for a pattern in history must necessarily include a look at the classical world. Not only is it a matter of our own close association with it, but also of the nature of that remarkable excerpt from human experience. The classical world arose, flourished, declined, ended. It gives us a picture of a complete cycle of civilization. Objection can naturally be raised to this way of putting it and of course, no passage in history is without its indefinite edges. Greece and Rome had their forebears and the descendants of the people who built up their civilization did not vanish from the face of the earth. But surely if any set of human phenomena can be isolated and looked at as we would look at, shall we say, an animal in a cage, it is that set which comprises the history of the classical world. Both Greece and Rome rose out of the twilight of prehistory, had their day and changed so profoundly that what succeeded them can, from any reasonable point of view, be considered new. The contrast with both Judaism and Mohammedanism is clear. Judaism is still very much alive and in its main content, religion, not much changed in many centuries. The same holds for Mohammedanism: that culture, once proclaimed, once spread, while it has adapted itself to local conditions, is still much what it was to begin with. But where are historic Greece and Rome? Mostly in piles of stone.

The heritage of the classical world, as contrasted with itself, is quite another matter, for the West has reminders of its predecessors at every turn. No moderately well-informed person needs to have that spelled out for him. To recall it, one has only to mention aesthetics, thought, language, law.

Since this inheritance is so vast and many-sided and penetrates so deeply into our lives, it is correspondingly difficult to characterize in a word or a formula. A single word, monotheism, serves more or less adequately to label Judaism. But no single word, no longest of words, will serve to ticket the world of Greece and Rome. There is indeed, no "ism" word for that purpose, except the ugly and inadequate word "classicalism." There is not even "Greekism" or "Rome-ness."

I
Greece

We couple "Greece and Rome" as if we could speak of them as a unit, which of course, we cannot. Disraeli, speaking of a feminine acquaintance, exclaimed ungallantly, "Poor so-and-so, she never can remember which came first, the Greeks or the Romans." Few of us probably are under that difficulty but we might find it hard to make a neat, simple distinction in kind between them. Their history has often been presented in a way not calculated to bring out the difference. "The glory that was Greece, the grandeur that was Rome" is not a bad try, but we should be able to go farther. "The beauty of holiness," someone remarked, "was a view congenial to the Hebrews, but the holiness of beauty was more appropriate for the Greeks." Such a saying has its point, too, but it does not mark Greek life as it does Hebrew.

Except in a loose sense, "Greece" never existed. The word had some geographical logic about it, it had some cultural and considerable linguistic. It had a mild infusion of institutional and customary reality in such forms as amphictyonic leagues, Delphic Oracles or Olympian games. But it marked no integer. Every school boy is taught the difference between Athens and Sparta plus small gestures to one or two other cities, but we take our measurements, as a rule, not on "Greece," but on Athens. Athens definitely was not Greece. Yet if there never had been an Athens, would subsequent ages have bothered much about Greek history? It is unlikely. Instead of "Greece and Rome" should we not write "Athens and Rome"? It was mainly Athens that created "the glory that was Greece" that extraordinary glory of architecture, sculpture, art and literature which by lucky accident came into our possession.

We Westerners were not legitimate heirs to the glory that was Greece. Little trace of blood connects us. We recognize that "the Greeks" were vaguely of the same stock as ourselves, that some of them, early migrants into the peninsula, were probably originally "northerners" and that their language sprouts from the same roots as other "Indo-European" tongues, but that is not much. "Race" may be real enough in terms of certain biological traits (such as skin colour), but fair hair and blue eyes do not imply brotherly love. "The glory that was Greece" does not come down to us through our genes.

Nor was there any historical continuity of consequence. "Greece" was transmuted into Byzantium and Byzantine culture passed over the Black Sea, giving to the vast interior, now Russia, an alphabet and a religion. There in the East, there was that much of continuity, but it was no continuity of the great days. They had gone. To the West, there was a minimum of anything transmitted. Over the centuries, the glory that was Greece had folded up, apparently forever. Although as a scholarly accomplishment Greek did not entirely die out, it was only in obscure holes and corners, such as southern Italy, that the Greek language survived and it was only by the fortuitous roundabout way of Moslemism that fragments of Greek literature came to the West. The glory that was Greece had to wait for the Renaissance before it was disinterred and made almost to live again. Then, like one of its own breath-taking statues, it shone forth, to lighten man's path, let us hope, forever.

"The glory that was Greece," that is, the civilization of Athens, thus comes down to us by only fragile links. We are taught to think of it as lying in our own past, as something to which we are rightful heirs. That claim does not seem sound. If at some point along the historical route the Turks, say, had dug up the glory that was Greece and came to understand it and profit by it, their right to it would be almost as legitimate as is ours. Their sophisticates would have drawn from its stores just as ours have done. As a matter of fact, something like that actually happened when the Arabs translated and used some of the great classics. While our ancestors were still not far from barbarism, the glory that was Greece was shining in Arab cities such as Cordova.

To Europeans of the Middle Ages, the Athenian culture of the great centuries would surely have seemed altogether strange and probably reprehensible. Blood sacrifices and considerable acceptance of homosexuality, how would they have looked to pious mediaeval eyes? No good Christian has ever approved the amours of the pagan gods. The great plays would probably have seemed irreligious and idolatrous, the philosophers talking in riddles and had the pagan gods not been got rid of by generations of spiritual warfare? The great beautiful temple of Olympia was deliberately destroyed by Justinian. Its columns still lie there for the tourist to gaze at (they ought to be put up again).

Add to the cultural gap, a religious revolution, and it becomes almost impossible for anything from classical Greece to cross that gulf and reach early mediaeval Europe. And to this day, very little of the Greek inheritance has passed down to popular levels. The average plain man knows (or used to know) far more about the life of Palestine than about that of Athens. The Greek inheritance is not a bone and sinew inheritance. It is an intellectual inheritance, one unsurpassed in its riches, but an inheritance of the literate, not of the people.

Yet those who have had the good fortune to discover Greek culture have never ceased to fall in love with it. Not only the beauty of its arts and the magic of its poetry, but the depth of its philosophy, the accomplishments of its scientists. It is a case of mind speaking to mind across the centuries. That is what the Western world has laid hold of – the Greek mind. Lucky for us that there has been recognition of the treasure. Lucky that even the schoolroom has not been able completely to alienate us from it. Lucky for us that some can see that there in Athens for a short space the mind was free and that mind can speak to mind. The great example of liberty all too soon terminated, alas! A beacon light is perhaps the essence of our heritage from Greece.

Apart from details, in contrast to Greek, Jewish history is relatively simple. It is the story of a people passing through tribulations and erecting for themselves a monolithic institution, monotheism. No such straightforward path leads through Greek history, which is categorized by the city state and by the relative absence of concern for past and future. The Greeks seem to have been as extroverted as the Hebrews were introverted. The result should not be too difficult for us moderns to understand. As long as we cherished our fixed religious beliefs, with convictions of beginning, growth and end, we were "Hebrews," but now that we have thrown them overboard and become "scientific," that is "with open minds," sceptical, we have become "Greeks." We look at life and nature with the eroding gaze of the intellect and go not one step beyond that which we confirm by observation and experiment. The attitude is quite consistent with forebodings of fate, with a dark mysticism, and it thus is not out of line with that mirrored in the great Greek poets. We have convinced ourselves that we are homeless particles in space, and if the Greek intellectuals had known as much as we do, they would have shared the conviction.

It is thus hard to find any thread through the Greek maze except the easily catalogued list of "causes" – the nature of the country, the infinite division that this effected (something probably exaggerated), the intensity of the rivalries, the relative scarcity of resources, and so on. We can follow the evolution of a specific state (invariably Athens) for some centuries, but the evolution of "Greece," the convictions and beliefs the Greeks had of themselves? Surely we seek for such generalities in vain. In this subjective sense, Greek experience does not present "a pattern for history."

In the more objective sense, and if it is taken city by city, it does. Athens grows up, matures, declines. The great triumphs of the Persian wars surcharge its people with zeal, with love for their city. The great poets speak. The Parthenon appears. Pericles makes his famous oration. That miracle of miracles, Greek sculpture, appears. Then the warmth cools. The philosophers appear. They degenerate into mere cleverness, "sophists" and "cynics." Freedom, so splendidly attained, shifts into something less orderly; if not chaos, verging that way. Athens is humbled. There are no more giant poets. The age of intensity, of zealous emotion, is over. Cool, analytical intelligence takes its place, reaching its apex in "The Master of them that know," Aristotle (384-322 B.C.). The clock runs down. But the moonlight of the Greek mind continues to shimmer over the world.

II

Rome

In contrast with Greece, the history of Rome is a straight line. The collection of huts by the riverside grows, becomes a town, a city, and thence, decade by decade, century by century, something like a nation, at last the world empire. In this sense, Roman history has a simplicity lacking in that of Greece. It is a matter of "wider still and wider, shall thy bounds be set." Good Romans would have endorsed the rest of the aspiration: "God who made thee mighty, make thee mightier yet!" On the arrogance of the words, the fate of the organisms referred to seems a fitting comment.

No collection of men knows where it is going and it is only after its life course is pretty well over that its general trail can be traced. Of few if any others than the Jews is there a constant belief in destiny, and destiny of a specific kind. No Roman of republican days knew that his Rome was to build an empire covering almost the entire world. But in the consolidation of the Italian peninsula and more especially in the victorious issue of the Punic wars, it was surely allowable to discern the hands of some kind of Providence. And later, where far-flung countries had been subdued into provinces, even the northern edges of the continent crossed, and with internal dissension ended, that hand surely had become not only discernible but evident. Rome, like many of her later children, had been given a mission. She had "divine" tasks to accomplish. It was all put into a few lines by Vergil:

> Let others beat out more smoothly the
> breathing brass,
> Draw out from the stone the living face.
> This I may accept.
> Let them plead better in the law courts.
> Let them describe more cleverly the
> movements of the heavens.
> And predict the risings of the stars.
> But thou, Roman, attempt to rule the
> peoples under thy sway – these shall be
> thy art: –

To impose the habits of peace, to spare
those who submit, and to put down the
proud.[1]

In the centuries since those lines were written, there have been so many variations on the same theme that it no longer conveys to us suggestions of mystical destiny though it is only yesterday that the "Land of Hope and Glory" ceased to be thrilled by the same impulses. And was it not as recently as the 1930s that great speech was made about "the 1,000 year Reich"? Roman imperialism, no matter how hard Vergil tried to dress it up in garments of worth and nobility was intrinsically as tawdry as other imperialisms, a compound of personal ambition, greed, the love of power, the excitement of violence, the satisfaction of conquest and the mystical unconscious urgings of the group mind ("We British," "Nous Français"!). The well-known passage of Tacitus which puts into the mouth of a British chieftain the exclamation that "they (the Romans) make a desert and call it peace" is probably closer to reality than high-flown notions about spreading the blessings of civilization.

So Roman history, insofar as the making of the empire goes, comes down to something ordinary – ordinary, brutal and bloody.

The republic is another matter and historians have readily recognized this in their division of the field into the two – republic and empire. Republican Rome presents us with a picture of public virtue and private worth, noble personages and noble attitudes. Victorious struggles against the foreign foe make their appeal to patriotism. Men of high character who will not break their word, call for our admiration, even if they are not fully within the light of substantiated fact. The struggle of the many against the few rouses our instincts of fairness and we rejoice at the triumph of the popular cause just as we feel sorrow to see the experiment running into the sands and ending in civil war, anarchy and despotism.

The history of the Roman republic gives us a clear evolutionary run. It is an example over the centuries of the keen Aristotelian analysis, according to which government runs through a pre-determined cycle, with power shifting from the one, to the few, to the many and back again. When absolutism has been achieved, evolution of this type stops and interest shifts into the details – it will always be interesting to learn a little more about some campaign on the German frontier – but in the history of the republic, there is a sense of process, events are leading us on in a sequence, the story is unrolling. So it is no wonder that the republic has never ceased to capture the attention of the historical investigator; no wonder that the generations which saw it die refused to believe in its death and kept its corpse unburied for centuries. This is not the place to examine the genuineness of those conceptions of which it lived long enough to boast. *Civis Romanus sum* embodies them and the words are wide enough to stretch over much which has been our own treasure – the rights and privileges of free men, the universality of law, and many other aspects of the political man which have never ceased to infuse their worth into the discussion and action of the centuries.

The Republic

The history of the republic illustrates not only the Aristotelian cycle but the pattern discernible in so many aspects of history. The light on the transition from monarchy to patrician rule is, it is true, dim, but apparently the expulsion of the king (credited to 509 B.C.) gave an incentive to the young republic which carried it forward for the next two centuries or so. The victory over the Carthaginians, which brings us well down into historic times, apparently furnishes a distinct sense of well-being that carries along the evolution still further. There is little suggestion of the succeeding phase, which seems prominent in other passages of history, the phase of intellectualism, with the doubts and erosions of certainty that intellectual activity invariably entails. That is left for the empire. Rome's history passes on: perhaps the victories of the Punic wars bring their nemesis – too much success, a bewilderment at the great place thrust upon Rome? At any rate, uncertainty creeps in, class contest ends, as perhaps it must end, in civil war, the fine initial thrust is no longer felt and authority comes in austerely to restore order.

In framing his classical succession of governmental states, Aristotle had under his eyes the kaleidoscopic phases of the innumerable Greek city states. They afforded ready illustrations for his analysis. He could have known little or nothing of Rome, so Rome, as illustrating the analysis, stands apart from Aristotle. Our immense wealth of political experience enables us to see how inexorable the logic of the succession is. One man as ruler, whether tyrant or monarch, must depute much power. Power deputed is power lost. Terrorism slowly loses its terror, and reaction builds up. A good modern example is Stalin, whose terroristic tactics have had to be greatly relaxed in Russia, where the one has given place to the few. One day, even in Russia, the few may give place to the many.

Perhaps the end-phase of the circle may already be discernible in the United States, in which country, despite every effort to keep power divided, it steadily accumulates in the presidency. In countries of parliamentary government, the same evolution is detectable: more and more power gravitates to the prime minister. Both president and prime minister are close to absolutism while in office. But the president has only a four year lease of power and the prime minister is always under the guns in the form of a vote of want of confidence. Our modern systems have worked remarkably well, but will they always work well? Remember F. D. Roosevelt's fourth term. Remember what public catastrophe might bring.

Passing of power to the few in the Roman republic might be compared with the loss of power by the English monarchy in the seventeenth century. In 1688, the "Parliamentary Monarchy" was established by the "Bloodless" or "Glorious" Revolution and kings ceased in fact if not in law to be sovereign. Parliamentary government, that is, power in the hands of loose parties and their leaders, ensued. At first power was in the hands of only a small circle. Gradually the circle widened and in the nineteenth century, the era of parliamentary democracy ensued. For many years now "the few," who are those in place and in places of influence, have had to govern by persuasion; almost, it might be said, by stealth, that is, by activities of which the average man can know nothing. In modern times in Great Britain, the contest between the few and the many goes on every day and all day. The labour unions are only one group among others which claim to speak for the many. Sometimes it seems as if the issue between the few and the many would be resolved, as so often before elsewhere, in violence. And after that? Restoration of order under a "strong man"? Who knows? The realities of the Aristotelian cycle in modern societies have not yet all been experienced. No one knows the exact position of our ship in the ocean of time and not even its compass course.

To look back to that ancient Roman past, such points seem clear enough: the decline of republican virtue, the civil wars and resulting confusion, the emergence of the "strong man" in the person of Augustus. Not that there had not been "strong men" before him – Marius, Sulla, Pompey, and Julius Caesar. But none of them was strong enough apparently, except Caesar, and everyone knows what happened to him (it nearly happened to Adolph Hitler, a similar but more sinister figure). Augustus reaped where Caesar had sown and the world rang with eulogies of his régime. Few men felt the loss of liberty. Would many feel it today?

The Empire

Julius Caesar had, in all but name destroyed the republic by the time of his assassination, 44 B.C. There followed a generation of confusion and civil war, ending in the triumph of his grand nephew, Octavius. Much in the mode of the traditional American city "boss," Octavius made himself "boss" of Rome without disturbing the ancient constitution. It would always have been legally possible for the citizens to return to the old forms, though in practice it would have been impossible, and no doubt good Romans would have wanted few things less than a return. Octavius, or Augustus as he became, was definitely not "imperator," just *princeps*, a word that could be translated as *Duce, Führer,* or simply *boss.* Luckily for Rome, he turned out to be a "lad of parts," and to mere ability in running things, he apparently added a measure of benevolence. The result was that remarkable phase of human affairs commonly known as "the

Augustan Age.'' Augustus achieved peace (for a time) and the doors of the
Temple of Janus were closed. The coincidence in time with that other,
obscure drama which was being played out in Palestine, was too remarkable for subsequent ages to allow it to pass. No doubt it inspired the Miltonic
lines:

> No war or battle's sound,
> Was heard the world around:
> The idle spear and shield were high uphung:
> The hookéd chariot stood
> Unstained with hostile blood;
> The trumpet spake not to the arméd throng,
> And kings sat still with awful eye,
> As if they surely knew their sovran Lord was by.

> But peaceful was the night
> Wherein the Prince of Light
> His reign of peace upon the earth began . . .[2]

"The Augustan Age" has made for itself as conspicuous a reputation in
literature as in other areas. Who can forget that it was the age of Vergil and
Horace, and that before that bright sunrise had "passed into the light of
common day," many another name had appeared to adore Rome's major
cultural achievement, her literature.

Augustus must have appeared to his Romans and in retrospect as larger
than life, the ideal. No wonder Paganism made him a god. He had every
right to the title: powerful, beneficent, assuring to the people under his
kindly sway, peace, prosperity and justice – a superman, *August* in every
sense of the word. Here was the *Patriot King* of the eighteenth century
Bolingbroke's maunderings, that perfect ruler who could temper justice
with mercy and set all right. It is an ideal that often flashes across the
human mind – the kindly father, *par excellence.* Christianity has been
realistic enough to know that such a ruler can never be found, not even
among the Popes, the successors of St. Peter though they be, and with the
mantle of "infallibility" about their shoulders. If we knew enough about
Augustus, we probably would soon find his feet, like other colossi, were
of clay, as, indeed, some of his contemporaries did.

The shortcomings of the successors of Augustus becoming apparent,
the usual eroding intellectual process soon set in. Excoriating writers
changed the calm, majestic atmosphere of the few good years to something quite different, to something bitter. Another trough in the historical
cycle was reached. The horrors of the imperial monsters, the Neros
(54-68) and their like, are legendary, if overstated. Rome was destined to
be rescued from another descent into chaos by the sunny afternoon of the
Antonine emperors.[3] That afternoon ended and Rome plunged into the

vicissitudes of the third century. From them, once more rescue came with Diocletian, 284-305, and his division of the empire into two, east and west. But at that, we are in another world of time and event, facing a new and troubled future. The old days of Rome, the city, are over. We are in that vastly different structure, the Roman empire.

It seems evident that in the early empire there was a widespread mood of pessimism. This may have arisen partly out of the old gods' wearing out for the sophisticated, partly from the feeling of submergence in the vastness of a universal empire. Something of this can be glimpsed in the remoteness from his government felt by many an American (and probably most Russians). After all, the average American – or Russian – is only one-quarter billionth part, more or less, of the whole. It would almost seem as if a new religion that would restore meaning to life was waiting to be born. It was, of course, but its cruel gestation took two more centuries.

The periodization in Roman history from the first century B.C. to the third A.D. seems plainly visible. Civil wars, virtual anarchy, the appearance of the strong man, Julius Caesar, his assassination, more civil war, the second strong man, Augustus Caesar,[4] order restored, the arts of peace flourishing. Degeneracy at the top, further disorder, the attacks of the intellectuals,[5] the Antonine recovery, then further severe disorder and once more order through the appearance of the strong men, first Diocletian, then Constantine. The cycle no doubt is endless and could probably be traced out in Byzantium during a thousand years. It provides us with one of our plainest *Patterns for History*.

It is not quite right to think of the empire as a long régime displaying no evolutionary tendency. There was evolution, quite evidently, but evolution downward. History has sharply recognized this in its emphasis on *The Decline*, recognized it more justly than in the picture often presented of *The Fall*.[6] *Fall* after a thousand years, yes, as Gibbon presented it, culminating in 1453, but not *Fall* in 476 A.D., as it is so often presented.

Everyone knows, too, that in those first imperial centuries, there was another evolution going on, the evolution of the Christian church. Arnold Toynbee has made much of this as a historical process. And it would be hard to make too much of it. Christianity, whatever it was, and it would be hard to say what it was, was destined to blot out Paganism for which the current and better term was Hellenism, except for odd bits. History records no more complete extinction of a culture, a culture which had satisfied the ancient world for many centuries.

The culture thus destroyed had religion as its nucleus, the religion involving the rites and ceremonies associated with the worship of the Olympian deities and their Roman parallels. That had begun as most other religions do, as a nature cult. It had expanded until it included more ''gods'' and ''goddessess'' than those with which modern evangelical sects can furnish the United States. It had become decidedly shop-worn even in the generations in which its future supplanter has not taken on much weight. But even at that late date it had retained enough conviction to accuse Christians of "atheism" because they would not perform the symbolic rites.

But can it be asserted that Roman culture, as a whole, was destroyed? It was the heart of it which was destroyed or superseded. The old religion was destroyed, insofar as Christian efforts could destroy it, but many elements of the old culture were simply superseded. We use the term "Paganism" rather too easily. The "pagans" who clung to the old religion called themselves simply "Hellenes." Originally, "paga" before it became a term of contempt, could have meant little more than "old fashioned" – the way of life lived by country people, the *pagus* being the countryside. Taking the old gods seriously was "old fashioned." More deeply, holding the old attitudes toward your fellow man, was or became, "old fashioned" and therefore, in logic, wicked. This subject, the transition from Paganism to Christianity, is a very large one, and it is far from the purpose of this piece of writing to describe it in detail.[7]

Yet everything considered, the transition from the one culture to the other was the most complete that the Western world has known. The only comparable example is the change made by those eastern Christians who shifted over from Christianity to Mohammedanism, and that was conquest, not revolution. Some would argue that the shift from Roman Catholicism to Protestantism was just as complete. That it was great needs no argument, especially where practically no trace of the old religion remained, as in seventeenth century New England. Even in such places, however, the memory of the old religion lingered. It was not dead, it was an active foe to be fought, so the transition to the new order was not total. Nor has it ever become so. It is a matter of two orders slowly making their uneasy accommodations. Nothing of the sort can be said of classical Paganism. Popular survival in folk custom is not the equivalent of philosophical, sophisticated survival.

Yet Rome survived, if not religiously, in a dozen other ways. Thomas Hobbes's word still has truth in it. Roman Catholicism is "the ghost of the Roman Empire sitting crowned upon the grave thereof." It is a very lively ghost and it has carried many mortal trappings along with it. Do these require naming? The Latin language, Latin literature, both ecclesiastical and lay, Latin as a formal subject of study (what a tremendous item that has been), Roman law in a sense,[8] lesser items such as those aspects of Paganism directly incorporated, for example, Christmas and Easter, and in the southern areas of Western Europe, a more or less continuous mode of life. The *lex scripta* has never ceased to be in force in southern France. And everywhere in Europe, except to the far northern lands, Rome lies visible in stone monuments, some of them mere rubble, others like the amphitheatre in Nîmes, still in ordinary use (though no longer for gladiatorial games!).

The further the European was removed from Rome, naturally the less Rome's influence. The Scandinavian countries were quite outside it. So was most of Germany. In Italy, Spain and southern France, it is probably correct to think of the Roman way of life going on century after century, allowance being made for attritions such as Arab conquests and for mere wearing out. In the rest of France, the Roman way of life, not having been universal was changed or disappeared more easily. In England, contrary to a strongly-held popular belief, no continuity whatever can be proved. Not a single pre-Anglo-Saxon bishopric church remains. There was little trace of the Latin language in the English too, until the Norman conquest[9] and no trace at all of Rome in Anglo-Saxon institutions. It is even doubtful if anything but a fragment of Roman London, a considerable city, remained to become English London. English life and institutions, apart from the church, were, as F. W. Maitland said, "the purest products of primitive polity."

III
Conclusion

Classical Rome looms large in modern life, simply because for centuries it was there. It is like a great volcano which has become extinct. There it is looming massively over the landscape, austere, but quiet. Not even the occasional plume of smoke gathers about the cone. But the lava streams that flowed from that cone are many, visible, thick. Some of them are indubitably still warm.

Some years ago, a French-Canadian priest remarked while in Rome and about Rome – "Rome est inépuisable." Rome is indeed inexhaustible – in history, in physical remains, in tradition, in literature. Of our popular culture, it was not the parent. Of our sophisticated, it was.

Both Greece and Rome, major constituents of our own civilization in so many ways, clearly, in the courses they ran through time, gave *A Pattern for History*. And were their ruins not "Preludes to Chaos"?

Notes

1. Vergil, *Aeneid*, Book VI, lines 844-853 (Author's translation).
2. Milton, *On the Morning of Christ's Nativity*, IV, V (1629)
3. Two excellent descriptions of Roman society during the mid-first century empire, say fifty years after Augustus, are Sir Samuel Dill,

Roman Society from Nero to Marcus Aurelius (Norwood, London, 1930; First Edition, 1905), and Jerome Carcopino, *Daily Life in Ancient Rome* (tr. from the French, Yale University Press, New Haven, 1940). For the horrors of the persecutions of the Christians, the frying-to-death, throwing to the beasts, and so on, as described at the time, see Anne Fremantle, *A Treasury of Early Christianity* (New York, Mentor Books, 1960) specifically pp. 173 ff. Dill is careful to note that in the midst of barbarism, there were circles of people who lived decent, kindly lives, such as the younger Pliny and Seneca.

4.   The successors of Augustus included Tiberius (14-37 A.D.), and Claudius (41-54). Then came Nero (54-68). The Flavian dynasty followed (69-96), consisting in the general Vespasian (67-79) and his sons Titus (79-81) and Domitian (81-96). To this group there succeeded the fairly long dynasty of the Antonines (96-180), of whom the chief were Nerva (96-98), Trajan (98-117), Hadrian (117-138), Antonius Pius (138-161) and Marcus Aurelius (161-180). These quite long reigns of men of great abilities as rulers brought the early empire to the climax of its evolution (usually regarded as reached about 150) in extent and in prosperity.

5.   Notably Tacitus and Juvenal.

6.   Gibbon's lucky title probably has had something to do since his volumes appeared, with the course of historical writing in the English-speaking countries. For the continent of Europe, with its more continuous tradition, the cut-off line does not seem quite so sharp.

7.   See G. Lowes Dickinson, *A Modern Symposium*, Allen Unwin, London, 1962 for an interesting short and illuminating discussion.

8.   Roman law as is well-known, has become the basis for the law of almost the entire white world with the exception of the English-speaking countries. It is hardly, however, a direct inheritance, but came mainly as a by-product of the twelfth century Renaissance. The canon law, which in turn, was mainly Roman in essence, was of course, a direct aspect of the church.

9.   Some twenty words are said to have been taken in, mainly church terms, e.g., *biscop,* bishop.

CHAPTER FIVE

Early Christianity

I
The Earliest Days

The obscure events that were occurring in Palestine during the last years of Augustus Caesar and those of his immediate successors (Tiberius, 14-37 A.D., Claudius, 41-54, Nero, 54-68) were destined to mount in their effect, higher and higher until they had given the world a new religion and another epoch. When Christianity eventually supplanted classical Paganism (or *Hellenism*), the first and the greatest of the revolutions of Western history had occurred. The old gods were no more, the old customs, beliefs and myths, by which ordinary men had lived for centuries, were no more. The culture, its literature, its philosophy, its way of life, withered. The old temples came down – often systematically wrecked – the new churches went up. The old barbarities of the arena disappeared, to be replaced in time by new barbarities, if different, yet scarcely less horrible. The old morals disappeared, the old ethics were transformed. The old political structures gradually crumbled. The old memories faded. In scarcely an item of life, except in the practices of the lowly, did the old Paganism survive the onslaughts of the new Christianity.

The Christian revolution began inconspicuously enough. A few simple men doing what many a man in their country had done before them, walking about holding religious meetings, gradually coming into conflict with authority and one of them called Jesus of Nazareth, their leader, singled out for the miserable Roman execution called crucifixion. The sequence with its culminating event was obscure and it is only indifferently attested, for the Gospel accounts are those of naive and simple men, men who would get little credence today beyond people of their own type.[1] But it was destined to reshape the world.

The conditions of life in Palestine under which Jesus was brought up and the kind of people from whom he came and among whom he moved are clear enough from the first three Gospels, which corroborate each other or at least depend on each other. As conveying atmosphere and reflecting the nature of their country, they would be accepted by scholars as good social history. The region about the "Sea of Galilee" was evidently a simple countryside, for the people who move through the Gospels are plain men and women, lower and lower-middle class in status. They evidently live happily enough, as plain people do. There is no evidence in the Gospels that they lacked food or clothing or other ordinary necessities. They encountered the ordinary troubles of the countryside, such as illness, and the occasional minor sex scandal. They were so much like our own people of similar social standing that the English-speaking world, especially its North American portion, has never found any difficulty in understanding them and accepting the stories handed on by those who wrote about them.

It has found no difficulty, indeed, in understanding the attitude, though not all the recorded sayings, of the man who evidently became "a troubler in Israel" and was later executed. Such troublers had been frequent in Israel before and have been numerous elsewhere since those days and never more so than in our own times, wherein a new way of salvation is proclaimed every day of the week. No doubt the Palestinians were well accustomed to them, too, for was not the history of Jewry the history of prophets, wise men, scribes, more particularly prophets, very upsetting prophets, some of them?

Why should Jesus,[2] just another prophet, have met the fate he did? His preaching had been strictly ethical, on themes on which many another prophet had held forth – denouncing his people for their sins and exhorting them to repentance. It was very much in the familiar pattern of Jewish life. He had left politics alone (he probably knew little about their higher ranges) except for the one statement that has come down to us and into which he is represented as having been trapped: "Render unto Caesar the things that are Caesar's and unto God the things that are God's." He got out of the trap as skilfully as any modern politician trained in the art of defensively and ambiguously answering questions. He made many strange statements, apparently, about the relationship between God and himself, but in that land of religious ecstasy, they probably were no stranger than many another's. They have been distorted for us by the verbiage in which we have received them. For example, when the term "Christ" began to be applied to him, we forget that it meant simply "the Anointed." The German word is *Der Gesalbte,* which conveys the original idea far more clearly than our own – the one upon whom "salve," ointment, has been placed. Much more of course was to be read into "anointing" than any mere physical act. Jesus began to consider himself or others to suggest that he "was called of God." This is not an unusual conviction for a man to have. Many a man has felt himself "called of God," that is, his nature has forced upon him the particular task he tries to accomplish.

The ethical teaching of Jesus was along more or less familiar lines of exhortation to righteousness but it was taken to uncomfortable logical extremes ("Forgive seventy times seven, turn the other cheek, sell everything you have and give to the poor" and many other such injunctions) which in some respects made it illogical and except under rare circumstances, impracticable. But there had been prophets before him just as extreme, annoying and impracticable. He was evidently a faith-healer of enormous success in an age when every community provided abundant material for the exercise of that art, and this may well account for many of the Biblical "miracles." But miracles (literally, "marvellous things") came every day and everywhere in those times, just as they do today ("unidentified flying objects"!) and no one except the sophisticates such as pagan Lucretius boggled at the course of nature being set aside.

The trouble probably was that his mission began to reach such proportions that it got out of control. In a simple countryside, hordes of people, whether 5,000 or 500, cannot be drawn together without distant authority getting to hear about it and taking an interest in it. Even in our day and our free society, great open air assemblages invite the attention of the police. As the movement rolled on, it must have rolled its leader with it and eventually it swept him up to Jerusalem, the ancient capital and not far from the seat of Roman control (Caesarea Philipi, on the coast).

As long as Jesus stayed in the country, he had evidently aroused little more than curiosity. As a countryman, he would not be familiar with city life. When he came up to Jerusalem and began cleaning up the temple in what must have seemed a very high-handed way (like Carry Nation of Kansas long ago smashing up saloons with her hatchet, in an effort to abolish the use of alcohol), it surely must have seemed to Jewish officialdom that he would have to be restrained – even tolerant public authority would have seen things in that light, and the officialdom of the day is not pictured as tolerant. And what was worse, among that turbulent people, large crowds and disorderly conduct would be sure to bring down the Roman soldiery upon the city.

Whatever the exact circumstances, the crucifixion took place and the greatest of Western revolutions began. We get an account of what happened through the Book of Acts, which book of all of those of the New Testament, carries on its own face the best guarantee of historical accuracy. Those who did not immediately fall away from the band that had gathered around the crucified leader were left bewildered and wondering what to do. Somehow or other they received a fresh impulse and the new creed began to grow. A similar situation was to arise some six centuries later, when the death of the next tremendous Semitic prophet, Mohammed, precipitated his followers into just the same situation of doubt and hopelessness. From it, these men were propelled into the remarkable course of events that in the short space of a century spread their creed across an area much larger than had been covered by the Roman empire at its largest. Early Christianity was to know no such expansion, either in extent or in type. Not until the time of Charlemagne (ninth century) did its representatives, pushing well beyond the bounds of imperial Rome, begin to offer the heathen an alternative of conversion or the sword.

II
The Emergence of Christianity
From Judaism

It is probable that but for a few individuals, the new sect would gradually have taken up its weight in Judaism and have settled down into some new variant of the old religion. Jesus, it is true, had been quite cavalier in his treatment of that most sacred of sacred cows for the orthodox, the law. "The Sabbath was made for man, not man for the Sabbath," he had shockingly declared. There had been other flouts. But even this sinfulness of doubt would have been smoothed out with time. Thanks to the "Dead Sea Scrolls," we know today that a segregated group of Jews had lived their own life for many years apart from the main body of their people. The followers of Jesus could well have followed some such course. But that was not to be. An infinitely wider destiny was to open to the new sect than could possibly have awaited it in Judaism.

According to the narrative in Chapter Ten of the Book of Acts, Peter, the disciple, had a vision; this, clearly enough, showed him that there would be no difference made between man and man, that is, between Jew and Gentile. "God is no respecter of persons," Peter found himself saying to the Roman centurion, Cornelius, "but in every nation, he that feareth him and worketh righteousness is accepted with him" (Acts X, vv. 34-35). Through the pious Cornelius, so the scripture reads, many others were converted, and evidently without embracing the formal aspects of Judaism, especially circumcision. Peter was heavily criticized by his fellow followers when he returned to Jerusalem "Thou wentest in to men that were uncircumcized and did eat with them" (Acts XI, v. 3). There could have been few graver ritualistic offences among the Jews of the day. Peter stood his ground and made the first breach in the wall.

Meanwhile, another man, to become an even greater example of the familiar "troublers in Israel," had been coming to the front. This was Saul of Tarsus, later to become Paul. Evidently a zealot, he had thrown himself into persecution of the followers of Jesus wherever he could find them, and it was on some such mission that he had the experience on the road to Damascus which turned him in the opposite way. There is no need to enlist the aid of pious miracle-ism to explain it: many a man, long brooding over his course of life, has suddenly come to the conclusion that he has been on the wrong road and has experienced this psychological turnabout that religious people call "conversion." If Paul had an epileptic fit at the same time, which from the narrative seems not unlikely, that too, apparently was much less uncommon than it would be today. Julius Caesar himself is said to have been epileptic ("he hath the falling sickness") and epilepsy gets much mention among the healing miracles.

At any rate, from being persecutor, Paul became exponent. And he discovered, or thought he had discovered for himself, the exact nature of the man who had been crucified. "And straightway he preached Christ in the synagogue, that he is the son of God" (Acts IX, v. 20). The new sect came in for persecution in Jerusalem and Saul escaped by being let down over the walls in a basket (Acts IX, v. 25). He then made various short journeys, spent a year quietly (Acts XI, v. 26) and finally having got the conservative members of the sect to accept him as one of themselves, set out on the first of his great missionary journeys. Along with Barnabas, he went from Antioch to Seleucia, to Cyprus, to Perga on the continent and thence back to Antioch (Acts XIII). Here Saul-Paul, being invited to speak in the synagogue, as a Jew, let go and told the congregation about Jesus and the crucifixion, that Jesus had been raised from the dead and was now immortal and to quote (vv. 38ff) "Be it known unto you therefore, men and brethren, that through this man is preached unto you the forgiveness of sins . . ."

After the talk "many of the Jews and religious proselytes followed Paul" (v. 43) who persuaded them not to allow a break to occur. The next Sabbath, Paul attracted an enormous audience, but the old "hard liners" "were filled with envy and spoke against those things . . . contradicting . . ." But (v. 46) "then Paul and Barnabas waxed bold and said 'It was necessary that the word of God should first have been spoken to you (the Jewish community) but seeing ye put it from you, and judge yourselves unworthy of everlasting life, WE TURN TO THE GENTILES.' "

Here was the decisive statement: "We turn to the Gentiles." As decisive as Luther's "Hier stehe ich . . ." of 1,500 years later.

Paul's innumerable missionary journeys followed and the result of them and presumably other such efforts by other individuals, was that the new sect expanded across the empire, breaking the ancient bonds of Judaism and universalizing itself within a century or so into a world religion.

A new name was soon applied to it. "The disciples were first called

Christians at Ephesus,'' the Book of Acts informs us. This must have been within a few years of the first migrations from Jerusalem, that is within the first generation after the crucifixion. The new name stuck, and the sect spread. Paul himself reached Rome. The journey is described in one of the most vivid and picturesque of biblical narratives (Acts XXVII, and XXVIII).[3]

If we only had a second Book of Acts! This first century, otherwise largely conjecture, must have been comparable to a fire spreading. Competition with Oriental mystery religions[4] such as Mithraism, was intense and it was not ended until the new religion, in the fourth century, got power into its hands, when apparently, it managed to choke them off. In those first centuries, the world of the Roman empire must have been religiously a vacuum, for the old gods were almost dead and had nothing to offer. Any new sect, however extreme or absurd, apparently could get a start among the urban multitudes which, drawn from everywhere under the sun (like the great American cities of our own day), had neither religious or ethnic roots, but floated like leaves on a stream. The phenomenon repeats itself today, when another God is dying. It is a phenomenon apparently just under the surface at all times everywhere, which only the stern hands of authority or disciplined custom keep submerged. Once that is relaxed, the official God is quickly replaced (though the old name or names may remain) by multitudes of gods and godlets.[5]

As the Pauline epistles testify, the rapid spread of the new religion was accompanied practically from the first by divisions, divisions about doctrine and about ethical and moral practices. It was only slowly that the loose, go-as-you-please morals of classical Paganism were displaced by the Jewish outlook with its intense convictions on what was right and what was wrong and the accompanying feeling of sin and guilt which has ever since been so prominent in Christianity. Among the hordes of new adherents, it must have taken unremitting, arduous fighting to wrestle down the centuries-old practices of Paganism, all, to those who knew nothing else, deeply rooted as life itself. There stand in evidence St. Paul's innumerable references to "meat offered to idols," "fornication, uncleanness, inordinate affection, evil concupiscence, and covetness, which is idolatry" (Colossians III, v. 5). What was "inordinate affection"? Unnatural sex practices?[6] And do the complexities of the sexual relationship stand at the base of Christian morality?

And what was the attraction of the new religion? It must have been something powerful enough to induce people everywhere to abandon old ways of life and take on this new and difficult one. There is always a challenge in difficulty and it will always be met by many superior people. But beyond that there was the simple promise whose power in a largely lower class and slave society must have been magnetic: forgiveness of sins and "life everlasting." Again, the Pauline epistles ring the changes on these two themes. The power of these promises does not come home to the modern Western world, whose knowledge and secularism makes them seem practically meaningless and whose course has been such an extraordinary combination of misfortune and prosperity. Never, however, at the lowest points of our misfortunes, in the midst of the horrors of two World Wars, has hope for our own future, as contrasted with "eternal life" forsaken us. We were convinced we should come through – as we have! It was different for the lowly under the empire, where subjection and slavery were the lot.

The spread of a great new religion can never be a simple matter and there are many other factors which contributed to the growth of Christianity. These have often been discussed by other writers. They cannot be detailed here. But it is necessary, from its bearing on the general thesis, to note one in particular: the new religion in due course caught up some of the intellectuals of the day and thus opened the door to the marriage of simple Bible Christianity with the abstractions of Greek philosophy. St. Paul himself was a semi-intellectual and he showed his acquaintance with some of the minor Greek classical writers. But mainly he was zealot and exhorter and it was after he passed off the scene that those major intellects who are embalmed in "the Church Fathers" made their appearance. No doubt their adhesion at the time was welcome, as would be the capture today of a Harvard professor by a Bible sect. But such men are dangerous. Tertullian (160-230A.D.) for example, could not be contained within strict orthodoxy and became a heretic.[7]

How great a burden for heresy is to be laid on the intellectual of those days may be uncertain. What is certain is the fact of heresy. The new creed had hardly got started before differences began to appear. How could it be otherwise? Adherents were scattered over wide spaces and communication between them was slow and irregular. For a good many years only verbal memories of the man Jesus remained and we know how quickly verbal tradition can become twisted into fantastic forms, especially among simple people. The beliefs that men in Asia Minor, shall we say, had about this man, what his teachings were, the words he put them in, what he did, must have varied enormously from similar notions obtaining in, say, Spain. The wonder is that any unity remained. The natural result was "heresy" upon "heresy," whatever "heresy" could have meant under the circumstances.

III
The Christian Church Takes Shape

And so it remained for many generations. One could hazard the guess that one of the main things saving Christianity from disintegration was persecution by the Roman authorities. It is an old Christian saying that "the blood of the martyrs is the seed of the church." In those early centuries, there were plenty of martyrs and there was plenty of blood. It may have saved the church. In justice, it would be necessary to add that the doctrinal and ethical survivals from Jesus and his immediate successors (e.g. the New Testament) were as powerful as they have always been in succeeding ages in holding the faithful and attracting converts. Christianity was purged with fire and it showed it had metal in it.

Despite division and persecution, the church increased in size and went from strength to strength. It developed its hierarchical ranks – deacon, priest, bishop, archbishop and patriarch. This parallelled the parcelling out into territorial administrations that has occurred throughout history in secular imperialism. The patriarch became a kind of Seleucian monarch, a spiritual ruler over the "faithful" living within his vast area. And so with the lesser ranks down to bishop, each became, as time went on, more or less of a ruler within his own domain or *diocese*. When the breakdown of imperial power in the West left many a distant bishop isolated (say in the sixth century) such men had to rely on themselves in both secular and spiritual matters.

So greatly did the church grow in numbers and influence that, after the last of the great persecutions under Diocletian, official recognition came. Under Constantine, an edict brought toleration, 313 A.D. and at last in 324, recognition as an official religion of the empire. Whether Constantine acted from purely political motives or whether he, too, had been touched within, it is too late in the day to decide. What he did is well-established. Not only did the church get recognition (which must have been something like the Communist party being declared the only official party in the United States) but a great council was held, the Council of Nicaea, 325 A.D., at which Constantine himself presided and at which an official doctrine was hammered out for the whole church, still good sixteen centuries later.

Does the course of the first three centuries of Christian history illustrate the thesis that these chapters attempt to elucidate? The thesis that a new culture, or an important chapter in an old one, is launched on a wave of zeal, enthusiasm, conviction, that the wave slowly loses its force, leading to a phase in which intellect succeeds zeal, that intellectualism brings tolerance and liberty, that liberty runs down into licence, with the resulting confusion going as far as anarchy and that only a strong exercise of authority restores order and brings about the beginning of a new cycle?

Definitely, it does. Never was there such a wave of emotional zeal (apart from Mohammedanism) as that which carried Christianity to the uttermost limits of the Roman empire and even beyond them in the first and second centuries. Never until the Reformation was the original foundation rent and wracked so grievously by internal division. While not all of this can be laid on the shoulders of intellectuals, they must bear a good share of it. The rundown is clearly reflected in the nature of early Christian writing:

> . . . Christian literature begins in spite of itself; first-hand, sometimes even first-person, account of the life of Jesus Christ; letters from His friends. Only gradually do the arguments begin, apologetics, creeds, statements of faith, definitions of dogma. And these first Christian writings are naive, full of grammatical errors, they lack in taste, in polish, what they make up in sincerity, in immediacy. But they show the whole Christian life, the thought, the behaviour, the arguments are honest, direct, and courageous . . .

> So long as the writers are purely practical and unselfconscious, writing only to remember, to reprove, to convince, and to refute, the early Christian writings *are* literature, and of the best. But from the moment when the authors roll the words around their tongues, when they seek to astonish, to impress, or even merely to emulate their pagan or wordly rivals, they fall into platitudes, into bombast, or into sterile rhetoric . . .[8]

From disintegration, by recantations, and by internal divisions, geographical and doctrinal, the church was saved by persecution and by an inner core of vitality arising, as Christians would have said, "out of the Holy Spirit," but also out of the freshness and decency of a new and hopeful gospel. In the third century, there may well have been almost as many "churches" as there were bishoprics. This would correspond to the libertarian phase of the cycle in other epochs. The internal condition of this decentralized church could have been anything but good, especially when we think of the confusions and disorders of the times. From this condition, the strong hand of Constantine saved the church.

With Nicaea, we are in a new cycle, a cycle to merge in the West, unfortunately, into the breakdown of empire and the return to disorder. Yet within three centuries, a new religion had emerged, clarified its own nature, triumphed over internal division and external rivals. It had secured official recognition and was using its new powers to expand and aggrandize itself. The old world from which it had arisen lay in ruins about it. The greatest revolution in the history of Western man had taken place.

Notes

1.   As for example, Jehovah's Witnesses and the numerous groups collectively called Pentecostals.

2.   Most authorities concede that Jesus was a historical, not a mythical, figure, but as it has recently asserted, it is impossible to write a biography

of him. (University of South Florida broadcast, February, 1978).

3.   It is of intense interest to all who, like the writer, have "sailed the sea in ships."

4.   See F. Cumont, *The Oriental Religions in Roman Paganism* Dover, (tr. 1911).

5.   These many range down to the love-goddesses manufactured in Los Angeles and the killer cults of the Mansons *et al.*

6.   For some good modern literary recreation of pagan practices, see that strange book by Robert Graves, *I, Claudius.* The reference is to the Emperor Claudius, 41-54 A.D., through whose eyes Graves tries to view the Rome of that day.

7.   For samples of Tertullian and many others, see Anne Fremantle, *A Treasury of Early Christianity, supra.*

8.   *Ibid.*, p. 223.

CHAPTER SIX

The World Turned Upside Down

PART I

Into the Valley

I
The Decline of Hellenism

There are two periods of profound upheaval and change in the history of the Western world. These are the three centuries or so during which Paganism was dying and Christianity was replacing it, and the modern period of some 200 years marked by the great revolutions and by the revolutionary upheavals of our own day. There is room for much difference in detail in reviews of these periods, but hardly for dispute about their having occurred. Many would add a third period as equally stormy: that which saw the Middle Ages ending and something very different taking their place.

For the first of these periods, specified by the hackneyed phrase "the Fall of Rome," there are as many explanations as there are writings on the subject. All of these probably have elements of truth in them. One, only, can be singled out for individual and brief examination here. Sir Samuel Dill, writing at the turn of the nineteenth-twentieth centuries, stated that the largest element in determining Rome's fate was the loss of freedom. Sir Samuel's authority is worthy of the highest respect, but it may be questioned whether in such belief, he was not rather too much a child of his times. He wrote at the very apogee of English freedom, the heir of over two centuries of profound belief in the rightness, justice and immutability of the principle of self-government. No one in the English-speaking world can fail to respond to the nobility of such convictions. Self-government under the law, the equality of all before the law which all have made, is as deeply rooted a belief as men may well have and its guardianship under enduring institutions is our greatest gift to mankind.

Unfortunately this intense sense of personal freedom does not seem necessary to all societies, many of which have flourished without it or with severe modifications of it. No people should be more aware of this than those of the late twentieth century, for we have had before our eyes cases of the grossest violation of freedom, individual and collective, of justice, cases of a tyranny quite on a level of anything the ancient world had to show. Without question, a sigh of relief went up from Germany when the tyranny of Hitler disappeared. Yet Germans had fought stoutly for Hitler, or for what they were persuaded he stood for, the "defence of the Fatherland." So too, Russians fought just as valiantly for the tyrannous Stalin. Tyrannies have evils that cannot be disguised, but they may go on for a long time. What the tyrant does is usually far away and it does not affect myself or my family. As long as it does not, we may shrug our shoulders.

Then there may come a "good" tyrant: he is called merely an autocrat, and if he can show claim to legitimacy, as Henry VIII or Louis XIV easily could do, he may be applauded, almost worshipped. But even to a Napoleon, success brings sanction. So regretfully, one must dismiss the adequacy of Samuel Dill's major thesis for "the Fall of Rome." But that the loss of freedom had clearly discernible consequences. In our modern tyrannies some kind of deliverance has usually seemed possible. In the sixteenth century, for the English there was always France across the water, and in the seventeenth, for the French there was always England. For republican and Napoleonic France, there was England. For Hitlerian Germany, escape routes lay open to men who could not stick the régime. For Stalin's Russia escape was more difficult, though even for it, there was always the possibility.

But for dissidents in the Roman empire, there seemed to be no escape, save, possibly one that few would take – abandoning civilization and seeking the barbarians. Otherwise, how escape from a rule that included the whole world? But there does not seem to have been much desire for escape. Conspiracies there were without number: few of them went beyond assassination which merely replaced one tyrant by another. Of reasoned constitutionalism, except of the nostalgic type, which sighed for a republic restored, there was none: there were no more discerning Polybiuses. Rome's government rested in one man. The few that in a more enlightened world might have led the way to more reasonable things, evidently were incapable of that, and the many were brutish and hopeless. Countries get the government they deserve, the saying is. An almost barbarian Rome, in which only a microscopic few were civilized got what it deserved.

For a long, complex period of human history, there can be no final, once-for-all explanation. It is also to be asked: did Rome "fall"? Rome, the city, we know ceased to be a capital and it was plundered by Alaric, the Goth, and half a century later by other war bands. At one time it was lost to the empire and later regained, only once more to be lost. Did this constitute "the Fall of Rome"?

That which had been created, the Roman empire, far outgrew that which had created it, the city of Rome. And as it grew, the mother city began to lessen in importance. When Constantine established Constantinople, his new eastern metropolis, (330), the trend to secondary status was hastened. Not long after that, the emperors ceased to live in Rome, or even to visit it, except occasionally ceremonially. They made their capital, insofar as they had a Western capital, first at Milan and then at Ravenna. During many years, no city in the West could properly be termed a capital. The emperors moved around, carting along with them, their officials, their servants, slaves and personal possessions. Even the imperial treasure appears to have moved about Europe along with the emperor. Centuries later, this was exactly the practice of the half-barbarian kings of England who maintained their treasure in the room or tent where they slept. Did such elementary modes of behaviour of a necessity equate the two civilizations?

There are several veils between us and the ancient world, and so well do they conceal it that even today with all the wealth of scholarship that has been directed upon it, we are far from certainty in most of the statements we make about it. First of all, there is the relative scarcity of source material. Much has been done to rectify this, especially in the collection and interpretation of inscriptions of every possible type and purpose. By such instrumentalities, historians have managed a splendid job of reconstruction, but no one would contend that all the gaps are filled. For some periods, source material is relatively abundant and for others, scarce. As the years go by, material increases in quantity, though not in quality. It seems to be more abundant for the so-called Dark Ages than for the height of the empire. Its mastery calls for high linguistic attainments and for many other supporting qualifications and no one but an expert will try to use it directly. As in most fields of history outside our own personal narrow space, we must trust to others.

Another difficulty in getting a clear view lies in the mists with which tradition, immemorial usage and sentiment surround the classical world. In our own day and especially in the New World, the classics have been relegated to the shelf, but indirectly they are still powerful. If a given perspective has for centuries dominated the schools, dominated the minds of scholars, dominated the polite traditions of the educated public, then it is difficult indeed to dig the original material out from under it and view it afresh.

A third difficulty for the present piece of writing arises out of the slippery nature of the quest. The object is to try to find the way through cultural changes and for this the subject matter must necessarily be indefinite. One cannot have recourse to the straightforward approach of many another type of inquiry, where a march through country well-marked with chronological signposts may be what is called for.

And finally, however apparently at home in his period, the writer moves through foreign territory, that semi-pagan, semi-Christian, semi-civilized, semi-barbarous territory of a time infinitely different from our own.

II
The Triumph of the Organized
Christian Church

Despite all this, it is possible, with the aid of the many excellent modern studies, to see the large features of the ancient world and at least to suggest why, as it were, under our very eyes, oaks keep changing into ash trees or dogs into cats, metamorphoses that the mysterious processes of history so often seem to resemble. For the purposes of this study, thanks to the repeated inspection of the old materials by good minds, the outlines stand out clearly and we can look at the ebb and flow of the historical tide as it goes on century after century. It seems that what we can see with especial clarity is exactly this tidal movement of history, in other words, that phenomenon to which the study is directed, the periodization of history and its accompanying "pulsations."

Periodization stands out with especial clarity in the transition from Paganism to Christianity, and also in some of the phases of the transition. We speak easily of "the Age of the Antonines," and of late there has been introduced the phrase "the Late Roman Revolution." This latter period has its own subdivisions, as does the long and painful transition from Paganism. Another good phrase is often heard; "late antiquity." These classifications stand out the more distinctly because they are farther off than those closer to ourselves and many of their details have faded.

There are various general considerations which if they do not "explain" what was occurring in the late Roman empire, at least throw a good deal of light on the history of the times. In the third century, life went out of the cities.[1] Since the empire was in some vital respects a congeries of cities, some of which were close to city-states, the decline in that area must be given weight. It is explained with relative ease, especially since something of the same general nature is happening around us. An account exists of a certain city, Nicomedia, whose "city fathers" undertook to build an aqueduct. Something caused failure. The aqueduct was abandoned, only to be begun afresh later on. The same thing happened and it was proposed to begin a third time. This was too much for the emperor, who could see that the city was being burdened by an impossible debt. He sent an inspector and the authority of the local "fathers" was by that much curtailed. One "inspection" to secure greater efficiency led to another, and eventually this became more or less general. In this way and others of the sort, central power gradually extinguished local authority. But that occurred slowly. The Athens of the middle of the fourth century has been described as a thriving university city.[2]

As for the parallel with today, central authorities everywhere, either for efficiency or because power feeds on power, trench on the municipalities. School boards, among our most democratic institutions, slowly are dessicated, their members left with the feeling that they have little genuine function. With us, this process of bureaucratic centralization has not gone to its logical limits and there is still life in local boards, commissions and councils. But give it a chance, come back in a hundred years and then see where central appetite for power has got to.[3]

In the empire, the ever increasing weight and expense of local duties naturally led local authorities to try to get out of them. This brought the extraordinary step of requiring officials to stay at their posts, and their sons after them. Nothing like this obtains in our world. The same general considerations led to peasants being required to stay on the land, thus opening the road to mediaeval serfdom. There was considerable variation in the two sections of the later empire. The peasantry of Asia Minor and of Syria remained prosperous and independent. Not so in the West, where there was being taken the route to the large, completely self-contained estate, equipped with slaves.

In the middle and later half of the third century, a degenerating situation was accentuated by two things: the uncertainties of the imperial succession[4] which led to innumerable emperors coming and going, with none at their posts long enough to accomplish much even had they had the ability, and also a tremendous inflation which almost destroyed the value of money. We moderns do not need to be informed about the evils of inflation, we have had too many bitter experiences of them. The two things combined greatly weakened the empire and presumably the loyalties of the people. As so often happens, authorities looked for a dog to kick and found it in the Christians. The mid-century persecution under the Emperor Decius was the result. The period from about 235 to 284 has been well termed "the Anarchy."

The imperial succession presented to the empire a problem for which no solution was ever reached. There was an uncertain tendency towards hereditary succession, but this never became a rule. There was a tendency, which could even be called a policy, towards adoption. This might have worked out quite well, if there had been any mode of substituting careful counsels of adoption for the mere choice of the ruler. There was the vestigial remnant of election, which may have psychologically been more important than it is usually esteemed, for the fiction of legitimacy seemed necessary for loyalty – Constantine was the only emperor, apparently, who succeeded in becoming illegitimately legitimate.

In one of the museums of Rome there is an interesting bronze tablet on which is engraved the *lex Vespasiana,* the law by which the Roman people hand over full power-of-attorney to Vespasian (69-79) to act on their behalf. Apparently some such grant of power was deemed necessary: it formed the base for legitimate succession and legitimate exercise of power. But when emperors came and went (at one time four in one year), legitimacy must have become a relative trifle.

The empire of course was not the only political organization which failed to find a satisfactory form of succession to power. Until its disappearance in 1806, its successor, the Holy Roman Empire, was in the same position. Great Britain has not to this day clearly and unequivocally decided that hereditary succession is the fundamental law. All it has done has been to regulate the succession by Act of Parliament, empirically.[5] France alone of the great states, secured, or practically secured, full recognition of the idea of hereditary succession through primogeniture and male descent.[6]

The name for the period, 235-285, the Anarchy, is no doubt just. From anarchy, the empire was rescued, as it had been before, by the appearance of a man, Diocletian. Diocletian (284-305) was no noble Roman of the old school; rather, a rough frontiersman, a kind of Andrew Jackson among Virginia aristocrats. Diocletian was strong enough to restore order, put new life into the army, protect the frontiers. As we all know, he it was who divided the empire into East and West, each under its own Augustus and each with the aid of more or less subordinate "Caesars." It was a valiant effort at decentralization and it had consequences which have lasted until our own day – though it could be reasonably maintained that the division was simply an admission of geographical and cultural fact.

Diocletian carried out the last persecution of the Christians. It furnished a number of martyrs to the church and thus strengthened its internal cohesion, bringing closer the great day when the numbers and status of the Christians would force first, toleration, then recognition. The severity of the persecution apparently has been exaggerated. While the empire represented civilization, it certainly did not stand for humanitarianism. There were probably more slaves than free citizens and for many of the slaves, life could not have been harder. The gladiatorial games were still going on. With such "adornments" of Roman life – there were others – it is hard to see imperial Rome as very much more than a modified barbarism. So not much indulgence could have been expected. Nevertheless, the number of outright executions is said not to have been unduly large for the times. A figure is cited for Palestine of thirty-seven, but "Maximin (Caesar of the East) sent obstinate cases of contumacy to the mines, having first blinded them in one eye and severed the tendons of one foot."[7]

Relief was not far off. After Diocletian's reign, there was a short, uneasy interval, then the victory of Constantine at the Milvian Bridge ("Hoc signo, vince" – "by this sign (the Cross) conquer!"), the toleration proclaimed through the Edict of Milan (313), Constantine's "conversion" and finally full acceptance as the official religion. Constantine's conversion may have been genuine. Why otherwise it has been asked, should he have associated himself with a small and relatively unimportant minority of his subjects? Not that he at once saw far into the nature of Christianity. That came slowly and he would not have himself baptized until shortly before his death, the idea apparently being that, well knowing he could not avoid sin, unbaptized he always would have the chance through baptism of escaping the consequences of his sins.

The conversion, after which many a prominent pagan no doubt found that he had always been a Christian anyway, quickly brought large results. Not only were the gladiatorial games prohibited (325) but Constantine took much interest in church affairs, especially in the divisions caused by doctrinal disputes. This was symbolized by the all-important General Council of Nicaea, 325,[8] in which the leaders of the two major camps, Athanasius and Arius, confronted each other. The decisions made at Nicaea separated the world almost as effectively as had Diocletian's. Its echoes have rolled down the centuries.

To trace out the issues debated at Nicaea in detail and describe them would and has required endless volumes.[9] Arius contended that since God is the "eternal and unknowable monad," the Son could not be of the same substance as the Father. This would make the Son something other than God, even less than God, exclaimed his opponents, aghast. The dispute projected into debate the words around which debate raged: "homoousian, or was it homoiousian?" "Of the same substance" or "of similar?" Just an iota, a jot between them, but about to tear the church apart. The assembled bishops, unable to agree and apparently willing to go on debating forever, Constantine himself ended the dispute (for that moment) by adding to the creed agreed-upon the words, consubstantialem patri, "homoousian to patri," "the Son, consubstantial with the Father." "The formula was only welcomed by the opponents of Arius because it was utterly unacceptable to him." And so ended the Council which was to mark a division in the church as deep and almost as long lasting as that which was to be projected into Western Europe by the Reformation.

Such words do not bring out the full import of Nicaea. The creed which was adopted there, however many hair-splitting disputes might be waged about it, became THE CREED for Christianity. Here were rock-bottom affirmations in which Christians believed and must believe:

> I believe in God the Father Almighty, Maker of Heaven and earth, and in Jesus Christ, His only Son, Our Lord, Who was conceived by the Holy Ghost, born of the Virgin Mary, suffered under Pontius Pilate, was crucified, died and was buried. He descended into hell. The third day, He rose from the dead. He ascended into Heaven. And sitteth on the right hand of God, the Father Almighty: from thence He shall come to judge the quick and the dead . . .[10]

The mystique of the Trinity was thus firmly established – the Triune God, the One in Three and Three in One. Scarcely a word of this document that was not to affect to their uttermost depths, almost every man and woman who would live from that day until our own.

The reach and profundity of such vast decisive pronouncements is not recognized when they are made: they have to sink in and sometimes take generations so to do. Nicaea in this respect may be compared with Magna Carta or the American Declaration of Independence, one of the supremely great and decisive points in history.

A speculation is allowable that the doctrine that suffered defeat at Nicaea, Monophysitism, foundation of Arianism, which continued influential in Syria, Palestine and Egypt, prepared those countries, four centuries later, for the easy triumph of a religion not too readily distinguished from the Arian version of the Christian creed – the triumph of Mohammedanism.

The decision reached at Nicaea was the first major and universal synthesizing of Christian doctrine. It drew a line which all could be forced to toe. Not for another 900 years was another of its reaches to be made, not until the Council of the Lateran in 1215 established the Doctrine of Transubstantiation. But Nicaea by no means brought immediate unity to the Christian world, though the Apostles' Creed is found in a Greek version of about 340.[11] Total uniformity was too much to expect, especially when abstract theological propositions came under the inspection of the subtle Greek mind. But eventually a high degree of uniformity came to prevail. Arianism, after some three centuries, shrank away and the church entered those long ages during which Christianity seemed as stable and as deeply rooted as had the Paganism ("Hellenism") that preceded it. Only in our day, or yesterday at latest, has the faith affirmed at Nicaea, ceased to dominate the European world.

III
The Full Energies of a
Growing Culture

The triumph of Christianity unleashed the full energies of growing culture. Its new shoots sprang up everywhere, piercing the old pagan thickets and at last obliterating them. We are at the crest of one of those innumerable ridges in human affairs where the air is clear, the view wide and the future seems illimitable. As we go down the valley, however, there is mist and at last the bottom is reached. Nicaea was the height, the sixth century was the swampy bottom. On the way down the slope, we go through the autumn brilliance of the "silver age," so-called, of Roman literature and of the new Christian culture, too, an age of some of the church's greatest men, but men who are less saints than intellectuals. The saintly Jerome and the almost equally saintly Augustine had an anything but saintly quarrel about a book Augustine was alleged to have written in which he made depreciatory remarks about some of Jerome's work. Augustine was in Carthage, Jerome at the other end of the eastern Mediterranean at Bethlehem. But he kept bombarding away (during the year 403-404) and eventually ended by practically telling Augustine "to put up or shut up," in quite unsaintly language. The two, Augustine especially, had descended from the plateau of Christian zeal to the "shelf" of intellectual wrangling.

The fires of the early fourth century, with memories of the martyrs just beyond it, seemed banked. The Christian philosophers and literary men had come in. It seemed a proper age for a Jerome to translate the Bible into the "vulgar" (common) tongue (Latin) or for St. Benedict to attempt to curb the zeal of the monks by his famous "Rule."[12] Ahead lay the blows of fate and temporal trails as yet unimagined.

In the new cycle, the conversion of Constantine is, if one event can be so, the decisive point. Where leaders were not converted, the church did not flourish: in Persia, for example, the Christians remained a minor sect. But in the empire, the church took full advantage of its new position and it went forward from greatness to greatness. It was to be only a matter of time before emperors themselves would discover they could not longer be gods but in theory, at least, only humble members of the universal church along with the slaves of their palaces. The effect on society, right down to our own day, of this innate egalitarianism of Christianity, however obstinately resisted by Christians, has been beyond measure.

Diocletian began to reign in 284. Constantine died in 337. There were less than ten years between the end of one reign and the beginning of the other. The whole period extended fifty-three years. If the reigns of the other emperors of the House of Constantine be counted in, down to Julian the Apostate, 361-363, and they were worthy successors to Constantine, though not of his magnitude, the period is seventy-seven years. If we follow the "Great Man" view of history, here is the explanation of the late Roman Revolution – two great men in fairly direct succession. There can be no question of the enormous place of a great man in history, but that does not settle the controversy for there are always other factors, some of them visible, many invisible. Yet it seems clear, given historical experience, that when men of sufficient stature gain power, the fortunes of the state and the happiness and prosperity of its citizens greatly increase. In the case of the Roman empire, the least that surely can be said is that the appearance of these two great men enabled that dilapidated old coach to go crawling along the road for quite a few more years.

There are many other matters which should be discussed in this look at "the late Roman Revolution," but most must be passed over. They all bring up the question as to what a revolution is. Most people think of revolutions in terms of blood in the streets, reigns of terror and the emergence of dictatorships. These are aspects of the short, sharp revolution to which the modern world has grown accustomed. With reasonable despatch, the English get round to cutting off the head of their king (1649). The French do the same (1793) and the Russians murder their Czar and his daughters (1917). These, however, are but the surface phenomena of revolution. The French Revolution comes out of the whole sweep of the eighteenth century Enlightenment, of which it was the culmination, and the Russian began with the corrosive ideas carried back home by the Czar's soldiers returning from Paris after Waterloo (1815).

The late Roman Revolution was of a different kind, though there were elements of similarity. Dictatorship there had been, to be overthrown by the lovers of liberty, if there had been any lovers of liberty. A new religion there was, to be substituted for the old, and this is the most specific revolutionary aspect of the "late Roman Revolution." But as revolutions go, the late Roman was stretched out in time and except for the church, lacked concentration and conscious direction. There does not seem to have been sense of the creation of a new world, the opening of the gates to Utopia, which accompanies modern revolutions. It was the New World above the skies, not the earthly that provided the driving force. Where did the "driving force" drive? Not to the restoration of any earthly city but as Augustine said, to a city not made with hands, the heavenly city, to the beatitudes of which all good Christians looked forward. Perhaps defeats and loss of territory, sack of cities, even rapine, slaughter and death, did not matter much. They would all be replaced soon. Had not soldiers marching over the shimmering deserts of Syria, actually caught glimpses of its shining towers upon the eastern horizon? No wonder we are in the great age of saints and holy men, of hermits and of monks. No wonder the course of empire trended steadily downward.

No one can, however, look at the age without noting the vast changes in men's affairs here below. The change in religion was the most conspicuous and the deepest; this must have fuller discussion below. But there were many others. One of these, often overlooked, took the shape, under Constantine, of practical reform. Reference has already been made to the disastrous inflation of the second half of the third century. Diocletian had already attempted to control this by his well-known Edict of Prices which could only be and was a failure. Constantine had much better luck. By the simple expedient of plundering the pagan temples of all their accumulated treasures, which were immense, he found enough gold to issue a new currency. His major coin was the *solidus*,[13] the origin of the "S" in L.S.D., *libri, solidi, denarii,* and for a thousand years afterwards it remained the standard and acceptable coin of the Eastern empire.[14] Its effect in restoring balance and certainty through every nook and cranny of life was apparently just as great as the restoration of the German currency after the inflation of the 1920s. Inflation and restoration is a repeated historical phenomenon, one instance not differing basically from another, but always treated as if it were something entirely new.

Elementary acquaintance with history at once brings to mind another big feature of the "Revolution," the "Barbarian Invasions." The subject is a confused one. Some authorities tend to minimize the amount of dislocation they caused, others give prominence. In the fifth century, Germanic tribesmen promenaded, sometimes almost at will, throughout Roman territory. No one denies that Rome itself was taken twice in that century. It is possible that in the distant past such events could be taken more lightly than they would today. But the sack of Rome by Alaric (410), brought on though it may have been by the Romans' own shortcomings, did make a vast impression on the age. The proud imperial city, founded 1,163 years before and hardly having had an enemy foot within its walls in all that time, had been sacked. And sacked by a lot of uncouth, half-savage barbarians, too.

Then there were the confiscations of land, by which the old inhabitants could lose as much as one third of their holdings. And in the last phase, the complete domination of the Barbarian and the supersession of the last of the emperors by a Barbarian king. It was all very well for Augustine to talk about the Heavenly City and derogate the earthly. But he lived in distant Africa, and Rome had been sacked!

What estimate is to be placed on all this? Take the matter of extent alone. We read easily of swarms of Barbarians, possible hundreds of thousands of warriors, crossing into Roman territory. The numbers are invariably incredible. How did scores of thousands of Barbarians – as time wears on they must be dignified by a capital – march as armies over vast distances, provisioning themselves, finding horses and carts and arms, keeping some minimum of discipline? Those who know something of the logistics of armies will know how incredible such feats were. How could the hordes be counted? A little experimenting in doing arithmetic with Roman numerals will give the answer: they could not be counted. The Latin word *mille* is translated not only "one thousand" but "countless." Moreover, as has so often been pointed out, by the fourth century many of the Barbarians had to all intents and purposes become Roman. That process went on more rapidly as time wore on. The great Roman general, Stilicho, who was executed (presumably for being too successful) 408 A.D., was a German. But then, in the Second World War, General Eisenhower and various other allied generals were successful. If multitudes of Barbarians came into the empire, their assimilation was rapid. Perhaps for most of them it was more an immigration than a conquest. When in 451, "Romans" met Huns in the classic Battle of Châlons, the "Romans" were mostly Germans.

Still, however the accounts are set up, it is indisputable fact that in the Battle of Adrianople, 378 A.D., a Roman emperor was slain and the Barbarians entered the territories of the empire to settle, and that only a short thirty-two years later a Barbarian chieftain sacked Rome – almost without resistance. Thirty-two years is not a long space of time for a mighty empire to crumble. And *crumble* is the word, for if the East recovered to fight another day, the West did not and another half-century saw the formal dissolution of 476.

It is surely wrong to attach too much significance to this formal "fall." In the West, and probably most of the East, too, the emperorship as such had had little significance for many years before 476, except as a kind of badge of that sense of legitimacy which is so deep-seated in human hearts. For some years the Western emperors had no more weight than the Mogul emperors of India after the British reduced them to impotence. The subjects of the emperors had apparently lost most of their sense of loyalty. To them the empire had come not to matter: it was the local situation that counted. And were the Barbarians less "civilized" than the Romans? Barbarians were less sophisticated than the Roman *illuminati*, but were they less civilized? A civilization that had produced the gladiatorial games, that officially committed mass murders,[15] the exposure of infants, slavery and the private slaughter of slaves may not have very substantial right to the term "civilized."[16]

The fifth century saw the empire fighting on many fronts, Barbarian inroads constituted only one of these.

IV
Rise and Decline in the Fifth Century:
The So-Called Silver Age

Along with wars without, there seems to have been much change, even turmoil, within. One form that this took was the rapid substitution of new men for old. At various periods of Roman history, we hear of "the decay of the old aristocracy," "the disappearance of the old families," the ascent to power and place of persons of humble origin. Several of the emperors were themselves of this type. Perhaps not too much should be made of it, for it is in the nature of aristocracies to decay – as the French saying is, "the staircases of history are noisy with the sound of wooden shoes going up and the soft tread of silken slippers coming down." Or as the piercing text of scripture puts it – *Deposuit superbos de sedibus et exaltavit humiles.* In the earlier centuries of Rome, the class pyramid was "about as steep as in eighteenth century England." Later on, however, especially from the fourth century, there was more flexibility: the pyramid was open at the bottom, though that does not mean that it was necessarily less steep.

This mitigation of traditional class rigidity was in itself a semi-revolutionary symptom (as in modern England) for strong assertion of equalitarianism is a necessary revolutionary weapon used against every overly-traditional society.

The effects of a class structure on society in general are infinite. In Rome, the city, the great aristocrats at one period backed away from the army and even from office, retreating to their own luxurious solitudes. At another they are found taking stand-offish attitudes to the German immigrants, segregating them, preventing their assimilation. After the recognition of Christianity, they find it useful to co-operate with the bishops and between them, as Rome, the city, and the West, declined, great man and great bishops came to manage their localities. Their education separated them from the ordinary man, and the bishops in particular, clung to the old culture, which few others could possess and came to express themselves in a high-sounding classical Latin that put still another barrier between them and the ordinary man.

Class is a social phenomenon of utmost interest and universal operation. It runs its logical sequence and once again illustrates the thesis this book seeks to maintain. Yet, since the margins of a social class are always blurred, it is hard to "isolate" a class at any given period of history. We hear of "new men" frequently. Since after Nero there was no Reign of Terror, with elimination of an entire class, as in France or Russia, there was not a sudden transition from one kind of class society to another. Except for the disasters of the sixth century, changes apparently were gradual and among the most conspicuous of them was the decline in the width and quality of education. There are no statistics of literacy from those days but the general impression one gets is of decline. Christians, however, were "people of the book" and although they were drawn from relatively humble classes, literacy, at least while they were still an oppressed minority, seems to have been fairly widespread among them. Otherwise there would not have been such a proliferation of tracts, letters and homilies. And we must remember that the Source of the religion once "stooping down, wrote with his finger in the sand," which for a mere carpenter's son, was a considerable accomplishment.

Education for the upper classes had always been readily available. It was essential to the government of the empire and to the administration of the army, as well as to the oratory of the Senate and the law courts. It was available and it was expensive and, as today, served to make a class apart. In a later century, a great man, a Charlemagne, could be unable to write and not suffer from it in the opinion of others. It is improbable that there were illiterate Roman emperors.

The simple old explanations that rested so much on the Barbarian invasions have been known to be inadequate, but the more subtle questions connected with the exhaustion of a culture have not received any excess of attention. In a strongly aristocratic society, the ambitions and ideas of the few go far to shape society as a whole. That something like a genuine revolution was close to the surface of life in the fourth century is to be inferred from the attempt of Julian the Apostate (361-363) to restore a Paganism that he hoped had been sufficiently house-cleaned to make it acceptable. Evidently there was not enough life left in the old religion for success, so after the two year reaction, the evolution of the new society was once more resumed. It was a society in which Christianity was now triumphant. "Thou has triumphed, Galilean" is the oft-quoted remark.

After Julian's counter-revolution, the Christian church was free to work out its destiny, practically unimpeded. Old aristocratic social values by no means disappeared, still less ceased to be influential. Some of them infiltrated the church: bishops stemming from patrician families began to be not uncommon. The church began to veer away from simple doctrines of love and charity and towards the importance and coldness that official status brings. But "under Christ, there is neither Jew nor Gentile, neither bond nor free." The essentially equalitarian nature of Christianity, overlaid though it so often has been by considerations quite the reverse of democratic, comes out from time to time in history: it is always insidiously present, and that is one of its most powerful moulding forces.

No Roman emperor would have had patience with the abstract notion of equality, except in that all his subjects must be equal in their subjection to himself, but even Constantine soon discovered that while tremendously powerful, he was no god, as Augustus before him had been, and that in certain matters, the church would give the law to him. Consequently, along with Paganism, the idea of complete, unfettered autocracy became more and more difficult to maintain. That may have been good enough for an Oriental monarch but not for a Christian emperor. Today we would have to substitute some other collective noun for "church," some such phrase as "public opinion," "free discussion," the right of "private judgment," and so on. Hence comes in that régime, lasting to our own day and still very much alive, under which we recognize two sources of authority, which in adjusting themselves to each other, help to maintain the freedom of us all. Lord Acton maintains that the idea of church and state coexisting in one society is one of the best, perhaps the ultimate, guarantee of freedom.

The powerful "shove" forward given by the two great emperors lasted for a hundred years more or less, but evidently the West was again in trouble in the first decade of the fifth century, as evidenced by the sack of Rome by Alaric in 410. How disorganized "the Romans," that is, the inhabitants of Rome, how far fallen from the great days, is evidenced by the disgraceful shilly-shallying that preceded Alaric's final act. His conduct before the sack had been no more befitting a "Barbarian" than was the habitual conduct of "the Romans." Yet this was the generation that produced a number of the most famous names in late Roman history, some of whom were also great on the scale of world history. Theodosius I, the Great, reigned from 379 to 395. Stilicho, the great general, lasted until 408, when, in an expression of gratitude often resorted to at that time, he was beheaded. Sir Samuel Dill speaks of the latter half of the fourth century, more particularly in respect to provincial society in Gaul, under the heading of "the renaissance" of the fourth century which extended from Constantine to Theodosius, as a kind of "Indian summer," between two periods of convulsion.[17] There were born in the Constantinian period, among others, the following: St. Martin, the evangelical preacher (316), Ammianus Marcellinus, the celebrated military historian (330), St. Jerome (347), St. Paulinus, the convert to asceticism (353), St. Augustine (354). St. Ambrose, the great Bishop of Milan, was born about 340 (dying about 397). There were also Ausonius, around whom Dill centres his study, and the poet Claudian (who disappears from history early in the fifth century). Of these names, two stand out in world history, St. Jerome (translator of the Bible into Latin, the so-called Vulgate), and, of course, St. Augustine. Among the four "learned doctors" of the early church, Roman Catholicism reckons Ambrose, Jerome and Augustine.

Most of these men finished their careers in the first third of the fifth century. Evidently that was not an age of pygmies. The period is well-named "Rome's silver age." It arouses many reflections upon the association of violence and intellectual creativity in a society.

Dill puts his finger on the major explanation for the decline of Rome in the fifth century, despite all this show of distinction, when he speaks of the exhaustion of a culture, and, by implication, of the uneasy restlessness that must occur before the old is over and done with and something new has taken its place. "The idolatry of mere literary form combined with poverty of ideas, the enthusiastic worship of great models without a breath of the spirit which gave them their enduring charm, immense literary ambition without the power to create a single work of real artistic excellence . . ."[18] Here he is speaking of traditional Roman literature, a narrower subject than that of a whole culture. For the culture as a whole, one turns to its political, economic and military phases, and in these he is safe enough in adhering to the conventional finding that the fifth century saw almost tragic decline. As literature is a reflection of life in general, however, a judgment on the literary efforts of an age may not be an unwise judgment on the age in general.

Dill gives the interesting case-history, well-known to specialists in the period, that of Paulinus, called of Nola (394-431), from the monastery in northeastern Spain to which he retreated. Old friends tried to shake him in his decision, not comprehending the inner urge, but he remained steadfast to the way of life he had deliberately chosen.

> The greatest Acquitanian noble of his time, who, before his thirtieth year, had held the consulship and the government of a province. He had had the best education of his day, was immensely rich and had married a rich wife. Suddenly he threw up all his good fortune and went off to the Monastery of St. Nola. There he 'withdrew from the world.' 'Hearts vowed to Christ have no welcome for the goddesses of song, they are barred to Appollo . . . God forbids me to give up my time to the vanities of leisure or of business and the literature of fable, that I may obey his laws and see his light . . . .'[19]

Paulinus did not flee "the world" because of the turmoil of the times. To some extent it was the other way round. He lost interest in the life to which he had been brought up and left it. He was not the only one.

> The biography of Melania the younger, a lady of a great Roman family, and of her equally noble husband, Pinianus, who in 404 decided to sell all their goods and give the money to the poor, and who later settled in Palestine, gives a vivid and circumstantial picture of the immense wealth of the senatorial aristocracy of Rome.[20]

Another who fled from the tumult of the metropolis was the great Jerome, who in 386 went off to Bethlehem in company with his Platonic friend Paula. She died there, having made a similar renunciation in order to follow the ascetic life.

It is easy to see why "Rome fell." The old culture had become riddled with new values. And these not of the kind that answers a rough soldiery with arms in its hand.

Yet such cases are not easy to interpret. They show clearly the penetration of Christian ascetic ideals into the classical world and from that time to this, instances of the same kind of devotional rigour have always been common. In fact, from the eleventh century to the fourteenth and later, the "one thing needful" in Western Christianity among the masses, if not the classes, the Christian ideal *par excellence,* and sometimes acted upon, was poverty. Wealth and poverty form as inexhaustible a topic as do state and church or free will and predestination.

V

Death of a Culture:
Another World Religion Steps
Into the Vacant Place

The idea of cultural exhaustion and replacement has been forced on our generation by events. Today we know at first hand what it is for mighty states to crash to the ground, dragging much of their culture with them. We know in detail what has happened in a score of instances, but have we made much progress in really explaining it?

The established Christian church had a fortunate few generations after its recognition by Constantine. It brought forth its great men, it made the most of the vast opportunities afforded by its promotion to the official religion of the empire. It erected its churches and basilicas, some of which still stand. It managed to incorporate the vagaries and the strength of monasticism and it embarked on its task of extending the Christian creed into regions far wider than the empire. It made its accommodations with some of the more popular and less gross aspects of Paganism as our Christmas and Easter exemplify. But the simple "gospel of goodness" of the early days is not conspicuous in the elaborate literary remainders that have come down to us from these centuries. There is a change in tone. The later writings are far more abstract than the early; more theoretical and semi-philosophical, far more concerned with the individual's personal fate as contrasted with his relationship to others.[21]

No doubt if the topic were explored in depth, it would demand a full dress history of religion in the period. It would have to indicate the results of pairing Greek philosophy into the original Christian vessel, an influence which overlaid and, for classical minds, probably obscured the essential teachings of Jesus about love, making them incomprehensible to many. It would have to evaluate the general air of pessimism, deepening into hopelessness, which apparently mounted higher and higher as the centuries wore on. Did this arise solely out of the uncertainties of life, its miseries (among which slavery must never be forgotten), the inability of a great scattered empire to focus loyalty, patriotism and purpose, or was there some still deeper groundswell to be found? Did the trouble lie mainly in the wearing out of the old gods and religious forms and rites which had satisfied their simple adherents over the centuries? In other words was the villain the increase of education, of knowledge, scientific but mainly pseudo-scientific, such as the *Chaldeans* (the astrologers) dispensed! Or was it the grim conviction of *necessity,* which out-Calvined Calvinism?

It was no doubt all this, and more. Few authorities fail to notice it. A seeking after some kind of solution, some say. Others say an effort on the part of the *illuminati* to catch glimpses of the supreme reality, that Platonic ideal, the prototype and model of all its faulty man-made and man-thought reflections to pierce, with Plotinus (205-270 A.D.) and his neo-Platonists, the evil that hung over life, separating us from the ultimate mysteries.

Whatever the situation and its explanation, it is clear that it left room for infinite explanations and the doctrines based on them. In the earlier centuries, the so-called mystery religions had come in and they satisfied the masses. Christianity itself had been one of them and the completeness and conviction of its explanation had lent to it power. But in the fifth century, the resurrection, chief of Christianity's symbols, was far in the past. How easy, then, for the newly-established church to drift in the direction of logical hair-splitting and ritualistic formalism!

But by the fifth century the church was far too firmly based and widely spread to fall before mere ossification. Moreover, it still had great battles to fight. One was with the old religion. That religion may have become nine-tenths mere traditionalism, but the hold of tradition is strong, and were there not on every hand visible evidences of the old order of things, the pagan shrines and temples, the more or less secret sacrifices? Many a Christian bishop made his reputation as a great destroyer of temples. "Marcellus, Bishop of Apamea (in Egypt) was a very active destroyer of temples, employing troops and hiring gladiators to quell the resistance of the peasantry   In Alexandria bishop Theophilus obtained permission from Theodosius (the emperor) to convert a temple of Dionysus into a church. He took advantage of this grant to parade the secret paraphernalia of the Dionysiac mysteries through the streets."[22] Such scenes were described from Soviet Russia in the fervour of its Revolution, but in reverse, the sacred vestments of the Orthodox priests become parallels to the "paraphernalia of the Dionysiac mysteries."[23]

Travellers in Greece invariably go to see Olympia, the site of the Olympic Games. In addition to the running field of the Games itself, another sight they are shown there is the temple of Jupiter destroyed by the emperor Justinian in his Christian zeal. There lie the beautiful columns, in serried rows, just as they fell over 1,400 years ago. They could easily be put up again. As a work of restoration they should be. That kind of Paganism is long since safely dead.

By the fifth century Paganism, "Hellenism" as it was more properly termed, was retreating to the hills or to the halls of the ultra-conservatives, who kept a little life going in it, just as did submerged United Empire Loyalists in the American states for some years after the Revolution. A worse enemy than Paganism was division, either heretical or schismatic. Arianism has already been mentioned: it was the chief dissenting sect. But there were others, some of which continue to this day, such as the Copts and the Nestorians. More serious was the Donatist schism in North Africa, which for many years maintained itself against the rest of the church. In 405, Donatism was officially advanced from schism to heresy. Importance is lent to it because of the position that St. Augustine, himself a North African bishop, took about it. At first he was all for persuasion through debate. ''But in a few years he had convinced himself that penal laws were an effective aid to moral suasion.''[24] In the centuries to come efforts to compel men unto salvation and the revolting cruelties they entailed were to bulk large.

From the fifth century onward, it becomes increasingly difficult for the historian to pursue the fortunes of East and West as if they still were really a united polity. They were both united and disunited. Since the founding of Constantinople, 324, the East had had its own metropolitan centre, which gave itself airs equal to Rome. These were tolerated, if disliked. But Constantinople was a capital and the emperors were often there. It grew larger and larger, as it must have done, given its geographical situation, for it commanded all the trade from the basin of the Black Sea, and was bridge between the Balkan area and the vastness of Asia.

Asia Minor and its neighbouring Near-East was dubbed in those years ''The Navel of the World'' and Constantinople was the navel of the navel. Constantine and his advisers when they rebuilt old Byzantium built better than they knew and for a thousand years after them, their city continued as it had begun, the metropolis of Christendom. Even the distant Scandinavians, the Varangians, coming overland along the interminable Russian rivers, eventually reached it across the Black Sea and to them it became *Micclegarth* – ''the big town.'' It remained ''the big town'' to the uttermost stretches of Western Europe, the point of origin of luxury goods, the last word in what was new and fashionable and most ''efficient'' in weapons or learning or theology. It was natural that the pope in the 660s, looking about for a successor to the late Archbishop of Canterbury, should decide on Theodore of Tarsus, a Greek, learned in the classical tongue of the Greeks and their literature, as well as in the arts and sciences of the great world from which he came. The fingers of a great metropolis reach far.

To Constantinople, Rome itself by that time had become secondary. To the rude barbarians of the Western islands, to whom Theodore was sent to bring light and learning, far-off Constantinople must have appeared as fantastic and as wonderful as the cities of the south to an Eskimo. Long did Constantinople hold its metropolitan position, the chief of cities, until, growing gradually farther removed from the rising West, eventually it perished (1453), to complete the gulf that by then had long before opened between them.

Notwithstanding the visible separation of the two halves of the empire after 323, the remarkable fact is that they recognized a unity in their duality. That held true even after Greek had displaced Latin as the major tongue of the Eastern empire. After the last emperor of the West had disappeared in 476, was there not, nevertheless, an emperor still? Of course there was, and if his authority became less and less effective, emperor he still remained. As the history of the West is usually presented, **this state of affairs is obscured. A Roman empire did not disappear in 476.** Constantinople remained still the navel of the world's navel.

In the sixth century, the affairs of the Eastern empire again seem to bear witness to the place of the great man in history, for two names dominate most of the period: Anastasius was emperor from 491 to 518, and Justinian, 527-565. Anastasius, like Constantine before him managed to cure some of the ills afflicting the coinage, and was successful with his finances. When he died, he is said to have left 320,000 pounds of gold in the treasury.[25]

The fame of the great luminary Justinian, of course, rests on his building of *Haggia Sophia,* the great church of Holy Wisdom, long since a Mohammedan mosque, and on his codification of the Roman Law. His reign was marred by three exhausting wars with the Persians. Never before had the empire faced another organized state, one as powerful as itself: this it did in Persia, under the two great kings, Khusro I and Khusro II.[26] The rise of Persia as a major power (after a thousand years!) foreshadowed the tripartite division of the world which remained until the fall of Constantinople to the Turks in 1453. It represented the opening phases of the second great attempt of the East to dominate the West. This went on intermittently for many centuries. It may be that in our own day, we are witnessing the third of these great millennial oscillations between East and West.

Justinian was a man who probably tried to do too much. He tried to restore the empire in the West and his famous general Belisarius, came close to doing so, he had his domestic project and his legal undertakings, his Persian and other wars. Belisarius was a great soldier. He recovered Italy and might with luck have recovered Africa and Spain. But Persia was another matter. Persia took Roman forces far off into the unfamiliar East. In the long run Justinian's accomplishments did not hold and after his death the Eastern empire sagged down into the confusion that so often has followed the death of a great man. That was shortly to be added to by the rapidity in the advance from the south of a new culture and a new religion, sternly monotheist in its doctrine. No saints or angels for it, no endless disputes about the various "persons" of the Trinity. In 637 the Muslims took Antioch, in 638 Jerusalem. The gulf had begun to open that has never closed, a gulf deeper and more uncrossable than any that existed between portions of the Christian world, a grand world gulf, one of the most decisive upheavals of all history, ancient or modern. By the time, the extraordinarily short time, in which that gulf had formed, all the south shore of the Mediterranean had passed from out of Christendom, most of the east shore, and eventually some of the north shore too, and its large islands. This huge eruption did not cease until it had rolled to the verges of the Atlantic, the Indian and the Pacific Oceans and had penetrated far into Africa. Compared with what it was to become, the Roman empire, East and West, had been as a child to a man.[27]

From the Antonines to Diocletian and Constantine. From Constantine to the great churchmen of the late fourth and early fifth centuries. From them to Justinian. Each time with disorder in between the ridges. Could there be a more vivid illustration of the periodization of history?

Notes

1.   A.H.M. Jones, *The Later Roman Empire,* (University of Oklahoma Press. 1964), Vol. I, p. 4ff.
2.   Peter Brown, *The World of Late Antiquity,* (Harcourt, Brace, Jovanovitch, New York, 1971), p. 70.
3.   In the modern Australian state of New South Wales, and possibly in others, power over the schools and teachers has passed almost completely to the Department of Education. The Deputy Minister moves teachers around from school to school at his discretion. He is like the general commanding an army or the bishop of a diocese.
4.   See Michael Grant, *The World of Rome* New York, (Mentor Books, 1960), chapter II.
5.   Act of Succession, 1703.
6.   With the barest tag-end of "election" retained in the Coronation ceremony.
7.   Jones, *op. cit.,* p. 72.
8.   A good and simple explanation of Nicaea, the decisions taken there and of the Creed is to be found in L. C. MacKinney, *The Medieval World,* (New York, 1947), pp. 65ff.
9.   For texts of the Creeds, and brief comments, see Fremantle, *op. cit.,* pp. 245ff.
10.   The traditional "Apostles' Creed."
11.   Fremantle, *op. cit.,* p. 275.
12.   For the documents, see Fremantle, *ibid.*

13.   Worth about $3.00 (of 1960 dollars).

14.   Changing its name to *bezant,* after Byzantium.

15.   Jones, *op. cit.,* I, p. 154.

16.   See the spirited defence of Christian conduct as opposed to pagan, by Octavius Januarius, as given by Marcus Felex (third century), printed in Fremantle, *op. cit.,* pp. 237ff.

17.   Dill, *op. cit.,* p. 172.

18.   *Ibid.,* p. 390.

19.   Sir Samuel Dill, *Roman Society in the Last Century of the Western Empire* (Meridian Books, reprinted from the Second Edition of 1899), pp. 390, 398.

20.   Jones, *op. cit.,* p. 172.

21.   Two useful documentary collections for the early writings are: W. C. McDermott and W. E. Caldwell, *Readings in the History of the Ancient World* (Rinehart and Company, New York, 1951); and Anne Fremantle, *A Treasury of Early Christianity, op. cit.* The remark applies even to such a classic as Augustine's great autobiography, *The Confessions.*

22.   Jones, *op. cit.,* I, p. 167.

23.   In the 1930s, the visitor to Russia had the opportunity to buy the robes of archbishops in the government shops of Leningrad.

24.   Jones, *op. cit.,* p. 209.

25.   *Ibid.,* p. 237.

26.   Khusro I, 510-579, Khusro II, (grandson) 591-628.

27.   For a brief *aperçu* of Persia in the sixth century and its clash with Constantinople, see Peter Brown, *The World of Late Antiquity, op. cit.,* pp. 160ff.

CHAPTER SEVEN

The World Turned Upside Down

PART II
The West at its Lowest Point

I

If despite its great emperors and its great soldiers, calamity befell the East, what is to be said of the West? The term "Dark Ages" used to be loosely flung about, applied to all or any of the centuries from about 600 to 1000. The term "the Miserable Ages" could well be applied to the West in that dismal century, the sixth. It does not take much inquiry to turn up large supplies of information on "the Dark Ages" and we probably know them in more detail than we do much of the classical period. Great writers are not to be found, it is true, but there are innumerable artistic remains, some of them of a high order. There is no suggestion that mechanical techniques declined: in fact, they apparently made some progress: it was during the "Dark Ages," for example, that improvements in the simple matter of harness increased the efficiency of the horse.

The "Dark Ages" were "dark" because the old classical way of life, with its favoured aristocratic few and its wide cultural inheritance, faded away, to be replaced by a new, very different culture which in its growing stages was necessarily crude.

"How wonderful must be the heavenly Jerusalem if this earthly city can shine so greatly!" exclaimed the good monk Fulgentius on a day in the year 500 A.D., realizing his ambitions of at last visiting the great metropolis.[1]

At the beginning of the sixth century, after all the vicissitudes of the fifth, the civil strife, the relegation to second place and the plunderings by the

Goths in 410 and 455, Rome was still by far the greatest city of the West. Not only in magnitude but in the aura that must surround a great metropolis which has ruled illimitable territories and whose founding thirteen centuries before had been celebrated by Vergil. In size alone, it has been remarkable for half a millennium, and now, towards the end of its days of glory, it still impressed all who saw it. "With regard to the wealth of its inhabitants their great and pre-eminent prosperity and their grand and glorious objects of luxury and pleasure . . . Without mentioning the splendours within the houses, the beautiful formation of the columns within their halls, their colonnades, their staircases, their towering heights . . . (this) city of wonderous beauty."[2] Twenty-four churches, the source goes on to claim, lie within it, two great basilicas, 323 great and spacious streets, 2 great capitols, 80 golden gods, 64 ivory gods, 46,603 dwelling houses and 1,797 houses of the magnates. The bakeries, the reservoirs and aqueducts of the water supply and the depots of the food supply; the theatres, the circuses, the park and the brothels.[3] The account is as breathless as that of a high pressure "developer" selling land in Florida to a northern small-townee. It is not that of someone fearful of the future.

One hundred years later, Rome, shrunken beyond imagination, was barely beginning its slow way to a painful recovery. Never again until Renaissance days, was it to come close to the splendour with which it entered the sixth century. The Roman of 600 A.D. might well have exclaimed with Mark Antony, "Oh, what a fall was there, my country men!"

The fateful century was marked by the effort of the Eastern empire to recover not merely its lost territory, but to give back to Rome, possibly in quite good faith, the liberty it deemed could come only from Roman citizenship and Roman law. Rome, after all, lay at the proud feet of a conqueror, Theodoric, the Goth (king 471-526). However large-minded a man he might be, and he seems to have risen to considerable heights, he had been born a frontier Barbarian Goth, and such in the eyes of all good Romans he must remain.

The normal violence of the times was great enough: the Gothic wars, desolating. The general of the Eastern empire under Justinian, Belisarius, was a great commander and he fought his wars economically as to casualties and the drain on the countryside. But the Goths wandered everywhere and as they wandered, they plundered. The conquest was never complete and it might have been better for Rome if it had never been attempted. Year after year the fighting went on, and the armies devoured the land, even when friendly. Add flood and earthquake, fire and plague, with famine in the wake. The countryside, we are told, over wide tracts was deserted, and refugees flocked into the city. To make matters worse, the Roman mob was ever unstable, apt to riot at any moment. Thus in 509, household servants of the senators and a disputed papal election caused

the mob "to begin to commit slaughter and murder upon the clergy . . .
they killed any they could find in the city, they stripped women of their
clothes . . . Dignissimus, priest of St. Peter's *ad Vincula,* and Geordanus,
priest of St. John and Paul, . . . they did beat to death with cudgel and
sword; also many other Christians . . ."[4] This may have been all in the
day's work in ancient times, always so much closer to violence than our
populations but it was the Gothic wars that did the major damage, so much
so that talk began to be heard of the complete evacuation of Rome –
"turning it back to a pasture field."

In 536, Belisarius, as victor over the Goths, re-entered conquered
Rome and re-established the empire. By 555, the Goths had been overcome and "Italy lay exhausted but liberated." "The country people had
been reduced to acorns and there were reports of multiple cannibalism."[5]
But once again the curse was to descend in the shape of the Lombard
invasions. These began in 568. "Long-haired, tough Aryan warriors,"
with long beards and hair as awesome as their fighting. Eventually much
of the north was wrested away from Roman rule (the name Lombardy
roughly marks the conquest) and a kind of peace of death descended.

It may be objected that too much emphasis is here given to Italy and that
it was in the seventh century that Europe reached its lowest point or
possibly even in the eighth. The battle of Tours, 732 A.D. is often pitched
as "the lowest point." How much "height" there was north of the Alps to
be "lowered" once Roman control gave way, it would be hard to say. It
must be remembered that Italy remained the metropolitan centre of the
West and that when metropolitanism collapses the shock is felt far and
wide – consider the repercussions in 1975 of the dangerous threat to the
solvency of New York City.

With Italy in a condition of anarchy and ruin, it is evident that the
functions of government would encounter strains that they could not bear
and sooner or later give way. Government apparently became reduced to
the sketchiest terms and there could only be one agency that could fill the
vacuum. This was the organized Christian church under the leadership of
the Bishop of Rome. It was natural that the church should take on and
extend charitable work and from one area of such work to another it
would have been an easy and logical step. Today we find difficulty in
understanding how a church could encroach on governmental powers and
eventually supersede them, but there are aspects of our own society that
are not entirely dissimilar. When, for example, during the great depression of the 1930s, whole countrysides in North America were on the point
of collapse, churches stepped in, providing huge supplies of food and
clothing. The distribution of these had to be administered, which implied
staff and adjudication between needs and areas. A minor quasi-
governmental structure came into existence. And in the important area of
education the church has never abdicated its functions. It often fights

hard to retain its rights. It has important property rights. Thus even in our own strong societies, the church is still there as a kind of stand-by government.

And the church of Rome by the sixth century had become a church very rich in landed wealth, which had come to it over the generations from donations and presumably from careful and shrewd investments. These reserves stood the church in good stead in the times of troubles.

Lastly, and providentially, the calamitous times brought forth their man, Gregory I, the Great. Gregory (540-604, pope, 590-604) was of ancient Rome family, had had a good education (something increasingly rare in his time) and for much of his middle life had been a civilian administrator. He had travelled and had spent several years at the court in Constantinople. He is described as a short, dark burly figure, a man of tireless application and energy. He has left a vast mass of writings. Gregory was one of the relatively few men who have shaped the future. He came to a collapsing Rome. Big buildings were disintegrating (one of the emperors had stripped them of their metal clamps and fastenings to make weapons), many were deserted. The aqueducts, those prides of Roman engineering, had often been broken in the sieges and usually defectively repaired. Many of them leaked, forming pools of stagnant water which brought malaria. Roman malaria was later to kill two visiting emperors. The old careful embankments of the Tiber, being neglected, gave way, and when the spring freshets came, low lying parts of the city were flooded, flooded deep. All civic services degenerated, education emphatically so. Professional people in Rome became rare.

Gregory is described as an outstanding administrator. No good administrator could have lacked occupation in those days. The church had estates scattered everywhere, especially in Sicily, and on these it depended for the sustenance of its clergy and for keeping alive the innumerable refugees who poured into Rome from a troubled countryside. From these estates it somehow found the money at times even to act as paymaster of the emperor's armies. It stood virtually alone, for the old aristocracy, some families of which had come down from the earliest times, after the pattern of aristocracies, had almost faded away. The historic senate dried up, almost for lack of members. "Breeding out" is repeating itself in our own day, especially in North America, carrying with it the rapid disappearance of the substantial and traditional classes, and their replacement from "below." This occurred, too, at the end of the great days of the Age of Faith in England owing to the Wars of the Roses. A secular change in people is probably related to a change in "the times." In Rome, the noble families that remained found themselves reduced to beggary. Many of their members entered monasteries or, heirless, handed over what was left of their estates, to the church, as did Gregory himself. The pope, willy-nilly became almsgiver on a huge scale, organizer of the city, paymaster of the army, defender, shield against the Lombards.

In constitutional law, Rome and its region about 550, had become a "Duchy," comparable with the other "Duchies" into which Italy had been divided by the emperors. But the civil power, never prominent, became more and more secondary. No "Duke of Rome" is even known by name until into the eighth century. Into this vacuum, the papacy virtually was forced. But, however shadowy the imperial power became, it continued to be freely acknowledged and loyalty to be accorded to it. In 664, the city had received the last visit of an emperor, Constans. He had been given imperial honours. But by 730 the pretence of imperial control was almost at an end. The emperor Leo in 729 confiscated the papal estates in Sicily. This was close to the last straw. The Exarchate of Ravenna, which was a kind of vice-royalty for imperial possessions in Italy, dragged on until 749 and the feeling for the emperor as "the fount of sovereignty" lasted for some years longer. But the day of the formal termination was at hand, for a half century later, not a long time for large changes, saw Charlemagne crowned, Christmas Day, 800, Emperor of the West. With the coronation, legitimacy was brought back to Rome and a new world order had begun.

Considerations of the power politics of the period lie outside the orbit of a book looking into the phenomenon of cultural change. But when the imperial capital in Italy was removed to Ravenna, a step had been taken which was deeply to influence the future. The Archbishopric of Ravenna became Constantinople's shield against Rome. Rome might have been the great imperial city, but it was yet to be proved that it was also the great centre of ecclesiastic imperialism. After all, in the East, St. Peter might be given a nod as "Prince of the Apostles," but he was not to be accepted as head of the whole Christian church. Few Westerners grasp the nature of this different place accorded in the Greek church to St. Peter from the high rank he is given in Roman Catholicism. While modern Protestants are not much concerned, the point explains much about the separation eventually occurring between Greek and Roman and this has come down to us, and its consequences have often been projected directly or indirectly into our lives. Instances abound: the Crimean War, the relations with Soviet Russia, with Greece and Turkey, as over Cyprus.

Ravenna, Rome and the Lombards formed a kind of triangle in the seventh century. Rome and Ravenna must keep up the connection with each other to guard against the heretic Lombards, who, left alone, would have overrun all of Italy – and perhaps have made it into a unity by the sword long centuries before that feat was accomplished. But Ravenna could not allow Rome headship of the church, Roman claims had to be watched and checked and the Lombards perhaps used as a counter-weight. Rome must keep open the route to Ravenna, whence could come imperial aid against the Lombard, but it could never admit anything savouring of equality or independence in a mere Archbishop of Ravenna. At last, after nearly three centuries of playing such games, there developed in the north, that which was to solve Rome's problem – a new power, the Franks. Clovis, first rude Frankish chieftain, had been propitiated by being dubbed "the Eldest Son of the Church." As the Franks solidified, especially as Merovingians[6] gave way to Carolingians[7] the popes began to see in them salvation from the Lombards and conceivably independence from the Eastern emperor.

After Gregory's day, the *de facto* situation, in which the church of Rome was slowly taking over the government of Rome, was being transmuted into something approaching closer and closer to the *de jure* (or legal) situation. Clever clerical minds could hardly fail to cast about for buttresses to suggestions, assertions and claims. Was not the Pope the actual power? Contempt on the "Duke of Rome"! If actual power and also God's vice-regent, why was he not the legal power? At last, the instrument was found. The emperor Constantine, he who had recognized the church and himself had died the first Christian emperor, had given to the Bishop of Rome those territories in central Italy which in fact he ruled. Of course he had, how could it be otherwise? And there, forged by clever clerical hands, was writing to show it – the Donation of Constantine!

The pope thus became a temporal sovereign. This was the legal foundation of his power throughout the Middle Ages. When at last, long centuries afterward, the Donation was detected as a forgery, it was rather late to dispute his power. Possession is nine points of the law, especially possession for some 700 years. The pope remains to this day a temporal if shrunken sovereign, as secure in the Vatican as Elizabeth in Buckingham Palace.

II
A New World Arising Under the
Leadership of the Church

Viewed from any angle that we may select, Gregory the Great stands out as a decisive figure for his age and for succeeding ages. Two of these angles in particular call for comment.

One lies in the important area of language. Gregory abandoned the Latin of his class, which apparently had become farther removed from common speech than is "the Queen's English" from Cockney. His sermons and other pronouncements, oral or written, we are told, were in popular style: at one point, he said he could not be bothered with the niceties of prepositions. His Latin must have gone in the direction of the tongue that was slowly turning into Italian and it probably hastened the rate of change. Since one of the conspicuous aspects of the Middle Ages was the breakdown of Latin (except in its official usage) and the growth of the Romance languages, Italian, French, Spanish and their offshoots, this is a matter of immense cultural importance. Wherever it occurs, and it occurs time and again over the long stretches of history, it is a marked accompaniment of cultural changes. In late antiquity, and early mediaevalism, classical Latin took a back seat. Later on, during the Renaissance, when new forces were at work, English and French changed rapidly. This they did again at the period of the Enlightenment – compare the Jacobean writers, for example, with those of the Queen Anne period. And today, as one writes, we are having an even more rapid shift. It is not the English of these pages that will survive but far more likely that to be read in the reports of a "big-league" baseball match or the rapid-fire conversation of a "gangster" telecast, or, ultimate horror, the jargon of "the sidewalks of New York."

The second angle from which Gregory is to be viewed is his place in the expansion of the church. Every ardent soul must be a missionary and Gregory was anything but an exception. Everyone knows the story which we are told decided him to send missionaries to England – the group of fair-haired Saxon captives exposed in Rome for sale as slaves. *"Non Angli sed Angeli,"* as he is supposed to have said. And the despatch followed of St. Augustine the Second, with his band of monks, his reception at Canterbury and the subsequent conversion of England. The story no doubt is substantially accurate and it sounds a note that was to ring for the next two centuries or more. The church had taken the offensive! Gregory seems to have been clear-sighted in his approach to the problems of his day. The strength of the empire was fading in the West, economic prosperity and military security were clearly fading with it, important provinces in the East had fallen to the Persians. New peoples had long been pushing into Italy and probably would continue to come. What could give cohesion to the mass, straighten out the confusions of a heterogeneous society? North Americans know or should know what it means to live in societies composed of people without roots, people from the ends of the earth, people strange to the accepted customs, the old speech, the old traditions. Much effort (but not too much thought) has gone towards overcoming the disabilities of such a society. "Instant citizenship," it might be termed. We tell ourselves that it works, that the "melting pot" melts.

For Gregory there was one social cement that would work: the Christian religion as he knew it. The old values had gone. What would replace them? The new values, the uniform, everlasting values of the Christian faith. By Gregory's time that set of values was different indeed from what modern thought holds to be the essence of Christianity. Modern thought in this respect is not far from the earliest Christian thought, dwelling on "a pure and contrite heart," having little interest in ceremonial, sacerdotalism and far-withdrawn mystic devotionalism. "What doth the Lord require of thee?'' asked the Jewish prophet and answered "To do justice and to love mercy.'' Gregorian Christianity included these virtues but as the product of its age it was full of a harsh asceticism and of a credulity which makes laughable reading today. Devils and demons large and small were constantly at their fiendish doings, though usually driven away by holy men. Miracles of every description, not least rising from the dead, everyone had seen or thought he had seen. Yet mediaeval credulity and love of the marvellous may have been no more intense than Roman, or even Greek. We hear much more about it and there were far fewer men of sophisticated education to withstand it. But credulity, even gross credulity, is always with us, just under the surface, if not actually out in the open, and there is many an evidence of it in our own mechanical, no-nonsense life. It is only in the most sophisticated areas of the earth that the belief in ghosts has been given up. Witchcraft still exists, even in the English-speaking world. But why should any other state of affairs be expected in a society whose religion is still based on belief in the supernatural?

Zeal, a crusading enthusiasm, carried the Christianity of the day far to the north. It was a creed far superior to the dark Paganism that it replaced. Yet it was neither the sophisticated and enlightened Paganism of the best Greeks and Romans nor of our own equally sophisticated and infinitely more humane moderns. But Gregory's immense influence arose just from his being essentially a man of his times. In Gregory and the new values of Christianity lay the key to the future: the key not only to a secure and peaceful Italy but to societies much larger, the societies of those who lay beyond the Alps: Gauls, Germans, Britons, English, and perhaps others further still. How much of a dreamer Gregory was, we do not know. The vision of a vast Christian north, a north almost without limit, all of it united in loving submission to Rome, may well have been his inspiration.

The attack on the north has been termed Christianity's first step outside the bounds of empire. That is not entirely accurate, since by Gregory's day, Ireland had already been evangelized by St. Patrick (about 389-461), whose mission had been an aspect of the zeal of monasticism. But like other matters, monastic fervour had declined in the sixth century and St. Patrick's mission was left to look after itself. Having taken deep root, however, by the seventh century, not only had it spread over all Ireland but even into Scotland and thence to the north of England. In the north of England, Irish missionaries encountered the Roman missionaries, bent on restoring to Christ that which had been abandoned by the Roman legions two centuries and more before.

Greogry became pope at a time when the future of the historic West could hardly have been darker. Was any vestige of civilization to survive? Was Rome (and all it had stood for) indeed to be "reduced to a pasture field"? By the year of his death, the tide had clearly turned. One more devastating assault was to come from the Lombards, but in the seventh century light is discernible. The slow climb up the opposite slope of the cultural valley had begun. It was to go on until the typical first phase, the enthusiastic march to a new world, had given way, as it always does, to those intellectualizing processes which act as brakes and ultimately destroy it, themselves to be succeeded by another abyss of anarchy.

The easy evangelization of "England," which remained firm in undeviating loyalty to the pope for over eight centuries – England rather than France should have been "the Eldest Son of the Church" – took the church of Rome a thousand miles farther north and gave it a strong counterweight to use against Constantinople. A century and a half of evangelizing efforts followed. These were to add other and still more extensive domains to Rome and to Christianity. They made up one of those "pulsations" of missionary zeal of which little in our history could be more significant.

In northern England, despite lapses elsewhere in the island, the new religion, a short two generations after Augustine, had securely established itself and found adherents who quickly assimilated what Rome had to offer them.[8]

This thrust of the church over the seas to the British Isles produced a kind of chain reaction, for English priests, evidently taking at once to the new religion, were in a short space of time rushing over to the continent and carrying the new faith beyond the Rhine. Differences with the Celtic priests had been settled in the Synod of Whitby (663 A.D.) and by the next century, England was able to produce great figures such as Bede (673-735). Bede was born into a society that could provide schools and books: however limited their scale, they were already there at his birth. A generation for them to develop must surely be a minimum, say about 630 to 680. 596 to 630 is another generation. A remarkable leap forward in a very short time.

The men who took the faith to the Germans, notably Willibrord, the Angle, missionary to the Frisians, and the great Winfrith (St. Boniface about 680-775) were of almost equal stature. It is hard to think of the society that produced such men as fiercely "barbarian" indeed as barbarian at all.

In the expansion of Christianity, St. Boniface, should be considered for a ranking somewhere up close to St. Paul. When we think of the very short space of time between the arrival of Augustine, 596, and the "pulsations" associated with such men as those just mentioned, it may provoke second thoughts about the nature of Anglo-Saxonism, as well about the time needed for a fresh civilization to spring up. In less than a century, the gap between Rome and the Celts is closed (662 A.D.). Then within a few years the great men are born – Bede, 673, Winfrith, 680. They are given good educations (a good deal is known of the Cathedral School at York), write good Latin and are competent to take their places in the great world, several of them to become leaders in it. Where would Anglo-Saxonism have climbed to if it had not been knocked over by the Danish invasions (beginning about 850)? Most of the bishops of the new continental dioceses were said to be English. Eighth century England must have been a regular powerhouse of religious zeal. The movement necessarily ran its logical evolutionary course. The new bishops or their successors "became great lords and weighty supporters of the state . . . They had little connection with the masses of the people, whom they ruled rather than served.[9]

Unfortunately we must take the good with the bad. Thus there are various assertions to the effect that England not only exported priests and scholars, but prostitutes. These "exports" were well-known in continental towns and some are said to have got as far south as Rome itself, there to become unpleasantly conspicuous.

Under Charlemagne two generations later (768-814), other Englishmen came to the front, not as the evangelists but as the intellectuals of the day. Among them, the most prominent was Alcuin (735-804). Alcuin was not a priest. He would not be considered much of a scholar by earlier or later standards, but he served his day. Yet, as a favourite of Charlemagne, he obtained so many monasteries that he was said to be "the lord of 20,000 persons."[10] When the storms of the ninth century smote Europe, the Carolingian "Renaissance," with its little wave of intellectualization, possibly because of the greed of men like Alcuin, was already waning and in the next age little more is heard of learning. The "pulsation" had run its course.[11] First, zeal drawn from spiritual fervour, stimulating proselytizing enthusiasm, then the coolness of the mind, the detached "scholar" toning down emotional exuberance, then the appearance of materialistic self-interest and, accentuated by the disorder of the times, the dissipation of the original impulse.

Notes

1.   For this and other quotations in this part of the text, my dependence is on Peter Llewellyn, *Rome in the Dark Ages* (Faber, London, 1971). This quotation is from p. 21.

2.   *Ibid.*, p. 27.

3.   *Ibid.*

4.   *Ibid.*, p. 42.

5.   *Ibid.*, p. 80.

6.   The dynasty founded by Clovis (466-511).

7.   The family which produced Charles Martel and Charlemagne.

8.   A. H. Thompson, *Bede, His Life, Times and Writings* (Oxford, Clarendon Press, 1935), p. 57.

9. Heinrich Fichtenau, *The Carolingian Empire, The Age of Charlemagne* (Harper "Torch" Books, New York), p. 17.
10. *Ibid.*, p. 86.
11. There will be found useful for the Carolingian "Renaissance" in addition to Fichtenau, Walter Ullmann, *A History of Political Thought in the Middle Ages* (Penguin, 1970), and J. H. Robinson, *Readings in European History* (Gunn and Co., Boston, 1904), Vol. 1. This latter is the best of the numerous books of "Readings."

CHAPTER EIGHT

The Great Age of Faith

From Anarchy Towards Ecstasy

During most of the ninth and a fair part of the tenth centuries, there was in reality neither church nor state in Western Europe. The powers and functions of the state were split into fragments and divided among innumerable local lords . . . The constitution of the church was little different. Each bishop was essentially independent of higher ecclesiastical authority. He rules his diocese according to his will and its traditional laws and customs . . . This fragmentation of authority resulted in something closely approaching anarchy in both church and state. The endless warfare of the warrior class kept the country in perpetual disorder. There could be little discipline in the church . . .[1]

Historians are in general agreement that the darkest of the "Dark Ages" was the period following the disintegration of Charlemagne's empire. Pirenne[2] calls the tenth century "the Century of Assassinations."

Among the first flickers of new life is to be prominently noted the founding of the Abbey of Cluny in 910 A.D. In the course of the next century and a half, the Abbey and its daughter houses, and especially the new order of the Cistercians (from their monastery at Cîteaux in France) were to become the seedbeds of clerical and ecclesiastical reform. It is easy to trace this current as it flowed across Europe until there was hardly a district, however remote, that was not affected by it. It is only necessary to mention the high points in the rebirth of civilization, all of them among the commonplaces of mediaeval history, to realize how pervasive and powerful was this genuine move upward – the new spirit animating the papacy under the emperor Henry III (1039-1056), the setting up of the College of Cardinals (1059), which ensured some order in the hitherto disgraceful papal elections, the Hildebrandine reforms under Hildebrand, pope Gregory VII (1073-1085), which included the effort to regulate priestly behaviour epitomized in the papal stand for clerical celibacy, the beginning of the long struggle between empire and papacy (which was to prove fatal to both) and especially the tremendous, tumultous movement known as the Crusades.

Few scenes have flashed down the centuries with more vividness than the humiliation of the Emperor, Henry IV (1050-1106), at Canossa in Italy, 1077. There on the northeastern slopes of the Apennines, 2,000 feet up, lay the castle in which pope Gregory had taken up his temporary abode. It was winter and the snow was on the ground. The details of the struggle between the two (the Investiture Controversy) hardly concern us. But Henry was beaten, and penitent. After many protestations of contrition on the part of the monarch, Gregory agreed to meet him and talk of the possibility of absolution. The issue, stripped of all its detail, was not moral but political: whose will was to prevail, pope's or emperor's? The emperor, duly crowned, inherited all the prestige that lay in an office once occupied by a Charlemagne, a Constantine, an Augustus, the prestige of an office that represented the headship of the entire Western world, the heritage of Rome. The pope, the Vicar of God, the "servant of the servants of God," the head of the church, merely represented Christ. The world of God, life or immortality, force or love, which was to prevail? In some such simple terms must the struggle have presented itself to the various participants in it. Gregory was in no hurry to receive the excommunicate sovereign. Henry came as a penitent and penitence let him show. The castle's gate remained closed. In the pope's own words, "There, laying aside all the trappings of royalty, he stood in wretchedness, barefooted and clad in woollen, for three days before the gate of the castle, and implored with profuse weeping, the aid and consolation of the apostolic mercy . . ."[3] In the person of the peasant's son, "mercy" was shown to the emperor but the struggle still had nearly two centuries to run!

Yet the politics of the great contest should not be allowed to conceal the rising religious zeal of the day. Already, three years before Canossa, after the Battle of Mantzikert, 1071, had laid all Asia up to the very gates of Constantinople under the heel of the Turk, the pope had made heartfelt appeal to the West for aid to the Greeks as suffering fellow Christians. Little response had come. But eventually the fire which had been smouldering for nearly two centuries burst into a blaze. Less than twenty years after Canossa, one of Gregory's successors, Urban II, journeyed to a great church council in Clermont, France, and there, in impassioned speeches, he exhorted his clergy and through his clergy, their feudatories, to take arms and wrest the holy places from the Moslems.

> O race of Franks, race from across the Mountains, race beloved and chosen of God . . . set apart from all other nations by the situation of your country as well as by your Catholic faith and the honour which you render to the Holy Church: to you our discourse is addressed, and for you our exhortations are intended.
>
> On whom is the labour of avenging these wrongs and of recovering this territory incumbent, if not on you – you, upon whom of all others, God has conferred remarkable glory in arms, great courage, bodily activity and strength to humble those who resist you. Let the deeds of your ancestors encourage you . . . Oh, most valiant soldiers and descendants of invincible ancestors . . . recall the valours of your progenitors! . . .
>
> Let hatred therefore depart from among you, let your quarrels end, let wars cease, and let all dissensions slumber . . . Enter upon the road to the Holy Sepulchre, wrest that land from the wicked race . . .
>
> When Pope Urban had said these things, he so centred in one purpose the desires of all who were present that all cried out: 'It is the will of God Deus vult! Deus vult!'[4]

It is impossible to read the records of the great address (and four accounts, in substantial agreement, have come down to us) without, even in these distant days, being touched by the fire and emotion that permeated it. Europe came alight and the First Crusade was launched. It was the highest crest in that great tidal wave of fervour which was to move forward for a century, that century which has been well named "the Age of Faith."

Religious emotion took many forms. In keeping with the spirit of the age, the crudest of direct action was often one of them.

> One day in the year 1115, upon a ship which was coasting the Flemish shores, a priest assassinated a man by cleaving his skull. The murderer had been impelled by piety and by zeal for the Catholic faith. The victim was a certain heretic, well-known in Louvain . . .[5]

Direct action also took many other forms. It expressed itself in the founding of countless monasteries and in numerous new religious orders, especially after 1040, in the magnificence of the great cathedrals, in the many outbreaks of heresies, old and new, and most spectacularly in the Crusades.

Cluny had been founded in 910. As a traditional aspect of Christian life, monasticism had slowly pushed forward but it was not until the eleventh century, in the reforming era usually associated with the emperor Henry III and the German popes of the time, that it seemed to break out as a fresh fire all over Europe. The century 1040-1140 has often been called the great age of Monasticism. Devotion to poverty, chastity and obedience, the threefold vow of the monk, penetrated the hearts of thousands and one of the greatest ages of Christian asceticism was the result.

Such ages are beyond the comprehension of the modern world, which has gone off in the other direction, into the fullest expressions of self-indulgence. They are, however, as conspicuous as could any social phenomenon be, in the long history of "Western civilization." As has been noted in a previous chapter, there was something like an ascetic movement in pagan times, headed by the Cynics, the poor philosophers who went about preaching renunciation as the road to happiness and holiness. There was the first vast wave of Christian monasticism originating in Egypt in the fifth century and flooding out both east and west until it reached into the forests of Germany, of Britain and that "last, best west," Ireland. And now in the eleventh century, the wave of asceticism mounted again, and it has never mounted higher. Before it was spent, innumerable new foundations had come into existence throughout Europe, all devoted to the life of prayer and meditation, all their members seeking each in his own way to "find God." The ways in which monasticism affected mediaeval life are innumerable and they are described in every good textbook. They cannot be analyzed afresh here. It is as the rolling wave of a new age of faith, shorn of all but slender exemplification, that monasticism must be regarded here.

The Crusades themselves, impressive as they are, are but sub-themes in the mounting mood of the times. The struggle with the Moslem and the papal struggle with the empire are but two aspects of it. The appearance of the new monastic orders during the twelfth century is another, Gothic architecture may be another. But then came Cathedral schools, codes of canon law, universities and everywhere the scholastic philosopher expounding, arguing and systematizing. Abelard (1079-1142) was the forerunner, a man the disintegrating consequences of whose cerebrations were foreseen by that mighty warrior in the faith, St. Bernard (1091-1153). To the modern age, Abelard, with his light touch and his clarity, is the more sympathetic figure of the two. And a century such as ours which has cast up so many aberrations from the accepted, may be in a better position to understand him than were those ages in which men thought they knew "exactly what is what." It seems clear that this nimble-witted intellectual who could lay all competitors low in the dialectic of discussion came to be regarded as a "smart aleck," earning quite another kind of reputation among his less gifted associates than he had among the brilliant.[6]

When, at nearly forty years of age Abelard seduced Héloise, his beautiful seventeen-year-old pupil, he must surely have recognized what a wall he was erecting between himself and the ordinary scholar of the day. The brothers of the lady, outraged, took it out on him in horribly brutal fashion. They seized him and castrated him. Abelard must have had strong survival value, for eventually he recovered his reputation as teacher and once more drew students to him – only, as was to be expected, to incur the hostility of the great Jack-the-Giant-Killer, St. Bernard. With a relish, Bernard was eventually able to announce his death to Héloise.

Abelard was a type of man that has become more clearly distinguishable in our own day than he was in the twelfth century. Today we would call him "an intellectual" and more or less understand him. Persons like him, of superior abilities, often find their very abilities cutting them off from their fellows. In school, they get labelled "brains" and the girls avoid them. Later on, they find it hard to share ordinary attitudes and interests, pronouncing them "obvious" or "shallow" or "silly." This does not endear them to those having the point of view of the average man. In Coriolanus's phrase, they have a hard job to "jump with common spirits." They are perpetual square pegs in round holes. They tend to be lacking in warmth and that may carry as far as their relations with the opposite sex: it is probable that they have fewer children than the less gifted. Catholic intellectuals often become celibates, as priests.

Intellectuals are men "who think too much," who "look right through the deeds of ordinary men." If their endowments are very high, these may submerge their other traits and they may come out having places in history, as prophets, major or minor, such as Rousseau or Karl Marx, or generals (like Field Marshal Bernard Montgomery) or even statesmen (such as Lenin). If their endowments while well above average, are not remarkably high, they may get no farther than the radicalism of the day, perhaps constructive, perhaps merely as thorns-in-sides. They may become little more than cranks: they may also help in giving society a step up. On most counts their lot is to be uncomfortable. Such a one was Abelard.

But it was as much against the dangers of his intellect as against the sins of his flesh that St. Bernard did battle. "What has Athens (that is, intellectualism) to do with Jerusalem (that is, Christian faith)?" he might have asked with the church Father Tertullian.[7]

Abelard's misfortune was to have been born a century before his time. Those who have had a little of the same painful experience will know how deep it can cut. It says something for the twelfth century that Abelard, so conspicuous a figure, did not go the way of hundreds of others who set themselves across the stream of history and were burned to death in consequence.

II
St. Bernard

St. Bernard came from a noble family in Burgundy. He was brought up in piety and at an early age, he entered the Cistercian Order. His austerities were reported as so severe as almost to endanger his life. Disgusted with the luxurious way of life that had come to prevail in the Order, he founded a monastery of his own at the age of twenty-five. This was Clairvaux, which he was to make famous. To Clairvaux there came one day, entering in as a family group, his father and all his brothers to join him in the life of the religious. The junior in his numerous family, his youthful ardency "converted" them all in one dramatic scene and brought them to give up their property and their home to enter the life of prayer. There remained only his sister "in the world" and she soon left it taking the veil with her husband's consent, Bernard was then reported as "converting" Suger, the great Abbot of St. Denys (d. 1151) and the well-known minister of Louis VII, king of France, persuading him "to terminate his worldly life and restore discipline in his monastery." Thenceforward, his career seems to have been a succession of remarkable "conversions" of persons engaged in "worldly" pursuits.

The age was full of such occurrences. In 1130, on the visit of pope Innocent II to Clairvaux, "the whole pontifical court was touched by the saintly demeanour of this band of monks." Bernard became an European figure. A pope of the period, Eugenius III, had been one of St. Bernard's own monks. "St Bernard took full advantage of his intimacy to press the interest of his monasteries."[8] He possessed, in other words, that combination of religious zeal and shrewdness which is not uncommon among men of his type.

From the beginning, as his asceticism and his denunciations of the luxury of Cluny indicate, St. Bernard had been unsparingly Puritan. This trait had a marked influence in the architecture of the period. The churches built under monks of Clairvaux were plain and unadorned, with little to come between the worshipper and the contemplation of God at the altar. Some of them survive and are illustrated in Christopher Brook's book, *The Twelfth Century Renaissance*.[9]

> We will not stigmatize the preposterous vast churches of the Cluniacs. We will look rather at the sumptuous ornaments encrusted with gold and gems, put there that money may breed money and pilgrims may give to monks alms that should be bestowed on the true poor. We will look at their cloisters with their monstrous capitals and arabesques, fit only to distract the idle from their books . . . Just heaven! Even if they are not shocked by the impropriety, they might at least blanch at their cost. (Pro Deo! Si non pudet ineptiarum, cur vel non piget expensarum).[10]

St. Bernard could be thought of as the Billy Graham of his age. Is the comparison valid? The audiences of both, the one twelfth century, the other twentieth, were about on the same level of sophistication, the religion the two expounded was almost identical. St. Bernard probably had had a much better education than Graham and he moved on a more impressive stage, among more highly placed people. Nor did he have to face twentieth century scepticism and since he was "gentlemen" born, social snobbishness. Otherwise, the two figures seem similar.

A devout and deeply religious Catholic like St. Bernard would have been shocked if heretical attitudes had been attributed to him. Yet his creed of poverty and devotion should in logic have brought him within sympathetic range of those following the great heresy that had for some decades been appearing all across the south of France and more particularly in the region of Toulouse. This was Catharism, a heresy similar to, but more extreme than that of the Albigenses. The main point of the Cathar doctrine was the evil of material things, and their complete renunciation by the most rigorous, the *perfectissimi*. The Waldensians, not so extreme, were not exterminated and to this day exist as an Italian Protestant denomination with their church on one of the principal streets in Rome. They have daughter congregations at many points in the New World. Apart from its doctrinal aspects, Catharism appealed to the middle classes and its adherents were conspicuous for their frugality, earnestness, sobriety and kindliness – qualities that invariably draw the unwelcome attentions of those who do not possess them, of the mob and hence of the government. In 1145 St. Bernard was urged to use his remarkable talents of preaching and exhortation to win back to the universal faith these heretics. He had some success at Albi (from which the term *Albigenses* is derived) and then moved on to Verfeil, a neighbouring town:

> Saint Bernard went into the church of Verfeil, to preach a sermon. He betook himself in the first place to the *seigneurs* of the town, to those knights whose protection had permitted the heretics to develop the ideas condemned. Seeing themselves pursued in this way, the knights left the church, followed by the crowd. Saint Bernard went out at their heels, and went on preaching on the public square. Some of the inhabitants went into their houses and made so much noise banging on the doors that those who had remained on the square were not able to hear St. Bernard's words "Then the holy man shook the 'dirt' from his feet, to witness that they were 'dirt' (poussière)! He left, and turning towards the town, he cursed it, saying, 'Verfeil ('Green Leaf'), may God wither thee!'[11]

Towards the hérétiques, Bernard displayed all the hatred manifested by the nineteenth century evangelical sects for the demon rum, or by the righteous Communist for the "Capitalist Beasts." (L'hérétique) "c'est un loup rapace qui sous des dehors de brébis s'agite dans votre terre . . ."[12] Heretics were to be hunted down. St. Bernard himself, like Augustine with respect to the Donatists, may or may not have approved of their being burned at the stake (les bûchers) but burned at the stake they soon were and when the stern canonist Lotario Conti became pope in 1198 (as Innocent III), mere preaching took second place to the rigour of the law. The crusade against the Albigensians led by Simon de Montfort duly followed. Its atrocities have been recalled in every age since. The time was approaching when legalism and orthodoxy would have far greater weight than piety, zeal and the occasional droplet of Christian love.

No prominent aspect of the times illustrates more conspicuously how zeal runs down than do the Crusades. The First Crusade was fire, pure and simple, "Christian" fire. It was based on something that is common in history, but virtually inexplicable, namely, faith, or the closely related word *zeal*. It is hard to understand why some ages, like some men, are filled with the intensity that literally "burns them up," while others are grey, unemotional, not rich in action, perhaps because of lack of conviction as to the possibility or wisdom of action – "disillusioned" is the word often used. As a rule, *faith* means religious faith, but in reference to almost any kind of "religion." The Mohammedan expansion was surely based on *faith*. So were the exploits of the French armies under, Napoleon. Communism in Russia has been fired by *faith*. So were Henry Ford's dreams (I presume they were his) of a "tin Lizzie" in every backyard. So, too, is the salesman of anything salable exhorted "to have faith" in the product he is selling. Those upswellings which have caused many countries or peoples literally to explode in burning accomplishment, to become possessed of "a sense of mission," satanic or not, have surely been based on a *faith* in something or other, if only in their own excellence. Faith will indeed move mountains.

The scriptural saying is eminently true of the Crusades, especially of the First Crusade, 1095-1099. There is no need to assume exalted spiritual conviction. The crudest will do. Many Crusaders no doubt had selfish "worldy" motives, but the driving force was faith and zeal. The accepted popular meaning of the term, Crusade, the Battle of the Cross (and what did the Cross symbolize?) need not be challenged. Possibly for most Crusaders the cross stood for something such as the modern Union Jack, Stars and Stripes or *Tricoleur,* plus a badge representing the New York Yankees, the Democratic party, General Motors and so on. The Second Crusade needed the torrent of St. Bernard's eloquence to get it moving – and it failed. The Third Crusade became a grand political manoeuvre among the sovereigns Philip Augustus (1180-1223), Richard I (1189-99), Frederick Barbarossa (1152-1190). The Fourth Crusade (1202-1204) turned into a plundering expedition against Constantinople. Later

Crusades, save for the flicker under Louis IX, lost religious meaning. They became mere aspects of politics, and "Crusaders" found more convenient "pagans" to slaughter.

III
The Intellectual

All zeal runs down. What replaces it? Intellectualism. Men being men, some of them begin to think about what others have been saying, believing and writing. The temperature falls. Something like that seems to have occurred in the last half of the twelfth century. Schools had been increasing in number for some decades, and for small numbers, good educations had become readily available. Abelard, and Saint Bernard too, are testimonies to its effectiveness. But it was after their deaths that the pace quickened. Before 1200 the various schools in Paris had drawn together into the University of Paris. Thenceforth an avalanche of philosophical and theological writing, all in the Latin tongue, descended upon the literate world.

It is fairly easy to imagine what happened if we look at our own world of this last century, say from 1850 on, for the similarities are many. When men get together in groups, discussion begins and among able men it is unlimited. Every modern academic knows that. The fervency of evangelism gives way before the assaults of mind, a simple doctrine to critical analysis. How many modern faculty meetings, it may be asked, are opened with prayer? The two currents may run alongside each other, as they have done in our day, and, to some extent, still do. Our world has no difficulty in accommodating itself to the fervour of the sects and the intellectualism of the universities. Eventually the intellectual prevails. To mix metaphors, intellectualism keeps pulling the petals off the flower until there are few remaining to pull off. What is left? Perhaps nothing worth keeping.

Broad historical explanations must never be pressed too far. Man is too complex an animal to be confined to a formula. But, with discretion, they can be used to help understand the great secular changes in history.

In this illustrative case, the world of the mediaeval renaissance, such explanations stand out clearly. It is true that the carryover of evangelical zeal was impressive: its thrust brought forth, among other things, two great orders of friars, Franciscans and Dominicans, and in the one of them, the Franciscans, there were released strong spiritual forces that kept on worrying official Christianity for several generations. St. Francis (1185-1226) came to be thought of as a kind of second Jesus, which was enough to worry any orthodox Christian! But after his decease, St. Francis was absorbed into Franciscanism (which signified merely an official cult of poverty, and this many a Franciscan took seriously, thereby expanding the Order's genuine spirituality, but restricting its influence) and St. Dominic (1170-1221) into the legal horrors of the Inquisition. The dominating currents of the thirteenth century were not spiritual but intellectual.

The true inheritors of the religious zeal of the twelfth and early thirteenth centuries were the meek and lowly and the persecuted – the innumerable heretical sects (many irregular Franciscans among them), that, suppressed in one place, kept bursting out in another all through the later Middle Ages.[13] But it is no accident that the greatest of the Dominicans was also the greatest of the intellectuals, St. Thomas Aquinas (1225-1274).

After St. Thomas's day, the unity of this remarkable period of human history, the "Age of Faith" or the "Mediaeval Renaissance," as it is variously called, slowly disappears. As sometimes happens, the amplest claim for that unity was made when it had already ceased to reflect the real position. This was the bull *Unam Sanctam* issued by Boniface VIII in 1302. The bull made the widest possible assertion of the unity of the church under the pope and of the supremacy of the papacy over all other authorities whatsoever. An account exists, possibly apocryphal proclaiming Boniface, a very old man for that period[14] seating himself on the papal throne, crying out "I am the vicar of God, I am the Emperor of the world." Whether he was foolish enough to indulge in such sentiments or not, he is known to have been an arrogant old man whose actions were not always marked by prudence. In the year 1300 there had been celebrated the thirteenth centennial of the Holy See and some 2,000,000 pilgrims are said to have visited Rome. Boniface was probably carried away by the acclaim he received, his arrogance reinforced. But the bull had hardly been issued before it was disregarded and before the ministers of Philip the Fair (1268-1314) took occasion to act. One of them, the lawyer Nogaret, was directed to go to Rome and actually arrest the pope, bringing him back to French territory. The bold plan was without precedent.

Nogaret arrived in Rome and found that Boniface was passing the summer at Anagni, in the mountains. He went there, with a few of his own men and accompanied by Italians of the Colonna family, enemies of Boniface. Arriving in Anagni, Nogaret attacked the pope's dwelling, broke open the door and found himself face to face with an old man arrayed in all the dignity of the canonical robes of the Vicar of Christ. Some of the Colonnas wished to kill him, but Nogaret showed some prudence (though not respect) and simply arrested him. There is a story that the pope was struck full in the face by one of the Italians. It may or may not be true. The times were rough and there was not much respect for persons, especially weaker persons. Whatever the truth, the old man preserved his calm, his dignity and the consciousness of his high office.

Eventually some kind of popular tumult arose in which aid came to him and he was able to go back to Rome. But the strain had been too great and within a month he was dead.

It might be supposed that the arrest and possible violence done to an old man of eighty years, to say nothing of the indignity heaped upon the head of the church, all mounting up to something close to the murder of a pope by the agency of the leading king in Christendom would have aroused an outcry similar to but exceeding the shock of horror felt throughout the West when in 1170 Thomas à Becket, Archbishop of Canterbury, was murdered on the steps of his own high altar by the four knights inspired by Henry II. "Will no one rid me of this troublesome priest?" No such shock of horror followed. Nogaret went back to France and later, thanks to the influence of the French king, a French pope was elected who in 1307, after some finessing, took up his residence at Avignon, a city of the French language though just outside the actual borders of France.

The epoch which may be said to have opened with the dramatic scene at Canossa, when a humbled emperor stood outside in the snow to crave the pope's forgiveness, had ended with the bullying of a pope, not by a great emperor, but by a much lesser magnate, the king of France.

The great age of faith was over.

Notes

1. Sydney Painter, *Church and State in the Middle Ages*, in Kenneth M. Setton and H. Winkler, *Great Problems in European Civilization* (Prentice Hall, New York, 1954), p. 135.
2. H. Pirenne, *A History of Europe* (Allen Unwin, New York, 1939).
3. Gregory to the Archbishops, etc. of the Germans, Gregory's *Register*, Lib. IV, No. 12, as quoted in Setton and Winkler, *op. cit.,*
4. From *Address of Pope Urban II at Clermont*, 1905, appealing for an Attempt to take Jerusalem from the Turks, in Robinson, *Readings op. cit.*, I, 312ff.
5. Michel Roquebert, *L'Epopée Cathare, 1198-1212: L'Invasion* (Toulouse, France, 1970), p. 47.
6. His well-known biographical letter to a friend makes this clear: *Historia Calamitatum.* See *inter alia* Philippe Wolff, *The Awakening of Europe* (Pelican, 1968), ch. 3.
7. Setton and Winkler, *op. cit.,* p. 47ff.
8. R. H. C. Davis, *King Stephen, 1135-1154* (Longmans, 1967).
9. Christopher Brook, *The Twelfth Century Renaissance* (Thames and Hudson, London, 1969), pp. 136-137.

10.   M. D. Knowles, *The Controversy Between Bernard and Peter the Venerable.* (Oxford University Press, 1955), p. 19, quoting from St. Bernard's *Apologia, circa* 1123 A.D.

11.   Roquebert, *L'Epopée Cathare, op. cit.,* p. 60.

12.   *Ibid.,* p. 58.

13.   See *inter alia,* Gordon Leff, *Heresy in the Later Middle Ages* (Manchester University Press, 1967).

14.   Said to have been seventy-seven when elected pope.

CHAPTER NINE

Cross Seas and Sudden Storms: From Faith to Doubt

I
The Dislocations of the Fourteenth Century

In that splendid year of jubilee, 1300, many a member of the Papal Curia no doubt found it easy to believe that he was an official of a world-wide government, of a city not made by hands but whose builder and maker was God, a power, not resting on armies, those swords of the flesh, but upon the Father in Heaven Himself, and the devotion He inspired in His children. Many a Roman citizen must have dreamed of the old days when Rome was indeed the capital of the world. But the great event was hardly over and the great document (*Unam sanctam*) hardly issued before harsh reality began to make itself felt. The successor to Boniface, in going to Avignon (in 1307), was making himself something close to a captive of an earthly monarch. The papacy was being degraded into a reflection of the king of France. Naturally, such interpretations did not come out at once. But the crack had appeared in the crystal and the years were to see it lengthen and widen, until finally the vessel broke in two.

The great symmetrical structure of scholastic knowledge erected by St. Thomas Aquinas in his *Summa Theologica* and by similar minds within the *Respublica Litterarum* met a not dissimilar fate. The symmetry of the thirteenth century's philosophical system was not long left undisturbed. William Ockham (1285-1349), for example, an Englishman and one of the greatest minds among the fourteenth century scholastics took the other side of the philosophical battleground and approached in his doctrine close to what we today would call pragmatism – let expediency be the test. From that position to heresy was not a lengthy step. Similarly, Marsiglio of Padua[1] was to question the very office of pope, its legitimacy and its necessity.

When ocean winds have blown, first from this direction and then from that, and back again, the sea gets into a dangerous and disorderly state. Waves come from almost every direction, crash against each other, often at right angles, delivering irregular and unpredictable thrusts against the vessel that is caught in these cross seas. Steering becomes difficult and even today in small ships, sometimes almost impossible. The mariner feels himself in the grip of tremendous and incalculable forces. Such a condition of the sea may succeed to one in which the long, rolling, swells have been coming, wave after wave, like troops marching, from a given direction, even if driven by heavy winds. Let the wind drop and turn, then set in another quarter, with the former sea running and a new one rising and a cross sea results, with all its inherent dangers. Let a new storm arise, still further to confuse the cross sea, and the ship is in danger indeed.

The simile may help to light up the nature of that period of time which succeeded the thirteen hundredth anniversary of the Christian church, A.D. 1300. For two centuries, the church of the West, the Roman Catholic church, was to be beset by cross seas and sudden storms. Eventually getting into less troubled waters, it found itself in sinking condition, dismasted, leaking, many of its crew dead or drowned, the others quarrelling bitterly among themselves. To abandon the metaphor, that of which the church had been head and shoulder, the rising new civilization of Western Europe, was first of all bereft of its old leadership and later, rent in twain by the bitter dissensions that collectively may be termed the Reformation. In the long two centuries in which every variety of division made itself manifest, the wonder was that this civilization went on, breasted its storms and cross seas, added to its geographical extent and vastly increased its internal contents of knowledge, of aesthetic creation and indeed of political extent and power.

The Christian church, East and West, had always been nominally one. By the middle of the eleventh century, however, the historical experience, usage and traditions of the East and the West had become so different that they had drifted into a more or less amicable separation, never again, despite occasional efforts, to come together.[2] This division of Christendom, still apparently as deep today as ever, rarely gets adequate attention in the study of European history. The interest of Westerners, all who were never within the orbit of the Eastern church, has become so concentrated on themselves over the centuries that they have had little attention to spare for that other great branch of civilization that succeeded the classical Roman empire. Yet for centuries, the words "the emperor" meant the emperor at Constantinople, and after that picturesque Christmas day in the year 800, when Charlemagne became "emperor of the West," there was still a "real" emperor in the world and his capital was Constantinople. Until well into the "High Middle Ages," until the Western barbarians wrecked the city in 1204, Constantinople continued to be THE CITY and Rome steadily sank back towards the status of a mere town.

In the period under discussion, after 1300, Constantinople continued to be a great city but not THE GREAT CITY, for rivals had arisen. But it was from the East that the Slavs in the depths of Russia had been evangelized and Constantinople itself continued to be what at least a few men of clear-sightedness and historical knowledge must have known even then, that it was the bastion of the West against the illimitable depths of Eastern savagery. Unfortunately, such knowledge and insight was nowhere freely available, save in narrow circles, mainly in the papal curia and even there too often it was obscured by the selfish parochialism of every day affairs. Efforts to recapture the ancient unity, such as those made by pope Urban II about 1090, and a later attempt in 1438-1439, proved futile. The Greek (or Byzantine) empire was left to its fate, to be extinguished in the capture of Constantinople by the Turks in 1453. Thenceforth, the West went on its own way and the area of Christendom was substantially reduced. The old metropolitan city no longer took its place in the general history of Europe. The chasm opened by this second great Moslem triumph was as decisive as had been the first and it remains to our day. "Christendom," whatever the term still meant in 1453, was being steadily pushed westward.

At first sight, it might appear far-fetched to associate the humiliation of pope Boniface VIII in 1303 with the Hundred Years' War, but if we look at the later history of Western Europe, it may be that subterranean connections are to be discerned. The transfer of the papal seat to Avignon resulted in a long succession of French popes. Monarchs other than the French and their friends did not welcome the new situation. Europe, in other words, whether anyone foresaw it at the time or not, was being divided into two camps, those who were for France and those who were not. Yet even at Avignon, French popes continued to secure the allegiance of the non-French, though gradually that allegiance cooled and first the shortcomings of French popes came to be laid open, then their faults criticized, then the corruptions of their court assailed, then the legality of allegiance to them put in question. Edward I of England had been one of the strongest of its kings and a faithful son of the church but his reign ended in 1307 and his son and successor, Edward II, turned out to be a mere "playboy" who alienated his subjects and sat on an uneasy throne until his deposition in 1327. His deposition was effected by one Mortimer, the lover of Edward's adulteress queen.

But that queen was the sister of the then King of France, Philip VI

(1328-1350), who had given his sister and her lover shelter, something that was not calculated to endear him to the young man, Edward III, who had just stepped into his murdered father's shoes. Edward, in 1327, was but seventeen years of age. His mother was his mother and he treated her with cold respect. Her lover Mortimer, he executed as a traitor. Ten years later he was in the full vigour of manhood, aged twenty-seven and politics would be joined to personal attitudes in his relations with the "wicked uncle" across the Channel. Philip held the throne of France by possession, which is "nine points of the law," and by claim of hereditary right. Nine years after Philip had secured that throne, both his hereditary right and his possession were to be challenged by Edward III, who assumed the title "King of France," a title his successors were still to wear long after it had become nothing more than a mere annoyance to the French.

Underlying such matters, some of them trivial, was the much deeper issue of the balance of power. The realization, if not in set words, yet in facts, that a major power must be prevented from holding the coast opposite England or as much of it as possible can be traced back to Henry II.[3] It probably had much to do with the unfortunate John's wars with Philip Augustus, which issued in the loss of the duchy that formed a good part of that coast, Normandy (1204). It underlay the great struggle which was not to terminate until the English had lost all their possessions in France except Calais.[4] It introduces us to the matter of the balance of power which has held a dominating position in European politics from that time to this. "Keep the French out of Flanders" was an ancient maxim of statecraft in England. Queen Elizabeth's "pocket pistol" sitting there to this day in Dover Castle exists to prove it – "Treat me well and keep me clean, and I'll carry a ball to Calais Green," the tablet fixed upon it by its maker's claims. Its makers were Flemings! Every major English war from those far-off days to our own has been fought primarily to keep a great power out of Flanders and Holland.

The Hundred Years' War (really 116 years), 1137-1453, kept the two countries in turmoil until it ended with the expulsion of the English. During all that long period there were few years in which English raiding parties did not storm ashore at one point or another in France, slaughtering, burning, devastating city and countryside. All the north of France felt the curse, as did those southwestern regions in which the English had retained footholds long after John had lost Normandy. Crécy (1346), Poitiers (1356), Agincourt (1415), the great showy English victories, were only high points in four generations of plunder and rapine. "Assassins, murderers, sea-wolves" the English became in French eyes, and rightfully so. The braggadocio of Shakespeare's Henry V, full of arrogant condescension to the inferior beings across the Channel, clothes the grim old facts with poetry, but it does not hide them from those who have knowledge and imagination about the time. In due course Jeanne D'Arc (Joan of Arc) appeared and her life – a martyrdom, as later it came to seem to the French – became the price of freedom.

But the end of that dreadful war, which separated the two countries even more effectively than John's loss of Normandy (the Norman conquest, it must be remembered, had almost made England into a French country – a "New France" across the Channel), by no means introduced tranquillity. France had suffered all the anguish of the *jacquerie,* as it was called, the peasants' revolt and its accompanying disturbances, which upset its government and destroyed the effectiveness of the only legal voice of its people, the States-General. It had to endure the long agony of the reign of an insane king – le roi fou – Charles VI (1380-1422).[5] Not until the English were gone for good, could reconstruction begin. Under the reign of Louis XI (1461-1483) with only secondary wars to be waged, those aspects of French life which have never ceased to be prominent, once more came to the fore. An abundant land, whose soil and climate were good, an industrious peasantry, such factors have always given France ready recovery from its ills. France is a phoenix: destroyed in one decade, it rises afresh in the next. Our own times illustrate the point.

The English had battened upon the Hundred Years' War. It provided a never-ending source of excitement, glory, wages, booty, women, no doubt especially women. Young fellows crossed the sea, hoping to return as their fathers before them, with stolen treasure, only made slightly legitimate by calling it the "spoils of war." They need take no responsibility for the issue of their amours and seductions. The wars enabled them to contrast their own happy superiority with the misery of the French whom they raided or battled, and when they returned, their English patriotism could grow apace. Even their kings at last stopped speaking French – Henry IV (1399-1413) was the first who confessed that English was his mother tongue. The Hundred Years' War thus takes a leading place in the formation of two nations, English and French. Indeed, if we think of the north, of a third, Scotland, for when the English went out of the front door, the Scots came in at the back. The Scots in a small way did to the north of England what the English soldiery were doing to the north of France.

Elsewhere in Europe, the political pot also never ceased to boil. The Spaniards continued their interminable war of expulsion against the Moors. The Italians fought each other in wars that did little harm and satisfied the participants' vanity or their greed. The Czechs in Bohemia – "That distant and unknown country," Neville Chamberlain was to call it in 1939, in a superlative expression of parochialism, whose capital was all of 500 miles from London – carried on for years their semi-religious, semi-nationalist war against the Germans.

II
Localism Shatters the
First Attempt At General Unity

The mention of the Czechs, opens another topic in this attempt to sketch the nature of the momentous two centuries. The rise of the nation-state is central to the history of the Europe of the High Middle Ages. Europe of the early centuries had been a welter of conflicting minuscule entities. Gradually these were drawn together. But how? Mainly by the power of the sword. The nation-state rests largely on the power of the sword in the hands of a strategically placed ruler, who either was or came to be a king.

The European nation-states were made by the king. They are not natural units but artificial structures of power. If natural unity were to be claimed, it should show itself most clearly in geographical terms and be found in islands. It is not, as the history of the British Isles amply illustrates. Since nothing succeeds like success, a political entity that could give order and continuity, success and the indefinable majesty that doth hedge a king, tended to become larger and larger. This in itself put an end to the multiplication of small states. In the loose society of the tenth and eleventh centuries the Normans had found it possible to found states and take to themselves the royal dignity. In the fifteenth century, however, the Dukes of Burgundy, though coming within an ace of founding a new kingdom, failed, because they shattered on the increasing national power of France (with considerable assistance from other sources such as the shortcomings of the dukes).[6] European history has been the emergence of larger and larger power structures. These have been only partially related to race and language.

Extension of sovereignty did not prevent the appearance of distinguished local cultures, as in Burgundy, especially in the "Low Countries" section of the Duchy. This growth of a new culture in the fifteenth century illustrates again the idea of the "pulsation": the Burgundian culture, from whatever causes, grows, expands and then to some degree declines, to become complicated by the religious and revolutionary upheavals of the sixteenth century.

When France had become something like a nation-state – as early as 1300 – it opened the fissure of "the Babylonian captivity" (1308-1378) across Europe. By the opening of that century, the fourteenth, non-Byzantine Europe from Poland westward had become something of a unity. It had acquired a loose common name – "Christendom." For all general purposes, save those of ordinary day-to-day life, it had a common language, Latin, and a common culture. This culture was based largely on the scholastic philosophy nurtured by the universities and the higher clergy, and its evidence may be seen in the glories of the Gothic cathedrals radiating out from France into Norway on the north and Italy on the south. It had a common metropolis, Paris, which was rapidly over-shadowing the ancient capital of Christendom. The University of Paris was not far from being THE UNIVERSITY with all others somewhat provincial in relation to it. The king of France was wealthier than other kings. His dominions were larger than those of other kings, stretching from the English Channel to the Mediterranean. France had risen as the concept of empire fell, weakened by the exhausting struggles of pope and emperor for a hegemony that had already lost its reality. France, too, had become the home of a great secular literature in the vernacular, a literature which found echoes in most European tongues. From several points of view, France had become a metropolitan country, arranged around a strong urban nucleus, Paris. As moderns today who are especially susceptible to the attractions of metropolitan life might put it, if you wished to be "where the action is," in about the year 1300, you went to Paris.

In fact, only the stubborn old Italian cities resisted. The great Gothic cathedral of Milan approximated the southern boundary of the northern culture, for Rome was still Rome, though small and stagnant, Florence Florence and Venice Venice.[7] The University of Bologna was older than that of Paris and Roman law was its foundation study. Sharp Italian minds could hardly abandon their centuries-old convictions, reinforced by daily experience, that beyond the Alps, the people had been, were and would be barbarians. A culture which could produce a Dante hardly needed to take seriously the love songs of wandering minstrels. Citizens who daily felt the thrust and creative competitiveness of urban life could hardly have believed that they had anything to learn from bucolic simplicity. Countries which could enchain the north in the intricacies of Lombard banking hardly needed to think they must take second place to upstart regions of forest, wild beasts and wilder men.

It has been estimated that before the Black Death, quite a few north Italian cities had populations ranging up to 100,000. Milan, Venice and Florence were of that order, but a number of others were not far behind. A land of cities of that size could not have been "mediaeval," a word which in modern ears invariably has an unpleasant ring. Its impelling forces represented a dynamic of life quite different from the past centuries and from what was still to keep northern Europe moving for some generations. The dynamics of Europe previously had been the effort of the individual to see God and find salvation, and, secularly, the local power struggle, termed in shorthand, *feudalism,* plus the great wrestling match between the two universals, pope and emperor. In "Christendom" (which was coming to mean Western, non-Moslem, Europe), Northern Italy was the first region to escape from the absurdities of feudalism, slowly at first, then beginning with the Crusades, with gathering speed. The new dynamic may be put in one word – commercialism.

The trader is an old and familiar figure in the world, but he had never succeeded in completely ridding himself of a certain ignominy. In practically every society of which we have record, the man who lives by gain has had something of the disreputable about him. *Homo mercator nunquam aut vix potest Deo placere,* cried St. Jerome – "the man of trade scarcely ever can be pleasing to God." The sentiment is of great depth. The Christian gospels inveigh against money. So do the classical fables such as those of Midas and his golden touch. *Mammon* "the false god of riches and avarice" has always and everywhere been under attack. Two "respectable" impulses only seem to have been universally admitted: fighting and prayer. The fighting man and the praying man, soldier and priest, it invariably has been to whom honour has been accorded. Even that still more elementary avocation of humanity, fornication, has been given its place of prominence partly because it has been regarded as an aspect of conquest, the most primitive conquest of all, the conquest of the female by the male.

But despite the constant disapproval of the "best" elements in society, the trader has always managed to sustain himself. He has existed on his own astuteness, his readiness to sacrifice all other qualities to one point: for what he has to trade getting more than it cost him. Today our Western life is so completely built upon that principle, that we seldom think twice about it and the most grievous of shortcomings has become a man's inability to keep a red stain out of his balance sheet.

The old Anglo-Saxon word *sellan* meant *to give*. It is a word that had degenerated in meaning. The lordly person (*hlaford: lord,* literally, "the loaf-giver") *gave:* he did not *sell.* It is a primitive notion, no doubt, but it points to the generous (and egotistic) streak in human nature, and it is universal, common to the civilized and to the savage. *Per contra,* the trader is grasping and mean, not to be tolerated by decent folk, except as a convenience, kept at a distance, made to feel his lowly status, at best patronized, often plundered (naturally always "in revenge," to get "back that out of which he has cheated us"). The attitude towards the trader is close to the psychology that underlies the "class line," the primitive feeling of superiority, and when society emerges from its mere turmoil of localized fighting, the trader has little chance of mingling with "the great": the *magnifices,* the *magnates,* the *proceres,* the *opulentes,* the *divitissimi,* the *nobiles,* as in mediaeval Europe they are variously called.

But traders have tough hides. They accept abuse in return for profits ("the customer is always right") and have little regard for self-respect – except in their private psychology, wherein abuse may bring on thoughts of revenge, or more commonly, of determination some day to get into the place of the abuser. It is all a familiar story, told long ago in his own inimitable fashion by Shakespeare.

It is against some such background as the foregoing that the struggle of the Italian towns with emperor Freidrich Rotbart is to be viewed. With what a height of imperial superciliousness must the great kaiser of the West have looked down upon those little men who bought and sold and dared resist his will! But it was the story of the Lilliputians. Eventually they bound the giant and finally got him out of their way. Then merchants, mere pedlars (Latin *pedites:* "foot men") could themselves become "respectable": a Doge of Venice could stand before kings. This ascent of the hucksters, to merchants, to bankers, to financiers, to princes, their women to the wives of kings (such as the Medici ladies in the distant sixteenth century), was a long climb, some five or six hundred years, but when they got there, and had made themselves utterly "respectable" (the mother-in-law of Mary, Queen of Scots was a Medici and herself Queen Regent of France; the wife of Henry IV of France was another), there were still plenty of their like on the rungs of the ladder below them.

In the intervening years the new dynamic introduced into European life by the merchant and his physical consequence, the town and city, had proven adequate to giving a purpose and a sense of direction to many large and countless small communities. Here was motivation. For centuries, petty barons had found quite adequate motivation in assaulting their neighbours' castles, carrying off their horses, cattle, serfs and wives; for centuries, the church, teaching men to seek spiritual goals, had provided motivation. Motivation for the crude fighting men of Europe was provided by the Crusades. Intellectual ratiocination had provided motivation for thousands of scholars. But by the fourteenth century all these media by which men seek to persuade themselves that life is worthwhile were wearing thin. Great princes and kings were imposing at least a minimum of order on disorderly barons, the church's hell fire was not quite as terrifying as it once had been, the scholars, having undermined the old ways of thinking and the old explanations, were getting tired of their own syllogisms. There was clearly a vacuum. Trade, the love of gain, with its mortal sins of covetousness and envy appealing to that which is in every man, but no less base for being in every man, could furnish a new drive in life.

Of all Europe west of Constantinople, the north Italian towns, where the new flame had already started to burn brightly, were best situated to respond to the new motivation. Their rise to heights of mercantile greatness has just been referred to. As usual, it had been facilitated both by the needs of those who had persuaded themselves that they were engaged on high and holy tasks, mainly the Crusaders, or by the fancies of their ladies, and by the invariably unscrupulousness of the middleman, whether he were called supplier, ship-owner, money-lender or banker. But the north Italian middlemen must have been of a special breed, for they did not hoard their money in miserly fashion, or even spend all of it on wine, women and song (though they, or their irresponsible young men, spent much of it that way). Instead, they spent it, and in increasing amounts, in the patronage of the arts. Imagine, if you can, a galaxy of imaginative and artistic bankers! Out of strength, as the Bible says, had come forth sweetness. The glories of the Italian Renaissance are found not only on native Italian genius, which must have contributed the larger share, but on the shrewdness, foresight, daring, sharp practices, lack of scruple, of the Italian businessman.

While northern Italy became a land of cities, with practically all the attributes of metropolitanism, except modern means of communications, northern Europe continued to be a region of villages.

To that statement, however, one exception must be made: a strong metropolitan region had grown up in Flanders, around such centres as Ghent and Bruges. Otherwise the north of Europe could boast not much more than Paris, already a city of perhaps nearly 100,000 and London which may have attained 60,000 before the Black Death.[8] By 1300, the two metropoli, the new north and the old south, seemed fairly in balance and which would have proved the victor in what might be looked upon as a contest for the domination of Europe, at least in areas of life not purely political, might well have been a matter of conjecture. Then came the harsh treatment of the papacy by the king of the Frankish barbarians, the manipulation of his removal of its seat from Rome to Avignon and the succession of French popes which he (or his lawyers) dictated. There could have been few more divisive acts. It would hardly be too much to see in it most of the future.

III
And Also Religious Unity

It is often assumed that from the early centuries onward, there was no dissent from orthodox Christianity. The never-ending rumblings of dissent down below the surface of official Christianity do not evoke much notice. Except, of course, with respect to the conspicuous figures of Wycliffe and Huss. The ordinary reader is rarely made aware that heresy was constant, various and widespread in the Middle Ages. Sometimes it boiled over, as in the cases of the Albigenses and the Waldenses, already discussed. Sometimes it could be contained: when an awkward enthusiast like Francis of Assissi appeared, his energies would be diverted or directed, though Franciscans were always sources of concern to officialdom. More often, it just went on furtively, confined to a group here and a group there. There never was a time between, say, 1100 and 1517, when heretics were not to be found in continental Europe.[9] This constant undertone to the life of the Middle Ages should be kept in mind, as it must have been at the time by every authority, lay and ecclesiastical.

Through all heresy ran a uniform pattern. The pattern was the Christ-like nature of poverty. It was earnestly debated whether Christ could have owned the very clothes in which he stood. Many a scriptural text was cited in support of the doctrine. The difficulty of a rich man getting into Heaven. The camel passing through the eye of a needle. Lazarus and Dives, that is, beggar and rich man. "Blessed are the meek, the poor in spirit . . ." "He hath put down the mighty from their seats and hath exalted them of low degree . . ." "The Son of man hath not where to lay his head." Exponents of the holiness of poverty rang the changes on such texts. The friars began as individuals "without a shirt to their backs" and a wing of the Franciscans stubbornly stuck to their original conceptions, though the main body of the Order and the Dominicans, like later Orders, took the convenient way out – the individual friar owned nothing, but that did not prevent the Order collectively accumulating property. Exponents of the doctrine were by no means confined to the friars. Poverty was the goal for masses of lay people, too, people, it is unnecessary to say, who did not for the most part belong to the possessing classes. The war waged between the official church and the exponents of the excellences of poverty went on unceasingly. Poverty was quite acceptable in theory at St. Peter's. In practice? That was another matter.

Poverty as an ideal easily associated itself with another tendency of the age, mysticism. Mysticism, implying some transcendence of the here and now, some kind of communication with things unseen, no doubt is as old as mankind, not dependent on any specific religion. There was many a mystic in classical times. In the Great Age of Faith, men were probably too extraverted to provide fertile soil for mysticism, though persons possessed by a high religious fervour must always have elements of mysticism about them, like the priest already referred to who was so filled with the spirit of the living God that he split the skull of the heretic whom he encountered. "The zeal of thy house hath eaten me up." But an age of action is hardly conducive to mysticism. That comes later, when men have a chance to sit down and brood. Characteristically Germany, that country which as late as the nineteenth century was said to be content to rule the clouds while France ruled the land and England the seas, supplied the best soil for the mysticism of the High Middle Ages. The names of the men whose attitudes and preaching bolstered mysticism are well-known. Two among others may be named, Meister Eckhart (1260-1328) and his disciple, John Tauler (1300-1361). Eckhart was philosopher and semi-intellectual as well as mystic. From such heights mysticism tailed off down to the humble anchorite, solitary in his or her cell outside the church, engaged in constant prayer, seeking God through ardent devotion. Later, Luther himself sought God, along with his fellow Augustinians, through prayer and fasting.[10]

In the Roman Catholic church mystics have never ceased to arise – Saint John to the Cross, for example, the great mystical poet. In Protestantism, the idea of mysticism is more diffused, less specifically directed to a vision of God, but in fervently religious experience, it is of much the same order. Since the mystic seeks a direct experience of God, a private communion with God, he always presents a problem to a church built on sacramentalism and the intermediacy of the priest between the faithful and God. But since mystics are not intellectuals and do not seek to deviate from the faith, they can hardly be arraigned as heretics. Mysticism in the mass represents waves of devotional fervour which with skill can be contained within the church and used by it or with arrogance pushed outside. The mysticism of thirteenth century St. Francis was contained and used. The mysticism of the fourteenth and fifteenth centuries arising within a church widely condemned as power-seeking and corrupt could hardly have been an element of strength. It must have been one of the innumerable forces that were leading to the same unseeable, destination.

There were still other storms, physical and spiritual. In the late 1340s, there swept up out of the distant east that horrible affliction known as the Black Death. Mediaeval statistics are unsafe but it is generally reckoned that as many as one-third of the people perished from it. In the city of Florence, for example, population was so reduced that it was not until the eighteenth century that the city regained its early fourteenth century size.[11] Other accounts go in the same direction. While there had been earlier visitations – one of great severity is recorded from about the year 166 A.D. – there had been nothing of the colossal magnitude of the Black Death. It has been termed the severest calamity ever to have afflicted the human race.[12] It had important social consequences in most European countries and these were felt for many years.[13] The Black Death was another of the sudden storms of the age.

A century on from the natural calamity of the Black Death, there broke out in England, the civil war known as the Wars of the Roses. For a generation, opposing armies trampled over English soil, bitterly dividing the great men of the land, or exterminating them. The rest of the people grew heartily tired of great men's wars and of the great men, and when Henry Tudor triumphed on Bosworth Field in 1485, they were ready to accept him – or probably anyone else – if he could keep order. He had the slenderest of titles to the throne, but he could keep order. And so began what is sometimes called "the Tudor Absolutism," another illustration of the everlasting procession of states – from order to liberty to anarchy back to order, however harsh the measures may be which are found necessary for order.

With the divisions at high levels in the church, war on every hand, the presence of pugnacious heretics in every town – some of them, such as the Brethren of the Free Spirit, of an impossibly extreme type – it would have been too much to expect that doctrinal disputes would not rise to a more sophisticated level than that of the simple man or woman. Strangely enough, it was in the most faithful daughter of mother church that the most formidable case arose. For centuries, nothing had troubled the undeviating and unimaginative loyalty of the English to the pope.[14] But French popes and English money going to them were evidently too much for national pride to take. English parliaments passed Acts of Provisors and Acts of Praemunire directed against the appointment of papal incumbents to comfortable English benefices and attempting to curtail some of the papal taxation, but these were not of major effect. It was the outspoken Professor John Wycliffe who caused the fuss. Wycliffe has been described as no Protestant, a distinction so often claimed for him, but rather as a rationalist, seeing through all the screens that surrounded pope and papacy, and as a rationalist of that thorough-going degree, many generations in advance of his time.

Wycliffe's movement, such as it was, would not have amounted to much if it had not fitted into the temper of the times. His followers, the Lollards, evidently found the country of the Peasants' Revolt (1381) receptive to the sermons they delivered, which apparently stressed equality. The equality of all souls before God both church and state could admit as harmless theory. Equality here and now, property rights included was quite another matter which it would take more than sermons to affect, as so it has gone down today. In the disordered state of England under Richard II (1377-1399) the Lollards had scope for their wandering and their preaching and when in the next reign, that of Henry IV, an attempt to suppress them was made, it was not completely successful and traces of Lollardry remained throughout the fifteenth century. Henry IV sat on an insecure throne and like any good politician, he made what moves he could to secure support. Evidently one stroke to make was to persecute the Lollards in order to win the church. Hence his statute, *de comburendo hereticos*, by which, for the first time, burning at the stake was introduced into England. It was to remain the favourite way of dealing with heretical obduracy for over two centuries – if your opponents will not agree with you, roast them![15]

Deep effects of Wycliffe's teaching and writing – and he wrote a great deal – came to the surface in "the distant and unknown country," Bohemia, that is Czecho-Slovakia. Richard II had married a Bohemian wife. This resulted in considerable coming and going between the two countries. Today many of Wycliffe's original manuscripts are to be found in the University of Prague (which had been founded in 1478, the earliest in eastern Europe). There was a scholar in Prague, a Czech, or Bohemian, who had evidently read in these manuscripts and had come very much under the influence of the doctrines they expounded. That scholar was John Huss. Huss in studying Wycliffe had responded eagerly to his doctrines and for much the same reasons. In England, the French were the enemy and French popes, as already noticed, were decidely unpopular. There is a strong nationalistic note in Wycliffe's writings which both comes out of rising English nationalism and encourages it. Into Bohemia, there had been for some two centuries a steady influx of Germans and the Germans who came to Bohemia were good Catholics. So to Czechs the church became "the Church of the Germans!" Huss could have hardly been anything else but anti-German. And insofar as doctrines of papal supremacy went, as a Bohemian nationalist, he could hardly have been other than anti-papal. It is a commonplace of history that Huss was given a safe conduct to the Council of Constance by the emperor Sigismund himself and that Sigismund repudiated the safe conduct, thus allowing the authorities of the Council to arrest Huss for heresy and burn him to death.

The betrayal and burning of Huss did not increase the popularity of the emperor with the Bohemians. To them he became simply, Judas. An uprising ensued which had both a religious and a national character. It proceeded against the Germans as intruders and foreigners and against the church as impure and corrupt. The idea was to go back to the earliest days of Christianity and build a simple Bible Commonwealth in which there should be no organized church and especially no priests. Wycliffe in England had been no friend of sacramentalism or of the doctrine of transubstantiation. The Taborites, as the Bible Commonwealth party were called, repudiated such matters in their entirety.[16] In so doing they provided for Europe its first considerable example of society – building "from the ground up," somewhat like similar attempts to do the same thing in America, such as that of the Puritans in Massachusetts Bay or the Mormons in Utah.

As might be expected, pious people, mystics in an age of mysticism, quacks and cranks of every description, flocked to Tabor, as the revolutionaries renamed the town they made their headquarters. A group of heretics known as the Brethren of the Free Spirit had long made themselves especially objectionable in certain parts of Europe, since their doctrine seemed to be that once one became one of the "redeemed" and "a free spirit," he was bound by no earthly law, that is he could do as he liked. The doctrine naturally led to many excesses, especially sexual excesses. In the disorder of the Bohemian revolution an offshoot of such heresies was begun in Bohemia by a certain Adam, and its adherents became known as Adamites. Settling on an island in a river, they founded an ideal community situated in a second Garden of Eden. They were completely communistic but went modern Communism one better in that they wore no clothes and were as primitive in their sexual communism as they were in their costumes. Such groups arise in most disturbed periods. The Adamites probably went no further than certain Californian groups of the 1960s; how could they? But they were not living in the twentieth century. In the fifteenth, authorities solved the problem simply – they exterminated them.

Bohemia went until 1434 without benefit of the traditional church. Was it then a Protestant country? It was more like that country would be in which some of our more extreme religious fanaticisms came to dominate society. Eventually disunion arose with the so-called Utraquists (who went little further taking communion in both kinds – *utra*) ready to compromise. As might be expected the Taborites were betrayed by the Bohemian nobles, who were quite ready to go back to mother church, if she would share the wealth. This she did, and with the spoils of monasteries and other church properties, the Czech nobles came back into the fold.

But the Czech experience had not gone for nothing. No such attack could be made on "the establishment" without leaving nasty wounds behind it. From Wycliffe to Huss to Luther may not be exactly a direct path, but it is a path. And perhaps more important than leadership, popular allegiance to the church was shaken, shaken to some considerable degree in England, shaken badly in Bohemia. Nor was it merely the effort of humble people to "get the priest off their backs." Priestly dominance, like the dominance of any other overly powerful class, invariably brings reaction. Not even humble people, despite their fears of the unknown, or more probably their women's, will continue forever to take orders and pay for taking them. But these movements against the tyranny of a class, or profession, can take the shape of mere sporadic uprisings. Far more serious difficulties arise from the increase in general understanding through the spread of education and the introduction of new knowledge. Both these forces are hard at work in our own societies: they have already practically destroyed the traditional beliefs and the end is not yet.

We do not associate the fourteenth and fifteenth centuries with popular enlightenment. Perhaps we should. Not popular in the sense of "universal," but at least in the sense of "widespread." New universities continued to be founded all during the period. Scholars gathered in them and went out from them; many less pretentious establishments came into existence, such as some of the great English "public schools"[17] or the great Dutch school at Deventer. The mariner's compass had come into use in the thirteenth century. "Lodestones" had been well-known in classical times – they are discussed by Lucretius – but no practical application ever seems to have been made of them. Partly through the instrumentality of the compass, new islands and new lands began to be brought into the European ken. The age of the Discoveries was at hand. Coastal trade over long distances was growing rapidly.[18] Most important of all, was the series of inventions which led to the revolutionary art of printing.[19] It is impossible to describe the exact effect of printing on history: it is a clear case for the imagination.

In the fourteenth century, the weakening in the papacy, the growing secularism, the emergence of national states, sapped the unity of "Christendom" and afforded opportunities for "ideological" differences to well up.

To cast up the accounts in this manner is to reveal a discrepancy between the two sides – extremely serious set-backs on the one hand, very real advances on the other. This leads some authorities to feel that the fourteenth and fifteenth centuries were not that "Age of Transition" which they have so often been called.[20] But surely they was a change in the historical climate, after the heights of the Age of Faith. Recession in one direction can readily be marked by achievement in others. Possibly mediaeval achievement was a reflection of the rapid economic progress which had marked those three centuries (say 1050-1350) that saw Europe's population grow, new lands made productive and new cities arise. Possibly the great burst of thirteenth century intellectualism rose on prosperity and fell on the calamities of the fourteenth century, especially the calamity of calamities, the Black Death.[21]

IV

The New Localisms of the Fifteenth Century,
Political and Religious

Many are the historians who speak of "turning points" in history. It is hard to identify a genuine "turning point" – history does not turn on ball bearings – but the idea may be of use in an attempt to identify a pattern for history. There is nothing climactic about the way in which the mediaeval Renaissance petered out. That came from much more subtle causes. Among these, surely the failure of faith should rank high. After the failure of St. Louis's Crusades (1254-1270), for example, while the popes did not cease to champion the idea, there was little response. Attention was directed elsewhere. Yet the old brilliance of the schools continued and universities multiplied. Still, cerebration, however brilliant, is no substitute for faith. It leads to disunity, not cohesion. "The dissidence of dissent" has often been remarked upon. And so a "silver age" succeeds "the age of gold."

In the thirteenth and fourteenth centuries, the new corporations, the universities harboured "dissent." As institutions they were, like other institutions, conservative. But they harboured dissent. And dissent was not far from heresy. The role they played in mediaeval society was not greatly different from the role they play in ours. They were and are places of dissent, of "academic freedom." As an untutored and anonymous correspondent of the writer's once put it, "the universities are the hell-holes of the earth." No doubt they are. Among their members, however, have been the men who have prevented the water from becoming stagnant, the makers of the future.

If dissent, freedom of thought and speech, go far enough, with every man, like the Athenians in St. Paul's day, each seeking some new thing, they may produce anarchy. But when it comes to a choice between security and the freedom of anarchy, men will invariably choose security. The choice may not be too decided and so freedom may stand its chance. In some such way, does one age give place to another and this presumably is what people have in mind when they talk about "turning points."

The shift by which twelfth and thirteenth century cultural unity gave way to cultural diversity becomes harder and harder to trace in bold, clear lines as European society increases in diversity and complexity. France opens the fissure of "the Babylonian captivity" across Catholic Europe and becomes something like a nation-state. Wycliffe's troubling doctrines in England are more than mere accidental by-products of this French deed – as is *the Hundred Year's War* itself. It was more than French chivalry that was blown to pieces there on the field of Crécy by that new invention of the devil, gunpowder.

In the fifteenth century, Bohemia breaks away, the first organized, semi-national attempt to loose the bonds of Rome. The popes try to maintain their former constitutional status and to resist the advance of peripheral forces by the delaying tactics they employ against Conciliarism. After a struggle they are successful. But the Conciliar struggle still further weakens the authority of the church. England goes off into anarchy of the Wars of the Roses. Another invention of the devil, or, so it must have seemed to many, printing, opened wider and wider the gates of the fortress of learning. Italy, spectacular metropolitan peninsula, blossomed once more, as it had done centuries before, in a hundred artistic and literary directions. New local literary life in the persons of Geoffrey Chaucer and others like him broke out in far-off England.

But the historical structures which had supported society for centuries, if they did not actually disappear, became weaker and weaker. The universal empire was reduced to a temporal state and that state divided in almost every way that the mind of man could imagine. The great semi-federal institution, the papacy, at one time had appeared as if it would give the law to all Europe and erect over all local authorities a great central government, legislating, taxing, directing. And now, the papacy itself had been reduced to a shadow of its former self. The triumph of "the states" was complete. It was as if the central government at Washington, under the impact of repeated blows such as those of the 1970s, had become a shadow and all real life had passed to the fifty American states. The hope of European unity had gone.

Is it not a wonder that the old centre of life, the church, one and undivided, the seamless robe of Christ, the Petrine Rock, stood firm as long as it did? Finally it, too, succumbed and in the sixteenth century, the Western world was launched again, as centuries before, on stern and turbulent seas.

> The period extending from the beginning of the fourteenth century to the middle of the fifteenth offers the spectacle of a disturbed and tormented society, struggling against the tradition which oppressed it, and which it could not contrive to shake off. The barrier which the past opposed to the thrust of the future held firm; it appeared to be still intact, and yet, undermined by invisible flaws, it suddenly gave way, and the energies which it had contained poured through the breach and gave the historic landscape an entirely new aspect.[22]

This fine statement could be made, almost word for word, of any period in which zeal has run down and the old order is changing, though not yet giving place to the new. It could be made of the yeastly religious bubblings which in Rome marked the first and second centuries.[23] It could be made of the chaotic twentieth century. One age had died, another was struggling to be born.

Such seems the pattern of history.

Notes

1.   His disturbing book *Defensor Pacis,* appeared in 1324.
2.   The year usually given as the parting is 1057.
3.   For a recent study of the balance of power, see Ludwig Dehio, *The Precarious Balance: Four Centuries of the European Power Struggle,* (New York, Knopf, Vintage Books, 1965).
4.   Which they eventually lost in 1558.
5.   A good appreciation of this dark period in French history is to be found in Joseph Calmette, *Les Dernières Etapes du Moyenne Age Français* (Paris, Hachette, 1944).
6.   See Paul M. Kendall, *Louis XI* (Norton, New York, 1971).
7.   The southern French kingdom of Naples was a partial exception.
8.   Josiah Cox Russell, *Medieval Regions and Their Cities* (University of Indiana Press, 1972).
9.   There are many discussions on mediaeval heresy. One of the best and most modern is Gordon Leff, *Heresy in the Latter Middle Ages* as cited above.
10.   See R. H. Bainton, *Here I Stand: A Life of Martin Luther* (New York, Mentor Books, 1955), ch. 3.
11.   G. A. Brucker, *Renaissance Florence* (Wiley, New York, 1969).
12.   *Ibid.,* "setting back historical development by at least two centuries."

13.   E.g., Statute of Labourers in England, 1351, Peasants' Revolt, 1383, and in France, the *jacquerie,* etc.

14.   See Z. N. Brooke, *The English Church and the Papacy* (Cambridge University Press, 1968).

15.   The martyrs under "Bloody Mary" are traditional in English history. Even in the seventeenth century James I caused a couple of priests to be burned.

16.   Tabor.

17.   Eton, Winchester.

18.   See, for example, E. M. Carus-Wilson, *Medieval Merchant Venturers* (London, 1954).

19.   Usually attributed to Johan Gutenberg, 1398-1468. Like other inventions, printing mounted up little by little from one adaptation to another, but Gutenberg is as a rule given the credit for making practicable moveable type.

20.   Professor Bertie Wilkinson, for example.

21.   See, *inter alia,* Robert-Henri Bautier, *The Economic Development of Medieval Europe* (Thames and Hudson, London, Library of European Civilization, 1971); Gene A. Brucker, *Renaissance Florence (1969);* and for the mediaeval period generally, the volume of essays by that outstanding mediaevalist, Joseph R. Strayer, *Medieval Statecraft and the Perspectives of History* (Princeton University Press, 1971).

22.   Pirenne, *A History of Europe, op. cit.,* p. 505.

23.   See Dill, *Roman Society from Nero to Marcus Aurelius, op. cit.*

CHAPTER TEN

The Great Divide

I

Revolutionary Italy:
Revolution Begins in Metropolitanism

There are points in the long chain of mountains that runs from Alaska to Cape Horn at which a person may stand with one foot in water flowing to the Pacific and the other in water flowing into the Atlantic, thousands of miles away. The crest of the mountains is "the divide." Separations in the courses of the waters of time are not as sharp as with some geographical watersheds, but as they recede in time they are invariably visible. In the history of the West, the greatest "divide" was the transition from Paganism ("Hellenism") to Christianity, but it is rivalled by the transition from "mediaevalism" to "modern times." The mere point that the old distinction between "mediaeval" and "modern" is so deeply engrained tends to confirm its validity.

The "Dark Ages" and the later Middle Ages – "the High Middle Ages," as they are called – often are represented as barriers to be broken before the arrival of a more important period – our own! The view may be legitimate, providing we are ready to agree that we ourselves may also be merely prelude, which turns history into an unending staircase. Since in the "Dark Ages," Europe was too fragmented and disordered to have much of a collective character, it may be legitimate to regard those days mainly as a period of incubation. This would not be the case with respect to the "High Middle Ages," which epoch had many aspects of a collectivity and is a distinct civilization of its own. It was the partial break-up of the mediaeval collectivity under the pressures from new sources of creative zeal that led to the major transitions usually referred to as "Renaissance and Reformation." These phases of history were in most respects quite distinct, but they join in marking the end of the previous epoch.

The break-up of a culture gives all the typical features of a revolution. As the old is swept aside, people, or at least some people, greet the new with triumph. "Joy is it in that spring to be alive." The world is being created over again and those who can run the rapids share in the ecstasy of remaking. A culturally revolutionary period necessarily has a somewhat transient aspect. Things are about to be established, the old building is not yet quite torn down but when it is . . .! When it is, then will come in the age of gold, the kingdom of Heaven, Utopia, the withering away of the state. Naturally, no age of gold ever does come in. We make some repairs, sometimes larger repairs, in the old building and it goes back into use until the job has to be done again.

It is hard to think of a clearer, more decided example of these transitional phases in history than that which is called the Renaissance, (except our own!), especially the Renaissance in Italy. This represents in a way the same kind of triumphant outburst as does the Great Age of Faith which had preceded it: a sense of achievement, of nearness to some kind of ultimate revelation, whether the nature of God or the nature of beauty. Some of its phases remind one strongly of our own day in their violence, their disorder and their contempt for anything but what they themselves were accomplishing. Each of the great epochs of which history is composed has been signalled by some kind of religious revival. Many would smile if the Renaissance in its beginnings were termed a religious movement. But a radically new attitude to life (in itself the essence of religion) and the introduction of a new scale of values which shapes human conduct may go so far as to provide the essentially religious quality of faith, faith in its own excellence and therefore hope. In this sense the Renaissance could be termed a religious movement without stretching the term too much. The movement as a whole has a fairly definite beginning and an even more definite termination. Without regard to its other aspects, this in itself makes it attractive to historians.

The Renaissance also illustrates with clarity the sequence that this book seeks to establish: it embodies the zeal generated by glimpses of a new destiny, goes on to the intellectualism that tends to replace it, produces the liberalism that leads to the brink of anarchy and ends by experiencing once more the establishment of authority and order.

Italy was the natural region of Europe for the Renaissance to begin in. Constantinople, the great metropolis whose shadow, even as late as the twelfth century, had fallen far into the West, had weakened under the hammer blows of the Turks. Its metropolitan status had been greatly lessened by the insane assaults of the Western Crusaders in 1204. The wonder is that the great city was to continue to survive for another two and a half centuries. When at last it fell and passed out of the Christian orbit, the event reawakened, at least for thoughtful people, all the fears that had dwelt in Western minds ever since, seven centuries before, the Moslems had sheared off those huge portions of the Western world that they still possess.

Without Constantinople, Europe would have been much longer getting clear from barbarism. But after the "Dark Ages," it was natural for civilization to begin to grow again in the region where its traditions were strongest, in Italy. In Italy, traces of Roman institutions, though weak, dying plants, had managed to survive. There were still organized municipalities, there were some schools, there were the shreds and patches of Roman law. Above all there was the papacy, which had had its own dark days, but had managed to outlive them, to go on to its greatest strength in the thirteenth century. Trade with the East had never quite ceased. The Crusades had been gigantic windfalls. The northern Barbarians may or may not have been fighting for Christ: Italian cities like Venice and Genoa, with Italian realism fought for gold, the gold of the northern Barbarians.

The Italian cities grew apace in the twelfth century and became so strong that they managed to defeat the most celebrated of the mediaeval emperors, Frederick Barbarossa. Freedom from the empire enabled them to evolve forms of self-government which had about them some aspects of democracy – democracy for a few, at any rate. They grew apace, nourished both by the Eastern trade and by their opportunities as middlemen for the northern towns at the other end of the Rhine trench, the towns of Flanders. More generally, they grew on the wave of economic growth that set in about 1050 and rose steadily to its crest in 1348, when the Black Death marked its fall.

Such matters were major: the Italian towns took the same advantage of them as cities everywhere have taken of their positions and their times. Venice, Milan, Florence, Genoa and various others became large for their times and eventually immensely prosperous. It was the same story that has been repeated again and again in the last two centuries and which has furnished the world not with one or two metropolitan centres but dozens. Much has been said in modern historical writing of "Western expansion," the spread of the white races and white civilization throughout the world. For all this, the Italian cities in the eleventh to fourteenth centuries furnished a dress rehearsal.

For the rest of Europe, they represented as glittering a pageant of success and magnificence as has done the United States in our own day. To explore the relationship between wealth and culture would take us far afield, but that they are close seems evident: we do not look for an advanced civilization among the Chippewyan Indians of the Mackenzie

River delta. The glory did not end with the Black Death, nor even with the cutting of the umbilical cord with the East by the Discoveries. But everything that goes up must come down and so, at long last, the Italian cities, at least in comparison with the parts of Europe facing the Atlantic, began to lose their topmost place. There were good reasons for that. But Italy was not finished. In the late sixteenth century its life passed into a resting stage, only to bloom again in the nineteenth century and once more to give the rest of the world a dazzling display of artistic achievement, this time mainly musical.

It may well be asked whether the specific matters to which the historian can point are, all of them, sufficient to account for the artistic genius which this relatively poor peninsula has continued to display, century after century. The usual explanation for the Renaissance achievement is wealth. No one will deny the need of some measure of well-being for cultural accomplishment, but it is surely wrong to hang the Italian Renaissance on wealth alone. For to mediaeval, Renaissance, and modern achievement, it must be remembered, is to be added that of classical days. It is true that great gulfs intervened between imperial Rome and the later Italy, not least those formed by the blood donations of innumerable strangers. But despite these, Italians descended from Italians, as do their descendants. So that it is not fair to subtract from them the classical inheritance.

Mussolini's theatrical revival of the phrase *Mare Nostrum* was empty, but there may be more subtle inheritances. The Italian peninsula is beautiful, has an easy climate and in some parts is favoured by nature with fertile soil. So are many other parts of the world which have never shown signs of being other Italy's. But genes are said to descend unchanged in the human organism from generation to generation. Yet biological inheritance of the subtler aspects of mankind, those emanating from mind (whatever *mind* is) must not be pressed too far. The social climate is possibly more important. The fact remains that this peninsula has contributed an enormous share of the Western world's artistic inheritance. It cannot have been all simply because of the availability of Carrara marble.

In the depths of the "Dark Ages," what light there was was furnished – Constantinople as a going concern, always excluded – mainly from Italy, though the important contributions from the other side of the continent, Ireland and England, must not be forgotten. Later, with the growth of the mediaeval civilization, the Italian peninsula showed the first signs of revival, as centres of studies grew up around the disciplines of law and medicine. (The University of Bologna proudly claims seniority to Paris.) It was in the thirteenth century that the trickle began to forecast the future artistic flood. It is sufficient only to mention two names, Giotto (1266-1337) and, of course, Dante (1265-1321), though "trickle" is quite too small a word to be applied to Dante.

The early fourteenth century contributed the other members of the pioneer "big three," Petrarch (1304-1374) and Boccaccio (1313-1375). Then great names become increasingly common and in the fifteenth century, they abound. At the end of that century, for example, there were living Bellini (1430-1516), Bramante (1444-1514), Botticelli (1444-1510), Fincino (1433-1499), Perugino (1445-1523), Leonardo de Vinci (1452-1519), Poliziano (1454-1497), Dannazaro (1459-1530), Pico della Mirandola (1463-1494), Machiavelli (1469-1527), Titian (1490-1576), Giorgione (1478-1510), Ariosto (1474-1533), Michelangelo (1475-1564), Guicciardini (1483-1540), Raphael (1483-1520), Andrea del Sarto (1486-1531), Aretino (1492-1556). These are those whose names appear in all the books: among the artists, there were many others. And a not inconsiderable personage among the sailors, one Christopher Columbus (1451-1506). It may be doubted whether any other age in history has produced and sustained such a galaxy of talent. Talent was by no means confined to the artists: it was universal. But then the story is too well-known for details to be necessary.

It is interesting to note, too, the generous life spans of many such men, compared to the northerners, where almost everyone seemed to die at latest in his fifties. This argues a degree of well-being (perhaps of mere cleanliness) not parallelled elsewhere. This would be logical and would arise from some of the same factors that produce the long life spans of our modern world. Evidently not every Renaissance Italian was assassinated.

> Italy (of the Renaissance) had become the richest, most dazzling, cultured, intelligent nation of Christendom. Italians had transformed the universe, or at least man's ideas about the universe.[1]

The richest, certainly, as benefits a metropolitan country – the richest, thanks to the communications to the north both by land and sea and thanks to the humble sheep, an animal that in destroying its owners' soil fills their pockets. Mediaeval Scotland was another country much of which was reduced to rock by the sheep. Castile was a conspicuous example, its mountains reduced to stony hill sides. Italy did not quite suffer this extreme. In Italy, Florence had become the great sheep city and its textiles went everywhere. Like the sheep-barons of mediaeval England, Florence rode to wealth on the backs of sheep. These animals also proved sturdy enough to carry the Florentine money-lender (banker, when he became rich and respectable) into the farthest reaches of Europe.

Was it pure prosperity that accounted for the Italian Renaissance? And for "Italian" should we read "Florentine"? Other cities shared, of course, notably Milan and Venice, but with the possible exception of Periclean Athens, was there ever such a city as Florence?[2]

There was a dark side:

Beneath the surface of brilliant social culture lurked gross appetites and savage passions, unrestrained by medieval piety, untutored by modern experience. Italian society exhibited an almost unexampled spectacle of literary, artistic and courtly refinement, crossed by brutalities of lust, treason, poisonings, assassinations, violence . . .[3]

The quotation brings up the problem of the relationship between artistic efflorescence and violence, a problem of much confusion. It would be foolish to think that artistic creativity cannot exist without violence, but much more foolish to believe that violence cannot exist without artistic creativity. The artist (using the word in a wide sense) cannot be an ordinary, humdrum person. He is nearly always more or less of a rebel, very much his own man, non-conforming. But there have been plenty of creative spirits in men of well-regulated, more or less ordinary life, some of them right in the midst of the Renaissance, Raphael and Michelangelo, for example. If Italy of the Renaissance was more violent than in preceding ages, that probably sprang from the many factors that were disturbing society at that time. A comparison might lie in the American "wild west" when the dream of unlimited wealth for everybody and limitless space to exploit it in, a continent to be seized, led to breakdowns of law and order.

Although in a previous century, the kingdom of Sicily had been described as the best governed, the most efficiently administered country in Europe, whether they differed greatly from preceding periods or not, there can be little doubt but that in most spheres of life (save perhaps the humble) Renaissance conditions in Italy approximated anarchy. Benvenuto Cellini is more or less typical:

Just after sunset, as this musketeer stood at his door with his sword in his hand, I with great address came close up to him with a long dagger and gave him a violent back-handed stroke . . . He . . . took to his heels. I pursued him and in four steps caught up to him, when, raising the dagger over his head, I hit exactly upon his collar bone and the middle of his neck. The weapon penetrated so deep into both that I found it impossible to recover it (here Cellini went into hiding for a few days. He then went back to see the Pope) . . The Pope (Clement VII) knew all that had happened . . . The Pontiff . . . frowned on me and with angry looks seemed to reprimand me . . . then looking attentively at me, he said, "Now that you have recovered your health, Benevenuto, take care of yourself.' I understood his meaning and told him that I should not neglect his advice.[4]

Let us hope that His Holiness had not been as thoroughly informed about Cellini's conduct as the latter imagined.

Absorption in the life of the moment with a jolly murder thrown in now and then, everything of yesterday unceremoniously dismissed as "old fashioned,'' worn out, here surely is revolution. Of that, there has been plenty of illustration in our own day. When the matters of yesterday consisted in the deepest concern for the fate of immortal souls, when they fixed the attention of every thinking man upon what was going to happen to him after he died and when, almost suddenly, this interest vastly diminished and men began to concern themselves with the excitement of the life about them, whether on high intellectual and artistic planes or on low and carnal, or on both at once, then evidently a vast historic shift was under way. Both in Italy and the sober north, for example, a system of thought that had carried the human intellect to great heights, Scholasticism, was first neglected, then kicked out. If the ancient pieties were seldom formally rejected, they everywhere came to be held in indifference where they were not received in ridicule:

> (The theologians) hedge themselves about with such an array of magisterial definite corollaries, propositions, explicate and implicate, and do so abound in subterfuges that chains forged by Vulcan himself could not hold them . . . The great and illustrious theologians (as they dub themselves) will only awaken when something like the following is propounded: – Does supernatural generation require time for its accomplishment? Has Christ a double relation of sonship? Is the proposition possible, 'God, the Father, hates the Son'? Might God have chosen to assume the form of a woman, a devil, an ass, a gourd or a stone?[5]

II
All Revolutionary Fires Die Down

Like most other epochs in history, the Renaissance falls into discernible sub-periods. Sub-periods in turn might be analyzed into the components that this book ascribes to the more conspicuous "ages": though the shorter the period examined, the less certain would the analysis become. Still, writers speak of "the period of the Regency" (that of George IV in England), of "*fin de siècle*" with reference to the end of the nineteenth century, of "Reconstruction" in the American post-Civil War period, and of others. It is always tempting to try to pin-point the nature of "the times."

The first period of the Renaissance is marked by the groping efforts of the fourteenth century and its triumphant "discovery" of antiquity – how much Petrarch regretted that he had not had the chance to learn Greek in his youth! Then in the early fifteenth century there was the rise of "humanism" and the triumphant overthrow of the past. It was this above all that furnished the basis for the cry boringly repeated in every textbook that the Renaissance meant the discovery of the individual, as if men had not always been individuals. There is no space to argue that point here. It may be covered by the simple statement that many a change in the pattern of life occurred in fifteenth century Italy and many new ideas occurred to Italians adapting themselves to these changes. None of them were more drastic than those encountered by late twentieth century man. Yet it is paradoxical that an age which was so determinedly repudiating its immediate past should at the same time have fallen head over heels in love with antiquity, with the classical world, with "the ancients" as they were commonly dubbed. But the paradox is everlastingly repeated in history, it is the immediate past which is repudiated. Periods more remote take on a romantic glow as they recede.

As it unrolled, the fifteenth century witnessed the intensification of the worship of antiquity the effects of which had already had marvellous results in saving from destruction much of the classical literary heritage. This had been reinforced by the last dying throbs of life from Constantinople with the flight to Italy of refugee scholars and their books. The arrival of Manuel Chrysoloras in Florence from that city in 1397 indicates the initiation of this new phase of the Renaissance. The period was marked not only by the lively interest in Greek (as the door to Greek literature) but by the more elusive aspects of a new age, by the rise of a critical spirit – Lorenzo Valla (1407-1575) who discovered that the "Donation of Constantine" was a fraud, is often cited in evidence of this – and especially of a secular spirit.

This word "secular" with respect to Italy raises difficulties. On a humble level, the old popular Paganism of classical days had been transformed, rather than abolished. There was little decrease in superstition, miracles continued to abound – St. Januarius's blood went on liquefying on its scheduled semi-annual performances and everywhere the *deus loci* continued to receive his respects in the shape of the adoration of the local saints. But such practices and such marvels are not altogether unknown in modern society, even in the most "advanced" of countries, and they may be on the increase.[6] They will never disappear until humanity comes to rise above them, which will be when humanity ceases to exist.

More importantly, increasing secularity meant loss of religious faith, and in Italy, the Faith, if the word is equated with "the Church," was not formally and openly repudiated. It was religious conviction which disappeared, not religious form. After all, pope Alexander VI, with his concubines and his incestuous son and daughter Caesar and Lucretia Borgia, continued to be a good Catholic. Protestants too easily intermingle the two terms *religion* and *morality:* the classical heritage fairly successfully kept them apart. It is quite probable, however, that *piety*, which may have to be distinguished from both terms, had decreased from the generations of the Great Age of Faith. It is quite probable that the sincerities of that inner experience which has universally marked the genuinely *religious* man, the mystic sense of communion with God which such souls crave, had decreased. In some such way Italian life by the fifteenth century had come to be secular.

Persons of the late middle age or older today (1970s) should have little difficulty in understanding what had happened, for their earlier years were passed in a day when the marks of religion were deep upon life. Moreover it is idle to measure Italian life by Western or Protestant standards. The tenth and eleventh century revival of religion which had taken such ardent form in the north had worn a different shape in Italy. In its schools it had been the legal aspects of life which had interested scholars rather more than its philosophical: that is, it was ritualistic observance, rather than the inner spirit which perhaps had dominated. Nor is there contradiction in assuming that in Italy as in other countries, there had always been many an ardent, utterly spiritual soul: St. Francis is testimony enough for that.

In the late fourteenth and the early fifteenth centuries, others of the familiar landmarks of the Renaissance appeared. A new Latin style, modelled on the classical masters, especially Cicero, was cultivated. Then in the course of the fifteenth century came a return to the native, "vulgar" tongue, marked by many literary works. The artistic glories of the fifteenth century tend, however, to crowd out the other achievements of this remarkable century. Who, for example, can stand and gaze at Ghiberti's doors to the Baptistery at Florence without echoing Michelangelo's exclamation "So beautiful that they might be the gates of Paradise." If a personal note may be introduced, that was the identical impression that they made on the writer when many years ago, he first stood and looked at them. How could human brain and hand do such work? The technical achievement in itself was miraculous. And over 500 years ago! Just as marvellous as flying to the moon.

Yet it may be asked why in an age of triumphant secularism, most works of art, right through the Renaissance, still have devout religious subject matter. Ghiberti's gates of Paradise picture Biblical scenes. So do Michelangelo's paintings on the ceiling of the Sistine Chapel. So do nine out of ten of the other artistic achievements of the era. The purely secular motif in art, though it became prominent, never crowded out the religious. The readiest answer lies in the deep currents of tradition that do not change their courses overnight, and in the organized forces of the age, in "the establishment" to use a favourite modern expression, which always buttresses things as they are and in the Renaissance delighted to buttress its artistic propaganda with its power and its wealth. Sooner or later, it is evident, art must reflect its age. Russian Communism has made much of this point, especially in buttressing the Marxist thesis of the transition from feudalism to bourgeoism to proletariansim, but it is surely self-evident.

The peak of architectural achievement was to come a little after the peak of artist. When the great age of building set in, and it was while Gothic cathedrals were still rising in the north, it was not Gothic that was being built in Italy, for Gothic had never penetrated far. Nothing mirrors as plainly the shift from one culture to another as does architecture and its accompanying sculpture (except men's clothing and their hair-styling), so that the fifteenth century is an age of experiment marked by a period of youth before attaining its prime, thus again illustrating the omnipresent nature of the process of evolution upon which emphasis was placed in the opening chapter of this book. In the statue *The Ecstasy of St. Teresa* (seventeenth century) decline has been alleged to follow:

> Bernini went very far – just how far one realizes when one remembers the historical St. Teresa, with her plain, dauntless, sensible face. The contrast with the swooning, sensuous beauty of the Cornaro Chapel is almost shocking. One can't help feeling that affluent Baroque, in its escape from the severities of the earlier fight against Protestantism ended by escaping from reality into a world of illusion. Art creates its own momentum and once set on this course, there was nothing it could do except become more and more sensational.[7]

In the beautiful statue referred to, St. Teresa is all Clark says about her, and more. Her ecstasy is love's ecstasy and her dream about an angel piercing her heart with a flaming golden arrow, has more than a suggestion of a Freudian image. Her beauty is too good to be true. But most people would prefer it so. People like honey.

Bernini's piazza before St. Peter's (seventeenth century) has some-times been criticized as being over-grandiose, signalling the arrival of architectural decadence, though it could be argued that the colonnade at least fulfils the worthy function of preserving an open space before the great cathedral, instead of allowing this to be built over by bureaucrats with visions limited to the prospects of new and comfortable offices. But St. Peter's itself majestically proclaims the peak. The money for its building collected in the north – the well-known purchase of indulgences' money – helped to split the church. But perhaps St. Peter's, the building, was worth a split in the Church!

By the end of the fifteenth century, the old Scholasticism had been rejected, the old pieties often scorned, a daring young man, to the horror of all good souls, in a mock restoration of pagan rites, had sacrificed a bull in the forum. Far greater was the horror this excited than the immoralities of popes, the frank assertion of one of them that since he had been given the papacy, he was going to enjoy it, the actual appearance in arms of another, the bastards of another, the gaiety, confusion, luxury, corruption, that surrounded them. While the papacy may have reached abysmal depths in the ninth century, it plunged still lower in the early sixteenth. "The period of the Renaissance popes" has become a byword for all that is in sharpest contrast to the religion of the Prince of Peace, the humble

Nazarene. The evolution had passed from liberalism to anarchy.

Yet an end was approaching. Even though Clement VII may have complacently passed over such little matters as the murder committed by Benvenuto Cellini – after all, he was a Medici – he was no Alexander VI. Nor was the new air stealing in in the third decade of the sixteenth century quite so genial for anarchic liberals as had been that prevailing in the previous generation. For this there were various good reasons. The break in the church was becoming more than an ordinary heresy. Charles V, the emperor upon whose dominions the sun never set, "the morning drum-beat of whose garrisons circled the globe," the potentate who took almost a proprietary interest in the papacy, was a sincere, glum Catholic. Then came the remarkable change in the occupants of the papacy. Paul III (1534-1549), Paul IV (1555-1559), Pius V (1566-1572) and Sixtus V (1585-1590) were all reforming popes. They have been termed the most zealous since the great days of Gregory VII.

Evidently the church was girding up its loins to fight. Why the shift? The shift from heads of a Christian church who were as "Christian" as their whores, to heads who had recaptured something of the old pieties? Why the shift? Was it because it was blowing cold out of the north? Many areas had been lost to Catholicism, apparently permanently. By the "Religious Peace of Augsburg" 1555, German princes had been given the right to decide the religion of their subjects. This could be considered, after a fashion, as a measure of religious liberty. The danger of the further spread of heresy must have had much to do with the new zeal for reform. There is nothing like competition for increasing the efforts of the merchant. The General Council, that of Trent, which met on and off between 1545 and 1563, marked the new zeal for reform. General Councils brought back no pleasant memories to Rome. It is hard to imagine that one would have been summoned except out of dire necessity. But they could be managed. Trent, threatening at times, was managed. The papacy came out of it stronger than it had gone into it. It advanced another step towards that absolute monarchy which was to be formally and ceremoniously proclaimed in the next General Council, 300 years into the future, the General Council of the Vatican, 1870.

Still more remarkable in eventual accomplishment than any meeting of churchmen was the fiery zeal that drove on the simple Spanish soldier, Ignatius Loyola. Here was the single-mindedness of the devotee, the passion for souls that has characterized other great ages of the Christian religion. Loyola's new Order, the Company of Jesus, was, as everyone knows, founded on military principles: its members were to be soldiers for Jesus (that exemplar of peace). The speed with which the ranks were filled, the rapid increase in the numbers within the Order, their militancy as crusaders, their vast success in holding at bay the Protestant heresies and in rolling them back in many a country, their world-wide distribution, the power in high places and in low which the members obtained, testify sufficiently to the success of Loyola's Order. If more were needed, more than adequate amounts could be found in the suspicion and hatred the Order quickly excited, among Catholic and Protestant alike.

With the two passages of history just referred to, the Council of Trent and the rise of the Jesuit Order, a new chapter opened. The age of Catholic Puritanism was at hand. In this way the Italian Renaissance is usually considered to have come to an end. Given the untidiness of history, the word *end* is too definite. "Slowed down," "changed its form," "its leading ideas having been worked out," some such phrases might be preferable to "come to an end." Whatever the best expression, there can be no question but that in the seventeenth century we are in a different world.

For Italy, that world was to be much duller than what had preceded it. In face of the wealth that poured across to Spain and the other West European countries from the lands beyond the Atlantic, the prosperity of its cities, if it did not actually decline calamitously, at least declined proportionately to that of the rising northern centres, conspicuously Amsterdam and London. The Italian peninsula as a whole had become that "geographical expression: which Metternich in the nineteenth century was scornfully to term it. Artists and intellectual vitality declined. But Italians continued to monopolize the papacy.

But the Italian Renaissance had proved as catching as a winter cold. It had spread to the north, where country after country in their turn had responded to its spirit. In England, for example, it was only in the reign of Elizabeth two or three hundred years after the first signs of the awakening had appeared in Italy, that the flame began to burn brightly. The English "Renaissance" – the term seems rather absurd in the case of England – within a few years rose to the heights of Shakespeare and then was lost in the sands of the seventeenth century, a brief but glorious shout of accomplishment to the world, which still hears it.

It should be noted, however, that continental influences had come in much earlier in the form of "the New Learning," "the Oxford Reformers" included the great names of Sir Thomas More and Erasmus, who lived at Cambridge for a time. This movement was one of intellectual liberalism, not a popular stir of artistic creativity, as was the Elizabethan Renaissance. The gap between More (d. 1535) and Shakespeare (b. 1564) could be taken as representing the phase of semi-anarchy that follows on the intellectual phase and preceding the phase of zeal or faith – in this instance nationalism, the faith of England. ("This precious jewel set in a silver sea, nought shall make us rue, if England to herself do rest but true.") It might be called Christianity, the better term was Anglicanism, Englishism.

In the grim years of the last half of the sixteenth century in France, there were matters more important to be attended to than poetry. France was in the middle of its religious wars: another age was dawning for it.

But while it is clear that the first rushes of enthusiasm died down, and accomplishment with them, the Renaissance, so-called, never actually died. In the seventeenth century, it was well into that intellectual phase which follows the enthusiastic. One thinks at once of Galileo. In this intellectualizing of the new world of civilization, so spectacular an aspect of the seventeenth century, prominence passed to the north, which is yet another illustration of how difficult it would be to say when the Renaissance *ended*. It is not dead yet. It will never die as long as the freedom of the mind endures. For that is its perpetual heritage to men. It allowed men to follow out their thoughts to whatever point that might lead them. With many a set-back, since those days the road has never been long closed. As one writes, the mind remains free. Only in those countries which have already attained Utopia is it still in fetters.

Notes

1.   Luigi Barzini, *The Italians* (Atheneum, New York, 1965, tenth printing), p. 25.
2.   A good study of Florence in brief compass is Gene A. Brucker, *Renaissance Florence, op. cit.*
3.   John Addington Sumons, *History of the Renaissance in Italy* (1894).
4.   Benvenuto Cellini, *The Life of Benvenuto Cellini,* written by himself.
5.   Erasmus, *The Praise of Folly* as quoted in Robinson, *op. cit.,* II, pp. 43-44.
6.   Note the increasing vogue of astrology.
7.   Kenneth Clark, *Civilisation: A Personal View* (Harper and Row London, 1969), p. 191. The spelling of the word "Civilisation" is Clark's.

CHAPTER ELEVEN

Pandora's Box

I

Renaissance and Reformation
Asked the Same Question

The old Greek myth has it that when Pandora, first of women, had opened the box which Zeus had given her, the trouble of the world flew out and could never again be confined. Under some such figure could thoughtful men in the sixteenth century well have considered the world about them. The old certainties had gone and new confusions assailed them, confusions in belief, in morals, in aesthetics, in geography, in politics, confusions in the services of the church of which they and their progenitors had immemorially been communicants.

The lid had been taken off Pandora's box and could it ever be put back on? For a century and a half or more men essayed the task, only at last to find that no lid would fit the box, which anyway had become so altered that it was no longer the box from which the lid had originally be removed.

When in the historic year 1517, Martin Luther posted his ninety-five theses on the church door in Wittenberg, the Italians who for two centuries had been creating that new world in the realms of culture which later generations were to call the Renaissance, could have had no idea that the stiff academic gesture away off in the wilds of Germany would one day symbolize the beginning of a movement that was to change man's fate and fortunes even more drastically than what they themselves were doing. Subsequent generations have coupled the two developments, so that they have often been looked at as if they had been one. As a recoil from such over simplifications, they have also been regarded as having had little to do with each other. The accident of alliteration has done almost as much as historical analysis to draw the two aspects of life together. "Renaissance and Reformation" are easily coupled.

Yet from still other points of view, they may be coupled justly. Men, events, times and places, separated the two. But both were attempts by human beings to find answers – or the answer – to the question that perpetually confronts humanity: What is man, this paragon of animals, what is the meaning of life or has it any meaning, what is the nature of the "unseen"? And if answers are attempted, how are they to be expressed? In some such strange way, the utmost paganisms of the Renaissance may be lined with the extremisms of the Reformation.

In its totality, the Renaissance, more especially in its Italian phenomena, may be regarded simply as an attempt to bring back into life the ordinary, natural human feelings and modes of conduct that many centuries of Hebraic Christianity had crowded to one side. Many are the books that have been written in explication of the two ideas, Hellenism and Hebraism. The two words may be used as shorthand terms for the sharpest dichotomy that separates man from man, society from society and the private selves within the individual's own private being. In varied form they seem to run the world around, creeping into all the great religions, bringing contention and uneasy compromise wherever they meet each other, but never true reconciliation.

In no aggregation of men have the two attitudes warred more constantly, more bitterly and more fruitfully than in our own Western world. The strife makes up a large part of the history of "the West": it is an objective of this book to light it up and try to suggest how it has worked out into historical change. Many names are given to the two sides of life: not only Paganism and Christianity, Hellenism and Hebraism, but more starkly, sin and salvation, selfishness and duty, pleasure and pain, laughter and tears, and various others. The two have been coupled with racialism: "the effete, pleasure-loving, frivolous southerners," the strong, stern, serious-minded northerners. This coupling is now reprobated, not only because of the arrogance implied in it, but because it is in error. That "effete," southern, tropical people, the Hindus, for example, are strongly Puritan in much of their conduct. The subject may be pursued indefinitely. The farther it is pursued, the less sharp become its contours.

For those whose natures put them on the Hebraic side, the artistic developments of the Renaissance form easy and obvious targets. The subjugation of the animal instincts had been and still is one of the primary objectives of Christian warfare in its battle against "the world, the flesh and the devil." And what was the artistic effort of the Renaissance but a frank recognition of the world and the flesh? For those whose natures made them "Hellenes," "Pagans," the gloomy claims of the spirit sacrificed life to illusion, made life a burden, required men to give all their efforts to the pursuit of shadows.

"Dost thou think because thou art virtuous, there shall be no cakes and ale?"[1]

For the spirit of the Renaissance to conjoin with the spirit of the Reformation, for the two to discover that they had some kind of common origin, and even a close relationship, would have been a surprising mutual accommodation. Yet that peculiar marriage had been effected once before in history, for was not the whole sweep of the church's expansion an illustration of it? The bond of union was to be found in the word compromise, and from the early centuries on, compromise had always guided the church as an organized institution. The pagan godlets had become Christian saints, the pagan festivals Christian holidays, pagan morality absorbed within the system of confession and penance. At times, the balance had swayed in one direction, at times in the other. Long prior to either the Renaissance or Reformation, creative re-awakenings of the spirit had marked the onsets of the great ages of faith, the missionary expansion into the east of Europe as they were later to mark the fiery ardour that lay behind the revivals of the eleventh and twelfth centuries. St. Gregory the Great, St. Boniface, Pope Gregory VII – "that monk Hildebrand" – St. Bernard, St. Francis, the lives of such men had marked the ages of recovery and of strength. Such men and such movements keep recurring in history – not only Luther, but Calvin, Wesley, the many American exhorters to righteousness, Lenin, Trotsky, Ghandi, Mao Tse-tung, all of them "makers and shakers."

For all these men, the foe is the same – absorption in the present and its trivialities, no thought of that "day of wrath, that dreadful day, when heaven and earth shall pass away."[2] delight in frivolity, idle dalliance, art for art's sake. The Puritan poet Longfellow put it all in verses that most of us had to learn in our childhood: "Life is real and life is earnest, and the grave is not its goal . . ." To this day, the stricter sects of Protestantism, the stricter devotees among Catholics, the most devoted Communists, hold in abhorrence all the more frivolous sides of life: they distrust beauty, they fear the arts, for do they not all waken up that devil within that leads to lust and sin?[3]

What could be more accurately calculated to lead to lust and sin than the alluring fleshly depictions of the fine arts? The story is old and familiar. The unclothed body of Eve, whether in stone or in paint, symbolizes sin and has ever been the target of the saint's or Puritan's shafts. For hundreds of years, no nude figure of woman appeared in the sculpture of the West, not until the thirteenth century, when a change of wind was beginning. When Renaissance art had reached almost its peak, there had occurred in its shrine, Florence, the extraordinary episode by which the gaunt ascetic Savonarola persuaded the Florentines to put all their "worldliness" aside and return to the worship of "the true God." Things had gone too far for that, however, and the Florentines recaptured their liberty by burning the would-be saint "as a heretic," that is, as a man devoted in unpleasant sincerity to the values for which Christianity stood.

If a marriage could be arranged between two such discordant life-views, what would be the basis? Reasonable compromise, had said the church, the recognition of the "built-in" weaknesses of humanity. Moderate reform, said the northern humanists such as More and Erasmus, reform of abuse based on an intellectual perception of excess. But More was beheaded and Erasmus ignored. The solution, or such solution as has at long last been found, lay in a direction that no one in the year 1500 could have perceived. It lay in the simple word *freedom*. For the creative artist in Italy, there had to be freedom for him to follow out his conceptions to whatever point his brain dictated. In the north, freedom, was, as it were, the Trojan Horse that Protestantism carried into Troy. It took generations for the armed men to find their way out and capture the city. But the essence of what was to become Protestantism was the spirit of individual freedom, the right to choose, to make your own decisions. "Every Christian man is a priest" cried Martin Luther, embracing in those prophetic words far more than he ever meant to embrace.

The triumph of Protestantism, where it triumphed, did not, however, end the old dichotomy. It is still with us, for once freedom is secured – any kind of freedom – it tends to be carried to excessive lengths. As old idols are cast down, their bronze is remelted and shaped into new ones. In the intervals, they lie in fragments. Thus out of the destruction of old fixed forms, through intermediate stages of liberalism and freedom (the two words must be distingushed) there invariably comes disorder verging towards chaos, and out of this, new, fixed forms arise. Luther in lifting one kind of yoke from men's shoulders prepared the way for the imposition of another in the rigours of Calvinistic predestination. The men of the Renaissance in celebrating the glories of man as man and not as semi-disembodied spirit, brought in the train of the celebration the sternness of the Counter-Reformation. Tridentine decrees and Puritanism from opposite sides seemed to have about them but little of the spirit of freedom. Yet freedom came again, and once again was shackled, down to our own days. History is a succession of pulsations. There is no end to the degree of refinement that may be given to such analysis. It must always remain full of "loose ends." In what cycle, for example, do we put the Hitlerian massacres of the Jews and total destruction of German freedom, 1939-1945?

II
The Reformation as Revolution

The period after the decisive break with which the year 1517 is associated represents another of those historical thunder storms that eventually clear the air. The anarchy of ideas and politics, mounting up to what is called "the Reformation"[4] leads to the Religious Wars and the Religious Wars may be interpreted as attempts to restore order, or, as some of their aspects must have seemed to persons living through them, re-establish the past. The attempts go on, giving rise to new concepts or order, civil and religious. In the seventeenth century, the new order emerges in form not nearly as symmetrical as the old but actually deeply rooted because based on new necessities. A new synthesis comes about and it in turn sets going new erosions.

The "Age of the Religious Wars" is usually taken as ending with the Peace of Westphalia in 1648. The date is too precise. Religious hatred, mounting up to bloodshed, is too old a story to end suddenly, like a car stopping. But the date suffices to mark off a boundary to the period in which kings were arrayed against kings and against subjects, states against states, citizens against citizens, upon what they claimed or thought to be, religious principles. Putting the matter in another way, the "Age of the Religious Wars" might be viewed as that revolutionary period, that difficult period of transition, between an old world and a new. It reminds one of the similar uneasy period in which Paganism was being defeated by Christianity. The old gods fought hard, they claimed many victims, and the new Faith when it triumphed, took generations to establish itself on that hard Petrine rock against which, the promise was, the gates of Hell would not prevail.

The period of the Religious Wars witnessed the destruction of an old faith, the shorthand term for which is mediaevalism, but when it had ended, the unity that had marked the earlier period never returned, and instead of there being one faith there were two, and one of these divided within itself. There was little to correspond to the former annihilating defeat suffered by Paganism, always due weight being given to the considerable elements of Paganism that still remained in one of the wings of the armies that had joined battle.[5] That element of Paganism still remains. It even tends to creep back into various areas of Protestantism. It will no doubt always be with humans, many of whom will never be able to persuade themselves to give up their marvels.

It was not only military turmoil that prevailed over the long four generations between 1517 and 1648. Almost every society suffered internal divisions, many of which continue to this day. Many parts of Europe broke away completely from the old order. Everywhere Christians demonstrated their notions of what was meant by Christian love by roasting each other live. It was the era of "the thumbscrew and the rack and (as Tennyson makes Sir Richard Grenville say) the devildoms of Spain." Not only of Spain, however, devildoms everywhere.[6] Tennyson reflected the horror, still felt deeply in his day, of the Spanish Inquisition, whose mass burnings of heretics had filled the Protestant world with loathing. These were the so called *"autos-da-fe"* the "Acts of Faith."

It was also an age which saw an unparallelled extension of the human orbit. The whole future of the race was changed by the discovery and colonization of the New World – largely by those same Spanish devils. The Italians reached their height of artistic development, the English produced their Shakespeare and in the next century, the seventeenth, men capped it all with the great move forward on the scientific front. How vast the stretch is, that scant century and a half between Luther's theses – between the inkwell he is held by legend to have thrown at a devil that appeared in his study, and Newton announcing (1687), his *Laws of Gravitation!* The High Middle Ages had been preoccupied with working out the logic of God and nature – reconciling faith and reason – but the seventeenth century made an attack on the nature of Nature itself. The world was changed. Why?

Facile explanations for what happened in this country or in that are not hard to find. In Spain, fresh from its age-old crusade against the Moors, with the riches of the New World pouring in, and would-be young crusaders, zealous for new fields of conquest and of plunder, crossing the seas to find them, it is the old story of zeal, zeal which thanks to the current situation, carried within it a large component of what may be termed religion or, possibly better, religious fervency. France, torn by civil war in the sixteenth century, had to wait until the seventeenth when, there too, religious zeal spurred Frenchmen to great deeds. In England, it was probably well-being producing a sense of Englishry which throve mightily on such events as the defeat of the Armada, plus the personal loyalty towards Elizabeth that brought forth the glories of the time. If favourable and easy environment, almost complete absence for centuries from foreign molestation of consequence, are the factors that bring forth a national culture, then surely national culture should have arisen in late sixteenth century England. The religious question had not divided the country into opposing halves, nor had rival claims to the throne. The foreign threat, when it materialized, was, thanks to the weather rather than to the valiant unreadiness of the English, averted: "Afflavit Deus et dissipati sunt." To such matters and others of the sort, "the Elizabethan Age" was presumably the answer. In England religious zeal here and there rode high, but it was tempered by the great compromise by which "the good old religion" went on presumptively unchanged – except in that it was fundamentally changed by the substitution of king (that is, in fact, the state) for pope.

For contemporaries, the year of Luther's bill-posting in itself, 1517, no more signified an epochal change than had 1492. Great events take time to work themselves out. Few clerics in the Vatican slept less soundly because an obscure monk in half-barbarous East Germany had nailed some debatable propositions on his own church door. And would Luther have mounted up even to the heights of a Huss had it not been that his ideas got coupled to the political exigencies of his Prince? It may have been merely Luther's times that gave to Luther his enduring place in history. The movement, the Reformation, with which his name is coupled became much larger than the man. Attempts to explain and interpret it have gone on from that day to this: as Preserved Smith, the distinguished American historian showed,[7] in the intervening four centuries, these have each reflected the tone and temper of their own day. The Reformation as one of the greatest of formative experiences in history continues to reflect itself in countless aspects of life and necessarily lends itself to innumerable endless "explanation."

If we think in terms of the new denomination that he founded, Lutheranism, we shall probably agree that Luther's impact on history was not as profound as that of the younger reformer, Calvin. "Justification by faith," his major theological position, was interesting to the intellectual theologian but how many martyrs did it produce? Lutheranism became the established religion of various of the German states and Scandinavia, but it did not change the world. Its adherents seldom became more than traditionalists. It did not have the upsetting impact of Calvinism. Left to itself, it might well have shrunk to a kind of later day Arianism, a thorn in the side of mother church, but not a thrust at her heart. Except in that the nature of the age made almost any disturbing idea contagious, Lutheranism left to itself might have quietly shrunk to minor proportions. Later on in history, in the nineteenth century, it became an important agency of Christian missionary effort beyond the seas. And in the eighteenth and nineteenth centuries, its adherents by carrying the church of their fathers to America greatly increased its geographic range. But it is hard to think of outstanding emotional qualities or intellectual theses that could be thought of as their own unique contribution to civilization, changing the world more or less to mirror them. In fact, it may be argued that Lutheranism, by its acceptance with little question, of the civil power as the supreme authority, stood merely for a conservatism that easily made its peace with the harsh power structures in which it found itself and thus aligned itself with the past rather than the future.

It could be argued, further, that Lutheranism by its emphasis on the spiritual side of man contributed to that "ruling of the clouds," that departure from the here and the now into the mists of theory which greatly added to the unease of nineteenth century Germany, spurring it forward towards that forceful conception of reality which was to prove so tragic when it got a state sufficiently strong to act upon it. That is not to deny to the Lutheran church its honourable share in the propagation of the Christian faith. It remains as one of the great Protestant denominations, but only as one among others. And Luther's personal courage in fighting against the religious system as it then stood, his incidental heroic ejaculations – *"Hier steke ich, vor Gott, ish kann nicht anders"* – "Every Christian man is a priest" and others such, gave to the Protestant world an inspiration of courageous self-determination which it has never lost.

Could the same be said of Anglicanism? Anglicanism represents the supremacy of state over church carried almost as far as can be. With Henry VIII appeared that horror of late Puritan divines, the Erastian Prince, "supreme Head of the Church in earth" as Henry was pleased to call himself. For nearly a century most of their subjects obediently did as king or queen saw fit, now "Protestant," now "Catholic." With plenty of dissent and many a rebel among them, the masses of England followed in their fathers' footsteps, apparently not much worried by the fates of their immortal souls. Not even the fierce storms of the seventeenth century civil wars jarred them out of their acquiescence or indifference, though these left a vigorous element of dissent in their wake.

In the nonchalance of its masses, Anglicanism presents parallels to Lutheranism. The Religious Peace of Augsburg, by which subjects were provided with the religion of their rulers, was not much different from the various sixteenth century changes and compromises in England by which the official religion was decreed from above.[8] The theological uncertainty which wavered about between predestination and free will was not dissimilar to theology on the continent. Arminius who in the early seventeenth century taught a watered-down kind of predestination, congenial to some of his Dutch fellow-citizens, found favour with Archbishop Laud. When it no longer mattered supremely, both Lutheranism on the continent and Anglicanism in England as official denominations pushed off into those regions of indifference and statism that seem to have satisfied most of their adherents ever since. In this they reflected rather faithfully the original natures of their evolution, for in neither Lutheranism nor Anglicanism was the revolutionary content marked. That was left to individuals. It is hard to imagine that the Luther of 1517 or even of some years later wished to break up the church in which he had been brought up. Salutary change was one matter: destruction quite another. Similarly, the majestic "Defender of the Faith" in England had no wish to destroy Catholicism, as was manifest by his executions of those who would not accept his version of it. It was another of history's ironies that those who founded these great strands in men's affairs wrought something far other than they had conceived.

III
Calvinism, the Protestant Sub-Revolution

The "weak tea" of Anglicanism had little in common with the fierce fire of conviction that burned next door to it, in Scotland. Scotland's zeal came from Geneva with John Knox (1514-1572) and in Geneva you can still see the church in which he preached, that church whose Renaissance façade is pasted incongruously on to its Gothic nave, apt symbol in itself of men who had turned their backs on the past. And, it may be added, of that stark austerity with respect to the amenities mounting to blindness and distrust that is to this day prominent in Calvinistic societies. There was no lack of the positive note about Calvinism. Surely there are no products of the Reformation that have bulked larger in the Western world than has Calvinism.

> On the death of Francis[9] a great crowd of learned and intelligent men, estimated at some 5,000 in number, took flight from Paris . . . The exiles all turned their faces towards Geneva . . . 'They found', says Michelet, 'that marvellous asylum placed in the very midst of three nations. Without territory or army she (e.g. Geneva) made up by intellect and spirit what was wanting in space, or time, or matter – Geneva is a city of the mind, built by Stoicism on the rock of Predestination' . . .''[10]

After possessing itself of Geneva, under the personal influence of Calvin himself, the creed this young man had formulated[11] spread down the Rhine and occupied Holland, whence it was later carried to America and to South Africa. For a generation, its adherents fought for their faith in France and it has never been extinguished in that country, despite the best efforts of a Richelieu and a Louis XIV. It deeply penetrated the church of England in the seventeenth century and that church has never lost the marks then left upon it. English colonists carried it to America where it found its most spacious days. In fact modern North America might almost be regarded as one huge monument to Calvinism. It is impossible for moderns of the English tongue to live a single day without directly or indirectly experiencing the effects that have flowed from the potent doctrine. If Lutheranism and Calvinism were each to be represented by monuments, while the outlines of the figures would be more or less the same, that erected to Calvinism would be several times the size of that put up for Lutheranism.

The central doctrine of John Calvin, to be found in his *Institutes of the Christian Religion* (1536) was, as everyone must know, *predestination.* Calvin puts it thus:

> Predestination we call the eternal decree of God, whereby he has determined with himself what he wills to become of every man. For all are not created to like estate, but to some eternal life and to some eternal damnation is foreordained . . .[12]

Working out from this proposition, Calvin stops up the holes that opponents might find in his logic. ''This is condemning the innocent young,'' it may be said. Oh, no, not at all. Original sin, or the defects of nature, is not an imposition, or punishment. It is simply part of one's inheritance. All men are not made guilty for one man's fault, but that fault deprives them of the ability to become of the elect. Why?

> We must be contented with this – that such gifts as it pleased the Lord to bestow upon the nature of man, he vested in Adam, and therefore when Adam lost them after he had received them, he lost them not only from himself but also from us all . . .

And is the God just, it will be asked, who can condemn men who have not first provoked him?

> To condemn to destruction whom he will agreeth rather with the wilfulness of a tyrant than with the lawful sentence of a judge . . . If such thoughts should at any time come into the minds of the godly, this should suffice to break their violent assaults . . . if they consider how great wickedness it is even so much as to inquire of the causes of the will of God . . . For the will of God is the highest rule of righteousness, that whatsoever he willeth, even for this that he willeth it, ought to be taken for righteousness. [13]

Calvinism left no loopholes. Its inexorable logic stopped up every exit from "the will of God."

But here was no novel creed, not, indeed, a particularly complicated or sophisticated creed. Once grant the complete omnipotence of God (the word should really stand in quotation marks) everything else follows. As well might the motor car roaring along the highway suddenly turn around and ask its driver questions about the speed as that microscopic speck, man, ask "God" questions about his plan of creation. The omnipotent "God" comes in easily once the idea of a Creator of the Universe has been accepted. It came into Greek mythology in the rather crude form of *fate* or *fortune*. The Old Testament is full of references to the all-powerful God ("A thousand years are but as a single day in the sight of the Lord"). It comes into early Christian ideology by a combination of the two, this easiest of routes. In the fourth century Augustine gaves literary expression to the doctrine and hands it on to subsequent centuries. It keeps cropping up throughout the Middle Ages, finds expression in Lutheranism and is given world currency by Calvinism. It lies at the base of Mohammedanism – the will of Allah. It was suggested earlier that Mohammed might well have taken it over from the Christians of the eastern Mediterranean who had been following the Arian "heresy" and making "God" into the "eternally unknownable monad," supreme in every particular over all and everything.

The doctrine, never ceasing to turn up, powerfully influences the thinking of many a modern scientist and the direction of his researches. It is a doctrine that must always lie close to the surface in any good mind. Perhaps the major matter wrong with it is simply that it is so severe that men while nominally accepting it will not really believe it: they refuse to be made into machines (much as some scientists want to make them into machines): "I propose to abolish autonomous man, the man who believes in freedom and dignity . . . 'How like a God,' said Hamlet. Pavlov, the behavioural scientist, emphasized 'How like a dog!' That was a step forward."[14]

Yet accepted Calvinism was, and by countless men. If not by the masses, yet, by the formative influential minds of the communities into which it penetrated. Moved by a strong, yet taciturn zeal, formidably, if narrowly, intellectual, Calvinism imposed on those who submitted to it something quite close to the fierce fatalism of the first Moslems. It met the old church in much the same kind of collision that had occurred between the Albigensians and St. Bernard.[15] But this time, two sides were far more evenly matched than they had been in the twelfth century, and the battle in consequence far more protracted. Not merely verbal battle, but many a bloody hard fought field as well. In all the fighting, the politics of persons, the simple power struggle, and the dynamics of class were so mixed up with the religious questions that no clear separation can be effected between them. Even in Scotland, a small and it might be thought, a relatively uncomplicated society, the assertion will hold. What was it in Scotland that drove a queen from her throne and established in her place the austerity of the Presbyterian kirk? Was it the amorous adventures of Mary, the ambitions of certain noblemen, the dislike of foreign influence, the leadership of John Knox, the zeal of religious conviction or a mixture of all these and many more? Who is to say?

Scotland was small, and valuable in French eyes mainly as a scourge to English backs. For both Catholics and Huguenots (as French Protestants came to be called), France itself, the kingdom, was the grand prize. The largest country in Europe under a single crown, the most populous, the most fertile of soil, potentially, when not paralyzing itself, the most powerful. Dissent might be tolerated in Geneva, itself a city of the French language, and it did not matter much in distant Scotland, but who could forecast the nature of a future in which France was uniformally Catholic or uniformally Protestant? Uniformity was the last word that could be applied to the France of the early stages of the Reformation: there were many *foci* of thought and action. The Court, the *Parlements,* the Sorbonne, the nobility, an increasingly important press, many a wealthy bourgeois and, of course, the clergy. And it was more than 5,000 refugees that had fled towards Geneva on the death of the more or less liberal Francis I in 1547. It was part of the soul of France.

There was much in Calvinism that made an appeal to the French. Some centuries previously, the University of Paris, reflecting the logical and intelligent French mind, had provided asylum for St. Thomas Aquinas, the man who wrote the most majestic of the mediaeval attempts to systematize life and knowledge, to reconcile faith and reason, the *Summa Theologica*. St. Thomas had probably found himself more at home in the University of Paris than in his native city, tumultuous Naples. And now, cast up by the debates and contentions of the Reformation, another Aquinas had come out of that same University, answering the same questions with the same clear, logical, elegance as the *Summa* itself had done three centuries before. But answering them, too, in a basically different way. The *Institutes of the Christian Religions,* now sent out on wings unknown to Aquinas, the printing press, made wide appeal to the logical, generalizing French intellect. It made appeal to the French nobility, who saw in its clear prescription of a "chosen few elected unto salvation" warrant for attempts to capture power, for must not the ancient French *noblesse* be of the chosen few?

> We are God's chosen few
> All others will be damned.
> There is no room in heaven for you
> We can't have heaven crammed.

Thus Dean Swift in the early eighteenth century, or in the later eighteenth Bobbie Burns' *Holy Willie:*

> O Thou, wha in the Heavens dost dwell,
> Wha, as it pleases best thysel',
> Sends ane to heaven and then to hell,
> A' for they glory,
> And no for ony guid or ill
> They've done afore thee!
> I bless and praise they matchless might,
> When thousands thou hast left in night,
> That I am here afore thy sight,
> For gifts an' grace
> A burnin' an' a shinin' light,
> To a' this place.

While the middle class "élitism" of Scotland, pictured in those lines, was different from the upper class *hauteur* of the nobles of France, the stubborn determination behind each, the arrogant conviction of superiority, was much the same. Calvin himself displayed all the hard-headed independence of those who are quite sure they have the answers. Addressing King Francis in his Preface, he tells him how glad he would be to be able to return from exile to his native land, but then, talking as that cat to that king, in a delightful specimen of unruffled self-sufficiency he remarks:

> Nor would I have you think that I here go about to make my own private

defence, whereby I might procure to myself a safe return to my native country, to which, I bear such affection of natural love as becometh me, yet as the case now is, I am not miscontent to remain abroad . . .[16]

Given the complex of forces in the France of the sixteenth century, there was no other road than war, civil war, bloody and horrible. The peace was maintained without open break until the 1560s but civil war filled most of the rest of the century. It is much too simple to see in these struggles merely a long duel between Catholic and Protestant, but they at least showed that France would not accept a Huguenot king. Tradition has handed it down that Henry IV scornfully cried that "Paris is worth a mass" and turned Catholic. It was not quite as easy as that. His accession did not terminate religious division in France, for the stubborn efforts of the Huguenots to maintain the rights that the Edict of Nantes (1598) had given them did not end until their last city of refuge, La Rochelle, after a long, cruel siege, was reduced by Cardinal Richelieu and brought under unconditional allegiance to the crown.

By the beginning of the seventeenth century, Calvinism was clearly the heart of the Protestant Reformation. It had maintained its independence in Switzerland, established itself here and there along the Rhine, freed the United Provinces from Spain and its Inquisition, captured Scotland and penetrated deeply into France. Lutheranism could not show such success, though, thanks largely to the dynastic interests of rulers, it secured the considerable accessions, the northern or Scandinavian countries, and some of the provinces on the eastern shore of the Baltic Sea. In Germany and Poland, the Jesuits had recaptured much of the territory that had been nominally Protestant. Germany's time of troubles was still a short distance into the future. It was in 1608 that civil war broke out in that country. For thirty years, it raged, leaving Germany desolate. Like the civil wars in France, it was only partially fought on religious grounds, for there was a complex of forces at work having some similarity to those which had existed in France when the Huguenot wars had broken out half a century previously. Eventually, in 1648, the Thirty Years' War was ended with the Peace of Westphalia, which was the first of the grand conferences by which nearly the whole of Europe came together in a formal effort at reconstruction, thus foreshadowing the sense of continental unity which our own day has seen increased. After the war Germany was left in a worse state of desolation than had marked France after her civil wars. Nor was the territorial distribution of Catholic and Protestant much changed.

Sixteenth century England shifted backward and forward as rulers changed. The "Erastian Prince," Henry VIII was succeeded by the boy king, Edward VI, whose reign signified a kind of Protestanism. Then came "Bloody Mary" and the martyrs burned under her, martyrdoms which left a deep mark on the whole of English history. Compromise came under Elizabeth and a certain measure of religious liberty – possibly it could be called "liberty if you do not claim it." With Stuart kings, came Catholic queens, the Protestantism of whose children could always be questioned. Many other factors accentuated the sense of division in the nation until in England too, as in France and Germany, eventually civil war broke out, and did not end until a king's head fell from his shoulders. Cromwell succeeds, a semi-king, and then comes the Restoration, 1660. Civil war and restoration give to England as decisive a turn in the historic road as France and Germany were experiencing at the same time. For all three, a new age comes in. Both Reformation and Counter-Reformation, or, if the reader prefer it, the Calvinists and the Jesuits, lose their wind. Zeal runs down.

Zeal began to run down first where one would have expected – where it had first blazed up. Good Calvinists in Holland did not take long in showing that fault of which George Canning was later to accuse them:

> In matters of commerce the fault of the Dutch
> Is off'ring too little and asking too much!

A mark of the good shrewd Calvinist everywhere. In England the Restoration gave free rein, with every possible public encouragement to all that which Puritanism abhorred. Charles II's countless mistresses – he began aged sixteen – the Restoration Parliament, the Restoration dramatists – Puritanism at bay everywhere, going "underground" though and once more to wake up in strenuous rebirth. In France, the evolution was delayed, for Louis XIV turned Godly. How effective his efforts were to make Parisians Catholics behave themselves, it is hard to say. Did it go much beyond the suppression of *Tartuffe?* The semi-Puritan strain in the French character, which is there clearly enough, when later it came out again, came out in forms quite different from those to which Englishmen were accustomed.

It was across the Atlantic that the best and the most determined attempts were made to establish the City of God. Both New France and New England were founded by people "who sought a heart's pure shrine," people determined to worship God in their own way and not to allow him to be worshipped in any other way, people who sought to purge themselves (and others) of annoyances of Adam's old sin, to keep the snake forever out of their Eden. They fought hard and they built colonies that for conforming piety, strict adherence to all the externals, and in all probability in moral earnestness and uprightness, came as close to the City of God on Earth as man is ever likely to attain. Both Puritan and Jesuit would have provided little space for Jesus in their religion. Meekness and holiness were hardly their line. Jesus might conceivably have done his best to escape them. They thought they were on opposite sides of the fence, Catholic and Puritan, but in reality, given a few minor mutual concessions, Puritan pastor would have been quite as much at home in ultra-Catholic Quebec as would Catholic Jesuit have been in Boston. Their code of morality was the same, from sex to Sunday, as was the place they claimed for themselves as clergy. Their fulminations against lewd dress in women were the same, as were their censures of idleness and idle diversions. But between them stood the spectral figures in the Vatican, so that striving for the same godly Eden, mortal enemies they remained.

But all zeal runs down, and in the eighteenth century even the zeal of Puritan and Jesuit was running down. An eighteenth century French bishop discovered heretics in the colony – nine of them! Young men in Boston, even the sons of clergy, nay, even the clergy, began to wear wigs. Along with God, "the world" had crossed the Atlantic.

The "run-down" of zeal takes different shapes, then, in different countries and different cultures but the deep currents in at least France, England, Scotland and Holland are similar. After the long age of passion, comes the period of reflection, in which fighting gives ground to the intellectualizing processes. A new age of political theorizing and philosophizing appears. Discussion by pamphleteering never ceases. In England, it becomes the day of Hobbes and of the innumerable pamphleteers of the civil war and Commonwealth periods. By 1660 men may have been beginning to grasp that fighting it out with words probably was better than with swords. More important still was the diversion of zeal into the area of commerce and industry. " 'Making money' is one of the most innocent of occupations," Adam Smith says somewhere or other, thus completely reversing the mediaeval view of the rich man and the poor man. Commerce draws adventurous spirits far across the seas. In both England and France, many such spirits were Protestant. In New France commerce was at first in Huguenot hands. It took state action, inspired and directly by Richelieu himself, to put it rather lamely back into the hands of "loyal subjects." The great divergence between the two ways of life roughly identified by the terms Protestant and Catholic, the two philosophies and moralities, already fairly visible in France as elsewhere, became more and more distinct, until at long last individualism and initiative, transferred to English hands, were to triumph over the hesitancies of a still semi-mediaeval Catholicism, not only in conquered New France but at many other points on the globe.

However the seventeenth century's slackening in religious intensity is explained, there can be little effective denial that it occurred. Its occurrence introduces us, almost dramatically, into a new world, a world of attitude and affairs as different from that of the Religious Wars as the New World then being explored was from the old, traditional home across the seas.

Notes

1. Shakespeare, *Twelfth Night,* II, 3, Sir Toby Belch to Malvolio.

2. The great mediaeval hymn *"Dies irae, dies illa Solvet saeclum in favilla . . ."*

3. After Calvin, the world had some three centuries of relief from major prophets. This will be expanded in a later chapter.

4. The German term is illuminating: *Die Glaubensverbesserung* – the bettering of belief.

5. Note, in passing, François Le Brun, *Les Hommes et la mort en Anjou aux 17e et 18e siècles* (La Haie-Mouton, Paris, 1971). A review of this book represents it as stating that "Christianity in its Tridentine form did not arrive in Anjou until late, and, even in the eighteenth century remained "l'un des éléments d'une religion populaire où foi et superstition se mêlent inextricablement." Review in *Canadian Historical Review,* September 1973, p. 326 by T. LeGoff.

6. See H. C. Lee, *The Spanish Inquisition.*

7. Preserved Smith, *The Age of the Reformation* (Macmillan, New York, 1920).

8. Some exception should no doubt be made for the martyrs under Queen Mary.

9. Francis 1st, King of France, 1515-1547.

10. G. W. Kitchin, *The History of France* (Clarendon Press, Oxford, 1885), II p. 258, quoting Michelet, *Histoire de France,* ed. of 1885, VIII, p. 483.

11. Calvin, 1509-1564. His book, 1536.

12. Robinson, *Readings, op. cit.,* II, p. 128.

13. *Ibid.,* p. 129.

14. *The Intercollegiate Review,* (VIII, 5, Summer, 1973, p. 243) quoting from B. F. Skinner, *Beyond Freedom and Dignity* (New York, Knopf, 1971), pp. 200-201.

15. See Chapter 9, p. 124.

16. Robinson, *Readings, op. cit.,* p. 241.

CHAPTER TWELVE

Calm after Storm

I
The New World of the Middle Classes

After the middle of the seventeenth century, a striking change of wind occurred in the European historical weather. While it by no means disappeared, the old religious bitterness ceased to hold the centre of the stage, and the passions of creed were slowly replaced by the interests of the intellect. The second phase of the great cycle, marked by the outbursts of the early sixteenth century, whether in creed or in art, was well under way by the end of the seventeenth century. In the early eighteenth it became clearly identifiable. By about mid-century, the third phase was evident, with rationality doing its normal task of disintegration. As is always the case with a great historic shift, it affected every aspect of life. Even war was altered. A certain ceremoniousness came in which helped ameliorate horrors – at least for the fortunate few. The punctilio which was beginning to characterize the duel began also to be found in warfare. An "affair of honour" between "gentlemen" could find a rough equivalent between generals in command of armies. When, for example, at the siege of Louisbourg in America, 1758, the English learned that the French defenders were becoming hard up for supplies, the commander, Amherst, gallantly sent in gifts of food to the wife of the French governor, Madame Drocourt. She, in return, sent out a number of bottles of good French wine. After the ceremonious interchange, the cannon opened up again. Such incidents seem somewhat ludicrous, but they indicate that the climate was becoming more genial. Good Christians even gave up the fun of roasting each other alive!

It is always much easier to describe the great changes in the historical climate than to account for them, and description may go on in infinite detail. Yet for the specific change which replaced the "age of religion" with the "age of reason," some general points seem clear. In the sixteenth century, the great central nation of the European scene, France, had been so torn apart by civil war that it could not play its usual part on the stage. In this long agony of civil strife and subsequent stabilization, two great men stand out plainly – first Henry IV (1589-1610), then Richelieu (1624-1642). And then came a king whose incredibly long reign at least gave continuity, Louis XIV, 1643-1715. History has refused to accord Louis the title he coveted, "The Great," but it cannot deny him considerable gifts and a vast influence on the world of his day, mostly not for its good. While minor internal disturbances continued[1] and foreign wars were fought, France under Louis XIV was as well governed as it had been accustomed to be, which is different from "well governed" – well enough to allow of its filling the role so often ascribed to it – "La grande nation."

England's civil wars came at the end of the period of religious wars and were of an entirely different character from those of France. During the years 1640-1660 political and constitutional discussion in England attained majestic heights, and warfare itself had a moderation that Europe seldom knew. England joined Switzerland and Holland in the ranks of those communities that led the way to the best aspects of later times. Her national life and institutions, the product of the slow, step-by-step march of centuries, though deflected temporarily by events in the seventeenth century, clearly led up to that characteristic which is the outstanding mark of English history, compromise. In England, with a minimum of carnage and destruction, history seemed to unfold in a logical and beneficial way. The vast phenomenon of an English world was at hand.

In "the Germanies," the ravages of the Thirty Years' War (1618-1648) were so severe and horrible that people of the German tongue could contribute little to the growth of civilization until the eighteenth century. For all their fighting, little had been settled.

Few observers of the period around 1660, however, would have been prepared for what was to follow, for the revolution in man's fundamental conceptions that was to occur in the last generation of the seventeenth century. In relatively few years, mens' perspectives were altered radically; a new type of man came in, new preoccupations, new philosophies, unlooked-for achievements in thought that pushed the old wrangles into corners, a new world of the mind just as impressive as the vast new world that daily continued to unroll beyond the seas. In the fifteenth and during the sixteenth century, Europe sowed. During the seventeenth she began to harvest.

Aspects of the times that looked backward rather than forward, of course, were numerous. Two may be cited. The one is the Cavalier reaction in England after the Restoration of 1660. The other is the Revocation by Louis XIV of the Edict of Nantes in 1685 and the dreary harassment of the French Huguenots by "the Most Christian King" (the honorific title of French kings). In England, Cavalier harassing of former Roundheads, Presbyterians, Independents, Quakers and others was severe but not bloody. By French standards it was nothing. It allowed of that contumacious individual, George Fox, the first Quaker, going on his way, denouncing "steeple houses" and other works of the devil, stripping off his clothes that he might be nearer to God and preaching in his nakedness without suffering more than some rough imprisonment. Only in the decent republics, Holland and Switzerland, could behaviour such as Fox's have been met with such light restraint. Punishing non-conforming ministers by exiling them from towns ("The Five Mile Act" and other similar measures) was severe but it did not draw blood. The attempts of James II, a Catholic, to extend a general measure of toleration were regarded as hypocritical and won little support, even from those to whom toleration was to be afforded, the non-conformists. In the end "good turned out to be the final goal of ill," James II was sent packing, Dutch William came over and there was passed the Toleration Act of 1689, a landmark, not only for religious liberty but in "the spirit of the age." Its provisions did not extend to Catholics: that would have been more than that age would have been capable of. Catholics, however, after 1689 were not disturbed, not in England. They were treated harshly in Ireland.

The great wars of the period after 1660 had ceased to be primarily religious, it is true, but the Catholic-Protestant antipathy still ran strong. Both English and French coercion of dissenters may be regarded as a secondary climax in the politics of religion. The great crest had been reached in the previous period. The period after 1660 saw the secondary crest and when that had spent its force (by the end of the century) only minor waves followed (as in England under Anne).

The persecution of the Huguenots which both preceded and followed Louis XIV's Revocation of the Edict of Nantes, 1685, was severe. It resulted in the escape from France of tens of thousands of her most valuable citizens. They fled to England, Prussia, the Carolinas, South Africa. It is ironic that one of the most successful of the German U-boat commanders in the First World War was a German of Huguenot descent, Armand de la Pérrière. The repeal of the Edict of Nantes is an unfortunate, sad, story in French history, which does no one concerned with it any credit. It is one of the most foolish acts committed by the rulers of this intelligent and short-sighted people, the French. (The massacre of St. Bartholomew had been another.) As an effort to turn back the hands of the clock, it was not successful, though it greatly weakened French Protestantism. It was an early factor in the long train of events leading to the Revolution. France, for all the brilliance of the Sun King,[2] came out of the seventeenth century many years behind England in nearly all the deeper matters comprehended in the word *civilization.*

Or must one say "nearly all the matters comprehended by English Protestants in the word *civilization"?* That is a case that may be argued, and the decision would depend much upon the point of view of the individuals arguing it. No one would question that there was a brilliant side to French civilization in the period. But English minds invariably judge by the presence of well-being and, imperatively, that quality, the twin of well-being, that is to say, freedom.

For the seventeenth century shift which with dramatic speed substituted a climate of intellect for one of emotion, explanation seems to rest on two assumptions, both of which will be familiar. One lies in Calvinism, the other in the expanding world.

John Calvin, with his expert refurbishing of ancient doctrines of determinism, has had a large place in the world. His responsibilitity for the modern commercial world has often been examined, notably by such German writers as E. Troeltsch and Max Weber[3] and by the Englishman, R. H. Tawney.[4] No one any longer believes that without qualification Calvinism was the parent of capitalism, for the history of the north Italian cities makes it clear that practically the whole apparatus of modern capitalism was developed in their day, and that of their Flemish and Hanseatic opposite numbers. How to avoid papal prohibitions of usury, easy ways around the doctrine of "the just price," such matters had provided no difficulties for clever Italian minds. Loans, banking, bills of exchange and other items in the more technical apparatus of international trade came into use long before the world had ever heard of John Calvin. One the other hand, it seems clear that certain aspects of the Calvinistic doctrines and practice fitted well into what most men do not need to be taught, where their own interests lie in a bargain. For Calvinism swept away various barriers to the amassing of wealth and it directly or indirectly provided incentives to it. Much of this was evolution within Calvinistic societies, some of it proceeded from emphasis on certain aspects of Calvinist doctrine. It is hardly fair to blame John Calvin too harshly for Calvinism.

Perhaps the central doctrine of Calvinism, election, bears more of a burden than John Calvin personally. "Elected unto salvation": a very nice situation to find yourself in, surely, in an age when no one disputed the realities of heaven and hell. But who could know whether they were "elected" or not? That was the rub. How to know? French Huguenot nobles, Condés, Colignys and their like, probably had little trouble deciding that they at least must be of "the Elect." How could God pass by a

Condé? Assuredness must have strengthened their arms, put the sword of righteousness in their hands.

And lesser men? They could pray and hope. And perhaps God would give a sign. Some went up in the scale, others down, some came through great spiritual and physical travail and others perished. Was God not giving a sign? "I know that I shall make my election sure." "God prospers the righteous man," not the unrighteous. Bible texts by the score could be quoted by "the righteous." "Depart from me, ye workers of iniquity. . . ." Necessarily it was the other man who worked iniquity. The godly man could surely come close to being certain of election. And if he had prospered, what better assurance than the prosperity with which God had blessed him. Yet he could never be quite sure. Hence the creative tension injected into Calvinism. It was necessary to fight to make your election sure.

Calvinistic societies never possessed themselves of great states, though they had a good try at it in France. Some have seen their failure in France as the failure of dour northernism and a creed not fitted to the Latin psychology. But it was in the south of France that Huguenotism was strongest and lasted best. It lasts to this day, and one may still enter Protestant churchs in Nîmes or Avignon. Moreover, it has been the south of France which has been vigorous in preserving liberal, or, rather, radical, attitudes. It is the modern south which cherishes "le mystique du gauche." Consider the place of origin of *La Marseillaise* Louis XIV's dragoons did not have the last word.

It is to the indirect effects of Calvinism that it is most profitable to direct attention. It is by no means necessary to imagine that everyone who was in some way drawn within the Calvinistic orbit was conversant with all the points made in *The Institutes of the Christian Religion*. What radiated out from a central core was something much more like an unconscious or semi-conscious complex of attitudes and influences, which possibly were all the more powerful for not being perceived. Calvinism opened certain doors, as has been noted above, and once they were opened, many types of men crowded through them. The major point made by Weber, for example, is not the identity but the high degree of correlation between Calvinistic and capitalistic societies, a correlation that with transmutations, continues to this day.

Argument about the precise influence of Calvinist doctrines in making the modern commercial world can go on indefinitely, but the fact of the modern commercial world's existence does not admit of argument. It is in the seventeenth century that the great commercial states become easily perceptible. The Spanish had had their empire in the New World for a century and they had done some considerable things for their civilization there, such as beginning universities and introducing printing. But their trading activities were little more than plundering expeditions. It was left to the northern nations to continue the commercial enterprise of the Italian cities but in the geographic spheres appropriate to them. Thus, as early as the 1500s the English had begun to reach around Scandinavia towards the White Sea, and the Dutch, former subjects of the Spanish crown, found their way to the Spanish Indies. As the beginning of the seventeenth century the chartered trading companies, as new legal entities, made their appearance in Holland, England and France (the French companies being Huguenot). Thenceforward it was like a fire spreading.

The story of colonial enterprise has often been told but there are general points about it that do not usually get emphasis. One is the relationship between colonial enterprise and the Industrial Revolution. This cannot be discussed here in detail but it seems obvious that the enormous and continuous "sellers' market" occasioned by the opening up of America, causing heavy pressure on metropolitan production, had a fairly direct association with the growth of production and the invention of new methods, thus opening a door to the stream of mechanical invention that has flowed in continuous and increasing volume ever since.[5]

Discussion of the point would lead into discussion of the staple trade as one of the main commercial aspects of history and that would be a subject in itself.[6] To take one example: the staple product, tobacco, pioneered by John Rolfe, turned out to be the foundation of the colony of Virginia and then of the city of Glasgow, which in the eighteenth century flourished by importing Virginian tobacco and sending out in return textiles, other necessities and young Scot's "factors." Other examples are legion, and drawn from all over the world. Human ingenuity naturally found means of satisfying the demands made upon it.

II
The Middle Class –
Its Easy Turn from Heart to Head:
The Modern Languages
Remade

The commercial and industrial revolutions[7] of the seventeenth and eighteenth centuries do not look satistically impressive compared with modern tables. But they should not be compared with astronomical modern tables; seventeenth and eighteenth century men of a fair span of life, with good memories, good educations and reflective minds surely could not have failed to be impressed with the material changes that they could see about them (and less easily, with the change in the spirit of their age). It is no accident that it was in the second half of the seventeenth century that some attempts were made to look at things statistically.[8] A view of things came in that allowed of change, and change "for the better," which was in contrast with the conviction that all the best things had happened in the ancient world, including God's gift of the one supreme moment of religion, the apex of history. At that point, men were not far from the notion of "progress," which was to take firm hold on various parts of the world in the eighteenth century and dominate it in the nineteenth – only when it had run to unreasonable lengths, to have its limitations pointed out in the twentieth, and even, to a degree, to be repudiated.

Ideas of "progress" must surely have been present in many Italian minds long before the new goddess was openly hailed in the eighteenth century. That century was not the only one to witness rapid strides in material accomplishment. The Europe of the eleventh century saw the beginnings of Italian material growth and not long after, the cities were in their full stride. The connection with Flanders and thence with the Hanse towns followed. In Germany many new cities had been founded, and the *Drang nach Osten* was strenuously pursued. Again, the fifteenth century saw the English trading actively with the ports to the south, along the Bay of Biscay, and some of their fishermen penetrating as far as the coastal waters of Iceland. The fifteenth century represented one of those vacua of values to which these pages have frequently drawn attention, but it was not a vacuum economically. And so with the period now under consideration. The world expanded and prosperity increased. So did the material apparatus of civilization, such as schools and in the New World, universities. It is that these transition periods in affairs, when one kind of world seems falling to pieces, are good periods for the material side of things? Perhaps the new values society needs float up, as it were, on new waves of well-being. The connection between economic and spiritual life must always be close, though ill-defined.

Notions about change which put things in terms of measurement are probably fundamental. The "architects" of mediaeval cathedrals knew a great deal about measurements. Images involving measurement must have occupied a prominent place in Leonardo Da Vinci's head. Evidently the concept gained force rapidly in the sixteenth century, for there was Copernicus (1473-1543) with his heliocentric thesis to prove it. There were plenty of other illustrations. Erasmus had an exact and tidy mind, for on his carefully edited text of the Greek New Testament rest much of his fame. Then there was his fellow-countryman, Vesalius, whose precision took the form of extremely exact observation and depiction of the anatomy of the human body. Is it too far-fetched to see the same desire for precision in that other Dutchman, Grotius (1583-1645), with his attempts to lay down *rules* of international law? The idea of precision shouts out from much of the Dutch painting of the seventeenth century – buildings in geometrical perspective, exact detail of furniture, floors, lights and shadows (along with much else) come in picture after picture.

Precision, whether in measurement or elsewhere (as in thought, for instance) lies only a step from the abstractions of mathematics. The seventeenth century has often been called "the mathematical century," for its years are studded with the names of great mathematicians, and their related fellow-astronomers, such as Johannes Kepler (1571-1630), Galileo (1564-1642), René Descartes (1596-1650), Edmund Halley (1656-1742) and above all, Isaac Newton (1642-1727), whose enunciation of the Laws of Gravitation in 1687 caught the imagination of contemporaries in every walk of life and went a long way to change the whole current of human thought. This is neatly reflected in the oft-quoted lines of the poet Pope:

> Nature and nature's laws lay hid in night
> God said, 'let Newton be' and all was light.

Newton could properly be coupled with two other great names from ages previous to his own, that of St. Thomas Aquinas, five centuries before him, and that of Calvin, too. The juxtaposition may seem odd, but both Aquinas and Calvin represented the zenith of the thought of their days, and by reason and logic each cleared up for their contemporaries large areas of human experience that had previously been dark and confused. Now it was the turn of the visible universe. What a perplexing, threatening mystery the heavens had always presented! All sorts of ideas flood the centuries, most of them highly nonsensical to us, few of them except some from the thought of classical Greece and Newton's predecessors, penetrating the mystery to the slightest degree. Even imperial Rome, the sun could still be regarded as god – "Sol Invictus." And now, Newton told people who could understand him just how it all worked – "all was light." Mathematical law governed it all.

The ancient lore of the spheres, their relationships to each other, the "music of the spheres," the belief in the "elements" (fire, earth, air, water) and similar notions – how firmly held all this was[9] – this received explanation of the universe – with its hierarchies of God, archangels, cherubim, angels; not even the very best minds were incredulous. Shakespeare is full of it, as is Milton. Then it was all blown away! The mental revolution this involved must have been of the deepest, and it all took place once Copernican ideas became fairly well-known in the seventeenth century. With three centuries more perspective since Newton, we today are making still another painful adjustment to the universe. We have added immensely to its dimensions and thereby to its mysteries. Newton now seems rather too simple for us, for the more we come to know, the more there seems still to be known. "All is light" no longer holds, for there are infinite reaches of space that we do not understand. The modern world is slowly coming to terms with its knowledge, man, or many men, is not as dismayed at the humble place he occupies in the scheme of things as were his predecessors. The old religions fit themselves into the new knowledge, accept it and start more or less afresh, perhaps finding in it a new source for the awe at the mystery of creation which has ever been the parent of religion.

How far away from actuality – or at least what we today believe to be actuality – even intelligent minds were, is amusingly and amazingly illustrated by Thomas Burnet (1635-1715) in his *Theory of the Earth* (1681). Burnet evidently was completely given to that idea of order and symmetry which had come into north European life from Renaissance Italy and which was to dominate most of the subsequent century. Consequently he looked out upon the earth and found that the Creator had made a poor job of it. Everything about the earth is untidy and mis-shapen.

'Hills, valleys, plains, lakes and marshes, sands and deserts' are simply strewn about: 'If the sea had been drawn around the earth in regular figures and borders, it might have been a great beauty to our globe.' As for the heavens, the stars lie carelessly scattered about, as if they had been sown in Heaven like seed by handfuls, and not skilful hand neither . . . If they had been placed in rank and order, if they had been all disposed into regular figures, and the little ones set with due regard to the greater, then all finished and made up into one fair piece or great composition according to the rules of art and symmetry the effect would have been far more pleasing . . .[10]

Burnet's only way of accounting for the sorry job God had made of Creation was by blaming it on man's original disobedience and the consequent wrath of God. Apparently this criticism of Creation was well received by "advanced" minds. John Evelyn, the well-known diarist, approved. Burnet continued to be read with interest into the eighteenth century, and surely constitutes not only a beautiful illustration of the mystery of the heavens which despite Newton, continued to baffle men, but also of the dominant notions of what came to be called "the Enlightenment" – the notions of symmetry, proportion, harmony, moderation, which mounted up into "elevated taste" the "taste" of the well-bred man.

The Newtonian revelation could have led logically enough to conceptions of a Divine Mind, and something of the sort occurred in the philosophy loosely called Deism. But the times were not remarkable for more than formal gestures towards the Mind, save in conservative devotees and later on, the folk movement of Methodism.

In France, despite absolutism, the climate of the day insofar as restraints on liberty permitted, was not much different from that in England. A similar galaxy of great names could be collected, bearers of many of which are describable almost equally well as philosophers or mathematicians. Blaise Pascal (1623-1662) will serve as an example. It might be put that in France the seventeenth century began in political and religious confusion, went on to order and legal orthodoxy, became marked by a high degree of intellectualism and ended in an easy but guarded scepticism.

The century evinced one almost curious diversion from this course, Jansenism. Cornelis Jansen, Bishop of Ypres (1585-1638), Dutch by birth, worked out a system of theology based on a modified form of predestination. There was much in the Roman Catholic past that could accept certain aspects of the doctrine of predestination – it was good Augustinianism but apparently when put in too stark a shape, it was judged too close to Calvinism for comfort. Jansen's disciples' attempts to found a school in France ("Port Royal") were viciously attacked by the Jesuits. Pascal lent his great name to their defence. The government seeing in the Jansenist organization, a suggestion of aristocratic revival and therefore a threat to the throne, seconded the attacks and suppressed the Jansenist establishment. It was not until the eighteenth century that the threatened rift was closed. But by that time, theological division was not heavy fighting ground. As one of the wits put it when the king ordered the destruction of the leading Jansenist establishment, the nunnery known as Port Royal – which, of course, even in the eighteenth century, had become, in a section of the popular mind, places of wonder and miracle:

> De par le roi: –
> Défense à Dieu
> De faire mirâcle
> En ce lieu.

> By the King: –
> God is forbidden
> To work miracles
> In this place.

Jansenism, a synonym, as it became, for quiet piety and strict morality, was little more than an episode in French history (though its indirect influence may have been considerable), for the main currents were elsewhere, running strong not on the religious but on the same intellectual course as in England.

The intellectualism of the seventeenth century received concrete expression in the form of the various national academies – some of which still endure. The French Academy was founded by Cardinal Richelieu, 1635, and at once received official, legal form. It was charged with the care and maintenance of the French language, as one of the devices by which the Cardinal sought to bring the whole kingdom, and beyond, into a single, cohesive unit which he hoped would prove strong enough to offset Spain plus the empire and dominate Europe – which, incidentally, during the next reign it did. The French Academy was as accurate a reflection of the French mind as Richelieu's statesmanship. It stood for order, precision, logic, but not for originality and the unruliness of creativity. It was as French as the legalism of Calvin's *Institutiones* (the Latin word would stand the translation *Laws*) or the mathematical symmetry of a French garden. The "native woodnotes wild" that warbled so loudly from the other side of the Channel could have evoked little response in France. The weight of the classical tradition was heavy and its nature appealed to the French mind. The qualities that came to be prized were order, dignity, logic, "good sense," that is, prudence and moderation. The contrast with the unmeasured volatility of Italian culture is evident, especially the Italian culture of the Renaissance. How would a Benvenuto Cellini have been treated at the court of Louis XIV? (He had soon made himself objectionable when he had appeared at that of Francis I).[11] And as for England, did not Shakespeare remain to the French a magnificent, unrestrained – barbarian![12]

The Royal Society is the most prominent example of related species in the English-speaking world. It was founded under Royal patronage, but naturally went its own way. At first its direction was not completely certain, but it soon settled down to the encouragement of what was then something quite new – the systematic investigation of natural phenomena, or that which the modern world calls "science." The idea had of course been adumbrated by Francis Bacon, but it was brought down to earth by the exceedingly able and imaginative group, a generation after Bacon, who gathered together in Oxford and London just after the Restoration. Charter members of the Society included such men as Robert Boyle (1627-1691), the enunciator of the "Boyle's Law" (of gases) presented to all of us in our school days, and pre-eminently Christopher Wren. Wren was typical: excellent draftsman, even making anatomical drawings for his friends, mathematician, architect. The brilliant coterie of scientists which sprang up were, most of them, well-known to each other. Many of them were doctors, and among these was the great John Locke (1623-1704), not only philosopher but medical man. Others among these pioneers were Thomas Willis, Thomas Sydenham (1624-1689), Charles Goodall (1642-1712), Richard Lower (1613-1691),[13] the latter of whom performed the first recorded blood transfusion, "turning the blood of a sheep into the veins of a man." It is not a recorded what happened to the man, but he was described as "a poor silly fellow," so perhaps no one worried much.

The shift from one "age" to another invariably occurs in every aspect of life. In small matters for example, "the fashions." In large, architecture. In day-to-day matters, the language. In more formal, literature. In architecture, the Gothic style did not last through the Reformation period. After an uncertain interval in the north, it was replaced by various versions of the revived classicism which had been displayed in mountain-range grandeur at St. Peter's at Rome. Until the nineteenth century attempted to revive mediaeval Gothic, every other architectural achievement in Europe, whatever its particular variation might be, whether baroque, rococo or what not, was in some measure a repetition of St. Peter's: among others, St. Paul's, London and the Greenwich Naval Hospital, both by Wren, of which it has been said that they are among the very few outstanding buildings erected in England since mediaeval days.

This extraordinary Roman shadow did not stop its extension in the Old World. It crossed to the New, and dozens of American "capitols," Washington included, echo it. At long last, after traversing the American prairies, it turned north and in the twentieth century, established itself in the legislative buildings of the four western provinces of Canada. It even got to Singapore, where classical domes ornament the centre of the city. The south Pacific, however, proved too much for it and it is not prominent in Australia. Thus the Italian Renaissance projected itself into the twentieth century. The mathematical symmetry of its straight lines and its hemispheres accorded well with the intellectualism of the late seventeenth century and the eighteenth. Architecture was making mind visible.

It may also have been making Calvinism visible. Gone were the old inviting nooks and crannies, the high gloom of lofty ceilings, the niches, sconces, the candles, the saints, that so well accorded with and induced the mysteries of the old religion. As the poet Pope, himself a Catholic, said, "all was light." That splendid inscription on the monument to the Puritan founders in Harvard Yard puts it "What have they need of lenses that can look direct in the eye of the sun?" Straight lines for a straightforward religion, with no nonsense about it, the religion that made America. George Fox got little thanks for his denunciations in England of "steeple houses," but he caught attention in influential places and his disciple William Penn, founded Pennsylvania, home of beneficent simplicity. Once the storms of the sixteenth century had breached the walls, "the march of mind," much hampering emotional baggage discarded, was not to be stayed. The mathematician was one aspect of it, the pietist, Quaker included, who thought out his own creed for himself, another. Doors opened in every direction.

These great secular changes seem to have been marked by distinct shifts in language. The subject is one for the specialist, but mediaeval scholasticism produced mediaeval Latin. Later, Wycliffe and English nationalism drove out the French language. Henry IV in 1399 "challenged the realm of England" and "in his modder (Mother) tongue." He was the first king of England to claim English as his mother tongue, 330 years after the Conquest. Tudor exuberance produced its own language. And today the bottom cards on the pack are muddying that "well of English, pure and undefiled," which has been the joy of those now passing off the stage. Since we possess no tape recordings of the speech of our fathers, we can only depend on its written forms, but they provide evidence in quantity. Try to find Shakespeare's low life rascals even fifty years later. The form and verbiage have disappeared. On a much different level, take a few sentences from Milton's *Areopagitica* (1644):

> . . . Now once again by all concurrence of signs, and by the general instinct of holy and devout men as they daily and solemnly express their thoughts, God is decreeing to begin some new and great period in his Church, even to the reforming of Reformation itself: what does He, then, but reveal Himself to His servants, and, as His manner is, first to us, though we mark not the method of His counsels and are unworthy. Behold now this vast city: a city of refuge, the mansion house of liberty, encompassed and surrounded with His protection; the shop of war hath not there more anvils and hammers waking, to fashion out the plates and instruments of armed Justice in defence of beleaguered Truth, than there be pens and heads there sitting by their studious lamps, musing, searching, revolving new notions and ideas wherewith to present, as with their homage and their fealty, the approaching Reformation, others as fast reading, trying all things, assenting to the force of reason and convincement. What could a man require more from a nation so pliant and so prone to seek after knowledge? What wants there to such a towardly and pregnant soil but wise and faithful labourers, to make a knowing people, a nation of prophets, of sages, and of worthies?

Compare the splendid roll and surge of this Miltonic prose, to say little of its content, with the smooth, everyday urbanity of another "non-conformist" writing only fifty-three years later (1697), Daniel Defoe in his *An Academy for Women:*

> . . . That Almighty First Cause, which made us all, is certainly the fountain of excellence, as It is of being, and by an invisible influence could have diffused equal qualities and perfections to all the creatures It has made, as the sun does its light, without the least ebb or diminution to Himself; and has given indeed to every individual sufficient to the figure His Providence had designed him in the world. I believe it might be defended if I should say that I do suppose God has given to all mankind equal gifts and capacities, in that He has given them all souls equally capable, and that the whole difference in mankind proceeds from either accidental differences in the make of their bodies or from the foolish difference of education . . .[14]

Here, in this second extract, is much good Calvinist doctrine, much facile piety, much plain common sense, an appreciation of abstract deity. Defoe was thirteen years old when Milton died: if they had met, they could have talked – as old man to young. But how different their speech would have been and how far apart its quality! Even though the words might have been the same, they would have carried different emotional charges. We talk of "the generation gap" today and of course it exists. But how about the "generation gap" in the years that saw the world, especially the English world, swinging from zeal, passion, conviction, to plain, smooth, even-tempered, reasonable intellectuality?

Defoe did well – He could have had no alternative – to put his religious references into cool abstractions: "That Almighty First Cause" very different, infinitely cooler, more remote, than "God . . . decreeing to begin some new and great period in His Church . . ."

Linguistic change evokes literary change. The extracts just given illustrate changes in prose style. Change in poetic style is even more marked. Compare the Miltonic blank verse with the jingly Alexandrines of Pope. Clever as these are, and he wrote them by the tens of thousands, they have nothing about them of the cloudy grandeur of Milton. Pope (1688-1744) was the major poet of his day. His works may occupy too much space and so give an exaggerated picture of the times.

> But adoration! give me something more
> Cries Lycé, on the borders of threescore
> Nought treads so silent as the foot of Time.
> Hence we mistake our autumn for our prime . . .

Which of Pope's poems with their smart sayings do these lines come from? From none. They are by a much less well-known man, Edward Young (1683-1765) in his *The Old Coquette*. Examples are endless: Swift, Addison, Prior, Gay (men born within twenty years of each other) sound the same note, cool, urbane witticism, sentiment of a lofty, frosty type, and nearly all of them using the same new device of the rhymed couplet. Prose followed the same paths. Imagine Gulliver coming out of late Elizabethan England! Urbanity was the word. It had a run of a hundred years more or less before it, too, was blown away by yet another change of wind.

III
France and England

Urbanity is a term that could well be used of most French literature of the seventeenth century, urbanity, and urbanity coupled with ceremonial grandeur. France being the senior country in cultural brilliance, much influence flowed across the Channel from it, more particularly after the two big settlements of 1660, the English Restoration and the actual beginning in France, after a long minority, of the reign of Louis XIV.

Louis XIV and Charles II were first cousins, but there the resemblance stopped. The English Restoration was the signal for the doors to open, as it were, and the literary expression of the relief from civil war is to be found in the gay Cavalier poems of the day:

Phyllis is my only joy
Faithless as the wind or seas,
Sometimes cunning, sometimes coy,
Yet she never fails to please:
If with a frown
I am cast down
Phyllis smiling
And beguiling
Makes me happier than before[15]

The Cavalier poets are echoed by the Restoration playwrights with their light touch and their risqué plots. Risqué, yes, but not vulgar: not like the earlier Shirley's (1596-1666) " 'Tis Pity she's a Whore" and other plays of that type. By far their best-known parallel in France, was Molière, and he had to keep within bounds. They would have seemed narrow bounds to the English men of letters. *Tartuffe*, was banned from the stage for a couple of years by the President of the Parlement of Paris:

> . . . Par suite des inimitiés que cette satire de l'hypocrasie souléva dans le partie des dévots, elle ne fût exposée au public que le 5 août, 1667; interdite de la lendemaine de cette première réprésentation par ordre du président Lamoignon, elle ne se réparut au théatre que le 5 février 1669. La polémique qu'elle excita dès son apparition fut des plus violentes et des plus passionées . . .[16]

Between French and English history there are both striking parallellisms and striking differences. The subject is a large one and to do justice to it, treatment would have to begin with the establishment north of the Channel by William the Conqueror of that strange New France, Norman England. For three centuries everyone who mattered in England either spoke French as his mother tongue or learned it. If there had been no English Channel, the island would have approximated a Britanny or a Provence, that is, an outlying French province. As it was, it managed to keep its own culture, which for long was French with a submerged Englishism, and heavily penetrated at all times by the superior brand across the water. It evolved a set of public institutions from the same roots as those of France but eventually of an entirely different genius. Many an explanation can be given for this, but probably the most fundamental is simply geographical – isolation and size. England was controllable from a given point, France was not. England as an island has been singularly free from invasion, France has been many a time overrun – as many times as it has overrun others. The area of France, until modern times, was simply too great for management: some local potentate somewhere could invariably defy the distant monarchy, some outsider was always ready to send troops over the border. Most other results follow: in fact and sometimes in law, great men refuse to accept obedience to the crown; no strong middle class arises; national feeling remains weak. Given the means of communication, in the Middle Ages and the early modern period, France was larger than the United States is today. The present age, the twentieth century, knows from bitter personal experience, something of the devastation that war can wreak. We have, however, a thousand aids to recovery that the past did not possess. Historians are so accustomed to writing of war that they cease to have much emotional response to the words they use. "The sack of the city"; "The spoils of war"; "The devastation of the countryside"; famine, slaughter, all these become "a tale of little meaning though the words are strong."

But a recent careful study shows in statistical detail what "campaigning" can mean to a countryside.[17] In a careful examination of local historical documents for a small village in Artois (just over the border from Flanders), the author, without stressing the cause, shows how the historic ups and downs of the village corresponded to the periods of war and peace. At the beginning of his study of the village of Isbergues, 1569, it had 105 proprietors holding 300 of the total of 516 hectares within the village.[18] "Cent cinquante ans plus tard, en 1720, on ne comptait plus qu'une cinquantaine de propriétaires résidants qui possédaient à peine 20 pour cent des terres. La conjoncture politique et démographique du 17e siècle explique sans doute dans une large mesure cette aliénation quasi – totale du terroir. Avec le retour à des conditions plus normales, c'est-à-dire, à tous fins pratiques, à partir de 1713, on assista à une lente récupération, véritable reconquête du terroir par ses habitants . . ." There was quite a striking increase in elementary literacy over the next long period. In 1721, 61 per cent of the more prosperous men could sign their names and 34 per cent of the women. In 1779 these figures were 75 per cent and 50 per cent. The labourers are manoeuvriers at about half these figures, with only a small fraction of their women able to sign their names.[19] In other words, from 1569 (just after the outbreak of the Wars of Religion) to 1713, the date of the Peace of Utrecht, war on and off for 144 years (more years on than off) had reduced this fertile countryside to something approaching desolation. For many a European area this was not more than average. No wonder humanity has had so slow a climb out of the pit of its own foolishness.

Nevertheless France had, in Paris, and had had for centuries, the largest city in the Western world, and that meant power; among other types of power, cultural power. Paris set the pace with all the prestige and magnetism that metropolitanism always gives. Until the seventeenth century it was a far greater capital than London. Yet French life always seemed in turmoil. Few kings were other than mediocrities, some were insane (Charles VI), some were nonentities (the three sons of Catherine de Medici). From Philip Augustus (1180-1223) to the Revolution only a handful stood out – Philip Augustus, Saint Louis, perhaps Philip the Fair, Louis XI, Henry IV, Louis XIV. In ages when so much hung on the head that wears the crown, the effect on the country as a whole plainly was immense: in general, that effect was misgovernment, disorder, financial incompetence, corruption and a mockery of justice. Have any European people been able to stand such chronic misgovernment as the French? No one would claim that England was the earthly paradise, kings or no kings, yet that country invariably could boast much more competent government than France. It was always regarded as well-governed – in the seventeenth century it was surpassed only by Holland – and from Elizabethan times, and perhaps before a haven of freedom: *Dominium polticum* Sir John Fortescue the Chief Justice, has proclaimed it in the early fifteenth century, no *dominium regale*, and by those words he had plainly meant a kingdom of some freedom as opposed to a kingdom of monarchical will.

The relationship between form of government and the cultural expression of a period in literature and the other arts is highly intricate and no set pattern for it has ever been precisely established. The arts in their turn reflect "the spirit of the times." The spirit of the times comes out of a multitude of causes, as this book has tried to show. The result is too complex for exact statement: no mathematical formula will emerge, though mathematical formulae will often help clear up a small patch of ground here and there as, for example, population studies.

England had its period of anarchy in the fifteenth century Wars of the Roses, got it over with, cleared up by the so-called Tudor Absolutism. Then came relaxation into some liberalism under Elizabeth. The seventeenth century struggle with the Stuarts, 1603-1688, could be regarded merely as an episode, a diversion of English history from its own proper current. Before the Stuarts, English history had long had well-defined shape. England was a land with well-understood, firmly established institutions deeply rooted in the centuries. In 1688, the year James II was expelled, the historic development was resumed and it has gone on unfolding ever since. An illustration of this lies in what was happening on the other side of the Atlantic. When the English colonies were established, their institutions were necessarily drawn from the mother country and they all were semi-popular in nature. The comparison here lies with New France, which was made into an absolutism in both church and state.

In France, thanks to a *noblesse* that never ceased to hope for a measure of actual individual sovereignty, disorder was historically nearer to the surface than in England. The striking period of disorder, was of course, the sixteenth century with its religious wars. To end that century of anarchy, however, not one period of absolute rule was required but two – Henry IV's and Richelieu's. Louis XIV added a third, the longest and most severe of all. If he could have given his country some measure of freedom, he would indeed have merited the title which never fitted him, Louis le Grand. His severe concentration of power was, moreover, probably unnecessary. The French rejoiced to find themselves free of civil war and possessed of a king they could respect and there was hardly a limit to the loyalty they were prepared to give him. There was no opposition of importance to the idea of absolute government. French society had not been made for constitutional freedom. In a country in which there was no sense of loyalty except to the family and to the superior, there was little for the idea of community, let alone political community and political freedom to rest upon. As André Siegfried observed, right down to this day, the idea of citizenship carrying with it the concept of public duty and public good has had few followers in France. This long period of absolute rule slowly broke down in the eighteenth century into the Revolution. In the nineteenth, there was a similar echo of English precedent, the French nineteenth parallelling the English seventeenth.

Once we leave general points, we are hurled into the discussion of specific historical developments and from them there is no emergence. Why this absence of public spirit in France? Why the failure to develop the original semi-popular institutions? Why the difference between "Parlement" and "Parliament"? Why the loss by the Estates-General of any semblance of financial control? Why the difference in "the liberties of the subject"? That did not all rest on *Magna Carta*. A thousand questions could be asked and each one would need a volume for its answer. Many of those volumes have, indeed, been written. It would be a noble ambition and a foolish one, to try to read them all.

France has always remembered her old motto: *Gesta Dei per Francos,* "The Acts of God performed through the Franks." No Frenchman can forget that the word "Frank" originally meant "free." No Frenchman would admit that he was not as "free" as an Englishman. But the word *free* is slippery. The French word *franc* has just about the same range of shadings as the English word *free* ("*avoir son franc parler:* to speak one's mind, etc."). The difference would seem to lie in the time-tempered stability of English institutions, so definite, so well-understood, so workable, as compared with their French counterparts of the old régime. But here, again, a stop must be put or the word *law* will intrude for its own interminable consideration. Can it not be contended, however, that throughout the France of the monarchy, there was a far larger component of will than under the English Monarchy? That seems self-evident.

Charles II of England by no means brought back French absolutism with him. "He had no like to go on his travels again," he used to say. James II apparently had, and did. For most people in England, the Restoration had been a restoration of freedom from the "rule of saints," saintliness being more than the ordinary man could take.

For France, 1660 on the other hand, marking the assumption of power by Louis XIV, ended two decades of relative, but disorderly complacency under Mazarin,[20] successor to Richelieu: even the Huguenots had been left alone. Louis XIV, however, brought French institutions and French life to their highest point of sharp regulation, the last conclusive step in that restoration of order that follows the supreme chaos of civil war. Hence, among many other things, the banning of Molière's *Tartuffe*.

Louis remains one of the most striking figures of French history and still a hero to many a Frenchman. In England his admirers were and are few. To the English world he is gold-plate not gold: the man who typifies absolutism (l'état, c'est moi") and who tried to dominate all Europe, an ambition in which, largely owing to England's Dutch king, he failed. Hence the increasing pressure on the Huguenots – the Edict of Nantes narrowly interpreted and used against religious dissidence. Hence the considered decision never to call together the Estates. Hence the establishment in the American colonies of absolute government. On the other hand, France became orderly and even sporadically prosperous. The usual results followed: minds woke up and despite the régime, some discussion went on. Hence one of the great ages – no, not great; conspicuous – of French literature. *Le roi soleil* shed his kindly rays upon men of letters – if they wrote how they ought to write. A great, powerful nation, within a stone's throw of dominating Europe, of beneficently giving the law to those whom it condescended to take under the protection of its greatness, could hardly have failed to produce an impressive culture. All the ceremonious pomposity of Bossuet (1627-1704), that master of funeral orations, and his like was in perfect keeping with the grandeur of Louis XIV.

In the France of Louis XIV, there were no St. Bernards. His age was not one of intense and deeply religious zeal such as had marked the beginnings of other new cycles, but it sounded sonorous drums, believed in itself and possessed a certain degree of emotional sincerity. Everyone in France "who mattered" saw at one time or another a bright ray of the distant sun. Many were blinded by it. The praises of the king never ceased to be sung. Many (himself included) really thought him to be "Louis le Grand." Add to the personal adulation, some of it deserved, the success of his troops in foreign war and the widening of the boundaries of France that resulted from them. This, the middle part of the reign, was the day of Turenne and of Condé, war leaders not merely distinguished, but great. Under Louis XIV, France had achieved a place in the world's affairs which she had never previously attained. All these considerations mounted up to a degree of emotional national fervour that brought forth the zealous energy, the hope, that always follows a period in which order has been restored. In a sense the period of, say, the 1670s, may be regarded as the equivalent in France of the mediaeval "age of faith": gentlemen fought under Louis almost as their ancestors had fought on crusade. But the character of the age was such as to provide easy targets for the intellectuals of succceeding generations. It splendidly kept up the old forms and from them the substance was visibly oozing.

If the long reign of Louis XIV had added political and religious freedom, even in modest measure, to its other glittering aspects, French literary culture might well have soared to vast heights. The seventeenth century names on which it rests are many, and among them there are a few of universal stature. Corneille (1606-1684), Racine (1639-1699), Molière (1622-1673), are more than merely national figures: they do not, however, stand in the front rank, as do Dante, Shakespeare, Goethe. In the late twelfth and the thirteenth centuries, France had given Europe its first general culture and had, through Paris, become Europe's metropolis. In the seventeenth century, it once more attained this rank – the centre of European civilization. But an essential was lacking – freedom from constraint. The age of the Sun King was brilliant, but it was limited. French civilization was admired and imitated everywhere, but Paris did not become another Athens or another Florence.

Notes

1.   See Boris Porchne, *Les Soulèvements populaires en France de 1622-1648* (Paris, 1963).
2.   Nancy Mitford, *The Sun King* (Hamilton, London, 1966), is a lively popular account.
3.   See E. Troeltsch, *The Social Teaching of the Christian Churches* (2 Vols., London, 1931). Tr. by Olive Wyon of *Die Soziallehren der Christlichen Kirchen und Gruppen* (Tübingen, 1912). Max Weber, *The Protestant Ethic and the Spirit of Capitalism* (Scribners, London, 1930). Tr. by Talcott Parsons of *Die Protestantische Ethik und der Geist des Kapitalismus* (1904).
4.   R. H. Tawney, *Religion and the Rise of Capitalism, A Historical Study* (Peter Smith, London, 1926; Pelican Books Edition, 1938). See also Michael Walzer, *The Revolution of the Saints: a study in the origin of radical politics* (Harvard University Press, 1965). A very good brief

exposition of Calvinism is Georgina Harkness; excellent brief illustrations of Calvinism in its New England form are to be found in John C. Miller, *The First Frontier: Life in Colonial America* (New York, 1966).
5.   Nicely illustrated in Humphrey Lloyd, *The Quaker Lloyds in the Industrial Revolution* (Hutchinson, London, 1975) and in Larzer Zeff, *Puritanism in America* (New York, Viking Press, 1975), both indirectly.
6.   The reader may be referred to A.R.M. Lower, *Great Britain's Woodyard: British America and the Timber Trade, 1763-1867* (Montreal and London, McGill-Queen's University Press, 1973).
7.   The two are often referred to as distinct historic phenomena. For purposes of clarity, no objection can be made to this, but the two are so much intermingled that they can hardly be regarded as different in kind.
8.   Sir William Petty, *Political Arithmetic* (1609) is an early example.
9.   A good description of the Elizabethan world-view is E. M. Hilyard's *The Elizabethan World Picture* (Modern Library Paperbacks, New York, 1955).
10.   See B. Sprague Allen, *Tides in English Taste (1619-1800)* (2 Vols., Rowman, New York, 1958, but written 1932), II, p. 159ff. The quotations are taken from this excellent book
11.   Symonds, *op. cit.,* p. 474.
12.   Cf. H. A. Taine, *passim, History of English Literature* (New York, A. L. Burt Co., n.d.). Tr. by Henri van Laun. Taine's work appeared originally in the 1850s.
13.   See *inter alia,* Sir George Clark, *A History of the Royal College of Physicians of London* (Oxford, Clarendon Press, 1964); Kenneth Dewhurst, *Doctor Thomas Sydenham, 1624-1689* (University of California Press, 1966); and Thomas Willis, *The Anatomy of the Brain and Nerves,* Wm. Feindel, ed., The Centennial Edition, 1664-1964 (Montreal, McGill University Press, 1965).
14.   A good study of Defoe is Michael Shinagel, *Daniel Defoe and Middle Class Gentility* (Harvard University Press, 1968).
15.   Sir Charles Sedley (1639-1701).
16.   Molière, *Le Misanthrope,* Emile Boully, ed., (Paris, Bélin Frères, n.d.) p. xvii.
17.   C. Pouez, *Démographie, Structures, Foncières, et Société: Evolution d'un Village d'Artois du XVI au XIXe Siècle* (Canadian Historical Association – Société historique du Canada), *Communications Historiques,* 1973, p. 269ff.
18.   One hectare is 2.47 acres.
19.   Pouez, *op. cit.*
20.   Galio Mazarin, later Cardinal Mazarin (1602-1661), and Italian, succeeded Richelieu as chief Minister of France. Though a Cardinal, he married Queen Anne, widow of Louis XIII and virtually brought up Louis XIV.

CHAPTER THIRTEEN

Calm after Storm:
The Enlightenment

In the eighteenth century, French culture was to have still other chances at universality (which it never quite attained). In that century men came to be able to breath more freely. "Under Louis XIV, men hardly dared to speak. Under Louis XV, men spoke low. Under Louis XVI, they spoke loud."[1] Insofar as freedom to write as you please goes, writers of the Restoration period in England had a three generation start on writers in France. Voltaire, Montesquieu and later Rousseau all had to accept the unwelcome hospitality of England from time to time when the police power in France came too close for comfort. In England after his failure to bar the Hanoverian Succession not by speech but by something that came close to a *coup d'état,* Henry St. John, Viscount Bolingbroke (1687-1751), found it wise to take refuge in France. This was a minor counter-account, for English martyrs to the cause of free speech during most of the eighteenth century were few indeed.

The French influence on the smaller insular society had long been manifest, though in form rather than substance, and decried. Shakespeare made fun of a French queen in his Henry V. But Charles I brought back a French queen to be his consort and like two previous French queens,[2] she brought French notions of absolutism along with her. Charles's two sons were both more French than English, his daughter became French, and again, French notions of absolutism found their application – luckily unsuccessfully – to England. In the eyes of the ordinary, sober, middle class man, the French were unstable, too talkative, frivolous, full of sexual intensity, with no wife faithful to no husband and *vice versa.*

Trivial fashions in manners and in clothes of course were French. If you went off without permission, you took "French leave."[3] French influence came far down the social ladder. It may have reached almost the bottom: "The polka dance, it came from France," exclaims Bobbie Burns.

Far above Bobbie's *milieu*, aristocratic Englishmen went across the Channel to come to some understanding of the great world beyond their doors and "to see life" *à la française*. Great English "milords," travelling in style with their coaches, might patronize French innkeepers and their like, but in the brilliance of Versailles, they remained, if not quite barbarians, at least somewhat rustic foreigners who could hardly be expected to know "what was what." When they returned home, they brought back with them foreign fashions, smart sayings and recollections of French amatory expertise, so different from the amiable mildness of the girls they had left behind them. There few returns of visits by French grandees. French "politesse" offered only a one-way street.

The explanation for the reason of English literary culture after 1660 assuming so many French traits thus becomes easy. What was written had to be fashionable, which meant, had to have some kind of French touch about it. The period which in general terms may be called the Age of Reason, divides rather distinctly into two halves, seventeenth and eighteenth century. The term *The Enlightenment*, usually reserved for the eighteenth century, is less definite in England than is *L'Éclairecissement* in France. A loose school of thought appeared, which was anything but orthodoxly Christian, Deism, but in a land where little conformity was required – less and less as the century went by – lack of orthodoxy was no great matter. The usual impression of the eighteenth century is of a period of religious and moral laxity, well depicted in William Hogarth's cartoons (Hogarth, 1697-1764).[4] It is not yet too far away from us not to have tags of memory still hanging to it. Many people must still have in their minds images of graceful ladies in fluttering clothes and powdered wig gaily receiving the addresses of equally picturesque gallants in knee breeches, silk stockings and white, powdered hair. It was, we like to dream, the age of the sedan chair, the fan and flirtation, and for gentlemen, drinking, cards, affairs of honour with pistols at dawn. In Paris, fine ladies sat in their *salons* entertaining their friends and admirers, all of whom said bright things. Everyone was excessively polite.

Such dreams are overdrawn but they have touches of reality in them, for there were *salons* in Paris in which an incredible number of bright things were said, and there were also a certain number of pistols at dawn. Perhaps not as many as a century before. Perhaps rather more bright things in the *salons*, not as many earnest. For seventeenth century heavyweight intellectualism did tend to pass into eighteenth century good manners and good conversation.

Good manners tended to exclude over-serious conviction. They left little place for evidences of feeling; none for the public display of emotion or enthusiasm. They left little place even for laughter. Throughout the eighteenth century, there runs adverse comment on "excessive laughter . . . an excessive Joy may be too boisterous in the Face to be pleasing . . ."[5] The above quotation is from Joseph Spence's *Crito* (1725). In his well-known *Letters to his Son*, Lord Chesterfield (1694-1773) constantly pursues the same line:

> Having mentioned laughing, I must particularly warn you against it; and I could heartily wish that you may often be seen to smile, but never heard to laugh . . . Frequent and loud laughter is the characteristic of folly and ill manners; it is the manner in which the mob express their silly joy at silly things . . . In my mind there is nothing so illiberal and so ill-bred as audible laughter. True wit or sense never yet made anybody laugh; they are above it: they please the mind and give a cheerfulness to the countenance. But it is low buffoonery or silly accidents that always excite laughter . . . a plain proof in my mind how low and unbecoming a thing laughter is, not to mention the disagreeable noise that it makes and the shocking distortion of the face that it occasions . . .[6]

Others who disapproved of laughter (not good humour) as "shocking distortion of the face" were William Hogarth and even the great William Pitt himself. "It is rare," he wrote, "to see in any one a graceful laughter; it is generally better to smile than laugh out . . ."

This disapproval of laughter may seem almost ridiculous to the modern, but it takes its place in a whole theory of behaviour, a theory that the classical period came close to evolving into a philosophy of life. It must be remembered that it had fairly close behind it the riotous Elizabethans, to say nothing of the turbulence of the Great Civil War . Laughter in any but polite, modest quantities, indicates *excess,* and perhaps that word is the key to all the rest. It had good classical ancestry: "nothing in excess" was the rule of a famous Greek philosopher, a rule by no means as yet in this late twentieth century wholly departed from. To the cultivated eighteenth century eye, the Gothic cathedral in its riot of arches, buttresses, gargoyles and the rest, exceeded canons of good taste. So did the old English country mansion, with its great hall, where master and men ate together, separated only by the dais, and all alike threw their bones and left-overs to the dogs that hovered around. It was such images in eighteenth century mind's-eyes that affixed to the "Gothic" past the denigratory epithets of which "horrid" was only one of the mildest.

Alongside injunction against immoderate laughter might be put the vogue of "courtesy books," so popular in the later part of the eighteenth century. These were intended for young ladies. They prescribed the precisely "correct" behaviour for practically every eventuality in life. How to enter a room, how to sit down, how to greet others and so on.

They were probably not very different in object from the "etiquette" books of our own day. And they probably sprang out of a background that had some similarity to those who use etiquette books today. The polite world of eighteenth century was doing its best to *civilize* itself, just as North Americans perpetually have to do when they cross that line which separates the simplicity of what is so often a country or small-town upbringing and face the sophistications of a more complex society and are also at an embarrassing loss on "how to behave."

Chesterton and his age did not have to go as far back as the Elizabethans for examples of what was to be avoided. Their own grandfathers' days would have sufficed. On one of his rambles with Charles II, Pepys observes nonchalantly "went about to find the king a whore!" The inquiry was apparently successful, but the quarters not the best. "We all got lousy," says Pepys, "Whereat was great merriment."

Substitute for the unruly Gothic past the ordered mathematics of Italian architecture, particularly as set forth by its great exponent, Palladio (1508-1580), and you had the classical architecture of the seventeenth to eighteenth centuries, with Christopher Wren as its leading genius and his London churches, still there and still beautiful to behold. Substitute for the crudities of mediaevalism the eighteenth century code of good manners and, necessarily, men refrained from excessive laughter. To expect them to carry the pattern into every corner of life, however, despite the philosophers, was too much. Great noblemen (like Lord Chesterfield) could so far unbend as to beget illegitimate children. Hogarth's cartoons and the eighteenth century novel do not give pictures of a society buttoning itself up in excessive restraint. Nevertheless, restraint in certain directions there was: the English code of civility, the "conduct becoming to a gentleman," was markedly an eighteenth century product. It was not for everyone, of course, but highly selective, for noble lords and others of "the quality." And how conscious noble lords and their like – the "twice two thousand Englishmen for whom the world was made" – seem to have been of their divine right in society. What had become of "Pym and his carls"?

But was not all that merely the frosting on the cake? Noble lords often were glad graciously to accept rich city heiresses as brides, as did Lord Halifax, born Charles Montague Dunk. But that is confusing the picture. The eighteenth century was the age of civility, its highly representative dance was the minuette. In England, it was the century in which the upper crust was earnestly living down the crudities of England's past when she had been merely a distant northern outpost of Italy, and was taking her place as a great metropolitan power.

Self-conscious efforts to follow codes of good manners implied no lack of vitality, vitality of all sorts. Wars were numerous, if increasingly punctilious. Science advanced. Literature flourished. Mid-eighteenth century man could well believe that he was living in wonderful times, his world advanced and progressive, far superior to anything in the past, in the dark, dirty *Gothic* past.

No complete description of a large society can be given, of course, so we have to put alongside our Hogarth cartoons, earnest souls such as Augustus Toplady, author of the hymn *Rock of Ages Cleft for Me,* and what has already been referred to as the folk movement of Methodism. The Wesleys themselves are good examples of the counter-currents that can run in a society. The two brothers, Charles and John (1707-1788, 1703-1791) came out of a quiet Anglican parsonage (two of the four survivors of eighteen, but they lived to great ages, and so did many others, which would not have been the case in their grandfathers' times) whose roots through both father and mother, Reverend Samuel Wesley and his wife, daughter of the Reverend Dr. Annesley went back into the milder aspects of mid-seventeenth century Puritanism (their creed became a kind of fusion of the old predestination and the free will and grace implied in the idea of *conversion*).

And how is the supreme example of English eighteenth century culture *The Messiah* (1742) to be accounted for? Its author, Händel, (1685-1759) was of German origin, it is true, and no doubt much influenced by the quiet and pious small-town church music of the country from which he came, a musical culture which was producing Händel's almost exact contemporary in age, Johann Sebastian Bach (1685-1750). It is hard to believe that *The Messiah* could come out of a highly dissolute, decadent society, either in its authorship or in the reception it received.

The upheaval of the civil war, the restoration of order by Oliver Cromwell and the Restoration of Charles II (in default of anything better to be done) takes us through a short historical cycle in itself, with many of the usual landmarks: the zeal of the Puritans at its peak, the number of dissident sects that appear at that peak (Levellers, Diggers, Baptists, Quakers, etc.) the failure of the Cromwellian Parliaments midst threatening clouds of anarchy, the imposition by Cromwell of a very unpopular attempt to end the confusion, all these plus the Restoration with its light cultural touch, and the still lighter morals of the restored, led into the eighteenth century and the English version of the *Enlightenment*.

Between the old world of the early seventeenth, and the new of the later, however, had been fixed the great, grand gulf of the Revolution of 1688. The triumph of freedom, and reasonable freedom, not the mere severity of "the Saints," opened the doors so wide that they have never since been closed. The English Revolution is the parent of the American, just as John Locke is the parent of Thomas Jefferson. It is the parent of parliamentary government and of limited monarchy. It is far more: it is the parent of constitutional freedom, not only for people of English speech but for all mankind that can measure up to it. For England "the principles of '88" dominated the eighteenth century. They produced the loose-textured period of the first two Georges and Walpole. They also produced William Pitt. They fenced in the out-dated notions of George III about the royal power. They were transmitted wherever men valued self-government.[7]

In France,[8] *L'Éclaircissement* means Montesquieu (1689-1755), Voltaire (1694-1778), Diderot (1713-1784), Condorcet (1743-1794), Jean-Jacques Rousseau (1712-1778), and various others of the same type. It meant, on the part of such men, capturing a new element in thought for Frenchmen, not only the idea of freedom but also institutions for it. The exiles of Montesquieu and Voltaire in England were put to good purpose: they may have been welcome to them, for they learned much and took back much. Through such men the English Revolution found its way into France. It shouted loudly enough through them to be heard by and influence the French Revolution. It is hard to imagine what it must have meant to Frenchmen of the middle eighteenth century to see the chains beginning to loosen, and, later, the depth of passion on both sides at the quaking and shaking of a society conservative beyond English imagination.

Consequently when Voltaire shouted out such epigrams as "I may not agree with anything you say, but I shall defend to the utmost your right to say it." "If there is no God, it would be necessary to invent one" or *"écrasez l'infâme"* (meaning clericalism) most Frenchmen were first puzzled, then annoyed. No doubt there were intellectuals here and there who could academically discuss a free society, but none had experienced one. So the yeast had a long time to work. Towards mid-century many pieces of writing increased the speed of fermentation: among these is always cited the great *Encyclopedia,* edited by Diderot, who also wrote an amazingly large part of it: even if authority at first prevented its publication (1752 on), its influence (as volume after volume appeared) went far. So slowly the ancient building began to yield to its structural faults.

Rousseau is perhaps not strictly of "the Enlightenment." He was a Swiss and a Protestant who had gone off from Geneva in a pique and who found what might be described as the Catholic church's "live-bait" in a certain Mme de Warenne whose business it was apparently to ensnare gullible Swiss Protestants by offering the ultimate inducement to conversion, her bed. At any rate she more or less made a man of him – until the next quarry came along! Rousseau found "nature" and outward freedom from Calvinistic restraint (never, inward) just over the border from Geneva and moving to Paris, he devoted the rest of his life mostly to publishing his doctrines, some of which are excellent, some of which are silly. Their influence – they were widely read in a society where literacy was now widespread – in preaching absence from restraint, following the law of nature, the sentimentalizing of freedom – ("Man was born free and everywhere he is in chains") – their sentimentalizing of life, such matters may have done as much damage as good. Countries with constitutional liberties would have been better off without them, for the element of anarchy in them was not far to seek.

Collectively, the writers of the middle century exercised a powerful influence throughout France, and through France, upon the whole of Europe. They did much to hasten the day when changes would come, and by the middle of the eighteenth century large numbers of people in France were realizing that changes must come. The periods of history in which France could have been considered well-governed were rare indeed. Far more often, the picture which nearly every outside observer gives is of an arrogant *noblesse*, a small and avaricious middle class and a countryside inhabited by a miserable peasantry, badly cultivated and over wide areas half deserted.

Naturally a counter-account can be made out. The monarchy was invariably able to raise large armies, often well equipped. In some districts at least, there was a decided rise in literacy in the eighteenth century. There was also a sharp increase in French commerce in the interval of peace. Between 1715 and 1743, exports were said to have exceeded those of England, and France to have become the major trading nation. All this reflects the basic soundness of a country blessed with large areas of good soil and a good climate. But the picture of rural misery is corroborated by French observers themselves, especially by the great engineer officer of Louis XIV, Vauban.

When the regency of Philip, Duke of Orleans (1715-1723) brought a measure of freedom, tongues were loosened everywhere and pens got to work. There followed during the middle years of the century, the peak of the Enlightenment, during which old modes of thought, old customs, old beliefs, were thoroughly discussed, usually destructively, and it became "the thing," among nobles and intellectuals alike, to turn and rend the ancient institutions. No people under the sun are better than the French at destructive criticism. The Enlightenment saw at its height as a

> marked characteristic of the age, the union of personal violence and depravity with strong feelings of humanity and a high-soaring philosophy, contemptuous of ancient creed and opinions . . .[9]

The author of the quotation stresses that independent of both top and bottom of society, a third "power" had arisen, which ramified throughout all of literate France:

> This power, call it mind, reason, public opinion, enlightenment, as we may . . . which spreads across Europe, which seizes greedily on all knowledge . . . this power . . . is destined, in a way, to be to the eighteenth century what the revelations of the Reformation were to the sixteenth . . .[10]

In time the wave of new interest thus referred to would bring a new age to Europe. Its immediate effects, joined to other factors, was to create that tension between old and new which is invariably to be found in periods of transition. Everywhere, old values and old customs, old beliefs, old superstitions, were crashing down under the assaults of the intellect. Such times are uncomfortable: there seems to be no solid ground beneath the ordinary man's feet.

In France, the middle and later years of the eighteenth century are filled with uncertainty, absence of values and, except in specific situations, absence of purpose. The void that portion of the century presents reminds one of the similar but much longer void when the Later Middle Ages were waiting to disappear before the new world of the Renaissance and Reformation. Europe or large parts of it, waited over a century then for the new age to be born. Later on, Russia was to wait nearly a century for its new age.

In eighteenth century Europe, the span between old and new was shorter. It could almost be pin-pointed, say from about the 1720s to the 1780s. Of all countries, France illustrates most plainly the historical "pulsation" which this book has sought to establish. "Le roi soleil," the decline of "the age of faith and zeal" along with the absolution, the shift to liberalism, the ensuing semi-anarchy, with everyone shouting everything at the same time, the increasing confusion of the last years after 1765 or so, the descent into the pit of revolution and then once again, the restoration of order under a strong personality – at which point the cycle begins again.

In England, the cycle is far less plainly marked than in France, but it is discernible. Its sign-posts are Cromwellianism, which raised England to importance as a continental power, the post-Restoration generation occupied in winding up the civil war accounts, the triumphs of Marlborough, thence the open and corrupt political society of the periods of the first two Georges. Then comes the uncomfortable first generation of George III, which saw the loss of the American colonies (through gross confusion and much folly in government)[11] and the virtual independence, for the time, of Ireland. It was the period in which the attempt to reform Parliament began.[12] All this mounted up high enough during the French Revolution to make a coercive government believe that it presaged revolution in England too.

The results of the Enlightenment in France, in a broad way, were the fall of the monarchy and the ushering in of a new age: the monarchy of a thousand years, of fifty kings, the proudest, the most powerful, the firmest-based, the most magnificent in Europe. Wider still, France set the pace for the Western world as a whole. The period had seen parliamentary government established once for all in England, it had seen the valiant Dutch securely established behind their line of barrier fortresses, the French denied their "natural" frontier, the Rhine, a new and powerful republic established in America (the French Revolution may be called a child of the American). It had witnessed the marvels of seventeenth century science, one of history's major "knowledge explosions," a good start on the miracles coming out of steam and the decline of the old fervours of religion. Catholic zeal, manifested everywhere in the Counter-Reformation, had slowly quieted down into the formalism which so often had overtaken the church. Calvinistic and Lutheran assertiveness, though much strengthened by the assaults of Louis XIV, was undergoing the same evolution. In England and more especially New England, some non-conformism was turning into Unitarianism, than which nothing could more perfectly represent the attitudes of the man of reason. German Quietism and English Methodism on the lower rungs of the ladder were, however, heralding a new dawn of a warmer, less rational sort. The "Age of Reason" by no means reached to the bottom of society, where depths remained unplumbed even by Methodism, as they had been over the centuries. But the exchange of "good taste," good manners, "refinement," for earlier, more primitive forms of conduct had been a real gain to civilization.

Social amenity had penetrated farther down than hitherto. International courtesy, if not peace, had become more marked. By the eighteenth century ("le beau siècle," as the French call it), the reasonable man was replacing the man of passion. Going along with all these changes in atmosphere went the physical concomitants of the commercial and industrial revolution. Supplies of the means of subsistence and their variety were becoming larger: population therefore was increasing. With more certain source of livelihood, well-being in general was promoted. The eighteenth century saw, not all by any means, but the worst of the Western world's miseries over and always, far out across the seas, there was visible that shining goddess, Hope.

Notes

1. W. S. Anderson, *Europe in the Eighteenth Century* (1963) gives a clear, pedestrian survey, basing the political on the social and economic chapters of history.
2. The wives of Edward II and of Henry IV.
3. The French reciprocated. "French leave" became "s'en aller à l'anglais." Birth control devices became "French letters" in "capôts à l'anglais."
4. David Green, *Sarah, Duchess of Marlborough* (London, 1967) gives an interesting look at one angle of eighteenth century life.
5. This and the following quotations are found in Sprague Allen, *Tides in*

English Taste, op. cit., II, Chapter III. This book was finished by the late Dr. Allen in 1932.

6.   Everyman Library.

7.   For one device of restraint, among others, see Robert R. Rea, *The English Press in Politics, 1770-1774* (University of Nebraska Press, 1962). It traces the appearance of a genuine public opinion in English politics.

8.   Sanche de Gramont, *Epitaph for Kings: The Long Decline of the French Monarchy and the Coming of the Revolution* (Hamilton, L. Ham., 1968) brings the eighteenth century to life.

9.   Kitchin, *op. cit.,* III, p. 422.

10.   *Ibid.,* p. 424.

11.   See, *inter alia,* Sir L. Namier and J. Brooke, *Charles Townshend,* (London, Macmillans, 1964).

12.   See Norris, *Shelburne and Reform,* for fiscal and financial reform especially.

CHAPTER FOURTEEN

Years of Ferment

I
Precursors of Romanticism

Each time that the historian confronts another "age," he realizes afresh how difficult it is to be definite about the turn of the tide. Many a competent modern professional would say, "Why, then, write about such things: why not fence off a small segment of the period you are dealing with and try by minute examination, to see in it 'just how things happened'?" The point has come up before in these pages. It is another way of stating that there are two modes of looking at history, one from a hill-top, as it were, and the other through a plant at one's feet. Both are legitimate, and those who go in for either will come out at the same point: however much they have tidied up their piece of historical garden, they will know that ultimate clarification still eludes them. Of no type of historical writing than of these pages is this more true. To try to explain how one age gives way to another is like trying to explain in ultimate terms why a sunny day gives way to a rainy day.

If ever some certainty can be reached, it is for the period which follows the Age of Light. Eighteenth century society within a generation or two gives way to the society of the early nineteenth century, which quickly erects its own new set of values, and these, in turn, are as quickly overturned by new and quite different currents of life. The changes occur, not only in one country, but in all. Once again, ultimate explanations in history are impossible, but if one whose nebulous nature may constitute its best defence is to be given, it simply is that one generation seldom has much respect for the one that precedes it. It associates its parents' values and modes of life with such notions as "old fashioned," "out of style" (nothing could be worse for youth) and, often, useless, false, hypocritical – with all the impatient rebellion of youth against parental restraint. Whatever the psychology of succession may be in primitive societies, where change is hardly perceptible,[1] there is no doubt about this juxtaposition in those with some degree of sophistication, as is borne out by the constant efforts of the old to train up the young in the way they should go! Periodically when traditional values wear thin, the natural rents in the social garment tear open more widely than normal. The deeper the old values (as, for example, belief in the old gods or belief in the superiority of white skins), the more reluctantly they are abandoned and the more grievous the wounds they leave behind them. It is then that we hear talk of "the generation gap." Sooner or later new values percolate through society as a whole. When that takes place in literature, a new age appears.

There is plenty of evidence that towards the first half of the eighteenth century, creative spirits began to get tired of mere brilliance and be dazzled by too much "Enlightenment." The change took place quite quickly. Pope and his heroic couplets retained their popularity, but various new voices began to be heard, indicating, if softly, the change of wind. These were the years in which James Thomson (1700-1748) won an international reputation: much of his poetry was about nature and its moods. One set of his verses actually showed *feeling*, than which nothing could have been much worse! This was something still familiar, *Rule Britannia*. *Rule Britannia* was sung as heartily in those days across the Atlantic as in Great Britain: that American world was to be prominent in the great shift of values.

Thomson was not alone: one thinks at once of Thomas Gray (1716-1771) and his famous *Elegy*, though his *The Bard* is a sharper departure from "pompous Alexandrines": its subject matter is a prophetic preview, placed in the mouth of a thirteenth century Welsh bard, of the course of history in subsequent centuries ("Ruin seize thee, ruthless King! Confusion on thy banner wait!"). Though Gray is not customarily allowed to be a Romantic, the poem in subject matter and air is a forecast of the years to come when "the Gothic past" would become a leading attraction.

A third writer who presages what was to come is William Collins (1721-1759); the author of the well-known verses "How sleep the brave who sink to rest by all their country's wishes blest . . ." Collins projects a romantic cat's-paw for the wind that would one day blow strong. His "Ode on the Popular Superstitions of the Highlands of Scotland, considered as the subject of poetry," surely as unattractive a title for a poem as well could be devised, recognizes the picturesque side of Highland life;

but as a view of the primitive by the sophisticated, it is as ridiculous in some passages as such views must always be. Collins intersperses his lines at frequent intervals with eighteenth century conventionalities: "mountains," "us threw his young Aurora forth."

The poem was made not long after "the '45," the great rebellion in support of Charles Edward, "the Young Pretender," so the place of that event in changing the nature of the times is to be noted. The rebellion is to be coupled with the interest then springing up in the primitive way of life – to the English, the Highlanders were as strange and wild as the Iroquois – and links up with the pseudo-folklore of *Ossians* which appeared a few years later. Interest in the primitive had already been more or less awakened by colonial experience. Men had begun to report back from America as soon as the discoveries were made. In fact, even in the early sixteenth century, one great voyage, that of Vasco da Gama, had already inspired an epic, that of the Portuguese Camoes (1524-1580). The very founding and growth of colonies indicates how large was the impact which the outer world had begun to make on Europe. Then there were the New World products, its "goodies," especially sugar, and according to James 1st, its "baddies" in tobacco. In France, enthusiasm for the conversion of the heathen in New France was a marked aspect of the Counter-Reformation in its seventeenth century stage. The Jesuit missions in Canada resulted not only in inspiring martyrdoms but also the publication over many years of an annual volume of *Relations* (chronicles of the year's activities) which reached excellent levels of authentic description and are much prized by historian and anthropologist today.

The English contribution in the seventeenth century was small, and few realized what solid foundation was being laid along the Atlantic coast by their expatriate countrymen. But an English pen made recompense for this in the eighteenth when in 1719, Daniel Defoe published his immortal *Robinson Crusoe*. "Robinson" swept over Europe. It opened the great world beyond the seas to European imaginations. In the sense that it was itself the product of travellers' tales and not of first-hand experience, it was a work of imagination. The interest in the primitive, scientific or literary, has never since lapsed. Defoe's *Moll Flanders* took its disreputable heroine to Virginia, but the book did not make the wide impression of *Crusoe*. In poetic literature, the apex of Augustinism was being reached just as the new forces were gathering which would blow it away.

The question may be well raised as to whether "the Enlightenment" ever penetrated far into English life and conduct. There were many changes in the eighteenth century, naturally, but when we recall how consistently and joyously English and Scottish poetic voices had shown their love of nature over the centuries, it is to be doubted whether the urbanism, the politeness, the formality, of the Enlightenment had made more than surface impressions. The French noble is invariably described as disliking, even hating, the country. The English gentry loved it and took active part in country life.

This change of cultural weather held in Germany as well as England, particularly in its manifestations of love for nature: in the former country Hagedorn (1708-1754) and others were "trying about 1730 to lift the German lyric out of the bands of a tired convention," and then came two great poets, Friedrich Klopstock (1724-1803) and Gotthold Lessing (1729-1781).[2] The men introduced "a quite new type of poetry." They had caught a new vision of Germanism and have been called "patriots in the best sense of that word," and this suggests the nature of their inspiration. Unlike predecessors, who leaned heavily on the French classics laden with pomposity, (which made their works formal and without life) these two men turned to England and found their inspirations in Shakespeare and Milton, whose distance in nature from the French Enlightenment needs no comment.[3]

The beginnings of the German revolt against *Die Aufklärung* were perhaps rather more self-conscious than the English, for there were chains to be broken which the English did not keenly feel, and it may be dated more precisely, thanks to the German compulsion to set forth schematic programs (Where would the German be without his *Weltanschauung* - his manifesto of his *World View?*). The proclamations by Goethe and his circle which came to be called *Sturm und Drang (Storm and Stress)* were of the 1770s. Lessing was twenty years older than Goethe, Johann Gottfried Herder (1744-1803) five years, but he was a more direct influence on the young Goethe as his mentor at Strasbourg and a major influence after in German cultural life. Greater influence still was Goethe's first love, Friederike, the pastor's daughter at Sessenheim.

> Friederika fitted so well into the natural background that she also opened the eyes of the poet to nature as an aspect of the soul. For the first time now, wood and valley, stream and mooonlight became living powers to him which, grasped without mythological or rhetorical intermediary, could without intermediary – make their poetic impact.[4]

In the seventeenth century, thanks in part to the Thirty Years' War, in part to political fragmentation, Germany as an area of European culture could have been disregarded, but in the latter half of the eighteenth century a remarkable renaissance occurred. Immauel Kant (1724-1804) the great philosopher, belongs to it. So do the musicians, such as Bach and Christoph Gluck (1714-1787). Add to them another major poet, Friedrich von Schiller (1759-1805). For greater or lesser periods, some of these men were gathered together in the little German town of Weimar. That little town had then only a few thousand people. It was the seat of a petty Archduchy, and one would think, a backwater of backwaters. Yet forth from it came some of the world's greatest poetry, such as *Faust*,

Wallenstein's Tod (Wallenstein's Death) and that splendid *Ode to Joy* of Schiller's[5] used by Beethoven in the Ninth Symphony. A remarkable group it was and how magnificently and delightfully these great figures must have stirred and stimulated each other. From any point of view the world was fortunate to have them. And characteristically, before they were scattered, out there came from among them, just before the century ended, another pronunciamento. And thereby, there was begun in Germany, by the clock, as it were, THE ROMANTIC MOVEMENT.

It is hard to join this vigorous cultural renaissance in Germany with either political or industrial evolution. Rather there seems to have been a quiet accumulation of well-being in the great towns, especially the ancient free cities. Goethe's pleasant pictures of his youth in Frankfurt, Leipzig, and Strasbourg *(Dichtung und Wahrheit)* paint middle class societies of comfort and an amiable social setting that to North Americans is quite familiar, much like the excellent provincial society of their own nineteenth century. A distinguished culture came out of New England's nineteenth century and to it Protestant Germany's eighteenth might well be compared.

It could be advanced that the rise of Prussia and Frederick the Great provided enough patriotic drive to give rise to the cultural outburst. That might be so. There is no reflection of it, however, in Goethe's autobiography. Johann Fichte (1762-1814) comes after, not before, the Renaissance. Herder, later, Goethe's companion at Weimar is credited along with Goethe, with formulating the doctrine of *Sturm und Drang*.[6] The title of the volume put out by them in 1772 (along with others) has a patriotic note about it – *Von deutscher Art und Kunst (Of German Ways and Art)*.

Political events have a heavy bearing on the swing from the *Age of Enlightenment* to the *Age of Romanticism*. During the eighteenth century, England and France waged four of the seven great wars that the historian Seeley appropriately called the Second Hundred Year's War. The struggle was to change the weight of both countries internationally and deeply to affect them internally. Englishmen came out of the War of the Spanish Succession (1703-1713) convinced that one Englishman was as good as three Frenchmen (when led by a Marlborough, at any rate) and that Frenchmen were a frivolous lot, living as slaves, under a despotism. "Rule Britannia" just fitted the times. Such attitudes were reinforced by the first world war, the Seven Years' War. In it, the two countries fought each other in Germany, in the Mediterranean, in the West Indies, in North America, in India, and through France's ally, Spain, in the distant Philippines. England ended the war everywhere victorious under her popular hero, William Pitt. This was the war that, once and for all, made Great Britain into an island, developing its own life apart from the continent: as the quip goes about the newspaper headline – "Great Storm: Continent Isolated." The enlargement of mind that must have come through successful war in every part of the world, together with the nation's self-consciously realizing its completely appropriate environment – the sea – one would think would have been quickly expressed in literature. That was the day of "Hearts of Oak" but such songs apart, the reflection in literature does not seem readily apparent. But how about" The Ancient Mariner," just a little later?

For England, the next war and the events leading up to it present a very different picture. George III, young, vigorous, stubborn and stupid, came to the throne in 1760. He reigned for sixty years and for the last thirty or so of them, was most of the time insane. His contribution to English life was the loss of the American colonies and the alienation of Catholic Ireland. Luckily, English parliamentary institutions proved tough enough to survive this blight, but the wound in the English heart caused by that civil war, the War of the American Revolution, lingered for many a day, as it still lingers in those colonial children of Great Britain's who found their cause lost. It broke the English-speaking world in two and there has never been a day since in which the effects of the break have not been evident.

The decade prior to the war, the 1760s, was one of much political confusion in Great Britain, with administrations coming in and going out in kaleidoscopic succesion – some six of them in the decade – and the king trying his best to make himself into his own prime minister. No wonder that after the colonies had gone, a private member of Parliament, Dunning, should introduce and have carried his well known resolution to the effect that "The power of the Crown has increased, is increasing and ought to be diminished."

The generation of British history that lies between the Peace of Paris, 1763, and the outbreak of the War of the French Revolution, 1793, might be regarded as the period of confusion that normally follows an "age of reason." It was not anarchy, still less chaos, simply uncertainty, poor judgement, weakness, too much success and too much money for the gilded youth. It was the age when Charles James Fox, as a young man, could lose fifteen thousand pounds in a night at the cards (but his father Henry had had custody of all the pay for the forces, pocketing the interest on it), when Charles could express "his astonishment at his own moderation" in India and the money of other returned "Nabobs" in corrupting Parliament. On the part of the king, very possibly it was his inability as a German (although he "gloried in the name of Briton") really to understand English institutions. Lord North's administration, which fought the disastrous war, is comparable to that of Neville Chamberlain in the 1930s, two weak men leading their country to the brink of ruin.

In the late 1740s, Admiral Anson took a squadron round the world. In the 1750s, great fleets and thousands of men crossed and recrossed the Atlantic. Nothing on the scale had ever occurred before. The feat was repeated, and by the French, too, during the War of American Independence. It was remarkable in itself and a remarkable illustration of how high European power and capacity had mounted before the Industrial Revolution had much more than entered its first stages. Power and capacity took two principal paths, geographical and industrial. In the 1760s and 1770s, Captain Cook laid open the Pacific in detail, the southern continent and New Zealand, the North American Pacific coast, towards the Arctic, the ocean south towards the Antarctic Circle. Industrially, Watt's steam engine had begun operating by 1764 and by the end of the century over a hundred of his engines had been installed. But there still remained to be achieved, the application of steam to transport, a revolution in itself. Many another mechanical invention dates from this last half of the eighteenth century. Cumulatively, they carried forward the Industrial Revolution to considerable lengths and had their reflections not only in increased production but the rapid growth of population and the increasing number of large towns. The links are evident between geographical expansion, urban life, a new note in politics and a new world in all the creative aspects of civilization.

While Britain went on from victory to victory, France remained in its normal state of royal profligacy and confusion, conjoined with the private thrift and industry which, given its wide area of fertile soil and good climate, enabled it ever to rise above misgovernment. Administrations may have changed frequently in England, but in France, as one official said at the height of the Seven Years' War, "we change our war ministers as often as we do our shirts." France, governmentally and financially, was to steer a steady downward course until the confusion ended in revolution. No country presents so clearly the successive phases of the typical evolution: from absolute rule and the pride and enthusiasm under the grand monarch to the loosening of restraint under Regency and Louis XV, with the turn to intellectualism which was the *Enlightenment,* the semi-anarchic freedom of the last years and eventually, the chaos of revolution, whence came order restored by the strong hand of Napoleon.

II
Rousseau, Methodism, Humanitarianism

Most new periods begin with a stirring in religion. This may involve the destruction of an old and the substitution of a new, as in the shift from the Classical world to the Christian, or it may take the form of new currents in the old channels. Whatever the specific historical situation, a major change of values must have manifold reflections in life and society. For the shift from the Enlightenment to Romanticism, there is to be considered in this connection, the place of Rousseau on the continent, and of Methodism and other religious phenomena in England.

There is a vast mass of assertion for the view that Rousseau was a major force in the continental turn-away from Classicism to Romanticism. He was regarded as a child of nature preaching a return to the life of nature, to simplicity, naturalness of morals, and to primitive goodness generally. He was a leading architect in the building of the idea of "the noble savage," but he knew nothing at first hand of the life of the noble savage and probably not much at second. Old Thomas Hobbes was nearer to the mark when he called life in a state of nature "nasty, brutish and short." Any number of people in France with colonial experience could have told Rousseau as much. The idyllic picture was widely accepted, however, and numbers of persons came to believe that "man was naturally good" and could lead a perfect existence, given a chance. French intellectuals could point to the utopia that under the kindly, just sway of the Quakers, they imagined existed in a new ideal commonwealth, Pennsylvania. Disillusion was to come, but it was to come slowly. Before it came, Rousseauism had a major place in sapping away the foundations of the Old régime, as well as in inspiring those pretty games of pastoral life played by Marie Antoinette, with her "milkmaids" and "farmers" and model mills. The idea of a return to simple life dies hard: it still continues to drive people off in search of "a lodge in some vast wilderness," as it has all through the years between then and now, and no doubt always will. But how much of that stems directly out of Rousseau's proclamations? Probably not very much. Probably far more of it from the actual opportunities afforded by the outer world for really finding the lodge in the wilderness.

At first sight, there would not appear to be any connection between the heterodox Swiss-French prophet Rousseau and the staid Anglican divine, John Wesley. But a subterranean semi-philosophical relationship could be traced. Rousseau's doctrine of individualism, perhaps a revolt from Genevan predestination, (how much of Rousseauism came out of a Genevan childhood, it may be asked) is comparable with Wesley's theological convictions. Wesley was a man whose whole heredity predisposed him to a life of serious devotion. At first this zeal ran in normal Anglican channels, but in his late thirties, it overflowed its banks and was influenced greatly by certain pious Moravians whom he met and respected. He seems to have received, almost suddenly, what he believed to be a consciousness of God's nearness to him and concern for him. Wesley's experience drove him out to preach the gospel he had thus received, and resulted (in the 1740s) in the birth of a new denomination which came to be called, (in derision) *Methodist*.

As noticed elsewhere, it is rather hard to reconcile the eighteenth century of Methodism, of *The Messiah* and such organizations as the Society for the Propagation of the Gospels, with the eighteenth century of the *Tom Jones's* or the Lord Chesterfields. We may picture the religious fervour set going by the Reformation as a river which was deflected from its course by the Restoration and, as it were, went underground. There, one would judge, it ran true and strong without taking much note of the fashionable world of its day, to emerge in full spate to the surface in the second great age of Puritanism often called Victorianism. This would make the English Enlightenment not much more than a surface move-ment, the true genius of the race getting its expression (even more con-spicuously in America than in England) in its Reformation heritage. The "Great Awakening" as it is called in America began about 1735. Methodism was its English expression (it also had its German counter-part) and before its first thrust was spent, it had established a new régime in religion first for the masses, later also for their "betters."

The essence of Wesleyanism was this personal, direct association with God and the conviction that once it was attained, a man was put in some state of grace which enabled him to lead a new life and to have a con-sciousness of "being saved." This was surely fairly close in conventional religious terms to what Rousseau was saying in secular terms. It became the now familiar doctrine of "conversion": God spoke to the individual and in a flash changed him. "If your sins be as scarlet, they are made whiter than snow." Ever since, Methodists the world over have been insisting on the phenomenon of conversion and insisting on their experi-ence of its reality. God may have fore-ordained degradation or salvation but to Methodists such conversions turned aside the old order of events and were evidences of a gift freely given and freely accepted. Methodism was a religion of freedom; as opposed to Calvinism, it rested on *free will*.

If God spoke to you, pardoned your sins and gave you assurance of entrance to eternal life – and what else was being "saved"? – then evidently you were in an exceedingly favourable position and the thought would be sure to creep in that not being "as other men are," you must have considerable liberty of action. Were you not "saved" and could you therefore be "lost"? This was the gate through which extremists in centuries past had moved on to hold themselves free of all the ordinary restraints: the "Brethren of the Free Spirit" of the fourteenth century had felt themselves free to act precisely as they wished, and there had been other sects of the sort. Methodism never got far along that road, though its adherents were often accused of hypocrisy.

It is unlikely that the paths of Bobbie Burns and the "Methodies" crossed, but in his Holy Willie, Burns drew a picture of what their enemies thought Methodists might be. It was in Presbyterian terms, but could be applied to any "unco guids."

> Oh Lord, thou kens what zeal I bear,
> When drinkers drink and swearers swear,
> And singin' there and dancin' here,
>   Wi' great and small,
> For I am keepit by thy fear
>   Free from them a'.

But yet, O Lord! Confess I must
At times I'm fashed wi' fleshly lust
An' sometimes, too, in wardly trust,
    Vile self gets in:
But thou remembers we are dust
    Defil' in sin.

O Lord! yestreen Thou kens, wi' Meg
Thy pardon I sincerely beg
O! may't ne'er be a livin' plague
    To my dishonour
An I'll ne'er lift a lawless leg
    Again upon her . . .[7]

Methodism was to survive these relatively mild afflictions and grow in Wesley's lifetime to be a force both in Great Britain and America. After his death, its expansion went on with much greater speed, and like most new movements, as it expanded it suffered division. Each division had its own characteristic, but they all drew from the working classes and they all depended for leadership on Wesley's innovation, the "local preacher," usually a layman of superior qualities who took occasional services. Wesley himself had never ceased to be a minister of the Anglican church and both a high churchman and a Tory. These traits were transmitted to the leadership of the *Wesleyan* Methodists, who never allowed their movement to become identified with the radicalism of the first half of the nineteenth century. Wesleyanism claimed to be in no respect a political movement.

It has been argued that in the nineteenth century this position of neutrality, keeping it away from extreme positions, saved Methodism from disintegration. The junior branches, founded by men who had chafed under the absence of denominational self-government during Wesley's life (no lay representation had been given in the church courts) and many of whom had never been within the folds of the established church, took on more popular tones at once and led the way to that democracy of government which marks practically all the modern Protestant churches.[8]

The great tide of Methodist expansion came in the first half of the nineteenth century and it was clearly a reflection of the gathering speed of the Industrial Revolution. The Industrial Revolution occasioned rapid increase in population, the growth of numerous large cities, the factory system – everything that drew men together and increased social tension. It has been argued that the local preacher system of Methodism by drawing off the most capable men from political agitation to the chapel pulpit conceivably averted social disturbances that could have deepened into revolution. Methodism could thus be accused of being another one of those opiates for the people upon which the modern Communists have poured scorn. To work out that point would take a volume. Briefly it can be agreed that all religion having a consolatory element about it, is a kind of opiate, the Communist religion included. Religion in this sense is a sedative, but it is also a stimulant, and it is from this side of it that there come "movements," major and minor, ancient and modern.

Methodism certainly did not lack the crusading, missionary urge,[9] more particularly in its dissident branches. Thus while these latter offically kept clear of labour extremism and of political movements like Chartism, the passage from Methodism to radicalism was an easy one. Even those of the brotherhood whose proclivities have been anything but radical have often manifested marked interest in steps for the amelioration of society. Methodism had so much social purpose concealed within its purely religious aspects that it could not avoid being a parent of radicalism. It never to this day has entirely lost the original zeal, and has remained a driving force in political movements of the left. All this would probably have horrified John Wesley, but it has been well said that Wesley was like a man rowing a boat – he faces backward but every stroke he took propelled him and his boat forward.

Methodism contributed to the English-speaking world what is now probably its most numerous and powerful denomination. Apart from the more technical aspects of its doctrines, its appeal has lain mainly in two points: one, its success in founding itself on the rising new classes resulting from the Industrial Revolution or, in the New World, an unsophisticated rural population increasing rapidly as settlers pressed onward to occupy the new lands: the other, the optimistic note in its idea of perfectibility, which fitted well into a new world in the making. As the lower classes of yesterday have become the middle classes of today, the appeal through social class has lessened. But the idea of perfectibility has always remained strong and, perhaps more than any other one consideration, it has inspired the innumerable "movements" for building a better world that have been characteristic of modern times. The point applies through a wide spectrum. Methodism has lent powerful aid not only for "banishing the bar" but for establishing the United Nations. Some of its idealistic crusades have been impracticable, some misguided because narrow, but none of them has been based upon a mere desire to conserve selfish vested interests.

Methodism, as often remarked, has always had a dualism in its nature. Founded in conservatism, it yet has been a consistent advocate of reforming changes. Cherishing the existing social order, its weight has often been used against the existing order. This duality has had its necessary results. Few men could keep up to the level of moral perfection at which Methodist teaching has aimed. Many have dropped out. Many, especially the successful, have become members of more congenial groups: as an Anglican once expressed it, with them, it was a case of "out of the church at the bottom and in at the top." Many have taken the route to Burn's Holy Willie in the "prayer" already quoted. Nevertheless, add up the sum as you will, it does not seem exaggeration to assert that in Methodism (and its allies) there has existed the most powerful of all the forces of the last three centuries seeking to establish a world "closer to the heart's desire."[10]

In Great Britain, the social weight of Methodism was long hampered by the very fact that its membership was drawn mainly from the lower classes. John Wesley was a "gentleman" in the starchy eighteenth century English sense. Few of his followers were. Consequently when other "gentlemen," such as William Wilberforce, also found their hearts filled with zeal for social betterment, or the love of God, whichever the reader prefers, close co-operation with Methodists was not easy. Yet the interesting point about the period does not lie in the difficulties presented but in the appearance of men actually ready to take seriously Christ's injunction to "love their neighbour as themselves." The attitude is of course as old as the injunction and no church has ever completely failed to recognize it. At the mediaeval height of prelatical haughtiness, at the very apex of the *autos da fe* of the Spanish Inquisition, there were also found instances of sheer Christian goodness, as for example, Father Las Casas during Cortez's bloody conquest of Mexico. The point about Methodism and its allies is that they arose in the period in which the established church seemed static, resting on its oars, more dead than alive. By their zeal and enthusiasm they awakened men, not only to the old truths of the Christian ethic, but to the need for their application to the world then so rapidly rising about them.

This new awareness became marked in the second half of the eighteenth century. One of its best illustrations is the determined war waged by certain Quakers, among whom Granville Sharp was prominent, against slavery, which to their credit the Quakers from their beginnings had opposed. But it took many forms. John Howard's efforts at amelioration of the horrors of the eighteenth century prison are well-known. So are those of Robert Raikes, the founder of the "Sunday School." Burke's (1729-1797) prolonged attack on Warren Hastings for his alleged injustices to the Begums of Oude in India is another expression of it, as is much of Blake's poetry. But it was the assault on the slave trade and the institution of slavery that gained the most public attention and drew in men from the upper layers of society, among whom William Wilberforce (1759-1833), good friend of the younger Pitt, is still widely remembered. Through Wilberforce and his circle, who from their places of residence, have long been nicknamed "the Clapham Sect" and sometimes "the Saints," the original Christian precept to "love thy neighbour as thyself" widened its new appeal and was closely associated with the Evangelicals on the "Low Church" wing of Anglicanism.

The Evangelicals, as good members of the established church, and as "gentlemen," not working class, were not open to the accusations of disloyalty so frequently levelled against the Methodists. Their left wing, under Wilberforce, gained a major victory when in 1808, Great Britain abolished the slave trade and some of them were to live to see, in 1833, the abolition throughout the British empire, of slavery as an institution.

Not even the change in the literary climate exceeded in depth and range this change in the attitude of men towards men. As an example, John Newton the author of the once popular hymn "How sweet the name of Jesus sounds in a believer's ear," when he wrote the hymn was actually sitting in the cabin of the ship of which he was then captain and that ship was a slave ship, its hold filled with miserable, chained, captive negroes. A few years later, he would probably have found it impossible to reconcile the two opposites, the Christian piety which he practised, probably quite sincerely, and the inhumanity of the trade in human flesh from which he was making his living. Or again, in 1755 a slave was punished by being burned to death. Not in the deep South, but of all places in the common of Cambridge. Cambridge Massachusetts! Within a stone's throw of Harvard, within four score years to be the very nucleus of abolitionism.[11]

Notes

1.   In primitive societies, those who have worn out their usefulness have often been abandoned or killed outright.
2.   That is, if we may call a man such as Lessing a poet, when his productions, dramas, in his case, were in prose: this seems, however, to conform with German usage.
3.   For Germany and its literature, see *inter alia*, J. G. Robertson, *The Literature of Germany* (London, Williams and Norgate, Home University Library). For more specific discussion, see *inter alia*, *Die Lyristichen Meisterstücke von Goethe, mit Einleitungen und Anmerkungen* von Richard M. Meyer (London, Meyer and Co., n.d.). See in general, the excellent collection of German lyrics in *The Oxford Book of German Verse*. For the eighteenth century, there looms up one gigantic figure, Goethe. See his *Dichtung und Wahrheit*, a partial autobiography and of great charm, also his fashionable novel of eighteenth century "sensibility," *The Sorrows of Werter (Werters Leiden*, 1774). The present writer claims no special knowledge in the area of German literature, but ever since his student days, he has been a lover of the German lyric and, of course, of Faust. May this cover a multitude of sins!
4.   Meyer, *op. cit.*, p. xii.

5.   Which opens: Freude, schöner Götterfunken
                      Tochter aus Elysium
                      Wir betreten, feuertrunken,
                      Himmlische, dein
                      Heiligtum . . .
6.   Robertson, *op. cit.*, p. 93.
7.   See also chapter 11, p. 162.
8.   Including the Anglican church itself except in England.
9.   In the second generation of the nineteenth century, attempts were made to carry Methodism to France. These all failed. The emotional displays of Methodism were not for the French.
10.   The modern Marxist might challenge this assertion.
11.   John C. Miller, *The First Frontier; Life in Colonial America*, (Dell Publishing Company, New York, 1955), p. 155.

CHAPTER FIFTEEN

Years of Ferment: Bubbles Everywhere

I

Romanticism

The strengthening forces of Protestantism and those emanating from the Enlightenment, more particularly Rousseau, meet in the later eighteenth century, a strange encounter! The men of the Enlightenment, as so often noted, were for reason, right or, at least, prudent conduct, ''correct'' behaviour, good manners. The type was widespread. It reached Scotland as well as England. But its Scottish form, as might be expected, with Calvinist rigour in the background, kept its feet on the ground. David Hume (1711-1776) and Adam Smith (1623-1790) give its nature: practical men, with solutions. Few eighteenth century minds have had more influence on subsequent thinking than has had that of Adam Smith, whose *Wealth of Nations* appeared in the very year of the American Declaration of Independence. Smith is credited with a root-and-branch solution to the American problem: hand over all British North America to the new Americans (not quite yet the *United States*). That probably would have altered the course of history. But it leaves sons of the then unborn child unconvinced and rather angry. Cool rational solutions to large problems seldom seem acceptable.

Wherever he acquired his ideas, whether from the French world to which he migrated or from his Swiss mountains or by revulsion against Calvinistic lock-step, Rousseau drove them all farther along the road. Children of nature, the natural life according to nature, above all the natural goodness of man: if society would only leave man alone, if he could get rid of the artificiality and tyranny of customs, conventions, laws, constitutions, institutions! Here was the key to the "golden age," "When man to man, the world o'er Shall brothers be and a' that." It would all be a matter of proper education and of course, of getting rid of the curse of class – and wealth.

The influence of Rousseau on the literary generation following him was obvious and immense, not only in France but in Germany and in England. Men writing with sentimental and revolutionary fervour – for the worship of the master demanded both qualities – abounded in England in the decades of the 1780s and 1790s, where they expounded their doctrines in didactic poetry, didactic dramas, didactic novels, didactic philosophies.[1] It is only his large calibre which prevents Jeremy Bentham (1748-1832) from being lumped in with the lesser "Jacobins." His fervent appeal to the French authorities to "Emancipate Your Colonies," which appeared about 1794, is typical. William Godwin (1756-1836) was another of the "advanced" thinkers of the day. Though he hardly rates with Bentham, his book *Political Justice*, still well remembered, lifts him above the crowd. In it and other writings, he argued himself into such an extreme position of individualism that he is said to have objected to an orchestra having a conductor – leave every musician to himself, that was the way to secure the best music. Godwin attempted to explain his ultra-speculative ideas by putting them into a novel, *Caleb Williams* (1794), in which the characters were supposed to bring the ideas down to earth. He and his wife, Mary Wollstonecraft, belonged to the most "advanced" of circles in the London of the 1790s and 1800s. It was one of their daughters, Mary, who married the young radical Percy Bysshe Shelley. Another daughter apparently decided to illustrate anarchism in her own person, for, in a really emphatic gesture of "advancement," she offered herself (in writing) to Lord Byron (whom she had never met) because she thought it would be socially beneficial for two such excellent people to produce offspring. Byron gallantly submitted to the ordeal.[2]

Each year of the 1790s saw appear in England poems and novels filled with valiant commoners standing up to dissolute, insolent lords, good girls of the lower classes repelling the advances of the rich men who sought to seduce them, upper class ladies giving up all for love, "the petty tyrants of the fields" suffering repentance and dissolving in tears of contrition. Much of this appeared too early for the French Revolution to have been its major source. The deduction is fair, that Rousseau, if not the actual source of it, was heavily influential in it. Similar writing, especially in the drama, appeared in Germany. August Kotzebue (1761-1819), chief of the successors to the *Sturm und Drang* movement is a dramatist of whom the German intellectual usually seems more or less ashamed. That is because his plays were not in a proper sense *literature*, but mere melodramas of the same "tear-jerking" kind as were appearing in England.

Crude as some of this literature was, it represented a revolution in social conceptions. It provided the finger writing on the wall against class distinction, ill-gotten gains, haughty tyranny over inferiors, all those aspects of society that nearly everyone in our modern Western world reprobates (often with tongue in cheek). It was thought worthy of the attention of William Pitt, when his administration decided that it represented a wide conspiracy to stage a French Revolution in England. The situation was quite similar to that which obtained after the Second World War towards Russian Communism. The extreme "left wing" literary products of the two periods were also similar in their naiveté, crudity and horrible didacticism. These late eighteenth century reflections of French Jacobinism became greatly modified as Republicanism – "Liberty, Equality, Fraternity" changed into Bonapartism. Although they had had their influence on some of the men who later became major figures, these, especially Wordsworth and Coleridge, sloughed them off – too emphatically in these two cases – and their work long ago entered the English pantheon.

Bobbie Burns put Rousseau-ism in a nutshell. To quote a few lines from "A man's a man for a' that":

. . . The coward slave, we pass him by
We dare be poor for a' that . . .

What though on hamely fare we dine
Wear hodden-gray and a' that:
Gie fools their silks and knaves their wine,
A man's a man for a' that . . .

You see yon birkie ca'd a lord,
Who struts and stares and a' that
Though hundreds worship at his word
He's but a coof for a' that . . .

Then let us pray that come it may
As come it will for a' that,
That sense and worth o'er all the earth
May bear the gree and a' that.
For a' that and a' that
It's coming yet for a' that
That man to man the warld o'er
Shall brothers be and a' that.

It seems a shame to mangle Burns' eloquent lines by cutting them short, but few readers will be without a copy of them surely. Burns, if he had met

John Wesley, would probably have numbered him among the "unco guid" to whom he addressed some famous lines – those beginning.

O ye who are sae guid yoursel
Sae pious and sae holy . . .

Ye've naught to do but mark and tell
Your neibours fauts and folly!

It is quite improbable that John Wesley had read Rousseau, still less likely that he got any inspiration from him. Bobbie Burns may or may not have known and been influenced by the gospel from France. At any rate, the two currents of social thought approach each other.

But then so many currents of thought and of action approached each other towards the end of the eighteenth century. In France they provided that grand display of fireworks whose reflections can be seen in the sky to this day, the French Revolution. In England, there was no revolution, just the fear of one and the repressive measures which that fear engendered. In both countries and in Germany, too, the age seethed with novelty and change. And just as in our own day, it was "the state of the times" that most forcefully impelled men to write.

It is always difficult to explain literary movements in terms of the social and political phenomena of the age, so whether there had been a French Revolution or not, there might have been a "Romantic movement" in literature, and the French Revolution might have occurred without there being any "Romantic movement" in literature. Whatever the final explanation, the eighteenth century wound up with an explosion in France of volcanic proportions and with the literary movement usually called "Romanticism."

Writing in 1936, F. L. Lucas[3] maintained that up to that year there had appeared 11,396 books on Romanticism. Forty years later, the score has probably turned the 12,000 point. It is a formidable pile and no one in his senses would try to do more than toy with it, pulling down a volume here and there that looks interesting and sampling it.[4]

Definitions of Romanticism are as numerous as the books about it. Too much light, say some, the excessive clarity of the earlier century, blinding not binding. Too much good sense. Too much reason, not enough heart. Lucas in the book just referred to, looks into one of the newer areas of knowledge for his explanation. Romanticism to him seems to represent the subconscious aspects of men's minds pushing out, asserting themselves demanding expression despite "reason's" attempt to repress them. He might say that in the same way in our own day all the filth of the centuries, the "four-letter words" repressed by innumerable generations, is forcing itself out into public utterance and acceptance. His interpretation is semi-Freudian. A Hindu scholar of the 1950s seems to accept this idea and widens it.[5] He considers the French Revolution itself as the explosion of volcanic forces breaking through to the surface, the volcanic forces of the theretofore carefully controlled human mind. In England, he finds a similar but milder explosion, decently confined between English banks in the form of the ''Gothic'' novel, the horrendous novel of dark dungeons, ruined castles, fierce barons, hapless maidens, ghosts, corpses, blood, which had a huge public towards the end of the eighteenth century and which probably had its moulding literary place in the work of some of the great poets (notably Coleridge and Byron) and of course in the mediaevalism of Sir Walter Scott. Horace Walpole's *Castle of Otranto* (1765) is usually regarded as the first ''Gothic'' novel, and from it the line runs directly, through Mrs. Radcliffe to Sir Walter Scott.

How heavily English literature – indeed European literature – has depended on mediaevalism ever since is surely evident to anyone with the slightest acquaintance with books. Not only Sir Walter Scott: earlier, Schiller with his *Die Räuber* and *Wallenstein's Tod,* among other historic dramas. Later, Tennyson and his *Idylls of the King,* and the huge stream of historic novels that never ceases to pour from the press. ''Gothicism,'' at its widest point is simply interest in the past, and as such, an underpinning of all historical writing. In its narrower connotations, it can never be neglected as a mark on the route from classicism to the nineteenth century.

Students of literature seem to give boundless flexibility to the chronology of the Romantic movement. Some authors prefer to be precise, assuming that the movement began with the German manifesto of 1798 already mentioned or with the publication in 1798 by Wordsworth and Coleridge of *The Lyrical Ballads,* and that it ended (not quite as exactly) with the disappearance from the scene of ''the big five'' – Blake, Wordsworth, Coleridge, Shelley, Keats. Some will not admit Byron into the pantheon. Some insist on Sir Walter Scott.

Germans like to end the Romantic revival with the death of Goethe in 1832, though Goethe was far too big to be confined to a literary period. And then there was Heinrich Heine, who surely was a Romantic, although he did not die until 1856. This is in fact, a well-known lyric of Heine's (beautifully set to music by Robert Schumann) which illustrates as exactly as words (and music) could what seems to be the essence of ''Romanticism'': *The Two Grenadiers (Die Beiden Grenadiere).* The lyric depicts two French grenadiers who had been captured in Russia during Napoleon's campaign of 1812. Making their way back to France after escape, they learn of the emperor's defeat and surrender. One of them exclaims that ''the song is over. I might stay and die with you. But I have wife and child at home, and they without me would die of hunger.'' The other strikes an attitude and in what must be the extreme of the Romantic pose, cries:

Was schert mich Weib, was schert mich Kind,
Ich trage weit bessres Verlangen
Lass sie betteln gehn, wenn sie hungrig sind –
Mein Kaiser, mein Kaiser gefangen!

What matters wife to me, what matters child?
Higher claims than those I answer
If they are hungry, let them go and beg
My Emperor, my Emperor is taken![6]

And he goes on to tell his comrade that when he dies, he is to take his body to French soil, where he will lie until once more he hears the cannon firing. Then the emperor will ride over his grave and he, his follower, will rise out of the grave to guard him.

This attitude of utter devotion, pictured by Heine, is as strange to us today as it would have been to the well-ordered, sensible people of the eighteenth century. It is to be found, very likely, among devoted followers of Mao Tse-tung and possibly in Russia (though there in diminishing numbers, as Communist fervour declines). It is the essence of the Romantic attitude, the transcendence of reason, the defiance of common sense, the sincere, sublime but impracticable and not wholly admirable expression of complete consecration. Not admirable because so far away from life that if often acted upon it would blow society to pieces. For the world to go on, men must put a good deal of water in their wine.

Many scholars refuse to see Romanticism in the limited terms of a "movement." They prefer to take a running start, as it were, and trace "Romantic" elements in literature to much earlier ages. Some see Romanticism as an ever present element in life which can be traced back through the ages, back to the classics, Latin and Greek. Here is the *Pervigilum Veneris*, the *Vigil of Venus*, a fourth century poem, which in its abandonment, is distinctly of the romantic *genre,* the prologue to the Middle Ages, it has been said of it, not self-possessed, but *possessed* :[7]

Tomorrow let him love who never yet has loved, and who has loved before.
The new green is born, green, green the old grey world becometh
In the spring lovers meet, the birds mate in the spring
And under nuptial showers the boughs of the grove are loosened.
Tomorrow let him love who never yet has loved, and who has loved before, let him love tomorrow.

Such enthusiasm, so utterly "non-eighteenth century"! Not even classical. But why stop at the fourth century? Why stop at the older Greek classics? Why not glance at the Biblical *Song of Solomon*? Romantic yearning, surely. Why stop at the limits of the written word? There is no need to stop there: pre-literate peoples still exist and their warrior dances or folk tales are as authentic expressions of the Romantic spirit as Homer's heroes, or Scott's.

A book such as this can hardly afford to dally in the company of single individuals. Bow then to the great Romantic poets, as you pass them, Mr. Author, and come back to your theme, which is how, why and, less strictly, when, one age passes into another.

In literary forms, the shift into the so-called Romantic period is plain enough: no one would mistake Keats for Cowper. The heroic couplet passes off the stage, though its echoes can be heard for many years and there are still people who have the knack of writing it and writing it quite well, too. But after 1800, it no longer is the major verse form. Blank verse begins to come in again. Wordsworth is using it as early as 1798.

> . . . For I have learned
> To look on nature, not as in the hour
> Of thoughtless youth: but hearing oft
> The still, sad music of humanity,
> Nor harsh, nor grating, though of ample power
> To chasten and subdue. . .[8]

Many other metres come in, too. The simple lyric, such as *Lucy Gray*, appears. And then, of course, there is *The Ancient Mariner* which must have burst upon an old fashioned poetic world (about 1800) as did the Mariner's ship into "the silent sea." Coleridge's *Ancient Mariner* and Heine's *Grenadiere* are clearly "brothers under the skin."

The common characteristics of the Romantic poets have long since been carefully enumerated and tabulated: not only presentation of the unusual, the exotic, the strange and the marvellous, but always some element of transcendence: Wordsworth's finding intimation of immortality in nature, Byron's rejoicing in society where none intrudes, stealing away "to mingle with the universe and feel what he can ne'er express, yet cannot all conceal." All this was in strong contrast with the "good sense," the proportion, the propriety, the moderation, the genteel repression of feeling exhibited by and advocated by the writers of the preceding age. It was close to the warmth of feeling, the *enthusiasm,* of Methodism, and a world away from it socially. For the eighteenth century, few words could have been more repellent than "enthusiasm." "A set of ignorant enthusiasts," exclaimed the first Anglican Bishop of Quebec in the 1790s, seeking to describe the troublers in his Eden, the Methodists. And here were "enthusiasts" of another status capturing the citadels of literature in the very metropolis of empire itself. Perhaps too much should not be made of eighteenth century censure of emotion. Such attitudes still prevail. No one wishes to exhibit his feelings in public. Inhibitions on a show of feeling, even on ordinary talk ("silence is golden") range through most ranks of northern societies.

II
Romanticism: Its Non-Literary Aspects.

Romanticism in literature has been given a larger share of attention than its manifestations in other spheres. The point is important, for when the times swung from eighteenth century classicism, they swung in every direction, though at different speeds in different places. As it is hardly necessary to say – every branch of the arts had its Romantic phase. In music, for example, the older Beethoven of the later Quartets would possibly have hardly recognized the young man who wrote "classical" music much in the manner of Mozart. For the non-expert in music to describe the music of two periods, Classical and Romantic, in technical detail is not possible, but music lovers everywhere grasp the differences satisfactorily enough: they do not put Schubert back into the era of Mozart. Great as is the charm and brightness of a Mozartian selection, it does not have that quality of ineffable longing, that unanalyzable appeal to the inner man – if you like, the soul – possessed by Schubert.

One could make the round of the arts in similar fashion. The change in architecture from "Palladian" to Gothic Revival comes more properly in the next chapter. The changes in religion too, are more appropriately considered there. Changes in painting and in the minor arts follow the same general pattern but as all pieces of writing must have limits, most of these have to be passed over. In general terms, in practically all aspects of life, the change from the one period to the next involved decrease of emphasis on form: the appeal must be to the evocative, the semi-mystical, the attainable unattainable.

If the phrase seems obscure, consider the big book of Sir Uvedale Price (1747-1829) on gardens – noblemen's gardens, of course.[9] Price wrote during the first years of the nineteenth century. Behind him lay several centuries of professional work on the English garden, and a large body of writing on the art of making gardens. From it no doubt a formidable theory of aesthetics could be compiled. During that long period, the old English garden, probably pretty unkempt, had lost favour to the formalities of Italian gardening *via* its French versions. Every English grandee had seen the gardens of Versailles; and through them and lesser French examples, the long arm of Italian Renaissance civilization stretched out once again over English life.

Price wrote when the art of gardening was beginning to feel the new, Romantic influence. His writing shows all the stiffness of the old classicism, but he is evidently open to the new world rising about him. He has little to say about those classical watchwords, symmetry and proportion, but much concern with "the picturesque," as compared with "the sublime and the beautiful," which terms are echoes of the Edmund Burke of 1757. In his eighteenth century formalism accompanied by concern with the new abstracts, Price is a more or less interesting half-way figure.

> . . . The neglect, which prevails in the works of modern improvers, of all that is picturesque, is owing to their exclusive attention to high polish and flowing lines. . . They neglect two of the most fruitful sources of human pleasure; the first, that great and universal source of pleasure, *variety* – the power of which is independent of beauty, but without which even beauty itself ceases to please; the second, *intricacy* – a quality which though distinct from variety is so connected and blended with it, that the one can hardly exist without the other. . . Intricacy in landscape might be defined, that disposition of objects, which, by a partial and uncertain concealment, excites and nourishes curiosity. . .

Here Sir Uvedale retreats into the coyness of a footnote.

> Many persons, who take little concern in the intricacy of oaks, beeches, and thorns, may find the effects of partial concealment in more interesting objects and may have experienced how differently the passions are moved by an open, licentious display of beauty, and by the unguarded disorder which sometimes escapes the care of modesty, and which coquetry sometimes so successfully imitates.

At this point Price evidently feels that he has reached the outer limits of plain speech for he takes refuge in Italian, which enables him to refer to proud breasts and scanty clothing. He is getting round to a discussion of the strategy involved in the way women manoeuvre, what Desmond Morris[10] calls "the erogenous zones" in women's clothing or its absence; but not living in our own unrestrained age, he goes back to the safer topic of the attractions that are presented in winding *picturesque* lanes. If he had written sixty years previously, he might not have been so restrained. His book has its interest as a product of the space between two ages, with eighteenth century Squire Westerns on one side of it and Victorian prudishness on the other.

In view of its dislike of "enthusiasm," the late eighteenth century attacked new fashions and ideas with a great deal of enthusiasm. Great men spent large sums in remodelling their gardens in accordance with the latest notions. Building "ruins" at good look-out points had been relatively common, but one noble lord went so far as to build a hermit's cell in his gardens (in a "grotto," of course) and to advertise for a "hermit" to live in it. But, illustrative of how complex is the interweaving between periods, already in as early as 1736, Queen Caroline, wife of George II, had had built in her garden an extraordinary structure known as "Merlin's Cave," after the famous magician of good King Arthur's day.[11] It was no more absurd than George IV's famous Pavilion of the 1820s at Brighton, England, still in existence; great people will have their fun. The Pavilion is probably the more interesting example of calculated irregularity – the "picturesque."

The transition from the symmetrical to the irregular – the "pictures-que" becomes almost by definition, the a-symmetrical – is easily observable not only in gardening and its accessories but in the things within the household, the ornaments, knick-knacks, minor *objets d'art* and especially the furniture, the area where "the mode" and people's anxiety to follow it always hastens the speed of change, though not as quickly as in the extreme example of fluctuation – ladies' "fashions." The straight lines and heavy design of seventeenth century oak furniture became lighter in the eighteenth century, when lighter woods, especially mahogany, began to come in and reached the peak of grace and symmetry with the second half of the eighteenth, the great age of the Adams brothers and Thomas Sheraton (1751-1806). Thence, slowly, curves crept in, until in the mid-nineteenth century "Victorian" furniture burst out in full riot of curves, bulbs, swellings-in swellings-out, in an orgy of ornamentation for ornamentations's sake.

Chairs *à la mode* were being made by Chippendale around 1750, and *la mode* of that period demanded about furniture at least a touch, at most, a great deal, of what was considered *Chinese*. The word introduces a large sub-topic in the coming of Romanticism, the place of Chinese and Indian influence on European taste and, deeper, on European attitudes.

Chinoiserie as an influence on art arose out of the trade with the Orient which, hardly known in the sixteenth century, increased rapidly towards the end of the seventeenth and became of major proportions in the eighteenth. The new trade encouraged *taste* not only in the literal meaning of that word – the taste of and for *tea* – but in the derived, for around tea a whole social ritual arose – tea cups, teapots, tea kettles, tea tables, all came in in increasing profusion. And along with the objects came the styles or supposed styles of the country from which the tea came.

Great Anna, whom three realms obey
Doth sometimes counsel take and sometimes *tea* ("tay")

wrote Pope in *The Rape of the Lock*. Tea ("tay," as of 1714) was not overly easy even for "Great Anna," Queen though she might be, ("great" though, she certainly was not) to secure in unlimited quantities. But as the great "East Indiamen" increased in numbers and carrying capacity, back they came with their holds full of the goods for which the sale in Europe seemed unlimited; lacquered furniture (a cult in itself), "Japanned" ware, "chintzes" and other textiles, and tea, tea, tea.

The vogue of *chinoiserie* required every fashionable or affluent hostess to furnish a *Chinese room*, and if she could not afford the real thing, she tried to get imitations made. For example, the French gradually pried out the secret of lacquering from the Chinese, and this spread eventually to England. In that way a considerable extension of range was given to some branches of European industry.

Here was one of the roots of the so-called Industrial Revolution, for the Eastern trade being far too much one way, it provoked a crisis in the English domestic production of textiles, threw weavers out of work, caused riots, with the usual accompaniments of smashed windows and destroyed stocks of goods. It called emphatically for return cargoes. Much of the eighteenth century was devoted to finding them; one interesting by-product of the search was the so-called "sing-sing box" playing a little tune, which acquired much favour in the eyes of the Chinese, so much so that it became one of the rocks on which the great Chinese trading house of Jardine, Mathieson was built.

But "sing-sing" boxes were hardly enough in themselves. The disproportion became ridiculous in the light of the small compass of some of the fabled "wealth of Ind'," as Thomas Pitt's diamond showed. While in India as a servant of the company, Thomas Pitt, grandfather of the great William, "procured" a huge diamond. How he got it remains something of a mystery, but Indian temples had idols and many idols were jewel-encrusted. We have to draw our own conclusions. At any rate, when the diamond, so it is related, was sold to the Regent of France, it fetched a huge sum which became the foundation of the Pitt family fortune.

Probably the Pitt diamond was not entered in any ship's manifest. But how was payment to be made for all the costly items that were? Sir Joshua Child, a late seventeenth century director, made light of the standard axiom that gold must only be imported, never exported, if a country were to prosper, and by carrying his point gave a jolt to those semi-sacred doctrines which later students have called "the Mercantile system." The solution to the Indian "drain of specie" was not found until cheap American cotton, cheap English labour and some power machinery were got together towards the end of the eighteenth century and the vast English cotton industry began to take shape, providing "the bagman's calico millennium" as Thomas Carlyle was to call it – the salesman's cotton heaven. Various efforts were made by law to prohibit imports into England of many Indian wares. But laws went for little when "ladies of quality" proved good at smuggling things through customs under capacious clothes, and equally proficient at bribing customs officers.

The vogue of *chinoiserie* and its by-products simply shows that the world was expanding in the eighteenth century and expanding, despite reason, proportion and symmetry; expanding, some would have said, because of the foolish shallow pates of women who were determined to be fashionable and "have nice things," despite silly man-made laws that would have restrained them. An expanding world – and *chinoiserie* seems to have swept over all Europe – had to mean expanding, or at least changing, fashions and attitudes. So symmetry, proportion and good taste got the worst of it and a door was opened for quite a new set of criteria. Let the word *chinoiserie* be expanded to exotic goods in general and there seems to be a good deal in the contention that here was an important root of Romanticism. Away with the old, the staid, the unchanging, away with immutable good tast. Bring in the new, the uneven, the bizarre, and, as all this was shortly to become the *picturesque*.[12]

III
Industry, Great Wars, Well-Being

If space could expand, so could time. The rediscovery of the Middle Ages is usually regarded as a late eighteenth century achievement, but popular impression and its reflections in taste must be distinguished from scholarly investigation; that came later. Interest in the old "Gothic" remains and love for the great monuments, such as the cathedrals, while it of course had waned with the change of religion, had never by any means ceased. Goethe in his *Dichtung und Wahrheit* speaks of the admiration and love awakened in him by the great Cathedral of Strasbourg, when he went to that city as a student in 1770.[13] There had always been knowledgeable defenders of "the old style of building" and well before Horace Walpole's pioneering adventure in using "the Gothic" in his new building of "Strawberry Hill" there had been care and even restoration of some of the old. We have to be careful to avoid too fully universalizing a change of style, whether in cathedrals or in wigs. The Gothic revival does not spring out of a vacuum. Like the Romantic revival in literature, it is a continuation of the past, as well as an imitation. As an architectural revolution, it consists in the number of the new structures to which it gives rise and in its huge geographical spread, embracing as it eventually did, the entire English-speaking world, wherever found, even India. Neo-Gothic architecture, still very much with us, made the transition from the Age of Light highly conspicuous. It took some generations to get rid of its eccentricities – its Caves of Merlin, or George IV's Brighton Pavilion, but eventually these were sloughed off and a new architectural aesthetic clearly established.

It would almost seem sometimes as if centuries had a habit of ending with "a big bang." The seventeenth century's demise was marked by the wars of Louis XIV and Marlborough, our own nineteenth by the volcanic eruption of 1914, and the eighteenth ended its course in the fires of revolution and dictatorship. The French Revolution blew the eighteenth century to pieces just as the First World War blew the nineteenth. In the primarily aesthetic fields of literature, and architecture such explosions do no irremediable damage. In other areas, economics and politics more particularly, the changes they work are written in the well-being and the blood of humanity.

It was the English in their happy insularity who were best able to take advantage of the economic changes. The eighteenth century advanced

England from a second rate power to a world power. Luckily for her, her wars were fought on other people's property and largely with other nations' soldiers. At Blenheim, 1704, Marlborough had only a handful of English soldiers under him. Even at Waterloo, Wellington had only about 30,000. War abroad and peace at home can be a forcing house for industrial production; it is no mystery why the eighteenth century is regarded as the century of "the Industrial Revolution," especially the Industrial Revolution in Great Britain. Like every other great shift in human situation, this one cast long shadows before it. Clever modern interpretations, indeed, seem almost to try to persuade us that it never occurred at all, that it was no more than an swelling-out of social processes long under way. That seems a matter of mere words. What would Francis Bacon have made of Thomas Newcomen's one-way steam pump? What did James Watt make out of it? No doubt the Industrial Revolution can be traced back to man's first use of metals, or beyond that to the invention of the bow and arrow. But what most people would agree on as the Industrial Revolution, the rapid succession of inventions that magnified production and especially the application to production of steam power was well under way by the end of the eighteenth century, destined to change the world. The men who understood its portent did not write poetry.

Such men could almost be regarded as a new breed. They were rapidly separating themselves from the rural life, gathering up machines for spinning and putting them into old barn, where they employed their neighbours to work them. Such a man was the grandfather of Sir Robert Peel, the later prime minister. Or they were sending ships into all manner of strange ports, buying tobacco from the planters in Virginia, growing sugar in the West Indies with slave labour, or making fortunes from the shipping that carried the slaves from Africa, as the ancestor of William Ewart Gladstone was supposed to have done. There were hard men among this new breed; at the moment, they were not much interested in running the country and left that to the traditional classes. But they knew what they wanted and had a way of getting it. If they felt that the overseas colonies were becoming rivals too vigorous to put up with, they knew how to get a new "Iron Act" out of government (1751) to restrain the upstarts. As a class they were probably not very nice men, but they were creating something that cut as deep into English life, and thence continental, as the goods they produced. They were creating a new class system.

"Praying, fighting and labouring men" was the mediaeval division of society, and deep into life had that gone. New centuries added new categories, not as fixed as the old; sailors and shipwrights, builders, weavers and the like. Then printers, and, by Elizabeth's reign, even dramatists and men of letters. Though the breed had long been known in small numbers, it remained mainly for the eighteenth century to add "captains of industry" – and the persons who under them, sank to lowlier and lowlier status. The English or Puritan Revolution, it was said then, and it still stands for the most part true, had been made "by the middling class of people." The French Revolution had its aristocratic participants, such as Mirabeau and "Philippe Egalité," but its power, too, seemed derived from the middle class, the more or less upper middle class of professional men and their like. It was captured, it must be remembered, by a middle class man, Napoleon Bonaparte. In the non-revolutionary countries, Great Britain, the Germanies, Austria, strong pockets of the older classes remained for long in strategic places; in the army, in law, in government. But eventually they, too yielded. The middle class, not remarkable for its meekness, yet like the meek, inherited the earth. If the transition to modern times is to be explained in a word, can there be one more satisfactory than what is dubbed "the Industrial Revolution"?

The Industrial Revolution brought both blessings and curses in its train, plenty of both. It seems rather clear that it raised the standard of well-being among considerable numbers of people, and this can be demon-strated by a rough statistical test. This consists in taking the span of life at various historical periods. The list used here is of "men of letters," poets and other literary figures, beginning with the sixteenth and seventeenth centuries. This class of persons was selected mainly because their life-spans were readily available but also because they represent a sector of society far from the bottom of affluence and not close to the top, either. The only English poet born in the sixteenth century to exceed the age of eighty apparently was Robert Herrick. Of literary persons born in the seventeenth century, some 9 per cent reached eighty or over, 15 per cent seventy to eighty, 13 per cent, sixty to seventy, 30 per cent, fifty to sixty, and 35 per cent died under the age of fifty. In the eighteenth century of a total of forty-four names, 16 per cent lived to eighty or over, 23 per cent died between seventy and eighty, 20 per cent between sixty and seventy (making 59 per cent living into their sixties), 14 per cent between fifty and sixty, and 30 per cent below the age of fifty. It would be easy to compile much longer lists, but the results probably would not be much different. In the eighteenth century, relatively fortunate people could expect to live considerably longer than their predecessors.

Coke, the great farmer who inherited some poor land in Norfolk, spent his life in redeeming it and lived to know that he had effected something like a revolution in English farming. Coke was a stalwart Whig and his country home was the scene year after year for the celebration of the Revolution of 1688, it being as much a part of his career to keep alive "the principles of '88" as to improve his land. He was not a radical – unless his marriage (in his seventies, to a young lady of eighteen, by whom he had several children) could be considered a radical act – but a man of liberal ideas, who looked back to a revolution, not forward to one. It was his like that, lacking in France, contributed to English well-being by increasing the food supply.[14]

Still more impressive testimony to the increasing well-being of Western man is rendered by the evident recoveries made from the great wars of the "Age of Reason." The German states are said to have been so desolated by the Thirty Years' War (1618-1648) that they took the rest of the century to recover, and France in the War of the Spanish Succession exhausted herself (causing Louis XIV to make the unprecedented gesture of an appeal to his people to rally round him). But after a generation of peace France was ready to fight again and the long period of warfare from 1743 to 1763 followed. In the later campaigns the situation probably became difficult, for a minister of Louis XV wrote impatiently to the hard-pressed Canadian colony – New France – that "when the house is on fire, one does not worry about the stables," but within a few years the country was ready to fight again against the hereditary foe in the War of the American Revolution. Another short interval of peace and then the close to a quarter of a century of warfare, the Revolutionary and Napoleonic Wars. But after 1815, France seemed to go on into relatively fair weather and her nineteenth century course was not that of a nation that had been exhausted by generations of warfare. France of course, like Great Britain, for the most part managed to fight her wars on other peoples' soil.

But warfare raged back and forth over the German lands, not by any means only in the Thirty Years' War. Yet Prussia raised itself into a kingdom in the eighteenth century. And the impression one gets from books like Goethe's *Dichtung und Wahrheit* is of German cities flourishing, the universities alive – in contrast to those of England, which were asleep – and of smiling countrysides about them. In both cases, much of this is to be put down mainly to space; Europe was not then the crowded continent that it has since become and warfare could go on with room for the warriors to march about without doing universal damage. But however the problem is viewed, recovery seems to have been quite rapid, and this no doubt is a testimonial to simple, hard-working people and an economy still close to the soil.

Great Britain in the eighteenth century had not changed into the industrial country of later years. It, too, could draw strength from a relatively simple economy – it did not need to import wheat until the 1790s. Its strength lay, however, in its intact insularity. In all the wars many were the good Britons who lay awake at night worrying whether the French would invade or not. But successful invasion never came, perhaps, even in 1805, was not seriously intended, despite Napoleon's great camp at Boulogne. And in the eighteenth century, Great Britain clinched her command of the sea, which opened to her the productions of the entire world.

Britannia needs no bulwarks,
No towers along the steep:
Her march is o'er the mountain waves,
Her home is on the deep.

The paradox of British life was not the island's ability to support eighteenth century warfare, but in spite of the brilliance of victory, the creation of a way of life in urban industrialism which entailed on succeeding generations burdens of unimagined weight.

"England rules the seas, France the land, and Germany – the clouds!" the old saying used to go. There was truth in it and its truth may have had much to do with the later movement for German unity. As for ruling the land, that does not seem to have been a profitable business. France gained nothing from her mid-century wars. She gained nothing from her assistance to the American colonies, except some uncertain goodwill and the spiteful satisfaction of seeing the English world divided. She gained nothing from her Napoleonic debauch. Frenchmen might exclaim "Ah, but her ideas!" Was France, then, the nation that ruled the clouds? But once more, after Waterloo, as in previous centuries (and the succeeding one), completely defeated, with the Cossacks camping in the parks of Paris, there she was, her soil under crop, the genial sun overhead, once more ready to start over again on the path of glory. But this time, luckily for the world, on minor adventures only.

While Frenchmen were being devoured on the battlefield or dying in the snows of Russia, Englishmen with little discomfort to themselves, were picking up the waste spaces of the outer world. One great contretemps there had been, the American Revolution. What Great Britain lost in that unnecessary and fratricidal struggle is shadowed forth by what has become of what she did not lose. She did not lose Canada and in the great wars of the twentieth century, Canada was to send to the mother country's defence (by far the major reason for her action), hundreds of thousands of her sons. This, few Englishmen know. Winston Churchill's wartime speeches and his war histories show hardly a trace of it. She did not lose that which she did not yet possess, Australia. But one year after the Peace of Versailles, 1783, Captain Philips embarked in British ships to found a colony in Australia. "All sailed with empire in their hearts," it has been said of his expedition. She did lose the thirteen American colonies. The wrench of heart for many, perhaps most of the colonists was severe. The future President, John Adams, once declared that every step he took away from his past, he took painfully. But when the wrench came, it tore up their ancient allegiance and made the British foreigners. The War of Independence was not a revolution in the extreme sense of the term; rather, it was a civil war. And a civil war which in interesting respects was the continuation of the Great Rebellion of the seventeenth century. In it brother fought against brother and son against father.

Benjamin Franklin's son became a United Empire Loyalist. The ancestor of the Jarvis family of Ontario was a man whose father remained in his old New England home. Many of Washington's officers had formerly been British – Montgomery who died at Quebec, 1775, Gates, the victor of Saratoga. As a civil war, waged in large part by "the middling class of people" against armies commanded by British aristocrats, it strengthened the middle class in America and by a commercial backlash, in Great Britain, too.

Great wars and two great revolutions are surely enough for one century. Even without them, the times were momentous. Many of the aspects of a mediaevalism that still remained were weakened and dying, much that was to come was waiting to be born. When the war ended at Waterloo, 1815, the eighteenth century ended. The century of ferment could give way to the Century of Hope.

Notes

1.   A good overview of this literary movement is afforded by Crane Brinton, *The Political Ideas of the English Romanticists* (Russell, New York, 1962, republication of London edition of 1926), chapter 1.
2.   Rosalie G. Grylls, *William Godwin and His World* (London, 1953). This book gives a fair picture of life among the ultra-intellectuals of London around the year 1800. It has good insights into the more ridiculous side of ultra-advancement and enough copulation to satisfy modern readers with similar propensities.
3.   *The Decline and Fall of the Romantic Ideal* (Cambridge University Press, 1936), p. 3.
4.   A short list of such samples, but of varying range: Lucas, *op. cit.;* C. M. Bowra. *The Romantic Imagination* (Harvard University Press, 1949). Crane Brinton, *The Political Ideas of the English Romanticists, op. cit.* Bonamy Dobrée, *Introduction to English Literature,* Vol. III, *Augustans and Romantics* (London, Cresset Press, 1940). B. Ifor Evans, *Literature and Science* (London, 1954). F. W. Stokoe, *German Influence in the English Romantic Period* (Cambridge University Press, 1926). Devendra P. Varma, *The Gothic Flame* (Russell, New York, 1957, re-issued 1966). For other than the purely literary aspects of Romanticism, Leslie Stephen, *English Thought in the Eighteenth Century,* (2 Vols., London, 1876). B. Sprague Allen, *Tides in English Taste, 1619-1800: A Background for the Study of Literature op. cit.,* (2 Vols., New York, 1958). Uvedale Price, *Essays on the Picturesque as compared with the Sublime and the Beautiful* (London, 1810). The Pelican *Guide to English Literature,* ed. Boris Ford, II, *From Blake to Byron* (1957).

5.   Varma, *The Gothic Flame, op. cit.*

6.   H. Heine, *Die Beiden Grenadiere*   (The Two Grenadiers).

7.   Lucas, *op. cit.*, p. 68.

8.   From *Lines written a few miles above Tintern Abbey.*

9.   See book list, footnote 5, *supra.*

10.   Author of *The Naked Ape, The Human Zoo,* etc., books of biological-anthropological popularization, published as Bantam Books, but originally in London by Jonathan Cape in the 1960s.

11.   Allen, *Tides in English Taste, op. cit.,* II, p. 136, reproduces a picture of it.

12.   A good short account of the cult of *chinoiserie* is to be found in Allen, *Tides in English Taste, op. cit.,* I, chapters IX-XII.

13.   It made precisely the same impression upon the present writer when he visited Strasbourg 180 years later. But 180 years later, just across from the Cathedral, there was a restaurant whose walls, reflecting the colonial experience, were covered with frescoes of life – the Congo! Time had rolled by, the world had expanded.

14.   For Coke of Norfolk, see Mrs. A. M. W. Stirling, *Coke of Norfolk and his Friends* (London, 1913).

CHAPTER SIXTEEN

Century of Hope

I
An Overview of the Century

Compared with the relative simplicity and straightforwardness of the eighteenth century, the nineteenth is complexity itself. Finding a pattern marking the hundred years that lie between Waterloo, 1815, and the outbreak of the first Great War in 1914 is a daunting task. It would be much easier to resort to something specific, another monograph, shall we say, among the thousands already written about it, than to look at the century as a whole and try to find some unity about it. Does it have any unity? Is it not rather a vast heap of odds and ends which may be sorted out into any arrangement desired?

The nineteenth century does have unity. The theme that marks it is the struggle of religion with science, or, more generally, with knowledge. The first part of the century is marked by revivals of orthodox Christianity, the second part by the triumph of knowledge. In between the two parts lies a battlefield whereon orthodoxy and science fight it out. We are back to the conception which previous chapters have sought to illustrate: emotion giving way to intellect. At the end of the century, there appear plain signs of that loss of a sense of direction which is precursor of a change in the historical climate, leading to loss of the old values and a period of confusion in which men grope for new. That, however, is something only emphatically developed in our own times.

230

In 1815, twenty-two years of almost constant war lay behind men. Dozens of gigantic battles had been fought, millions of men had been killed, as many maimed, as many uprooted from their homes and family life. No wonder that after at long last, when Napoleon had been safely hived up in St. Helena, the average man and the unaverage too, should have longed for peace and quiet. It would have been a miracle if conservative attitudes had not come to the fore. They were to be given expression not only in the political settlements by which, under the term Legitimism, the hands of the clock, it was hoped, would simply be turned back, but also by various writers who undertook to put the idea, Legitimism, in semi-philosophic terms; such were Joseph de Maistre[1] and Louis de Bonald in France, such had been Edmund Burke in Great Britain.

But something else had come out of the wars in addition to mere conservatism. The old world had been laid in ruin; now was the opportunity to build a better one. Despotism had been cast down. Slaughter had ended. Hope appeared. Hope is necessarily individual. Hope inspires, but it is individual persons that it inspires. The word should be used in the plural, rather than in the singular. In 1815, the hopes of European mankind varied. Great words like justice or well-being had to be embodied in achievement. That task would not be easy.

Here lay the initial rift in the post-war Europe. Peace and order, yes. But change and new life, too. The hard paradoxical saying of the Prince of Peace was to be born in upon men; "I came not to bring peace but a sword."

Demolished by the guns of war along with much other and less valuable material, had been the eighteenth century "Age of Reason." That age had scorned its past, the gloomy old "Gothic" past. Now the new age was to show itself equally impatient of it, of its predecessor's formalities and its aridities. "Let us have life," the Romantics had long been saying, "not mere manners." They had found many spokesmen. Perhaps Goethe had put the point as compactly as well as it could be;

Grau, theurer Freund, ist alle Theorie,
Und grün des Lebens goldner Baum.[2]

Gray, dear friend, is all theory
And green Life's golden tree.

Well could another poet sing, "The World's great age begins anew." That line in itself goes far to explain the nature of the next generation; a generation of conflict between old and new, each with its own idea.

Underlying the conflict there could be heard more loudly each year, another sound, the sound of the mounting changes in production which cumulatively go by the name of the Industrial Revolution. The Industrial Revolution, with its mills and machines, its ceaseless flow of new inventions, creates new classes, powers all "movements," impels new philosophies, deepens all divisions.

The century presents a few pivotal dates, 1830 and 1832, 1848, 1859, 1864, 1870, and 1914. Upon the events associated with these years, the course of history turns.

The generation of confused movements, conservatism struggling with reform and both playing their roles vis-à-vis increasing industrialism, ends in 1848, the "Year of Revolutions." Thenceforth begins another period of about a generation, marked by pitched battles between old and new. During it, the pope (Pio Nono) proclaims of himself alone the new dogma of "the Immaculate Conception" (1854), of himself alone issues "the Syllabus of Errors" (1864) and in the Vatican Council of 1870 procures the Decree of Papal Infallibility. On the other side of the battlefield an epoch-making document appears in Charles Darwin's *Origin of Species* (1859). Thenceforth, the sweep of mind symbolized by Darwin's great thesis goes on in mounting crescendo. Many are the counter-attacks from the right but slowly the tide of battle turns and it now seems clear that victory went to the new legions of science. The century ends with a measure of success for a counter-attack by the right, but it was a success something like "the Battle of the Bulge" in the Second World War – encouraging from the German point of view, but destined to failure, failure symbolized by one man's name – Dreyfus. As with so many passages of history, the English-speaking world, nourished by isolation, reinforced by the New World, stands as partial exception to these statements.

In 1914, the nineteenth century is blown sky high. When the pieces come down after the war, another period of history opens.

II
Post-War Reaction

In the Napoleonic wars, every state in Europe had been mauled about, its rulers displaced, Napoleonic puppets put in their places, an Austrian princess given in marriage to the Italo-French arriviste. Napoleon, it is said, became fond of referring to the emperor of Austria, brother-in-law of the late Louis XVI, as "my uncle." Marie Antoinette, Louis's wife, was the sister of this man who became emperor of Austria and was forced to give his daughter to Napoleon. When Louis de Bourbon, son of the late Louis XVI, came back to Paris as Louis XVIII, it became a saying that "he had been brought back in the baggage train of the allies." It was not an unmixed reception he got from Paris. The short reigns of the two returned, "legitimate" Bourbons, Louis XVIII, 1814-1824 and his brother Charles X, 1824-1830, while tolerably peaceful, could hardly have been other than attempts at conservatism. But the French people were not prepared to go back to the days before '89 and so the Revolution came to be for them, and for the rest of the century continued to be, the basic question.

Discussion of the burning question naturally was constant and given the French mentality, eloquent, stormy, filled with narrow, logical realism and the unrealism of wide sweeping generalization.

Its classical examples seldom seemed to get much beyond great general terms. In its first period two such men were outstanding; Joseph de Maistre (1754-1821) and Louis de Bonald (1753-1840). Both of them were "unreconstructed" royalists and both wrote in severe, even unmeasured, terms, of the results of the revolutionary period. "Government is by its very nature unlimited. No king can be bound by law or promise, nor can he be denied recourse to any measures that may suggest themselves to him." De Maistre had been Sardinian ambassador to Russia, 1803-1817, and in Russia evidently he had studied an "ideal" régime. De Bonald was no less extreme; "When God wished to punish France, he took away the Bourbons from her governance," he wrote. De Bonald had been an *émigré*, returned, made his peace with Napoleon, became a peer of France in 1823, and in 1830 refused to take the oath of allegiance to Louis Philippe. His son became Archbishop of Lyons.

Both these men were extreme authoritarians and it is hardly fair to couple them, as is often done, with a man of a different outlook, Edmund Burke. Burke had launched his thunders against the Revolution, especially the days of the Terror, and he had become more and more conservative as he grew older, but he could be said to be well over a century in advance of the French thinkers, although dead (1797) well before they became of consequence. It would be amusing to think of Burke asserting for George III the authority they demanded for a monarch. Burke was a constitutionalist, and his doctrine allowed for changes that were demonstrably necessary. It was not against all change whatsoever. Today he probably would be classed as a "middle of the road" conservative, not as a "diehard." At any rate the degree of opposition to the forces of the age in France up to 1830 could hardly have been matched in England, where Tory ministries could contain such men as Wallace and William Huskisson, enact liberalizing trade laws[3] and even emancipate the Roman Catholics from their legal disabilities. "Catholic Emancipation," 1829. Typically, English attitudes to Roman Catholicism had always been full of anomalies. The Duke of Norfolk, the senior peer, had always been Catholic and his duty at Coronations had been to administer to the king the anti-Papal oath of the Act of Succession. Alexander Pope, as a Catholic does not seem to have complained of his lot. It was in Ireland that the full weight of anti-Catholic measures had been felt.

Nevertheless, to paint British governmental action after the wars in *couleurs de rose* would be completely misleading. Local manifestations of

French Revolutionary Jacobinism had badly scared the secure classes. The new machine industry, threatening, so workmen thought, to throw them out of work, scared the lower classes. The heavy post-war depression after 1815 scared the middle classes. The sudden shift from years of war to years of peace, the uncertainties which peace brought with it – peace hath its terrors no less than war – all such matters led to an uneasy, even a cruel, period after Waterloo, a period in which what were probably no more than riots of the discontented and the threatened, were met by severe repression. Those were the days of the "Spa Field riots" (1816), the "Manchester Martyrs" (1819), the "Cato Street Conspiracy" (1820). This it must be said, was a genuine conspiracy by extremists, a conspiracy involving a plan to murder cabinet ministers. It was not widespread and other such examples of fright and disorder. For a time, *habeas corpus* was suspended and the Criminal Laws, which had always been unbelievably severe, were strengthened by additional acts. Through such offences as *blasphemy*, they could, and were used to suppress opinion, as well as actions. The excess of severity is usually put down to the reactionaries in the cabinet of Lord Liverpool; among them, Viscount Castlereagh was singled out. As foreign minister, he had had a good deal to do with the reactionary nature of the war settlement at Vienna, with its principle of *Legitimism*. But Castlereagh balanced his account by committing suicide in 1822 and thereafter reaction of an extreme kind ebbed, leaving English evolution to go on its usual empiric course, though with enough of right-wing Toryism in it to make a hard fight against reform of Parliament and eventually in that way, to bring the country close to a revolutionary outbreak.[4]

By contrast with Great Britain or even, indeed, France, the German Confederation (1815) under the lead of Prince Metternich, presented the very essence of arbitrary government. The Carlsbad Decrees of 1819 gave to the authorities the right and duty of suppressing practically everything in the way of opinion that did not meet with their approval. The Decrees were specifically aimed at the Universities:

1. A special representative of the ruler shall be appointed for each university with appropriate instructions and extended powers. . . The functions of this agent shall be to see to the strictest enforcement of existing laws and disciplinary regulations; to observe carefully the spirit which is shown by the instructors in their public lectures and regular courses, and without directly interfering in scientific matters, or in the method of teaching, to give a salutary direction to the instruction, having in view the future attitudes of the students. . .

2. The confederated governments mutually pledge themselves to remove from the universities, or other public educational institutions

all teachers who by obvious deviation from their duties or by exceeding the limits of their functions or by the abuse of their legitimate influence over the youthful minds or by propagating harmful doctrines hostile to public institutions shall have unmistakably proved their unfitness for the important offices assigned to them. . .

The Decrees went on at considerable length and in the section devoted to Press Laws gave the authorities full right to suppress newspapers, or prohibit their publication.

The Decrees were so extreme that they may have helped to their own weakening. If they had been fully and indefinitely maintained in force, there never could have been any pretension again to liberty in the German Confederation.[5]

The westerly winds off the Gulf Stream, those winds that advance the seasons from west-south-west to east-north-east (as opposed to the simple south-to-north pattern in America) and keep Copenhagen in winter as warm as Milan, blow over Europe right into the depths of Russia. Napoleon had "blown over" Europe in much the same way as the wind but with even more drastic results. His retreat had brought Russian soldiers across Europe and they had seen Paris. It must have been hard for intelligent Russian officers to return to the arbitrariness that constituted government in Russia after seeing the West. They were metaphorically the west wind thawing the Russian snow. The Czar Alexander had blown hot and cold by turns, now despotic, now liberal to the point of embarrassment. Alexander's successor, his brother Nicholas, was a stern cold autocrat with no room for the advanced idealistic notions that had blown eastward. Some of the military men who had brought them sought to translate them into political action. But their half-hearted revolt, the first Russian movement towards constitutionalism, was easily suppressed, the so-called "Decembrist" movement of 1825.

With Russia extraordinary things could happen and one of the most extraordinary was the way in which the idea of "the Holy Alliance" originated, to be passed through the brain of the Czar Alexander and thence into the high councils of Europe. As might be anticipated, the story concerned a woman. Julie Barbe de Vietinghof was born at Riga in Latvia in 1764. She was a "Balt," as the old German-Russian aristocracy of those provinces were termed. Of strict Lutheran parentage, at the age of eighteen, Julie was married to another "Balt," Baron de Krüdener. He was fifteen years older than she was and had already been divorced twice. By the lady's family, he was considered an excellent match having all the prospects of an excellent diplomatic career ahead of him. But for Julie, it was merely a *mariage de convenance*. She was destined to find that she possessed a power far more powerful than the power wielded by the diplomat – the power to attract love. Her first *affaire* was with a young

French officer. Under his protection, disguised as a servant, she travelled about Europe. The *affaire* was not her last pilgrimage in amorous rhapsody. For many years, she moved restlessly from city to city, now in the company of a man, now alone.

Her marriage held by a thread but was not discontinued. Her lovers included various French *émigrés* and a priest, Abbé Becker. As she grew older, to balance the decline of her beauty, she tried to attract attention by the audacity of her toilettes. In early middle age, she fell in with various German pietists of obscure origin and through some of them she possibly genuinely, "got religion." It is a familiar phenomenon with many high-strung, beautiful and clever women as their youth recedes. Their need for attention, and possibly affection, drives them to seek publicity and in this art Julie surpassed the most expert of modern American advertisers. Her loves, her religion, her literary forays – apparently with a certain merit – and her entrancingly successful attempts at notoriety, went on for some years.

Towards the end of the great wars, just before Waterloo, she found herself near the Czar's headquarters in the neighbourhood of Heidelberg. The news of the allied defeats at Ligny and Quatre Bras reached Alexander, the czar, and plunged him into depression. At that moment, Julie arrived on the scene. She is said to have pushed past the astonished attendants and found the Czar alone. The interview lasted for three hours. "When she left him, Alexander's eyes were full of tears." By her fervency, to say nothing of her charm, she had converted him, made an old-fashioned Christian of him, this man who had been brought up without religion. Thereafter he was devout. The episode recalls the story of the late Clare Luce and the pope; after a similar interview, the agitated pope is said to have been heard exclaiming "But, my dear Mrs. Luce, I already am a Catholic." At any rate, out of this neurotic pair of minds came the inflated statement known to history as "the Holy Alliance." Three sovereigns declare in the name of the Trinity "their irrevocable determination to be guided in their public and private conduct entirely by the rules of justice, love and truth contained in the Christian religion. . ."

The so-called Holy Alliance, thus so solemnly grounded in Christian principle, was not taken as seriously by the others as by Alexander. An English statesman called its documentary form "a piece of sublime mystification and nonsense." Others spoke of the Alliance as "a trade union of kings to repress liberty." But when a century later President Woodrow Wilson went to France after the First World War and met Clemenceau, that ironical Frenchman, somewhat astonished at the innocence of the well brought-up son of the Presbyterian manse, scornfully remarked "He speaks like Jesus Christ." The two situations were not dissimilar. A glimpse of ultimate idealism breaks through the murk and people, well-knowing that splendid declarations of principle are easily made by great autocrats and presidents well secured from the necessity of implementing them, make fun of it. The Kellogg-Briand Pact for the abolition of war (1928) is another example. But where did the great attempts in political architecture come from, these structures of our own day, the Hague Court of 1907, the League of Nations, the United Nations?

As for Julie de Krüdener, having allowed her tongue to wag too freely about the origin of the famous document, she lost the czar's favour and passed the remainder of her life in the restless performance of good works.[6] After that, thirty years of stern rule for Russia until another czar with other ideas ascended the throne.

Life and history took such a decided turn after 1815 as to warrant a brief apperçu of the subsequent sequence down to our own day. Romanticism begins to displace classicism about 1770: that is familiar. It reaches its apex in the immediate post-Revolutionary decade, say about 1800 before Napoleon's real nature and motives have become too obvious. It declines after 1830, when the intellectual phase begins to mount. Intellectualism (Science) has a clear run (with the minor "kick-back" of the social gospel and perhaps the major, of idealistic socialism) until the next phase of disintegration say post-1914 (liberalism, permissiveness, anarchy). It is in this phase that we are at present. Can the first "cat's-paws" of authoritarianism, mysticism, feeling-emotion be discerned (1978)?

Notwithstanding the ease with which ideas—and notions—were able to sweep over the whole of Europe, each leading country produced its own version of them: European civilization, as preceding centuries had illustrated, was diverse in its uniformity, uniform in its diversity. In the generation after Waterloo, Italy, France, the Germanies, Great Britain, even Russia, produced individual answers to the deep problems presented to that age. The deepest of the problems, inspiring the conservative reaction referred to above, arose out of the question of religion. The age of George IV and William IV in Great Britain, of the Restoration and the July Monarchy in France, do not on the surface appear to have been overwhelmingly religious in nature, but if they are looked at below the surface, it is not hard to perceive deep concern about the foundations of belief. It is to be remembered that everywhere in the westernmost countries the growing force of the Industrial Revolution was creating a new world, with new classes of men and new attitudes towards life and that parallel to it, in the unfree countries, emotion was gathering up which must burst forth into revolt, revolt based on those essentially religious dynamics, the hatred of tyranny, the yearning for freedom and the intense passion for the group into which men are born, that we call nationalism.

Many a historian has seen in the challenge to the old, familiar beliefs one of the root causes of the French Revolution. Another root cause, it has been proclaimed over and over again, was the teachings of Rousseau. The Revolution occurred, Europe underwent its twenty-two years of war and the trials of war and when peace came again, the world looked quite different to the sons from what it had to the fathers. Out of such circumstances, the phase of history known formally as "the Romantic movement" proceeded. Life came to seem larger than Newtonian formulae, men ceased to be much interested in a kind of mathematical monasticism (few, really ever had been – not when a good dinner or a pretty woman came along, anyway). Romanticism opened the doors through which the world that the last two chapters have tried to describe could be seen. Again, Goethe's golden tree of life, no ash-grey theories.

The intimate relationship between Romanticism and religion in some of its aspects is easily established. The Romantic person in whatever sphere of life his interests centre, seeks to transcend the present, to push at the limits of the possible, to grasp the ungraspable – romantic explorers must get to the source of the rivers, to the top of the mountain. They must conquer Everest. So must the religious Romantic: he puts it that he must find God. Men have always been caught up in that search: religious romanticism is nothing new. But in certain ages, it expands, increases its following, makes a mark on the public mind. Such an age seems to have occurred in post-Waterloo Europe. Not only was the humanitarian atmosphere of society becoming much more conspicuous than in the previous century but there was evident throughout the whole range of Western Christianity a new life and a vast increase in vigour. This change in religious atmosphere occurred more or less simultaneously in the English-speaking world, in Germany, in France and to some degree in Italy too. Here was the typical religious revival which heralded the approach of what was to be in many respects a new world. It is easy to put down this shift in values to one sole cause – reaction against nearly a quarter century of war and disturbance. The Revolutionary and Napoleonic cataclysm, of course, should be given its due weight, which was vast. People were utterly sick of war. France is supposed to have lost two or three million of her sons in the fighting and the rest of Europe probably lost as many or more. No wonder reaction set in: anything for a quiet life must have been the unconscious thought of most Europeans.

Great Britain was the only state in western Europe that had remained unconquered, the only one in Europe that had not known the Napoleonic soldier on her soil. Yet in Great Britain the conservative reaction was possibly sharper than in other countries, sharper than in France where it did not exclude much freedom of discussion. Great Britain had felt its institutions seriously in danger: not only actual threat of invasion but subversion from within by those subtle invaders, ideas, and by the semi-revolutionary effects of the new machines. Those were the days of the machine breakers – the "Luddite rioters" – and the more pernicious individuals who everywhere where speaking for the submerged: the preachers and local preachers of the fast-spreading new denomination, the Methodists. It did not avail that "local preachers" by mounting the pulpits of the Methodist chapels were diverted from the early nineteenth century equivalent of the mob-orator's soap box. The Methodist was a new and despicable religious innovator and as such, found little favour from those who were not far removed from him in faith, the Evangelicals of the established church, for the great horrible English gulf of caste yawned between them.

Reaction, the natural turn to conservatism after a period of disturbance, then, may be accounted a large factor in the sudden post-war shift in values, but these things do not explain it all. The classes that had been most marked by eighteenth century scepticism very possibly were scared back into orthodoxy, more or less deeply felt – after all, the established church was *their* church and it existed almost as much to affirm English-ism as Christianity – but the lower middle and lower classes had not been touched by such matters, which were of the great world above their heads. Many of them were now shepherded out of the virtual Paganism of their fathers into the new fold of Methodism. Among the new literate, who every year were increasingly numerous, there would be few familiar with Voltaire and Rousseau, many who read works of pious devotion. The traditions of a nation do not change overnight and the traditions of Great Britain were, with relatively minor exceptions, wholly orthodoxly Christian.

Add to general considerations, the severe assistance of the law and the courts – the prohibitions against "undesirable" writers such as Tom Paine, the prosecutions for blasphemy, the many "free thinkers" who, their books suppressed, were given heavy fines and long terms of impris-onment. From the point of view of liberty, the generation after Waterloo does not constitute the most distinguished page in British history. Britons could boast of their political liberty but those who departed from some form of Christian orthodoxy as "free thinkers," even as Unitarians, often had a rough time of it. As atheists, they would as soon have been received into the homes of "respectable" (a word much in vogue) people as rattlesnakes. Luckily there were no more hangings, drawings and quarter-ings, while burning-at-the-stake had long since become merely an evil memory. Yet prosecutions went on until the middle of the century and afterwards, though in diminishing numbers. Full liberty of conscience could hardly be considered accorded in Great Britain until in the 1880s when Charles Bradlaugh, an avowed atheist, after long debate, was al-lowed to take his seat in Parliament.[7]

III
The Post-War Shift in Values

Neither reaction nor persecution are adequate in themselves to explain the rapid shift of values in British life after 1815. From Paganism at the bottom to scepticism at the top, Britain quickly moved to hold the position of the most orthodox country religiously in Europe outside of Spain – the only one of the major countries, indeed, in which traditional Christianity once more became strong and cherished throughout the entire range of society. Across the ocean, her daughters, especially the United States, followed in her footsteps, or set the pace. To this day it is the English-speaking countries in which Protestantism is still most alive. "The spirit bloweth whithersoever it listeth." Whatever the explanation, there can be no doubt about the fact, especially beginning with the post-war generation, say from about 1830. No leadership came from the court, under two monarchs whose examples few decent men or women would have wished to follow.

But when the young Victoria came to the throne in 1837, a very different story began to unfold. Here was a monarch who could be idealized and given a representative character. As her reign wore on and her prolific domesticity unfolded (she had nine children), more and more she reflected the times about her and it is just that her name should be given to the age. There can be no question about the general nature which that age assumed. The typical person became the sober church-goer, the contributor to good causes, the earnest observer of the British Sunday. The Victorian age saw established and dominant that neo-Puritanism, which was a close reflection of seventeenth century Puritanism in its severity of observance and of its moral code. Humans being humans, naturally there were many individual failures to live up to the generally accepted standards especially in sexual relationships.

Yet no age in history, surely, has managed to impose a more rigorous code of sex on people than did the Victorian. The slightest allusion to natural functions in mixed company would have been regarded as unpardonable impropriety. In New England, so it was said, even the tables had to have their legs covered: in fact no Victorian lady had a pair of legs, only carefully concealed "limbs." Smells which once had been honest stinks, became odours. Babies appeared "out of the nowhere into here," brought by the doctor, found under blackberry bushes.

The Victorian novel, forced to admit the intrusion of nature into the lives of some of its characters, did its best, as Dickens made one of them say, to avoid bringing the blush of shame to the young maid's cheek, but Victorianism did not remove the streetwalker from the London streets. It probably did not have much to do with the percentage of "fallen women" in the total population, but that is a subject on which we have no statistics,

no "scientific" evidence on the sexual *mores* of the Victorians as compared with our own is to be had. But there can be no question of what
was the dominant conviction of what they ought to be. It was the attitude
which gives to the age its antiquated, unacceptable ring, "Victorianism,"
something to laugh at. The reaction of the great-grandsons to the habits of
their great-grandfathers was emphatic.

Victorian Puritanism is too large a subject to be canvassed here in any
depth, but "if you wish its monument, look around you," for it still is
strong and vigorous over large areas of our own society. In Victorian
days, it was probably most evident among the rising middle classes and
those below them who were touched by Methodism: these classes in our
own days have moved on towards other life patterns, but Victorianism
still holds almost untouched among millions of the "lower middles"
where it remains the buttress of their faith and their behaviour. Is it too
much to say that Victorianism remade the world, the English-speaking
world anyway, in its own image?

Victorian Puritanism being closely correlated with non-conformism has
had a bad press in Great Britain, where most of the prominent literary
figures were from the traditional classes or took their colour from them.
Newman, Disraeli, Carlyle, Arnold, Ruskin, have had unkind things to
say about the barrenness of this or that aspect of Victorian life and some of
them about most aspects of it. In all the unkindnesses, the same elements
are criticized. Victorian Puritanism is hopelessly middle class. It is taking
England out of its traditional course, that happy past of limited monarchy,
limited aristocracy, limited democracy (so Burke and Disraeli after him).
The middle class are mere money-grubbers. They are narrow minded.
They have no ideals and no imagination. They are giving England up to a
wholly materialistic way of life. Doing so, they are destroying England's
beautiful countryside, building railways through it – so Ruskin. Or they
are catering government to cater to fools – so Carlyle. In short, they have
triumphed over the old order, that old aristocratic order which for par-
venus like Disraeli and even for cultured Matthew Arnold, embodied
civilization in its higher form.

If history be read from another angle, it would seem that the major
preoccupations of that same aristocracy were sport, fighting as an English
variety of sport, good living, with conservation of all privileges, and
fornication, most emphatically fornication. Whatever the exact truth
(which can never be ascertained), it is evident that the dominantly puritan
atmosphere of nineteenth century England set up many tensions, and
equally evident that for both sides of the debate, "religion" was a matter
of primary importance. The large point for the present study is that there
can be no doubt that in the new century, a sharp shift of attitude, of values,
occurred. And not only in England, but throughout the European world.

To change religious attitudes in one direction is to change them in many and so after the wars, the mystical side of Christianity once more began to find its place. It affected mainly the educated few. The rational acceptance by "the reasonable man" of first causes began to find competition from those aspects of life which turn on life's mysteries, on "the communion of the soul with its maker" and not least, on the attempts made to translate yearnings, the emotional needs of men into visible form through the agencies of age-old but somewhat neglected devices: the "visible church," with its ceremonies, its vestments, its approach to the historic usages of that other church which was just at that moment, 1829 given, in Protestant England, the legal right to exist.

John Henry Newman was born in 1801, the child of relatively prosperous parents. His school and college days stretched over the post-war period. Pious airs surrounded him from birth and in the "Oxford movement" he found similar atmosphere. His whole career was to be an amplification of the piety of his youth. As a scholar and a stylist, he was greatly gifted. When in the autumn of 1845 he became a convert to Roman Catholicism, the act created a major sensation in England. It also, it has been said, "knocked the bottom out of the Oxford movement." There had been a considerable number of Anglican parsons "going over to Rome" and with Newman's spectacular exit from the church of England, much of the old Protestant anti-papal emotion was once more stirred up. It says a good deal for British tolerance that in 1851, the government of the day accepted for enactment "The Ecclesiastical Titles Bill" which, with limitations, allowed the church of Rome once more to erect bishoprics in Great Britain. The redoubtable Palmerston, it is said, on being informed that another group of clergymen had "just gone over," exclaimed: "Report to me when the greengrocers begin to go over: then I shall become alarmed." Few "greengrocers," however, then or subsequently were reported as "going over." The "Oxford movement" ran its course. In essence it had been little more than an indulgence in the higher nostalgia for those who felt comforted by their own devotion to traditionalism. It had no strongly, fortified philosophical basis, though much traditional learning. Eventually it subsided into that branch of the established church which finds its satisfaction in ritual.

Newman's *Apologia pro vita sua* (1864) has justly been adjudged to "rank with St. Augustine's *Confessions* and Pascal's *Thoughts* as one of the classics of religious autobiography."[8] To grasp the nature of the Oxford movement and the Anglican revival of the nineteenth century, one need read no further than Newman. An illustration of the diveristy and intensity of these nineteenth century convictions is afforded by the two Newman brothers, John and Frank. While John Henry became a Catholic, Frank went the other way and evolved into something close to atheism.[9]

The two branches of the British religious revival were very different. It is not apparent that the High Church Anglicans – Anglo-Catholics, as they later came to be called – were at that time much concerned with the condition of their fellow men. Theirs was a subjective and individual attitude. To the outsider, it seems a selfish attitude: seek God in prayer and the mysteries of the sacraments, seek your own relationship with God, establish beyond doubt that the path you are taking is the true path which others must follow or disregard at their peril.

There is, however, one heritage of the Oxford movement still surviving which few, surely, would wish to see lost, that is to say, the great classical hymns of the nineteenth century known and loved wherever the English tongue is spoken. Newman's own "Lead, Kindly Light" is among the best known of these:

Lead, Kindly Light, amid the encircling gloom
Lead Thou me on
The night is dark and I am far from home
Lead Thou me on.

Keep Thou my feet, I do not ask to see
The distant scene:[10] one step enough for me . . .

Alongside this great poem of Newman's might equally well be put "Abide with me" by Henry Francis Lyte, 1793-1847:

Abide with me; fast falls the eventide
The darkness deepens, Lord with me abide;
When other helpers fail the comforts flee,
Help of the helpless, O abide with me . . .

The hymn, it will be recalled, continues:

Swift to its close ebbs out life's little day
Earth's joys grow dim, its glories fade away,
Change and decay in all around I see.
O Thou who changest not, abide with me . . .

Apart from the controversies, apart from theological speculation, no higher expressions of the innermost religious spirit, that intense urge to trust in something greater than the self, surely could be found.

No stronger contrast could have been offered to Anglican ritualism of this type than Methodism. John Wesley constantly insisted that religion must be a link between men. His followers early came to be called "the Connection." One found oneself in his fellows, not in monastic solitude. Wesley would have nothing to do with that side of Christianity, which he would have found merely a form of self-indulgence. No cloistered virtue for him. "The world is my parish," he exclaimed.

However hidden under the semi-magic of sacramentalism, concern for one's fellow man had always been the driving force behind efforts to extend the bounds of Christianity. It had inspired the missionary movements of the early centuries, and after the Reformation, that of the Jesuits. Calvinism, with its selfish doctrine of "the Elect" had not been conducive to this missionary effort. In the North American wildernesses of the seventeenth century, it had not been the Puritans who had striven for Indian souls but the Jesuits. The most drastic of the Puritans had always been ready to "turn upon the Amalekites and slay them," thus giving rise to the later American saying that the only good Indian is a dead Indian. Later on, even Jesuit fervour had abated and in the eighteenth century, as has been said, missionary zeal was scarcely detectable, corresponding to the torpor that overtook the church generally and from which Methodism helped to rouse it. The Roman Catholic reaction was delayed but when it came – mainly after about 1830 – it came vigorously. For Protestantism, the new sap rising in the branches was apparent in the new missionary movements towards the end of the eighteenth century. These were at first largely the work of simple men, such as Henry Cary, who went out to India in the 1790s. There, much to the consternation of the officers of the East India Company, he began preaching typical Protestant evangelism introducing those Western viruses of notions about salvation, equality of man, love of God, brotherhood of men, that were to work underground in India and link with the whole concept of a liberal civilization.

Cary was not long alone. New missionary societies were organized and new fields sought. Anglicans of the "Low Church" wing were naturally drawn in. By the middle of the century Protestant missionary activity had penetrated innumerable lands forlorn:

> From Greenland's icy mountains,
> From India's coral strand,
> Where Afric's sunny fountains
> Roll down their golden sand,
> From many an ancient river,
> From many a palmy plain
> They call us to deliver
> Their land from error's chain.

Protestant missionary endeavour, reflecting back home, had become one of the major cultural forces of the era. While the Protestant missionary movement both in numbers and funds was preponderantly of the English-speaking world, German, Dutch and other north European peoples had also sent their representatives abroad. The tide had set strongly to America, and many an American missionary had joined his efforts with those of his English associates. Even the weak little colony of Nova Scotia in the 1840s managed to send a missionary out to the distant New Hebrides, whence came back stirring accounts of barbaric customs, such as the ritual strangling of widows and of the triumph of the gospel over them.

The nineteenth century missionary movement carried many of the more generous aspects of Western civilization throughout the world and offered a counterweight to the more invidious. Its efforts to improve the physical conditions of the "natives" as well as to "save their souls" was well-meaning and sensible (though often narrow minded). As the nineteenth century wore on and the scientific age took over, physical well-being received more and more emphasis, "medical missionaries" became more and more prominent, the emphasis on health and well-being greater and greater. In our own day this well-meant attitude has had its backlash in its contribution to prolongation of the life span in the more backward parts of the world, especially Asia, whence have come heavy pressures on food supply, overpopulation and the famines which those originally impelled by good intentions may have hoped they had succeeded in eliminating forever.

Despite their apparent total difference, the two aspects of nineteenth century religion in England had this at least in common: without stretching words too much, they could each be said to be aspects of romanticism, that is, if the term may be used in more than a mere technical way. All aspects of this nineteenth century religious revival represented that spirit of "ineffable longing" which has well been said to constitute the essence of Romanticism. "Ineffable longing" it may have been, probably was, what inspired the ardours of Newman. "Ineffable longing," it probably was what inspired the efforts of John Wesley, or of William Wilberforce. The Newmanites concentrated heavily on the ineffable longing within their own beings for some kind of mysticism, the Wesleyans and the Evangelicals found themselves moved by more concrete human experiences. The Newmanites represented one commandment, "love God," the others, the second, "and thy neighbour as thyself."

"Ineffable longing," without necessary relationship with any religious feelings, it probably was, too, that lay behind another aspect of British Romanticism, that which is usually termed "Imperialism." The empire builders have usually been dreamers. They have felt themselves to have great tasks which they are called to accomplish. They have been driven by the same kind of internal compulsions as probably impelled the religious men. Often they, in fact, were not dissimilar from religious men, having the same sense of the mysterious, the same feeling of being creatures of destiny. They have related closely to those who would come under the next heading to be touched on. As actors on the edges of the civilized world, they formed links with the explorers. It was not only Charles Napier in India ("Peccavi" – "I have Scind"), but John Franklin in the Arctic wastes who carried this high sense of resolve in their hearts. Such men were forerunners of those who thought of the burden of empire, rather than its building, of "white men's burdens," "weary Titans" and other such admirable objects. All of them had their reward, no doubt. They all formed factors in that vast burst of energy that marked the earlier Victorians.

A similar aspect of British life also reflected the same burst of energy. It represented, not high spiritual or political aims, but pure high animal spirits. As has been noted, the loss of the American colonies had affected British vitality only temporarily. It seemed a misfortune, not a tragedy. "Family feeling" about it seemed at a minimum, and the founding of Australia was its compensation. After the wars, with British sails on every horizon, the great days of empire ensued.

Moderns, who know water only as something that comes out of taps, find it somewhat hard to recapture the strength and depth of this penetration into British life of the sea, the life of the sea, the lore of the sea. Those were the days of the "mariners of England who guard our native seas" (in the poet's words), of poems about "Breakers on the weather bow and hissing white the sea," of those who "never were on the dull, tame shore but they loved the great sea more and more," of Byronic addresses to Ocean. They were the days of the jacktar, the heroic folk figure who could range himself along side the longbowmen of the ancient battles, the days of strange adventures in far off places, of kings of the cannibal islands and all the rest, days that have passed into our language in many a familiar phrase – we still talk of keeping things on an even keel and suspect what is wrong with a man who has "three sheets in the wind." The sea and the life of the sea, the innumerable tales, novels and songs in which it was framed, found the best of settings against the background of the Romantic movement and it joins up with Romanticism in its other phases of the missionary movement and of sheer imperialism. When battle's troubled night was past, the meteor flag of England did then terrific wave. Once more, also, God became a British subject and once more, as a later singer proclaimed it, He was concerned with setting the bounds of empire wider and wider, in order that His earthly favourite might become "mightier yet."

The nineteenth century European advanced upon the more primitive peoples, so it has been put, with his Bible under one arm and a bottle of rum under the other – that is, with his humanitarian civilization and his commerical civilization. Each of these may have been equally hard on the recipients of his "gifts," "the natives." As for "the natives," what no Westerner would do, was to leave them alone.

Notes

1. De Maistre was of French family origin, though a Savoyard by birth.
2. Goethe, *Faust,* Part One, II, 2038-2039. The speech, incidentally, is by Mephistopheles.

3.   See Alex. Brady, *William Huskisson and Liberal Reform* (Kelley, 1928).

4.   J. R. Butler, *The Passing of the Great Reform Bill* (Kelley, 1914).

5.   Text in Robinson, *Readings, op. cit.,* II, pp. 546-550.

6.   The more detailed story of this extraordinary woman is given by George Brandes in Vol. III (*The Reaction in France*) of his *Main Currents in Nineteenth Century Literature* (Haskell, New York, 1923).

7.   A standard book on this subject is J. M. Robertson, *A History of Free Thought in the Nineteenth Century* (Dawson, London, 1929, reprinted 2 Vols., 1969). This work, while full of meticulous detail put together with skill, is overdone propaganda and exhortation, which detract from the impression it makes, if not from its value, becoming rather boring.

8.   Charles Sarolea, introducing the *Vita* in the *Everyman's Library* edition.

9.   A good recent study is William Robbins, *The Newman Brothers, An Essay in Comparative Intellectual History* (Heinemann's, London, 1966).

10.   As succinct and accurate a description of the English mentality in general as could be imagined – a mentality that sustains Englishmen in the great foreign threats, for they simply cannot imagine what might happen tomorrow.

CHAPTER SEVENTEEN

Secular Religion

I
Reason, Faith and the German Thinkers

In Germany, the return of mysticism took its own German way. Ordinary people retained their traditional more or less desiccated Lutheranism, but the German philosopher rose to giddy heights. It was in 1781 that Immanuel Kant (1724-1804) published one of the most influential of books, both for his own time and succeeding generations. This was *The Critique of Pure Reason*. Kant reasoned that "there were more things in heaven and earth than are dreamed of by your philosophers" and that the way of pure knowledge, or science, was incapable of dealing with such things – beauty, for example. There came a point where faith must be introduced.

If one had gone to Königsberg in East Prussia when it was still a German city, he would certainly have been shown the house in which Kant had lived. Every afternoon, the story then still current went, he emerged from his study at half past four, took the same walk over a half hour's course and returned. People set their watches by his appearance at his door. Sooner or later his books came out of the same house. It seems a narrow existence and no wonder his books are difficult and to all but the professional, "dry-as-dust." Their effect, however, was vast. To introduce the notion of *faith* for *science* to share the world with, left it open to individuals to have their own *faith* and abandon the firm truths of science. Kant's

248

philosophy gave a good basis for the Romantic revolt from a mathematical world. He had many successors, each one of them providing his own variant of his ideas, Johann Fichte (1762-1814), Friedrich Schleiermacher (1768-1834), Georg Hegel (1770-1831), Arthur Schopenhauer (1788-1860), Friedrich Nietzsche (1844-1900) and many other lesser lights. In the early and middle nineteenth century Germany was indeed ruling the clouds.

That was the period in Germany which saw flourish in utmost luxuriance the legendary Germany professor:

> Those were the days in which the familiar type of the scholar was generated, of the man who complained that the public library allowed him only thirteen hours a day to read, the man who spent thirty years on one volume, the man who wrote on Homer in 1806 and was still writing on him in 1870, the man who discovered the 358 passages in which Dietys has imitated Sallust . . .[1]

Hegel, we are informed "comfortably finishing his book at Jena during the battle (one of Napoleon's great battles, Jena, 1806) and, starting for his publishers in the morning, was surprised to find the streets were full of Frenchmen."[2]

Hegel's was perhaps the most prominent name in the scholarly succession. Hegel among other matters, erected the idea of "the State" into the most complete form of reality and introduced the notion of "historicity" – a satisfactory account of anything whatever must proceed from the history of the matter in question. For example, we can only understand Parliament by knowing the history of Parliament. This is a point of view that appeals strongly to the historian but it has its limitations. It is a lifetime's occupation to know in detail *the history* of Parliament.[3] Its correlation provides more difficulty still. History, we are told, is the final judge – "World history is world judgement"[4] is the famous phrase. It comes close to the familiar "whatever is, is right"? Does that mean that the Nazi slaughter-camps were right"? Oh, but history has passed judgement on them, it will be said.

The subject evidently lends itself to endless speculation. And while knowledge is power, it is not supreme power. It is said that at the Frankfurt Parliament of 1848, where a strong attempt was made to work out a liberal constitution for a United Germany, and where the German academic was prominent – one hundred members were professors – professors could be counted on to recount the exact steps by which the English Long Parliament imposed its will on Charles I but proved wanting when it came to imposing an imperial crown on the head of the King of Prussia, occasioning his obnoxious remark that "he had no desire to receive a crown out of the gutter." History as explanation of everything comes close to justification of everything.

If the German philosopher would not accept the mathematical God of the eighteenth century, neither did he provide for his people much of a revival of a more traditional deity. No new version of a loving father appeared. Instead, along with Hegel, more and more emphasis seems to have been placed on that most complex, most historical, that greatest of human structures, the state. The state as the sum of human achievement. But for what? Many ideals could be ascribed to it but one easy concept came to dominate: the state as power. From that it was a short step to the state as war-waging machine. The translation of philosophical concept into reality was swiftly made.

In the cultural shift of the nineteenth century, another, but closely related group of German scholars took quite as large a place as the philosophers. These were the Biblical scholars. It was an old game to attack the scriptures from various rationalistic points of view, something that could give rise to endless angry argument never settled. But close scholarly investigation from the historical point of view, with the aid of textual and linguistic learning, even of the youthful discipline of anthropology, was another matter. The result of a generation or two of investigation, mainly in the German universities, which were intellectually alive, whereas those of England had been intellectually dead, was to reduce the Bible to literature, folk myth or pious asseveration. The foundations of "belief" were almost completely swept away, and when in 1835, David Friedrich Strauss (1808-1874) published his *Leben Jesu* he virtually ruled out anything but purely secular considerations: all the traditional beliefs, "God, the Son," virgin birth, miracles, ascension, were ruthlessly swept away. The net result of German Biblical criticism, most of it the work of Lutheran clergymen, was to leave historical Christianity in ruins for every educated man.

In Germany, more especially Prussia, as in Great Britain, the exponents of the new Biblical exegesis had a hard time of it: invariably they were dismissed from their posts and found the academic doors closed. Zurich in Switzerland afforded a partial refuge, but even Zurich had its limits of tolerance when it came to public opinion as contrasted with the judgement of the few. The general impression one gets, however, as between Germany and Great Britain in the first part of the nineteenth century, is of a far easier atmosphere for religious dissent or criticism in Germany than in Great Britain. In Germany, before 1870, there was a multitude of small sovereign states of varying types and one or other of these often afforded shelter to the heretic. Moreover, Britain was on the march, her cities leaping upward in population, her trade increasing and the empire expanding. "Onward, Christian Soldiers," was the watchword, not "Abide with me." A country profoundly empirical and "practical," highly anti-intellectual, could hardly be bothered with the cloudy speculations coming out of Germany. In any onward rush, the laggard is apt to get short shift. The Industrial Revolution was an onward rush.

"A land of damned professors," said Lord Palmerston of Germany in the 1850s. A decade later, he would have had to use other words.

II
Secular Religion

France presents still another variation on the first half of the century's theme, religion. The story is complex. This great country had always lain at the centre of Europe, not only geographically, but culturally. Its associations with Roman Catholicism had extended over the centuries and they embraced practically every aspect of human affairs. The Calvinist aggressions of the sixteenth century had been turned back, Henry IV had found "Paris worth a mass" and the eighteenth century had seen the triumph of formal orthodoxy in doctrine and observance. But not the orthodoxy of papalism, for Gallicanism (that is, nationalism under the crown) had never ceased to dispute the pope's claims to power over the French church. Napoleon bullied the pope into being present at his coronation in Notre Dame (though not allowed to crown him – Napoleon did that for himself) and into accepting in *The Concordat* of 1802 "a humiliating surrender of that spiritual independence which alone gives real life to a professedly spiritual body."[5]

On the restoration of the Bourbons, the church confidently expected to go back into its old place, that is, as the counterpart of the state in every aspect of life. Some Jesuits, under an assumed name, returned. Apparently, a wave of Catholic evangelism swept over the country, for it was reported that the country was covered with "missions" (that is, the Roman Catholic equivalent of left-wing Protestant "revival meetings").[6] How deeply the wave captured popular conviction and changed attitudes in a land where for centuries the village church bells had been sounding in rural ears, who is to say? Louis XVIII became orthodox, if not exactly a *dévot*. "Blue-bloodism" became prominent and visible: the long lines of fashionable equipages outside churches on occasions of ceremony carried ancient coats of arms. An aristocracy that had been politely sceptical in the eighteenth century was once more orthodox in the nineteenth, if not necessarily "spiritual." It could hardly have been otherwise in the France of the Bourbon Restoration, a country of the most ancient Catholic traditions, now with the ancient monarchy restored, to guard them, a country in which dissident movements had been harshly crushed long before.

Yet the religious revival had its two sides in France, as it did in Great Britain. French minds were too lively to permit the triumph of mere stodgy reaction. Catholic religious revival had its liberal wing, whose leadership devolved upon Félicité Lamennais (1782-1854). Lamennais had become a priest in 1816 and in attitude a reactionary ultramontane, but his attitude changed and by middle life, he had come to see that only a thorough-going alteration in the church could meet the new conditions with which it was faced. His *Paroles d'un croyant* (1834) became one of the most influential books of the generation. Eventually he thought himself out of the church. In their innocence, he and a few friends had decided to go to Rome and put their proposals before the pope: all they asked was that Rome accept the idea of a free church within the state, divorced from the state, standing on its own feet (as Roman Catholicism did in the United States). They might as well have asked the pope to turn Protestant. They came back crestfallen and papal condemnation duly followed (1834): the church in France was to pursue its historic path. The result was a generation of war within its bosom, the liberal Catholics, under such great men as Charles Montalembert (1810-1870), continuing to advance their views as best they could, some in rebellion or desertion, some in an uneasy conformity. After 1848, the contest was to become so intermingled with political considerations – the efforts of Napoleon III to sit on both sides of the fence at the same time – that its religious foundations are easily lost sight of. Liberal Catholicism, as a movement in the first half of the nineteenth century, may not have won its battle, but it had inflicted a serious wound on reactionary orthodoxy, and later on, the marks were to become visible.

It was not only in the area of religion that the keen French mind displayed itself. The eighteenth century had been disturbing enough in the region of pure speculation, the French Revolution had pushed every type of problem forward and now, in the generation after Napoleon, the results of the Industrial Revolution were forcing themselves on thought. Factories may not have sprouted as fast in France as in England, but they were coming and even without them the commercial tone of life was making itself forcefully felt. Under Louis Philippe (1830-1848), "the Citizen King," the upper bourgeoisie practically controlled the state. A "bourgeois," by one definition, was anyone who wore decent clothes and spoke good French. According to another and much more bitter, "la bourgeoisie de 1814, gorgée de biens nationaux, la seule chose qu'elle eût compris des institutions de '89, était libérale, révolutionaire même. 1848 l'a rendu réactionaire, catholique et plus que jamais monarchique."[7]

For a number of years, François Guizot, the Protestant historian, a gifted but narrow man – "a great intellect with blinkers" – was prime minister. His best advice to his fellow-countrymen has become notorious – "Enrichissez-vous": "make money!" Enough Frenchmen followed his advice to bring eighteen years of prosperity to France. Eighteen years, too, of what France has seldom had – good government, honest and progressive government, with encouragement to good family life, peace and prosperity all round. Apparently that was not the kind of world

Frenchmen wanted, for in 1848, without any profound reason, occurred the "Revolution from contempt" as it came to be called, and another phase of history set in.

"France was bored" is a well-known verdict on the reign of Louis Philippe. Louis Philippe clearly seems to have been boring. It is said that any group of loiterers by lining up and cheering could get him to come to the veranda of his palace, ceremoniously strike an attitude and bow his respect to "his loyal subjects."* It is further said that the appropriate skills on the part of some wit in the group could induce him to sing the Marseillaise with them – out of tune! He chanced one day to have presented to him the well-known poet Alfred de Musset. He mistook the poet for a certain minor official of the same name and until his reign ended, continued to greet him as such, never having discovered the poet: poets have been rated high in France – higher than minor civil servants! France was bored or some Frenchmen were bored. They preferred King Stork to King Log. Louis Philippe went on his travels.

It was "peace and progress," or what those words involved that so greatly disturbed the remarkable men who devoted themselves to thinking about the course society was taking under the drive of money and the machine. The Industrial Revolution as such may not have progressed as far in France as in England, but the era of the Revolution and Napoleon had seen the transfer from church and nobility of vast areas of land from the former owners to the upper peasantry and to men who, availing themselves of the opportunities for amassing wealth which war always affords to the astute, quickly came to be identified as a new, or virtually new, order of society, the *bourgeoisie*. They were pictured as hard, grasping, merciless in pursuit of their legal rights, materialistic in the worst sense; that is, without culture or ideals, except selfish gratification. They have remained, to become the stock pattern of the "capitalist beast" of later communism. They soon found their way into French literature. Indirect pictures of them appear in Marie Stendhal's (1783-1842) *Le Rouge et le Noir* and more explicitly in Honoré de Balzac's *Eugénie Grandet*, 1833, especially in the initial descriptions of Charles, "Le Cousin de Paris," and the way he had been brought up by his too successful father in the latter's climb from poor boy to rich man and his subsequent sudden fall.

In England, the spectacular growth of the factory and of commerce brought forth little equivalent to the writers and thinkers who appeared in France after the Restoration. The rebellious flash of around 1820 had gone out. William Cobbet (1763-1835) was the voice of an older England, not of the foes of industrialism. William Blake in an earlier day, had been, but he was gone. Richard Cobden and John Bright were themselves

* The authority is the late Professor C. K. Webster in a lecture anecdote at Harvard.

entrepreneurs. Jeremy Bentham and the Mills were of the middle classes and their doctrines for the middle class. It was only slowly that John Stuart Mill came round to something more humane than Benthamism. Thomas Carlyle loosed off in all directions at once, and his main on-slaughts, apparently directed against "getting and spending" like those of John Ruskin, came in the second, rather than the first half of the century. In Great Britain, by the nineteenth century, individual enterprise, private initiative, was so thoroughly entrenched that a full-scale attack on it could hardly have been imagined. No seer of stature sprang from among the English third estate. But in France, seers abounded, and powerful figures some of them were. The French railway era, which was to give much opportunity for wealth, began in earnest in the 1840s, about the same time as the English. But long before that, the seers had been expounding their doctrines. They were contemporary, not with the later publicists of Great Britain, but with men like Robert Owen (1771-1858), though with infinitely greater command of the pen than anything Owenism produced. Yet some of them could, like Mill, be regarded as systematic thinkers.[8] Among them, many be noted, the great names of Claude Saint-Simon, Charles Fourier, Louis Blanc and Pierre Joseph Proudhon. All these men were social missionaries.

> The Citizen, Charles Henri de Saint-Simon, a former nobleman, de-clares his desire of purifying by a Republican baptism, the stain of his origin. He has asked to be relieved of a name which remains him of an inequality that reason had condemned long before our constitution had passed sentence upon it.

The citizen became (temporarily) Charles Henri Bonhomme.[9] When Saint-Simon shifted into Charles Henri Bonhomme, he was thirty years of age, having been born in 1760. He died in 1825. His active years thus were passed during the Revolution, Napoleon and the Restoration reign of Louis XVIII. He wrote voluminously and after his death, his disciples came to form a school. Saint-Simonism established itself almost as a creed. One of the disciples had been his secretary, Auguste Comte. Comte gave to his master's ideas a much harder shape and in his hands they became the body of thought known as "positivism." They were influential in their day, but as not strictly pertinent to the purposes of this study, they must be passed over here.

The large point about Saint-Simon is that his thinking about the nature of society shaped itself into something close to what today we would call socialism, or even communism. "Saint-Simonism may be said to be the first really challenging criticism of the principle of competition as the basis of the economic order, the first really compelling statement of the social problem . . . There are few evils of industrialism that Saint-Simon did not denounce, or at least glimpse."[10] Criticism of such a pioneer was and has been easy, but he remains "the real initiator of socialist thought" and his successors perhaps only refined and elaborated on his doctrines. Necessarily, he had nothing like the mass of data that was later to accumulate on industrialism, for in his lifetime it was only its initial aspects that had manifested themselves.

In a book of this sort it is not appropriate to go into detail with respect to the doctrines enunciated by Saint-Simon and his successors. Of these, the most conspicuous were Fourier, Louis Blanc and Proudhon. Charles Fourier was a Utopian and he had his own dreams of a perfect society, which he tried to carry out in actuality by founding communities that should be self-contained and, presumably, sinless. Like Robert Owen, to find the best location for these, he was driven to the vast empty continent where space seemed to offer freedom, America.

The story of Utopian societies in America is interesting and it is long. Utopian societies have taken innumerable shapes and have had many different fates. The attempts still go on: they have had a strong recrudescence in our modern world, some of them having been intensely religious, others as intensely secular. The Hutterites, a "spinoff" from the Mennonites, have founded self-contained colonies throughout North America: they continue to practise an intensively agrarian religious communism and still maintain themselves against the hostility of their surroundings and even of governments. Many secular foundations similarly seeking escape, freedom in solitude, have been founded of recent years, especially in the United States, where the opportunities offered to them in the State of California have been very much availed of. An interesting light on them in quite succinct form was cast by a "story" (in the journalistic sense) by John Norheimer which appeared in the New York *Times*,[11] headed *A Long Shadow Cast on the Brotherhood of the Sun*. The details are hardly necessary. "The Brotherhood of the Sun" is, or was, a collective community near Santa Barbara, California, that originally consisted in people who had "opted out," left society, and formed an agricultural commune. Apparently, from an economic point of view, they were quite successful and came to possess many assets. Money being the root of all trouble, they found the task of bridging the gap between isolated communism and the society about them leading them into deep water: probity in the membership was only one factor in their problems, the jealousy and hostility of the nearby "world" being another.

Attempts to find a lodge in some vast wilderness, to live your own life, simply *to escape,* have probably gone on from the indefinite past to the present. They are general aspects of human life of which hermitism and monasticism are particular. It was the confusion of the times (though that is putting it too simply) which drove fifth century hermits out into the Egyptian desert and made sixth century Westerners take to the hills and caves. That wholesale flight from life involved just as bizarre examples of conduct as have been brought to view in our own day. For example, Edward Gibbon somewhere tells of holy men and women, monks and nuns, as they were called at the time, who sought to conquer the lust of the flesh by sleeping together. The historian dryly adds that nature often conquered piety. It is to the vast credit of the church that in a struggle conducted over centuries of time it brought some order and system into the lives of those who wished to "forsake the world." California may have been seeing the beginnings for a new monastic movement.

So much for Fourierism and its parallels. They are not in the main stream.

Louis Blanc was a more practical man: his idea was that much private industry should be transferred to the state, the conditions of production made decent, and gradually the private *entrepreneur* would surrender his hold. Blanc's ideas have in some respect been realized in our own day when so much industry has come under public control and when "the right to work" has received some formal recognition. But that was not possible in the late 1840s. "Natural Workshops" set up as a sequence to the Revolution of 1848 failed and Blanc, who bore the responsibility for them, ceased to be either prophet or pilot.

P.-J. Proudhon is the theorist who is always remembered for his re-sounding declaration that "Property is theft." The statement taken in its context is not quite as startling as alone. It was startling enough, however, "pour épater les bourgeois" and taken with others of the sort, the writings of which it formed a part helped in causing the downfall of the Second Republic and the dictatorship of Louis Napoleon. The *bourgeoisie* (a far more invidious word in French than *middle class* in English) had been badly frightened. They took no chances. The "strong man" seemed the answer.

Proudhon appeared to be fond of these *point blanc* declarations. "L'effet le plus remarquable de la division du travail est la déchéance de la littérateur," he raps out.[12] Many pages before and after the statement must be read to understand it. The general rule he seems to be working out is that a man who does everything for himself, like Robinson Crusoe, is in a more fortunate position, at least is a more completely integrated person, than the individual who has been reduced to routine activities. He cites the inglorious role of the postman, who has nothing to do but walk. Another lot of persons who have been reduced by the division of labour to inferior status consists in the printing trades:

> Gutenberg et ses industrieux compagnons, Furst et Scheffer, eussent-ils jamais cru que, par la division du travail, leur sublime invention tomberait dans le domaine de l'ignorance, j'ai presque dit de l'idiotisme? Il est peu d'hommes aussi faibles d'intelligence, aussi peu *lettrés* que la masse des ouvriers attachés aux diverses branches de

l'industrie typographique, compositeurs, pressiers, fondeurs, relieurs et papetiers. Le typographe que l'on rencontrait encore en temps des Etiennes, est devenu presqu'un abstraction. L'emploi des femmes pour la composition des caractères a frappé au coeur cette noble industrie, et en a consommé l'avilissement. J'ai vu une composatrice, et c'était une des meilleures, qui ne savait pas lire, et ne connaissait des lettrés que la figure. Tout l'art s'est retiré dans la specialité des protes (*foremen*) et correcteurs, savants modestes, que l'impertinence des auteurs et patrons humilie encore, et dans quelques ouvriers véritablement artistes. La presse, en un mot, tombée dans la mécanisme, n'est plus, par son personnel, au niveau de la civilisation: il ne restera bientôt d'elle que des monuments.[13]

And so his writing goes on, exploring almost interminably the problems to which the tendencies of modern life, mainly the machine, necessarily lead. The quotation gives a passage not so important in itself, but very well illustrating method and tone. French scholars have found it hard to classify Proudhon, for his point of view veered about a great deal. But no one could place him on the side of *la bourgeoisie.*

This cleavage seems to have gone far deeper in France than in England, where the victims of the factory system were left to speak for themselves, or through efforts arising from their like such as the leaders of the Chartists. In England, there were also conservative humanitarians, such as Lord Shaftesbury, who not only spoke for them, but acted, too. And to his name should be added a future prime minister, Benjamin Disraeli, who depicted the terrors of industrial life in his political novels, especially in his *Sybil, or the Two Nations* (1845). The *Two Nations* were the *rich* and the *poor,* who lived in two separate worlds, with little community of interest, knowledge or culture. In France, this same class of person existed and one of them was a very great man, no less a man than the poet Victor Hugo (1802-1885).

"J'ai . . .
Plaidé pour les petits et les misérables
J'ai réclamé des droits pour la femme et l'enfant . . ."

But "Le passé ne veut pas s'en aller . . ."[14]

No doubt Hugo was first a poet, next a humanitarian and at last a systematic thinker: his voice, nevertheless, carried weight and it did not lose any when later on, he preferred to go into exile rather than accept the despotism of Napoleon III. Yet Hugo's father had been one of Napoleon 1st's generals. In his day, he had no opposite numbers in England – possibly because they had already appeared.

The above paragraphs do not pretend to be a discussion of the socialistic thinkers of mid-century France: they merely call attention to their existence in order to try to place them in the historic stream of the century.

Their merit is that they saw the order of things that had vanished in the Revolution, penetrated the nature of that order which seemed to have replaced it and prophesied about the order they thought would come. They were the kind of men they were and propounded the kind of doctrines they propounded because they saw through, or thought they saw through, the hollowness of materialism. Life seemed to be about to make men mere machine tenders.

The Revolution had been carried through because some men had had visions of a better future. The better future still seemed far off. Here were ideas that might bring it closer. The French socialistic thinkers were as truly *religious* thinkers as any Jewish prophet or mediaeval saint. Their "Holiness" lay in the paths they elected to follow, the doctrines they enunciated. It represented that effort to bring forth heaven on earth which is the driving force of every revolution. Revolution, that is, is a genuine religious experience. It finds for those who link themselves to it a way of salvation. It could be put that every great revolution is a religious revolution, just as every great religious movement is itself a revolution (each with its appropriate allowance of hysteria).

It was certainly a revolutionary situation which changed Paganism into Christianity, as previous chapters have argued. It was a revolutionary condition which brought Protestantism out of Catholicism. It was revolution that produced the rule of Cromwellian saints out of the old church of England. American republicanism was a revolutionary creed. The French Revolution directly assailed the old religion to put a new one in its place. The revolutionary events of 1848, aiming at the establishment of a new order of things, were to be termed religious. The Russian Revolution was as religious a movement as had been the destruction of Paganism by Christianity. It must be accepted that any deep conviction, or indeed any dominating emotional feeling, held with intensity and sincerity, is religious. This waives the question of the nature of the god that such things involve.

The question at issue here is not the exact relationship of these doctrines to later doctrines of socialism or communism. French Saint-Simon seems clearly to point forward to Marx. Proudhon could be used for Marxist purposes. It was Marx's task to take all the messages and work them out into his system of "scientific socialism." He was not the first Jew to upset the world. Nor can it be assumed that the world now replaced in some countries by Marxism was greatly inferior to the Communist régimes that have replaced it. Humanity, or fractions of it, catches bright gleams of the future Eden, but it usually ends up in grasping for the pot of gold at the foot of the rainbow: much bother, much excitement, much gesticulation and hot-tempered argument, usually many blows and much blood and then humans settle back, not into exactly the same old ruts, but into ruts that seem good enough – until the next time!

The problems of nineteenth century France naturally were not confined to the area of production. All during the century, as has been said, one continuous fight went on over the place of the church in the state. The church insisted on making it a question of religion. Others saw in it primarily a matter of power. When traditional or authoritarian régimes were in power, the church got more or less what it wanted. When the government represented a departure from traditionalism, privileges – rights, churchmen would have said – were curtailed. After 1815, the very centre of the battlefield the school; which was to have the child, church or state? If children were to be schooled, they must not be put into "God-less" schools. It is a position firmly maintained by the church to this day, one that has given rise to wars of greater or lesser intensity in every country where there is any considerable Catholic population. Many solutions have been propounded, none have healed the breach.

Not only in France, but everywhere else, the fight goes on. In France, it was waged with a maximum of bitterness and with a kaleidoscopic succession of changes with which the outside observer finds difficult to cope. By the end of the century, it was hoped that disestablishment of the church would at last remove the apple of discord. Disestablishment duly took place (1904) but the apple of discord remained. Those who live in countries where the question of "separate schools" looms large (as it does in that to which the present writer belongs) know how deep is the controversy and sharp the bitterness which the question produces. Church and state have fought many of their modern battles in the schools. In a measure two worlds are pitted against each other there, two ways of life, two philosophies, each complex, neither one as pure in heart as its adherents would like to deem it.

Apart from the succession of psychological states whose portrayal is attempted here, the history of France sounds an intriguing echo to that of the England of a century or so before it. The parallel between the Parliamentary Revolution and the French is clear. In 1793, as in 1649, a king was beheaded. In both, revolution ended in military dictatorship and that, in both, in restoration. In neither country was restoration any solution to the problem of government. Two reigns and twenty-eight years ended it in England; two reigns and fifteen in France. Constitutionalism came to dominate the English scene, where Parliamentary government has remained unchallenged, but France was not finished with its ups and downs. The parallel fails after 1848 and France goes on to various changes of régime which, in milder form, endure to this day. In government, as in other areas, the pulsations of history in both countries are similar.

That is at least in part because modern Europe has once more been slowly finding its way to a kind of unity. It was loosely unified once under pope and emperor. It dissolved into fragments as a result of the Reformation on the continent and nationalism in England. When the bitternesses of religion died down somewhat, some sense of the ancient unity could return. And then in the nineteenth century the great changes began which have never since ceased and which make the whole world hear the whispers spoken anywhere.

III
Germany and Italy

Some attention has already been given to Germany. The early nineteenth century was the generation of the Germanic Confederation, dominated by Metternich, chancellor of Austria-Hungary (1809-1848), arch-reactionary but by no means bloodless – a "bloodless" tyrant would hardly have won the favours of so charming and capable a woman as the Princess de Lieven, who became his mistress. Despite Metternich, Prussia gradually came to the front (her eventual dominance in Germany was prophesied by the historian Johann Droysen after the failure of the Frankfurt Parliament[15]), partially because of reaction against him, or reaction of the Protestant north against the Catholic south, or, one would like to think, of Germans who wanted a free society against those contented with more or less beneficent domination. More or less beneficent it must have been, despite Carlsbad Decrees, for German poetry flourished, German learning in every branch flourished and most appealing of all, German music right in the dictator's capital, Vienna, for was it not the age of Beethoven, Schubert, Schumann, and many another lesser genius?

Hegel's doctrines of the state[16] did not help the cause of a free Germany much. Most German scholars fitted into the mould. Even the great Leopold von Ranke, successor of Hegel, could not see far beyond the national state, and for most Germans, the national state could be a small principality. Ideas of union came slowly, nor was there ever in Germany the strong thrust for freedom found long before in England. When '48 came, though the Austrians got rid of Metternich, Germans did not lead Europe into the promised land. "Religious" revival in Germany had meant revival, not of faith but of philosophy. The professors at Frankfurt had not proved that knowledge is power.

In the third of the great modern cultures of Europe,[17] Italy, post-Napoleonic revival took still another form. It is possible that Napoleon might have made Italy a nation – anything would have been possible from that source – but he did not and the peninsula returned to its age-old state of disunity. "Italy is only a geographical expression" was Metternich's well-known taunt. It was far more than that, of course. The Austrian yoke (over Venice and Lombardy) was not light and native efforts towards freedom earned the sympathies of liberal minds from other peoples:

Over all between the Po
And the eastern Alpine snow,
Under the mighty Austrian,
Sin smiled as Sin only can
And since that time, aye, long before
Both have ruled from shore to shore.

Thus Shelley.[18]

The yearnings for nationalism that had been manifest in Dante's time, over five centuries before, and during the Renaissance, once more made their appearance in the generation after Napoleon. The secret societies, Carbonari and the like, worked underground and then a prophet made his appearance, Guiseppe Mazzini (1805-1872). Mazzini preached the doctrine of benevolent nationalism, nationalism that by evoking and strengthening the forces of a people, would enable them to contribute to the world's stock of civilization. For his pains, he was exiled. So matters stood when in 1846, a new pope was elected, Pius IX.

Pio Nona was hailed as a liberal and he covered Rome with inspiring inscriptions carrying the ancient letters, S.P.Q.R. – *senatus populusque Romanus* – The Roman Senate and People. His liberalism did not get much farther than the inscriptions, for in 1848, "The Year of Revolutions," Italian nationalists hurried him out of his own city and he called loudly upon the ancient powers for his defence. They gave it. Pius, who continued as pope until 1878, ceased to be a liberal. At half-century, Italy's condition apparently was little changed, the south under the king of Naples, the middle under the pope – the ancient states of the church – and the north divided between the kingdon of Sardinia and the Austrian conqueror.

IV
The Unity of the Period,
1815-1848

The first generation after Waterloo, or the first half of the century, as it is convenient to call it, if we look below the surface, shows considerable unity. Unity in the midst of great diversity. It is not improper to think of this unity as "religious." It must be added hastily, religious in both the limited and wider use of the term. The "Oxford movement" attempted to breathe new life into the old forms, but the much deeper revival of traditional religion identified with the Methodists, the other non-conformists and the Evangelicals changed the world. It brought about the re-birth of Puritanism and made the nineteenth century re-echo the seventeenth. It was closely identified with the spread of British power and with American expansion in North America and later in the Pacific. It was the parent of what is now disparagingly called "Victorianism." It sponsored the immensely potent Protestant missionary movement. And it was closely linked with the development of the Industrial Revolution in all its aspects.

The mixture of these various components is not to be resolved. They were mixed inseparably as great world forces and they were mixed in the minds and hearts of men. Consequently it should occasion no surprise if we find the "hardest boiled" businessman of the time genuinely concerned with the welfare of his fellows, even those of different colours and cultures. Examples in illustration abound. To give one: that hard-headed Scot, the Reverend Archdeacon John Strachan, later Bishop of Toronto, was assiduous in his climb to power and wealth, and in securing the ascendancy of his adopted church, but he was a contributor to "good causes," even to those of the Methodists whom in the power game, he did his best to beat. Further, he persuaded his brother-in-law, James McGill, a hard-fisted old Montreal fur-trader who could not have possessed unmixed charity towards the Indian from whom he made his money, to leave his fortune for the purpose of founding a university, the present McGill University. McGill was childless.

Hymns of praise might well be sung to rich childless couples, for the possibility of their leaving their wealth to good public objects seems considerable. But it is not necessary to predicate childless couples: the tobacco family, the Wills, in England, founded Bristol University (not the only instance of good works resting on smoke, the Dukes being another: hymns of praise might also be sung to tobacco magnates). The Industrial Revolution has had many consequences in addition to the factory assembly line.

In France, it is possible, if one wishes, to call the renewed energies of the Roman Catholic church after 1815 a revival in religion: a revival of the church, at any rate, and no doubt with many individual clergy, men, a revival of faith. Liberal Catholicism failed against the conservatism of Rome, and in a sense had to go underground for many years: it came to the surface again in the twentieth century in the movement known as Modernism just before the First World War and more particularly in the General Councils held at the instance of John XXIII. Protestantism in France, in the period produced conspicuous individuals such as François Guizot, but as a religious denomination it was not impressive: it had probably embraced too firmly the less pleasant aspects of Calvinism.

The "religious" revival of moment in France was quite outside the church, as the preceding pages have attempted to show. It consisted in the philosophy that tried to meet the onslaughts of the materialistic way of life, which its exponents discerned to lie in the machine and the Industrial Revolution generally. They provided a marked contrast to the English thinkers of the day, nearly all of whom accepted the way in which the world was unfolding without much more than marginal dissent. In this, the French thinkers might have found themselves in agreement with the church, had not the church been imprisoned in its conceptions of dogma and authority. As it was, the two ships sailed on different courses. The French socialistic philosophers began something far greater than they knew. They began the struggle to subordinate the machine, to restrain and constrain "rugged individualism," the rights of private enterprise, unlimited individualism – *laissez-faire* – and civilize the "hard-headed, two-fisted, he-man" of future American folklore.

The day would come when the most case-hardened business man, *entrepreneur* or engineer would have to pay heed to words like "the social responsibility of business," "the conservation of the environment" and similar matters. But to bring that day to pass it would require many decades of further philosophizing, much furious debate, the sharpest of political struggles and in one great country, the agonies of revolution.

Notes

1.   Acton, essay on *German Schools of History,* (1886). Acton was himself one of them! Modern American scholarship in many respects is repeating the pattern.
2.   It is also said, however, that he was turned out of his house to make way for the Frenchmen.
3.   See the large book by Enoch Powell on *The House of Lords* (J. Enoch Powell and Keith Wallis), *The House of Lords in the Middle Ages* (Wiedenfeld and Nicolson, London, 1968) – several hundred pages of data, but not a definitive *History.*
4.   *Die Weltgeschichte ist das Weltgericht.*
5.   Roger Soltau, *French Political Thought in the Nineteenth Century,* (Yale University Press, 1931), p. 64.
6.   Albert-Léon Gérard, *French Civilization in the Nineteenth Century,* (New York, 1919), pp. 89ff.
7.   P.-J. Proudhon, *Du Principe Féderative* (1863).
8.   Auguste Comte comes closest to this, a "system" founder, but he was not a revolutionary.
9.   Soltau, *op. cit.,* p. 136.
10.   *Ibid.,* p. 147.
11.   Reprinted in *The Kingston* (Ontario) *Whig-Standard,* April 8, 1975.
12.   P.-J. Proudhon, *Système de Contradictions Economiques ou Philosophie de la Misère,* Introduction Roger Picard en *Ouevres Complètes,* (Paris, 1933), p. 146.
13.   *Ibid.,* p. 144.

14.   Quoted in George Brandes, *The French Romantics* (Russell, New York, 1966, reprint of 1905 ed.), p. 369.
15.   Acton, *op. cit.*, p. 397.
16.   See p. 234 ff.
17.   Russia, the fourth, hardly comes into the picture in the first half of the century.
18.   *Lines written among the Euganean Hills*, 246ff.

CHAPTER EIGHTEEN

Century of Hope:
Mid-Century Battle

The Ancient Faith: The New Knowledge

By mid-century, the demon of accomplishment had taken such strong possession of the Western world, especially of its English-speaking portions, that there was not much room left for the subjective concerns of such persons as members of the Oxford movement. Newman's niceties could easily be passed by in a time devoted to the all-absorbing task of building and exploiting what was literally a new world. The Industrial Revolution was roaring ahead like a forest fire. Those were the days when Great Britain, France and other countries were being covered with their network of railways. The seas were being conquered by the steamer. The electric telegraph was obliterating the miles. New cities, not only in the New World, but in Europe too, were springing up like mushrooms. And every day quiet men, not much in the public eye, were burrowing farther and farther into the secrets of nature, with eventual results that no one could foretell.

In the midst of so much change, it was unavoidable that every aspect of the human situation should come in for examination, and, of course, particularly the basic aspect of life, religion. As a small example, when John Stuart Mill published his essay *On the Subject of Women,* which was a dispassionate examination of the relations of men and women in society, it immediately became a matter of wide general interest and requests were received for its translation into many European languages. In a world that was rapidly changing and old forms and customs being sloughed off, the place of woman in society naturally called for much discussion. There were virtually no areas of life of which the same could not be said. The vast problem of race relationships posed by negro slavery, for example, had to be opened out, even if the results were the horrors of civil war.

"The euthanasia of metaphysics was setting in about 1850" wrote Lord Acton in the 1880s. In other words, the old abstract dialectical approach no longer satisfied a world that was more and more immersed in the realities of the practical. In France, as the last chapter has tried to show, the social philosophers had leapt over the actualities of the Industrial Revolution and had already explored its apparent destined results. In Great Britain, so completely was the country in the spell of the new life, these French writers had at first few opposite numbers. Few good Protestants feared the Industrial Revolution and in contrast with France, there was (until later) no major conflict of philosophies. Major challenges to chaotic industrialism were not to come until some of its worst consequences became too apparent to be disregarded any longer. It was left to the poets and the novelists of mid-century, rather than to the social observers, to be the watch dogs of humanitarianism – to them and to the occasional concerned individual, such as Lord Shaftesbury, a man who struggled hard to avert the worst consequences of the factory system.

The sweeping flood of life could not fail to well up around the deepest and most firmly held of man's beliefs. For the average man, religion as he had always known it, the religion of his fathers, was probably good enough. For the esoteric spirits, such as John Newman and Edward Pusey, there were the mysteries of tradition and the delights of ritual. But for the man of good educational status who could not be satisfied with such solutions, the man who was trying to think things out, the age could be a horrible one; he saw the old walls crumbling and no new structures rising to replace them. He could not easily accept the old simplicities, nor could the urgings of his heart, his whole past, allow him easily to reject them. Inner battles, deep and bitter, were often the result.

Naturally no class of persons reflected the crisis of belief more faithfully than the poets. The older generation had settled its accounts one way or another, in accordance with their individual natures. Wordsworth and Coleridge had become rather starchy conservatives. Shelley's blatant atheism had ended with drowning, and in any case, it did not fit the new age. Somehow a transition had to be made, a New World accepted without boisterous rejection of the old. In France, the battle could wax louder than in Great Britain, for there, there was all the strength of the ancient church to rally the faithful, together with the background of political reaction supplied by the successes of Napoleon Bonaparte. In the English-speaking world, the crisis of religion had to be worked out, as it were, in the private mind.

The poets registered their social protest, but their voices were mild. They did not carry the strong tones that in a period when factory slavery was hardly begun had drawn from Blake the denunciation of the "dark Satanic mills" and the query (still unanswered) as to "where we shall build Jerusalem in England's green and pleasant land." Elizabeth Barrett Browning was one among the concerned, a gentle rather than a powerful voice, as in her *Cry of the Children* and her *Curse for a Nation*. The *Curse for a Nation* is aimed at the smugness and complacency of successful mid-Victorian England, which can see humanity's woes abroad and at home will do little about them;

> For all day the wheels are droning, turning
> Their wind comes in our faces,
> Till our hearts burn, our heads, with pulses burning
> And the walls turn in their places:
> Turns the sky in the high windows, bland and reeling,
> Turns the long light that drops adown the wall,
> Turn the black flies that crawl along the ceiling:
> All are turning, all the day, and we with all,
> And all day the iron wheels are droning:
> And sometimes we could pray,
> 'Oh, ye wheels' (breaking out in a mad moaning)
> 'Stop, be silent for today'.

Elizabeth Browning's husband, Robert, was a more buoyant person than his wife. "God's in His heaven, all's right with the world," he could exclaim.

But that was just the trouble. Was God still in his heaven? Among thoughtful mid-century men, there were few who could be sure. Elizabeth herself reflected the uncertainties of her generation, neither robustly orthodox nor outrageously atheist – uncertain, as in her sonnet *Perplexed Music*;

> Experience, like a pale musician, holds
> A dulcimer of patience in his hand
> Whence harmonies we cannot understand,
> Of God's will in his world, the strain unfolds
> In sad, perplexed minors. Deathly colds
> Fall on us while we hear and countermand
> Our sanguine heart back from the fancy-land
> With nightingales in visionary wolds,
> We murmur 'Where is any certain tune
> Of measured music, in such notes as these?

Naturally, it was not the battle of philosophies which the ordinary man saw. What impressed him was the railway that would carry him in a few hours over spaces that had formerly taken days, the Atlantic crossed regularly by steamer in two weeks in place of the three-month struggles of the sailing ships, the marvels of the electric telegraph, the vast uprush in the population, with new towns, Manchester, Birmingham, Chicago, or Sydney on the far side of the globe, springing up with the speed of light. India and the Far East were being reached by steam. Cutting canals through the Isthmuses of Suez and Panama could be talked of. It was these "marvels" that must have impressed the ordinary man. The problems that marvels would create would come later, to be solved as they came along by the same ingenuity as created them. In the meantime, it was "the march of mind" that was triumphing. Even the discerning, with a few exceptions, could say with the poet Arthur Clough (1819-1861):

. . . And not by eastern windows only,
When daylight comes, comes in the light.
In front the sun climbs slow, how slowly,
But westward, look, the land is bright!

By "westward," Clough may or may not have meant the New World. It would be legitimate to interpret him as having meant that, for there indeed lay brightness for apparently all mankind. Ships streamed across the oceans laden with immigrants. Stories came back of lands of liberty, and of untold riches, too; California, land of unlimited gold, in the late 1840s, Australia, the same, about the same time. No wonder that the actual religion of the English-speaking world, whatever its creeds and its services may have been, became and for most people remains the religion of progress.

Yet it was Clough who wrote one of the most poignant of the poems expressing religious perplexity, *Easter Day* (1840). The poem is divided into two parts. The last stanza of the first part runs;

Here on our Easter Day
We, rise, we come, and lo! we find Him not,
Gardener nor other, on the sacred spot;
Where they have laid Him, there is none to say,
No sound, nor in, nor out – no word
Of whom to seek the dead or meet the living Lord.
There is no glistering of an angel's wings,
There is no voice of heavenly, clear behest;
Let us go hence, and think upon these things
In silence, which is best.
Is He not risen? No –
But lies and moulders low.
Christ is not risen?

The second part of the poem effects reconciliation of doubt and faith;

Though He be dead, He is not dead,
In the true creed
He is yet risen indeed:
Christ is yet risen.

The poem goes on to exhort the faithful few who found Him not, not to despair, but to go about their honourable daily tasks, and concludes by showing that all is by no means over, whatever happens:

. . . Whate'er befell
Earth is not hell; now, too, as when it first began
Life is yet life and man is man . . .
Hope conquers cowardice, joy grief . . .
Though dead, not dead;
Not gone, though fled:
Not lost, though vanished.
In the great gospel and true creed.
He is yet risen indeed,
Christ is yet risen.

This beautiful poem puts the dilemma of the century extremely well, and succinctly. Acton somewhere speaks of the period as "the anguish of an age that desperately wanted to believe and yet, with every day that passed, was convincing itself that belief was impossible," *belief* being understood to mean traditional Christian belief.

Clough's poem illustrates this anguish. It is further delineated in verses still popular, Edward FitzGerald's *Rubaiyat of Omar Khayyam*, though how much of this is FitzGerald and how much Omar, it is impossible to tell. Its sentiments echo the languishing decadence found in every age. But it fits well into the atmosphere of a time of doubt:

. . . I came like water and like wind I go

Into this universe and why, not knowing
Nor whence, like water willy-nilly flowing,
And out of it, as wind along the waste,
I know not whither, will-nilly blowing.

Up from Earth's centre through the Seventh gate,
I rose, and on the throne of Saturn sate,
And many a knot unravel'd by the road,
But not the Master knot of human fate.

There was the door to which I found no key,
There was the veil through which I might not see . . .

The "Master-knot of human fate"; that was the point precisely.

One poet there was above all others who pondered that riddle, and like all others could return no answer, Alfred Tennyson (1809-1892). Tennyson was worried about what the machine might have in store for mankind. In lines that turned out to have far prophetic reach, he wrote, in his poem *Locksley Hall* (1843), putting the words into the mouth of the speaker of the dramatic monologue which is the poem;

> For I dipt into the future far as human eye could see,
> Saw the Vision of the World and all the wonder that would be;
>
> Saw the heavens fill with commerce, argosies of magic sails,
> Pilots of the purple twilight dropping down with costly bales:
>
> Heard the heavens fill with shouting, and there rained a ghastly dew
> From the nations' airy navies grappling in the central blue . . .[1]

Professor F.E.L. Priestley in the course of a careful inspection of *Locksley Hall*, rather condescendingly remarks that "these lines are the most familiar in the poem, and are quoted almost annually, out of context, in the newspapers, usually as testimony of Tennyson's powers of technological prophecy . . ." The present writer reads more than his share of newspapers, but he has never come across these annual quotations. If they do occur, these do not detract from the poet's "powers of technological phophecy." This prediction – how horribly it came to pass – beats anything in Jules Verne. Tennyson goes on, more optimistically, to write about something else he foresaw, "The Parliament of man, the federation of the world." We have not got that far yet, one hundred and thirty years later. But how far did Saxon England get in 500 years? Farther down in the poem, he brings another "bogey" of that time, apparently about to be removed permanently but now in our own day, once more frightening us. This was the doctrine of Dr. Thomas Malthus who believed that people would always breed faster than the production of food would increase, so that the only agencies that would keep men and the means of subsistence in balance would be those grim necessities – war, famine and disease. The wheat fields and the earth of the New World put Malthus to rout, apparently, but his ghost has come back to haunt us today and in that great country India, Malthus can call out triumphantly, "I told you so."

> Slowly comes a hungry people, as a lion creeping nigher,
> Glares at one that nods and winks behind a slowly dieing fire

Then, since the motif of the poem is of one disappointed in love, Tennyson talks romantically of going to some unknown southern land, marrying a native woman and living a natural life "the passions cramped no longer." But he soon reflects,

Mated with a squalid savage – what to me were sun or clime?
I the heir of all the ages in the foremost files of time –

And he finally bursts out "Better fifty years of Europe than a cycle of Cathay." The poem is a sharp reflection of the hopes and fears, the hesitations and the uncertainties marking belief in the England of the 1840s.

Tennyson is full of this topic. The great poem *Ulysses* reflects it in the indomitable spirit of the old man, his determination not to be beaten by time. *The Lotus-eaters* introduces religious doubt;

. . . they (the gods) lie beside their nectar and the bolts are
hurl'd
Far below them in the valleys, and the clouds are lightly
curl'd
Round their golden houses girdled with the gleaming world:
Where they smile in secret, looking over wasted lands,
Blight and famine, plague and earthquake, roaring deeps and fiery
sands,
Clanging fights and flaming towns, and sinking ships and
praying hands.
But they smile, they find a music centred in a doleful song
Steaming up, a lamentation and an ancient tale of wrong,
Like a tale of little meaning, though the words are strong . . .

Tennyson was not the first to complain of the indifference of "the gods" – "they kill us for their sport." In his major poem *In Memoriam*, however, he approaches the topic in the knowledge of science that lay at his disposal, which was considerable. Readers will recall that the poem was begun because of the grief this poet felt for his close friend Arthur Hallam, son of the historian, Henry, a young man of great promise cut off in his early manhood. Its composition went on over the years and when it ended, the whole poem had virtually become an attempt to inquire into "the ways of God with man," to understand the sorry scheme of things entire, as FitzGerald puts it. The theme is addressed most directly in the groups of verses numbered LIV, LV and LVI. Some of the lines are so familiar that they have passed into the language as aphorisms – "Oh, yet we trust that good will be the final goal of ill," "An infant crying in the night, and with no language but a cry." The verses demanding direct quotation are in LXV and LXVI;

Are God and Nature then at strife,
   That Nature lends such evil dreams?
   So careful of the type she seems,
So careless of the single life:

That I, considering everywhere,
  Her secret meaning in her deeds,
  And finding that of fifty seeds,
She often brings but one to bear,

  . . .

I stretch lame hands of faith, and grope
  And gather dust and chaff, and call
  To what I feel is Lord o'r all,
And faintly trust the larger hope.

So careful of the type? But no.
  From scarped cliff and quarried stone
  She cries, 'A thousand types are gone;
I care for nothing, all shall go'.

Thou makest thine appeal to me;
  I bring to life, I bring to death,
  The spirit does but mean the breath:
I know no more'. And he, shall he,

Man, her last work, who seemed so fair,
  Such splendid purpose in his eyes,
  Who roll'd the psalm to wintry skies:
Who built him fanes of fruitless prayer:

Who trusted God was love indeed,
  And love Creation's final law,
  Tho' Nature, red in tooth and claw
With ravine, shrieked against his creed

Who loved, who suffered countless ills
  Who battled for the True, the Just,
  Be blown about the desert dust,
Or sealed within the iron hills?

No more? A monster, then, a dream,
  A discord. Dragons of the prime,
  Who tare each other in their slime,
Were mellow music match'd with him.

Tennyson has been criticized as not being strong enough, unable to resolve his doubts and striking out a line that men can live by. He might have answered, in his own words, "there lives more faith in honest doubt, believe me, than in half your creeds." It was an age of doubt, with all the traditional beliefs on trial and little prospect of acquittal. The precedent is Lucretius, as already quoted in Chapter 3.

Tennyson's verses might well have been post-Darwinian. They were not. They preceded that bomb-shell by a number of years. Yet when it came, the *Origin of Species*, 1859, bomb-shell it was. The poet ended his poem with an affirmation of faith;

> That God, which ever lives and loves
>> One God, one law, one element
>> And one far-off divine event
> To which the whole creation moves.

For God, read nature, and we are not far from Lucretius again. For Lucretius, read modern astronomy and we probably have shorthand terms for the same thing. The three expositions of the "nature of things" do not greatly differ.

II
The Bomb-Shell of 1859;
Darwin's *Origin of Species*

But a few years later, appeared the *Origin of Species* (1859). Tennyson had tried to raise a ladder up to Heaven, Darwin without ill-will, pulled it down. Man was simply a product of nature, like ants and elephants or oak trees. It had been hard enough four centuries before for men to endure the suggestion that the earth was not the centre of the universe, harder still for the unsophisticated to accept a mathematical formula for that universe. And now came a book to tell them that an honest man was no more the noblest work of God than a crocodile. Darwin's neat explanation, that different forms of life came about because of infinite small modifications over huge periods of time, modifications which brought the creature into closer and closer harmony with its environment and thus enabled it to survive, simply put the finishing touch to ideas that had been growing up long before him. Sir Charles Lyell (1797-1875), the geologist, had given infinite extension to time; the German philosophers, especially Hegel, had made prominent the idea of evolution through history. Many of the basic concepts were older still: natural law, the great chain of being, and others such. But nothing brought the notion so directly home to men as Darwin's book and his theory. No wonder it was explosive.

The explosion proved to be not one grand burst and then rest, for it is still going on in one form or another. God's in his heaven? Many millions ardently contend that he is. For men will not accept the conclusion, however logical, and "scientific," that they are mere bits of meaningless matter. Whatever their formal creeds have become or will become, they will fight hard for their free will. "Oh, the sun will blaze up and roast everything one of these days," say the astronomers, "just take a look through a telescope: you can see blasted suns in every direction."[2] Men turn the other eye to the telescope. The species may have another million years yet, prognosticated Sir Charles Darwin, grandson of the immortal Charles.[3] "Compared with the five or six thousand of recorded history, that seems a reasonable span," says the average man, "let us wait and see."

Darwin's book provoked bitter controversies throughout the English-speaking world and far beyond. He was attacked by the zealots and by others who were just profoundly hurt at his conception, which was, of course, twisted about out of recognition. "Mr. Darwin may claim an ape as an ancestor, if he will," it was put, "I do not." Or "let him find his 'missing link,' if he can." Well, the missing link, or links, have been found today, and few educated people will refuse the line of descent that Darwin offered. It does not seem to subtract much from our good opinion of ourselves, either.

Darwin's defenders were as ardent as his attackers. Chief among them was Thomas Huxley (1825-1895), grandfather of biologist Julian and novelist Aldous, two brilliant men, but Aldous (1894-1963) giving a diet to his readers which, though of great brilliance of style and conception, yet left a bitter taste in the mouth. For H.G. Wells, product of the early twentieth century, the evolutionary future of man had seemed inviting, thrilling, indeed. In another generation, the shine was going off it. Aldous Huxley faced the nothingness with whose preparing his grandfather had had so much to do. Smiling his bitter, brave smile, he painted for us the picture presented in his *Brave New World*, a clever, even a convincing picture. Men glanced at it and passed by, muttering "if this be the future, give me the past,"[4]

The battle over Darwinism occupies the central ridge of the nineteenth century landscape. Its fury dies down within a couple of decades after the publication of *The Origin of Species*, but gunshots continued to be heard from obscure regions such as Tennessee as late as the 1920s. The famous Scopes's monkey trial of 1925 was a rearguard action designed to keep the teaching of evolution out of the schools of that state. Today, the battle seems over. Man is troubled but his head, if bloody, is still unbowed. Moreover, he has many other horrors to worry about."Hope conquers cowardice, joy, grief."

The net effect of the Darwinian controversy was a clear victory for knowledge over faith. If the first part of the century was religious, the second part was scientific. The vast, secure and apparently beneficent domination of science over men seemed come to stay, and who could predict limitation to it?

Once more, an age which like others before it, had begun with zeal, had come under the sway of knowledge, the saint had given way to the savant, faith to reason.

In the various European cultures, the mid-century battle took the local shapes that might have been expected. In Italy, nationalism continued for many to be a substitute religion. Nationalism afforded abundant outlet for energy and action. Under Camillo Cavour (1810-1861, premier, 1852-1859, 1860-1861), the Kingdom of Sardinia extended its powers and emerged as the practical nucleus for a nation. In the war with Austria, of 1859, Sardinia received the unexpected support of Napoleon III and incorporated some of the former Austrian possessions. Success augmented nationalist fervour. Then came the hero Guiseppe Garibaldi (1807-1882) who demolished the kingdom of the two Sicilies (Naples). It was heady stuff, not to be ended until, taking advantage of the Franco-Prussian war and the withdrawal of the French bayonets on which the pope had been sitting, the Italians entered Rome itself (1870). Italian Catholicism survived the shock easily enough, since the twin existence of church and state was a way of life for Italians and the Catholic religion did not, as the pope soon found, depend upon his retaining his traditional "States of the Church." Italians who had taken deeply to heart the inner spirit of Christianity had never been impressive in numbers or influence. Italian Catholicism was largely a matter of tradition, law and institutions, not of personal conviction.

In Germany, intellectualism had for so long been such a dominating influence that one new doctrine more could probably make little difference. The home of philosophy, of Biblical criticism, of history, despite reactionary Prussia, was well in advance of the rest of Europe.

In France, the battle between old and new, as might be expected, was both stormy and prolonged. French social progressives, orators and poets had overthrown the liberal monarchy, only to see it replaced in four years by a semi-despotic empire. Napoleon III was not a despot in the sense of Napoleon I and streaks of liberalism seemed constantly coming to the top in him and as often disappearing again. His joining the Italians against Austria, for example, has been held to have been a response to something he really cared about – nationalism, especially nationalism in Italy, whose people were his people. Yet he took his pay for his help, insisting on Cavour's handing over Nice and Savoy to France, and then, after his troops had defeated the Austrians, suddenly withdrawing. At home, the reins were at first held tightly over the press and over the intellectual in general. Victor Hugo retired to the Island of Jersey in self-exile, to constitute himself for many years a thorn in the side of the emperor.

At first look it is hard to understand why the liberal France of Louis Philippe should so easily give up its self-government and most of its freedom to put itself under the yoke of its forefathers. But remember the preaching of the prophets, remember the signs of proletarian unrest, remember the actual outbreaks, as the risings in Lyons in the 1830s, and the picture becomes clearer. The bourgeoisie were frightened. They threw in their hands. As between property and liberalism, they chose property. In so doing they gave to the term *bourgeois* a burden which it has never shaken off.

The first decade of the Second Empire illustrates how the sun is apt to shine with equal warmth on the just and the unjust, for it was a period of unparalleled prosperity. The France of the period is described as a country of exuberant and long-lasting "boom," a period of financiers and swindlers, with gaiety and immorality abounding. And along with them very considerable cultural brilliance, too. France in the 1850s has been likened to Bismarck's Germany of the 1870s-1880s, or, even better, to the United States in the hectic days of western expansion.[5] This prosperity enabled the country to support without difficulty two wars in the one decade, the Crimean and the Austrian.

Monarchy so well accords with Catholicism that the church had little difficulty in accommodating itself to other aspects of the period, among them its vulgar materialism. In fact, it regained something of its old place, for naturally Napoleon, himself a Catholic from mere expediency, had to support it, even to the extent of laying a heavy hand on non-Catholics; various Protestant churches were closed,[6] though in the Austrian War (and again in 1867) he came close to riding two horses at once. That was the beginning of his difficulties, which were to increase in the next decade, partly from the same cause, with this dreadful fellow Garibaldi forcing the pace in Italy against the church. At home, religious fires were stoked as against anything savouring of liberalism by the powerful and vulgar journalist, Louis Veuillot (1813-1883). Veuillot was ultra-Catholic in the style of de Maistre but without much pretension to his master's culture and none to his manners. He waged war in the bitterest and most extreme terms with all who opposed his views of the Catholic religion, whether nominally of the faithful or heretics. "He was sorry that Luther had not been burned as well as Huss and nothing was more natural or necessary than the putting to death of the heretic convicted by the church and handed over to the secular arm" (presumably for burning).[7]

Veuillot might have done no more harm than many another local hothead had he not found favour in the highest place, the Vatican itself. The story is well-known, and might be regarded as the first act in the drama, possibly the tragic drama, that was leading to the very heart of the struggle between the old world and the new, between formal religion and advancing knowledge, scientific and other. Veuillot, thanks in part to his championship of the pope, found himself in much favour in that quarter. The pope was Pio Nono, Pius IX, who had begun his reign as something of a liberal, but whose liberalism quickly vanished with the events of 1848. In 1854 Pio Nono had broken precedent by himself proclaiming, without advice, the new dogma of the Immaculate Conception. Dogmas previously proclaimed had usually had to wait until there was very substantial support for them from below. Sometimes as with Transubstantiation (1273) they had had virtually to be forced on the church. But Immaculate Conception came out of itself, as if designed for a test of allegiance. Veuillot stood to his papal guns and an understanding grew up between him and Pio Nono. Their relations became close, and Veuillot's influence began to introduce itself into papal policy – so much so that an eminent Catholic, listening to a denunciation of Ultramontanism, quietly observed that it was not Ultramontanism from which the church was suffering, but Cismontanism – the church's policy was being made in the office of Veuillot's newspaper. Nobody attributed infallibility to Veuillot, however.

The strange relationship went on as a matter of mutual reinforcement and at last it came to a head in another shot heard round the world, the so-called Syllabus of Errors. "This famous document was little else than the promulgation as the official doctrine of the church of the political philosophy of de Maistre as re-edited by Veuillot."[8] The Syllabus, a document of some length, was a catalogue and condemnation of practically every view, attitude or practice of the thoughtful and intelligent sectors of modern civilization. It makes strange reading today: to illustrate:

It is an error to believe that:
  . . . Human reason, without any regard to God, is the sole arbiter of truth and falsehood, of good and evil . . . Every man is free to embrace and profess the religion he shall believe true, guided by the light of reason . . . Protestantism is nothing more than another form of the same true Christian religion in which it is possible to be equally pleasing to God as in the Catholic Church. In the case of conflicting laws between the two powers, the civil law ought to prevail . . . In the present day it is no longer expedient that the Catholic religion shall be held as the only religion of the state to the exclusion of all other modes of worship . . .

And finally: -

Anathema on those who should maintain that the Roman Pontiff can and ought to reconcile himself to and agree with progress, liberalism, and contemporary civilization.

In such an outburst it is hard to say whether it was the voice of the Roman pontiff speaking or the voice of Louis Veuillot. Few laymen can ever have been so influential. But influential within their own circle or not, and there were two sides to that, few men, between them, have done more disservice to the cause they seek to serve. The Syllabus surprised and shocked Catholic intellectuals, it outraged Protestant zealots, and fanned anew those Reformation fires which had never gone out. Even such Catholics as Newman seemed puzzled and did not know whether the Syllabus was to be rated as dogmatic teaching or something less rigid. Here was a modern Joshua commanding the sun to stand still. Naturally the sun did not obey. Refutation began at once, investigation continued as before.

The political effects of the Syllabus were as drastic as the doctrinal. If ever a political dogma had been winning the assent of men, it was that of the complete authority of the state within its own borders. International law, always a weak plant was in the 1860s no more than a dubious collection of international practices. The Syllabus frontally attacked the strong citadel of national law. This made no considerable difference in homogeneous Protestant nations, such as Great Britain, where the question had long since been settled, but in divided states, such as the new German empire of 1870, it was to add to their division. In the interesting experiment in bi-racialism begun three years after the Syllabus appeared, that of the new Dominion of Canada (wherein about half the population was Catholic and about a third, French Catholic), the reinforcement to Ultramontanism furnished by the Syllabus and the subsequent events in Rome, set going a bitter internal strife which deepened all the rancours of race and creed and threatened the very life of the new country.

France heavily felt the new strains. At the time imperial authority was showing signs of relaxing its severities and with relaxation, the active minds of France which had never ceased to play a great part in French life despite censorship, were counting for more and more. Comte had died in 1857, but Jules Michelet was still alive (d. 1874), as were George Sand and Hippolite Taine. (Alexis de Tocqueville, that good Catholic of fine, sane, liberal mind had died in 1859, but Charles Montalembert was still living (he died in 1870). Ernest Renan was at his prime. The French church by no means welcomed the Syllabus in unanimity, for there were many liberal Catholics (such as Bishop Dupanloup). By reinforcing all the diehard elements in French Catholicism, the Syllabus may have led them once more into the breach but there many of them filled the walls up with their Catholic dead, another illustration, if one is needed, of how frequently extremism brings about its own cure.

Events in what mounts up in retrospect to a vast cultural revolution were following thick and fast upon each other in that generation that stretches from 1848 to 1878. Not only the first occupation of Rome (1848), the Syllabus of Errors, the launching of Darwinism, but the dogma of Papal Infallibility, the second occupation of Rome (September 20, 1870), the downfall of Napoleon III, and the *Kulturkampf*. In 1866 Bismarck succeeded by his war with Austria in pushing the ancient empire of the Hapsburgs out of the Germanic Confederation (which he succeeded in having transformed into "the North German Federation"), thus greatly increasing in the latter the weight of northern Protestantism. In 1861, Victor Emmanuel had been proclaimed king of Italy and only Rome, held by French bayonets, remained to be gained. In 1870, those bayonets were withdrawn, to be used against the Germans (France declared war July 19, 1870), and the Italians marched into the ancient capital.

The shock was felt throughout the Catholic world. In far off French Canada, most faithful daughter of the church, an expeditionary force was raised to go to the pope's relief. At the parting service, held in the great Cathedral of Notre Dame, Montreal, one of the officiating clergy was so overwhelmed with the grandeur of the gesture, a modern Crusade in very deed, that in his sermon, overcome with emotion, he lost his voice and could not go on; "la lame use le fourreau," it was said in appreciation of his spiritual intensity, "the sword wears out the scabbard."

Just before the French evacuated Rome and left the pope to his fate, a still more historic event than the reappearance of the ancient city as the capital of a modern nation, had taken place within it. This was the Council of the Vatican, first ecumenical council of the church since that of Trent in the sixteenth century. The point at issue was the position of the pope in relationship to the church. The fifteenth century struggle at the great councils of that century had left the question of final sovereignty undecided. Pope or Council? The Council of Trent had moved the papacy closer to absolutism. The Council of the Vatican placed the coping-stone on that arch:

> . . . the sacred Council approving, we teach and define that is a dogma divinely revealed that the Roman Pontiff, when he speaks *ex cathedra*, that is when in discharge of the office of pastor and doctor of all Christians, by virtue of his supreme Apostolic authority, by defining a doctrine of faith or morals. . . is possessed of that infallibility with which the divine Redeemer willed that His Church should be endowed . . . [9]

The arrangements within the sessions of the Councils, the natures and memberships of the committees set up and such like provisions ensured easy majority for the papal proposals. There was some grumbling behind backs but no concerted opposition. After the decision some good Catholics had difficulty accepting the new dogma, but eventually practically all submitted. Few left the church. The step was not only logical but from the Roman Catholic point of view, necessary, for with the humiliation of Austria, the prospect of the secularization of Rome and the constant possibility of a secular republic in France, the papacy no longer had a political arm to lean on (with the exception of Spain, not a very sturdy arm) and had to depend upon itself and the cohesion of the faithful.

The church was to find itself in the old position recommended by Lamennais and his friends in the 1830s; a free church in a free state – *libera chiesa en stato libero* – as Cavour had described it.

This was to cut right across the grain of historic Catholicism, which put all the weight on *a free church*, free to prescribe the rules of faith and conduct, free to preach and teach as it saw fit. It was the position to which it had already adapted itself in the United States and in Great Britain and against which it was to fight a losing battle in France over the next thirty-five years. Nor was it able to see that freedom of that sort would bring it closer to its traditional Christian role than would its centuries old attempt to maintain itself as a state within a state.

The battle between Roman Catholicism and the state in Germany was an extension of the issues that must exist between the two sets of authorities. Lord Acton once proclaimed that their existence in the same society had been the historic guarantee of freedom, for clearly if there were two sovereignties directing the lives of the same people, neither one of them could be completely despotic. The thesis is rather thin, but the Roman Catholic church's struggle against Protestant states helps to buttress it. In modern times, "advanced" states could easily sweep away individual conscientious resistance to divorce, birth control and abortion, but as the church digs itself in on such issues, it is not easy to change the ancient laws.

In the nineteenth century, there was also a battle equally prolonged and waged just as obstinately in the field of education. This battle has continued with greater or lesser intensity down to our own day. "Give me a child up to the age of seven, and you can have him for the rest of his life," one of the later popes was reported to have said. "As the twig is bent so the tree grows." The schoolyard was to be the principal battlefield in France for the remainder of the century. While Roman Catholicism was not defeated on the playing fields of France, it suffered heavy casualties, for in France, as elsewhere, the common school has made vast contributions to secularism (as to democracy and equality, which are not such controversial areas, however important).

In Bismarck's Germany, the issue lay in familiar areas – the control of the schools, the privileges of ecclesiastical corporations and related matters. The Syllabus and the Dogma of Infallibility ignited combustible material in every direction, not only in the countries dominantly Protestant. A wave of anti-Catholicism swept over Europe and across the Atlantic: "Rum, Romanism and Rebellion" as principal enemies of the Union were picked on as targets in a Presidential election in the United States a little later, and in the ultra-Catholic province of Quebec, *le parti rouge*, an anti-clerical Liberal group, carried on a courageous fight from the pulpit against "influence indue."[10] Priests, it was alleged, often would proclaim that "les cieux sont bleus, l'enfer rouge."

In Germany with its extensive program of state socialism, touching many sides of life in addition to education, collision was predictable. German liberals were apparently quite ready to invoke the direct power of the state, and to call in the police to enforce the law with a heavy hand.[11] They were charged with deserting the principles of liberalism in thus encouraging and participating in the resort to main strength. This divided them. In beginning of his campaign Bismarck had proclaimed that "We shall not go to Canossa," but to Canossa he eventually went, and the more obnoxious provisions of his decrees were quietly withdrawn.

Similar issues arose in other countries. Monastic communities and the Jesuit Order were prohibited in several. Even in Italy, secularism took some long strides forward, a civil marriage service alone, for instance, being decreed as lawful.

The struggle arising out of the Pio Nono-Veuillot alliance thus conserved some important areas of life to the church but by arousing the old suspicions of papal power and resuscitating the always present Protestant hatred (the word is not too strong) of Catholicism, it probably had its most important results, the weakening of the church and the strengthening of secularism. Papal Infallibility in practice proved as fallible as most other human attempts to turn back the hands of the clock. The "march of mind" which for three centuries had gone on from conquest to conquest, was to prove as irresistible as the conquests of Alexander of old – and perhaps as fruitless. Who is to say?

Notes

1. *Queen's Quarterly* (Kingston, Ontario, Queen's University), Vol. 81, No. 4, Winter, 1974, p. 520.
2. So proclaims George Gamow, in his *Biography of the Earth* (Mentor Books, New York, 1948).
3. Sir Charles Darwin, *The Next Million Years* (Greenwood, Westport, Connecticut, 1953).
4. A similar picture is present in his *After Many a Summer*.
5. Gérard, *French Civilization in the Nineteenth Century, op. cit.*, pp. 124ff.
6. See Soltau, *op. cit.*, p. 170.
7. *Ibid.*, p. 187, quoting Veuillot.
8. *Ibid.*, p. 193.
9. The doctrine was officially proclaimed January 18, 1870.
10. "Influence indue" was the use of priestly influence, by persuasion or threat from the pulpit, in Parliamentary elections to secure votes for candidates of *les Castors,* the ultra ultramontane wing of the Conservative party.
11. Carlton J.H. Hayes, *A Generation of Materialism 1871-1900* (New York, Harper and Row, 1941), p. 86.

CHAPTER NINETEEN

The Earthly Paradise in Sight

I

The Great Age of Teutonism
and Imperialism

On the 18th of January, 1871, in the Palace at Versailles, that palace of the Sun King himself, the Sun King whose Versailles had been admired and imitated by a score of petty German princelings in an age when every German had felt himself a bucolic in the presence of citizens of *La Grande Nation,* that palace which symbolized the very heart of defeated France, the palace of a people lying at the proud heel of their conqueror, the king of Prussia proclaimed the re-establishment of the German empire. In that palace, built by "the eldest son of the (Roman Catholic) church, the ceremony was conducted in a Lutheran Protestant setting. A Lutheran Protestant sermon was preached."[1] The ancient Reich of Charlemagne and of Friederich Rotbart was re-established, and on the soil of the hereditary enemy, the enemy whose soldiers had carried devastation to German homes a thousand times in the thousand years of the precarious past.

Could the humiliation of a proud nation have been more complete?

A short year before, the pope had had himself proclaimed as the world's supreme religious and ecclesiastical authority. Many another occurrence of weighty significance for the future of mankind was also to come to pass in that eventful year. In May, Great Britain and the United States had signed the Treaty of Washington thereby giving legal end to the rift that the American Civil War had caused to appear between the two great English-speaking powers. On July 19 of that same overcrammed summer, France, almost light-heartedly, had declared war on the Germans, evidently in an effort to prevent the consolidation of German power under the aegis of Prussia. While the war was going on, Russia took the opportunity, no one saying her nay, to tear up the *Black Sea* clauses of the treaty by which the Crimean War had been concluded, those clauses that forbade her to maintain a navy on the Black Sea. On September 2, Napoleon III, his army shattered, surrendered at Sedan and became a German prisoner of war. Two days later, September 4, the French people repudiated the empire and began to work their way towards a republic. On the 20th of September, Italian troops marched into Rome and Pio Nono, the Pope, retired to the Vatican Palace, where he and his successors were to remain for fifty-nine years, "prisoners" of the Italian state. Surely enough for one brief summer.

The proclamation of the German empire on January 18, was followed in the spring by the Peace of Frankfurt. Germany took back Alsace and Lorraine, provinces which the Sun King in his greatness had added to his crown. The French frontier was shoved back from the Rhine and to a people well aware of their past the blood shed over many centuries to defend themselves from the Eastern barbarians must have seemed shed in vain.

With France's humiliation there was in the rest of Europe little understanding and less sympathy. For this was the great age of Germanism. To the northern peoples, wherever they might be around the world, the Franco-Prussian war had had some of the aspects of a duel between the polarities of the age, between fresh northern vigour and effete southernism, between Protestantism and popery, between the Reformation and the Renaissance, between the wholesomeness, the manliness, the essential innocence of the Teuton and the over-sophistication, the frivolity, the immorality of the Latin. To mention such matters today is almost to draw a laugh, but to the age they were real and warm, the incentives to thought and to action.

The concept of *race* was of course ancient: but it had been given definite form and shape by such writers as Joseph comte de Gobineau, ironically himself a Frenchman.

He used to imagine a majestic descent for himself: French, but a German noble of the blood of Charlemagne. De Gobineau became an influence in certain German circles far out of proportion to his talents or his soundness; in fact, he could hardly have been less sound, though his writings had a pseudo-scientific air about them;

> In Northern Europe, the materialistic strain, contributed by the best of the Germanic tribes, has been continuously strengthened by the influx

of Celts and Slavs. But as the white peoples drifted more and more to the south, the male influences gradually lost their force and were absorbed by an excess of female elements, which finally triumphed. We must allow some exceptions to this, for example in Piedmont and Northern Spain.[2]

The concept of *race*, however, went far beyond superficial writers. It penetrated into every crevice of human thought and probably could be rated as a dominant way of thinking during the last half of the century. Emotions roused by the wars of the northern peoples against the Italian Napoleon Bonaparte and his French associates followed familiar paths. North against south, Protestant against Catholic, fair against dark. Pious people could remind themselves that angels were flaxen-haired. Who sighed for the dark when he could find the light? The devil was black, was he not? Such notions were all too easy, but their influence was world-wide, and the world over they fashioned the attitudes of the colonizing peoples to "the natives." It took the uttermost of Christian grace to discover that in the sight of God black men might have white souls.

The idea of race represented the historical interpretation of the centuries for had not European history begun with the triumphs of the Germans over the effete and worn-out Romans? All history, and many historians, echoed Germanism. In England a great historian, Bishop William Stubbs, began his *Constitutional History of England* with recitation of how the youthful Teutons had swept over Europe in a kind of cleansing flood, carrying away the rubbish of the ancient centuries. Queen Victoria, wholly German in blood, was also German in her sympathies. Her daughter married the heir to the German throne. She had sighed with relief when the machinations of "those two wicked old men," as she called them, John Russell and Viscount Palmerston, had been foiled and the Germans allowed to go on uninterruptedly with their pressure on neighbouring Denmark. On both sides of the Atlantic, pulpit and press rang with condemnation of French immorality and frivolity, commendation of German manly vigour. The English world was Teutonic and proud of it. Luckily its pride stopped short of the edge of the cliff over which Germany many years later was to tumble. Meanwhile, this, the 1870s, was the day of Germanism.

A much more conspicuous year than 1870 could hardly be selected. Fifty-five years from Waterloo to Sedan. Once again German troops in the enemy's capital. Eighteen seventy may serve to mark "a tide in the affairs of men." It was to be the new Germany that was to take that tide at the flood. To it the Industrial Revolution had come late, but when it had come, the gates had swung open wide. The generation after 1870 saw imperial Germany advance on every front, finally to try for "World Power or Downfall" (in the words of one of its military writers). For that generation of Germans, the immense sense of well-being, a primary constituent in the heady wind of the new nationalism, furnished the zeal, the energy, the faith, that commonly lies at the base of a great shift in civilization.

A humiliated France for a time turned inward. "A republic is that form of government which divides France the least," said M. Adolphe Thiers, the new leader. A rather negative base upon which to build a new structure. But France must never be discounted. She rests solidly on her soil, and her soil provides the energies of her people. Moreover, she draws immense strength from her deep-rooted civilization and even today, despite all the blows she has received, her children probably would find it hard to believe that France is not the centre of the world. If in the nineteenth century, she could have had harmony within and have decided the direction in which she wished to go, she might once more have become, in many respects, that centre of the world which seemed to have been her historic role. But the late eighteenth century, culminating in the Revolution, had unleashed so many forces and so divergent that a steady course was not to be steered. Hence the kaleidoscope of régimes, attitudes and aspirations, down almost to this day.

The root of French disharmony is plainly to be seen. When the tides of the Reformation were sweeping over Europe, they submerged France in civil war. It was not merely a matter of the new religion against the old. Far more was it French nationalism against the supra-national papacy. In England that contest had been decided by the strong measures of Henry VIII and Elizabeth. A national church had been set up and the dominance and interference of Rome put to an end. But France was not to go that route. To Henry IV, "Paris was worth a mass" and so the division between church and state was perpetuated. Throughout the following centuries, it was never ended. To Rome, Gallicanism remained a running sore down to 1904. To the state, ultramontanism was a threat, a symbol of a sovereignty within a sovereignty. At last, after decades of friction, the French government cut the Gordian knot and disestablished the Roman Catholic church in France, making it into a private body, like other incorporated bodies. At long last, France was mistress in her own house. If France had solved the problem in the sixteenth century by establishing the often threatened national church of France, she probably would not have been such a divided country in the nineteenth.

The great misfortune of France has therefore been that it missed the Reformation.

France in the generation that lay ahead of 1870 was to continue to face extremely serious internal division. The struggle with church, suspended on a public basis during the empire, was to go on and become more acute. More and more men turned their backs on the ancient faith. A new generation of workmen arose who began to feel their power and probe for a place in the public life. But more and more securely, the church with its ancient appeal and its aggressive religious Orders, entrenched itself in the conservative elements of French society, not only the old aristocratic families but also the aspiring layers of its upper middle classes.

Towards the end of the century France was able to secure an alliance with the power on "the other side," that is, the power on the other side of the enemy, or potential enemy, Germany (1893); thus renewing a foreign policy that had strongly marked her affairs in the eighteenth century. Furthermore, by the late 1890s her expansive energies had once more so far asserted themselves as to challenge the British efforts in Africa. But the result of that had been the humiliation of Colonel Marchand at Fashoda (1898) on the upper Nile and the destruction of that dream of French imperialists – a corridor stretching across Africa from west to east. The general populace of France was not deeply concerned with imperialist adventure, but among its armed services, there were some who could have echoed the later words of General de Gaulle and thought in terms of "the hereditary enemy, by which they did not mean Germany." They were not dominant: most French people seemed to agree with Georges Clemenceau; "the place for our soldiers is on the Rhine."

French imperialists nevertheless were powerful. Many of them had been trained in the renewed Jesuit colleges, trained in a code that so well suited the high-minded authoritarian attitudes of the military adventurer in far places. But even these gambollings among the lions and elephants of Africa or the ruined palaces of Indo-China seemed to be dogged by retribution, for there was to arise a personal incident in the French army which ended by dividing the whole nation in still another fashion. This was the celebrated Dreyfus affair which, beginning in 1894, was not concluded until the first decade of the twentieth century. Alfred Dreyfus, a Jewish officer, had been accused of betrayal of military secrets to "the enemy" (the German government), had been put upon his trial and found guilty. After a long interval doubts as to the justice of the verdict had arisen and almost all France, it seemed, turned to the question of where justice lay. At long last, the previous findings of guilt were reversed, Dreyfus's honour fully restored. It was a magnificent display, every step of it visible to the entire civilized world, of the quest for justice. Yet the Dreyfus affair badly divided a France which already had divisions enough. But in the persistency and humanity with which some of her sons determined that justice must be done, the national sense of integrity must surely have been strongly buttressed. France, too, like Germany, may have found, in some measure at least, the energy, the faith in herself, that commonly lies at the heart of a great shift in civilization.

For Great Britain, the same general assessment may be made. The series of domestic passages-at-arms in which William Gladstone and Benjamin Disraeli exchanged sword cuts were after all little more than ripples on the stream, but the Irish ulcer began to suppurate more painfully than it had done since the days of the great Daniel O'Connell and the potato famine years of the 1840s.

At the end of the long bridge over the River Shannon leading into the City of Limerick, stands a great round stone tower. It commands the bridge and the city. It is called "King John's Tower," for it was built by the English forces of occupation under that monarch in the year – 1203! It was continuously occupied by English garrisons from 1203 to 1922, 719 years. Then in 1922, the English left. The Catholic Irish had got them "off their backs."

The conclusion seems clear enough. Irish nationalism, apparently unquenchable over the centuries, was simply the unending reaction against the original English conquest. Few English Conservatives could understand these twin problems of nationalism and conquest. "What Ireland needs is twenty years of resolute government," said Lord Salisbury when prime minister in the 1880s. A few years later, Arthur Balfour, to be his successor, publicly questioned whether there was any such entity as an Irish nation. The poetic intuition of Matthew Arnold, in his *Irish Essays* (1882) did not get him beyond current expediency. Liberals, under Gladstone took a different view. Receiving the Queen's summons to form a government after the end of the Disraeli régime in 1880, the great man, at the moment engaged in his vigorous hobby of cutting down trees with an axe, dropped his axe, drew himself up with dignified presence and exclaimed in appropriate solemnity: "My mission is to pacify Ireland"! He did not succeed in securing "home rule" for Ireland, but he had seen the way out, the goal that was not reached for many a long year. Ireland remained the divisive factor, the unpleasant cloud in the British sky.

Apart from the Irish question, the country was prosperous and the empire expanding. The union of the North American provinces into one great Dominion had been brought about in 1867; a second nation was being built there by the British North Americans, now become Canadians, in conscious compensation for the loss of the first in the American Revolution.

In Australia another nation, occupying the whole of the world's last continent, was being built, and early in the new century it received its form and shape as the Commonwealth of Australia. A new strong society, unique and progressive, was rising in New Zealand. While South Africa presented serious problems, it, too, seemed to be following the same general lines of evolution. English liberty, English constitutionalism, English adroitness, English capital, and the apparently irresistible strength of the English language – such factors were enabling Englishmen everywhere to create new Englands in apparent facsimiles of the old. The great Dominions had none of them begun to forget their origins and when in 1887 Queen Victoria celebrated her Golden Jubilee and still more, when in 1897, she celebrated her Diamond, heart-warming testimonies of affection came up from all of them to the motherland.

Those were the days when commercial concerns delighted to distribute calendars depicting the British bulldog guarding the Union Jack, with the label affixed "We hold thee safe" or with maps of the world showing in the deep red colouring those portions of it, by no means small, which lay within the British empire. Those were the days of the semi-heroic verse of Rudyard Kipling. They were the days when Cecil Rhodes (1853-1902), looking out from Capetown, could see Cairo 5,000 miles away on the northern horizon. They were the days of an energy and self-confidence, mounting up to a faith that commonly lies at the heart of a great shift in civilization.

With imperial expansion, evangelical Christianity went hand in hand. The world could not "be won for Christ" without a measure of order; order followed the flag, "God" only a step behind. Missionaries received the protection of the flag. Converts were children of God (minor children) just as surely as were factory hands. When in the 1880s, Scottish Presbyterian missionaries found hostile Arab slave traders on the shores of the distant Lake Nyasa in Africa, their church organized a monster petition asking for protection and interference. The petition was presented to Lord Salisbury, the prime minister, who had not shown himself anxious to act. As the leader of the deputation put a bound volume of petitioners' names upon the prime minister's desk, he exclaimed "This is the voice of Scotland." As he thumped down another, his voice rose as he exclaimed "And this is the voice of Scotland." It went on. The voice of Scotland became more and more emphatic as volume after volume descended upon Salisbury's desk. Eventually Nyasaland was proclaimed a Protectorate and the missionaries were able to oust the Arab slave traders.

"The voice of Scotland" and other such voices were heard in many other parts of the world. The details need not be repeated. Imperialism and late Victorian Christianity had many a link.

A similar portrait is to be made of the United States: recovery from the divisions of the civil war completed, the resumption of the current of internal expansion and prosperity that Americans had come to take for granted; the vast expansion of population with innumerable new states brought into the Union and innumerable great cities rising within them; the conviction of the many excellences of American life; the genuine feelings of generosity that moved so many American hearts; all these, in the American case too, provided the energy, the zeal and the faith that lie at the heart of one of the great shifts in civilization.

The American experience in the outer world differed only in detail from that of European nations. It was marked by sheer expansionism, as in the great continental additions to American territory (such as California (1845), strategic considerations (such as Alaska (1867) and Hawaii (1898), belief in the American way of life and the usual mixture of motives that marked evangelical zeal (as in the Philippines or Hawaii). In the Philippines, president McKinley felt much the same concern for his "little brown brothers" as Cecil Rhodes was feeling about the same time for his black brethren north of the Cape. Other colonizing nations showed little difference: some were possibly less hypocritical than others. But is hypocrisy the right word? In colonial expansion, there was a mixture of motives which it is not possible completely to sort out.

The expansion of the English-speaking world, while vast, was not so extensive as entirely to shut out the efforts and claims of other peoples. Bismarck is said to have exclaimed, in conjunction with the settlement of one of the colonial African disputes, that "England is a great gouty giant that screams aloud in apprehension lest anyone coming near step on her toes," which perhaps was a natural view for a German to take, but Germany founded her colonial African empire without British intervention. And France increased hers; after all it was 5,000 miles from the Cape to Cairo and almost as far from the west across the continent to the east. Dimensions such as that gave much elbow room, and Africa fortunately was divided up without a war.

Then there was the interior of Asia. Within its vastness, English and Russians had already become aware of each other's presence.' The expansion of Russia is as vast in scale as the expansion of Britain and it extends over a much longer period, beginning even before the consolidation of the Principality of Moscow in the early Middle Ages[4] and quite evidently not yet having stopped. But so far, it has not resulted in a full-dress "class A" war, only two "class B" conflicts, the Crimean, 1854-1856, and the Russo-Japanese, 1904-1905, both fought to check Russian expansion. The whole period since the Second World War could, however, properly be regarded as a duel between Russia and the West, with the United States playing the role played for a century by Great Britain, the barrier to Russian expansion.

During the period down to the First World War, Russia built no new nations, images of herself, in the depths of Asia or elsewhere, for she encountered indigenous peoples who might be conquered but not entirely obliterated. "It is impossible to keep peace with uncivilized tribes," the Russian General Skobelev is reported as having airily said in 1878, after a "battle" in which his soldiers had slaughtered some 25,000 of the "uncivilized." But a mere 25,000 did not destroy "the natives" and when they had thus been pacified, the attempt at Russification could go on. The degree of success achieved is not easy to ascertain but apparently it was roughly comparable with that achieved by the British in India. At any rate, Russian has become a kind of official *lingua franca* as did English in India, and in both countries, the railway and other communications caused semblances of Western civilization to penetrate everywhere (Indians might say that the word *civilization* should be put in quotation marks). The major distinction is obvious; no Russian government can be expected to endow any of the territories within its grasp with independence[5]. The northern areas of Siberia seem more like *Colonies* in the traditional sense, being offshoots of Russia proper, carrying with them the language and the way of life.

Under the drive of European, or "Western" expansion, it could have been imagined towards the close of the nineteenth century that the whole world, on the crest of this wave of well-being, was about to make a great move forward. The human race was increasing rapidly in numbers, the health of mankind was vastly better than it had ever been in the past, man's span of years added to, infectious diseases were being conquered, famine, thanks to a net of rapid communication, seemed to be virtually eliminated, (even in India whose people increased their numbers with bewildering speed). Technological progress was being made at a dizzying rate: the smoke of the steamship was seen on every horizon; the wonders of electricity were rapidly unfolding; the internal combustion engine was beginning to move carriages. In darkest Africa and on every tropical island, the old, cruel gods were yielding to the Christian God. John R. Mott, the American, coined the slogan "The World for Christ in this Generation" and organized his "*International Student Christian Movement*" (beginning about 1890) in support of that objective. New schools, new hospitals, new colleges opened daily, not only for the favoured white but for the peoples of all nations.

What could the boring portrait of "eternal life" with its golden streets, the harps of heaven, the shadowy paradise after death, have been to the terrestrial paradise which the unprejudiced observer with knowledge fitting him to compare that age with its predecessors, could see rising around him? Surely a golden age, a golden age of realistic qualities, not mere dreams, might have seemed to be opening. At the end of the nineteenth century, it looked as if the race had moved forward and its leading members might have been justified in believing that they stood at the top of man's upward path.

Was there then no spot on the sun? There is no age without spots. The period ending the century had its share. Wars, for example. The Chino-Japanese war of 1895, the Turkish-Greek war of 1896, the Spanish-American war of 1898, the British-Boer war of 1899. While all these might have been regarded as "class C" wars, they form a very fair collection of "spots." To them may be added the Russo-Japanese war, the Balkan wars of 1912, and, then, in grand culmination, the First World War of 1914. But were these outbreaks in themselves (with the exception of the last) prophecies of a coming change in the atmosphere of civilization such as those previously looked at in these pages? Probably not, for war of varying intensity we have always had with us. Wars themselves may be mere symptoms of deeper causes.

If one such cause could be found for all these wars, it almost certainly would be growing nationalism, the effort of organized human groups to make themselves masters in their own houses. But why had not these outbreaks occurred long before? In some areas they had, but unsuccessfully (notoriously Poland). The nationalistic wars of the last period of the nineteenth century, many of which were successful, proceeded out of the general well-being of the world, as more or less described above.

But why this general well-being? If that question could be satisfactorily answered, the explanation of "progress" would be plain. The mounting technological accomplishments (technical accomplishment rests on myriads of bits of inventiveness) must never be discounted, for through them, little by little, and with each step a little longer than the previous one, the gain becomes cumulative and vast. How much less startling to go from steam to internal combustion than from animal power to steam! Then there is the extension of the sovereign power of states, which means the extension of the areas of comparative peace, with the presumed accompaniment, prosperity. And a blanket explanation could be put forward, which would almost mock all the rest − "progress in civilization." Why larger states? Why more peace? Why machines? Had man become more humane, more sensible, as the centuries unrolled? Or stripped of all his accessories of place and power, was he still the same selfish, egotistic ape that he had always been? Education had spread, or at least *schooling*, but had wisdom? Religion? What has religion to do with peace? Principles are rained in blood, are they not? "I came not to bring peace, but a sword."

II
Inside Imperialism:
Discordant Voices, but Few Bounds
to Optimism

It is impossible to cast the exact balance of an age; every one uses different currencies. But some general items may be put down as partial answers to the perpetual questions: "is the world getting better − or worse?"

Sic et non, Yes and No.

As late as about 1800, English law provided the death penalty for scores of offences, some trivial: "as well be hung for a sheep as a lamb!" Within a generation and a half or so, the list had been reduced to moderate proportions. On the other hand, until a little before mid-century there was no prohibition against employing women in the most horrible aspects of coal mining. And they were so employed. Slaves were freed in 1833, the

British government compensating the owners. In the earlier parts of the century, ships carrying emigrants to North America had the lightest of restrictions placed on them and many an emigrant never reached the other side. Every dead passenger meant more room for those left. The last British restrictions on Jews as citizens were removed by 1858. Twenty years later, Charles Bradlaugh was not allowed to take his seat in Parliament because he was neither Jew nor Christian. So the list could go on – endlessly. The sum of all items was clearly on the plus side. Nineteen hundred was far milder in temper than 1800.

There can be a more generalized approach. What has been the message of "the prophets" in the last century or two? In the eighteenth century in France there were all the declarations of the "men of reason" which finally nagged others into the action of '89. In Great Britain there was the call to repentance, conversion and the orderly "methodical" life issued by Wesley and his disciples. After the war with Napoleon, there were the vague declarations of the lower class unfortunates such as Orator Hunt. There was William Cobbett, then Robert Owen. But before 1850, as has been noted, there was little equivalent in Great Britain to the major social proclamations relatively common in France – the Saint-Simonians, the Fourierists and others.

In Great Britain, Thomas Malthus, David Ricardo, *laissez-faire* and the policeman state held the field. Look after yourself, that was the motto. Even William Wilberforce and Zachary Macauley seemed more touched by the misfortunes of black slaves than by those of English labourers. It is true that Francis Place secured a nominal withdrawal of the Combination Laws, but Richard Cobden later could tell honest workmen to bargain for their wages face to face with their masters and, "if they did not wish to do that, let them save twenty pounds and emigrate to America."

Then within a short time, Great Britain found her "prophets," too. Their names are known to all: Thomas Carlyle 1795-1881; John Ruskin, 1819-1900; Matthew Arnold, 1822-1888, and various lesser lights. To them add the great mid-Victorian novelists, especially Charles Dickens, all of whom had their say on the "condition of England question," some of the poets, notably Elizabeth Barrett Browning, and we have as formidable a list of people who were anxious "to do something about it" as their opposite numbers in France had been earlier. These people all spoke with highly individual voices and their messages came in very different shapes but in them there was a certain common content; a desire for an improvement in society towards what they considered justice. They might be religious or without religion (as was George Eliot), of the establishment, like Arnold, or outside it, like "General" William Booth (1829-1912), founder of the Salvation Army. Several of them were conservative, though not Conservatives. None of them was a reactionary or even a high tory, with the possible exception of Anthony Trollope, and he was satirical at the ease and wealth of the Church of England.

To North Americans, most of the English "prophets" carry an alien tone, for obtruding into every page they wrote was the idea of social class. Few people on the western side of the Atlantic grasp the rigidities of the English class structure, rigid even in our day, triply rigid in preceding ages. Aristocrats, middle classes, lower classes, how the prophets rang the changes on the realities behind these words! And how hard were the realities they represented! Because of this deep-seated sense of class, a major literary figure like Matthew Arnold makes hard reading today. Carlyle, as a Scot, is fairly free of it. With most, it is constantly present (but Dickens is invariably and exuberantly middle class), the bedrock of English life.

The dissonances the English class structure awoke provided much of the stuff of English social evolution for the whole sweep of the nineteenth century in internal politics is the struggle forward against class privilege towards democracy. The various Reform Acts were major battles in the class war. When universal male suffrage had been won, the battle for universal female suffrage began. Until well into the new century, the twentieth, the English conservatism that insists on gradualism, after losing the battle of "principle," limited the suffrage to females above the age of thirty; this was swept away and the war for women's "liberty" in the fullest possible sense went on and goes on. In all the conflicts, the "prophets" have been prominent, but so deep is the English sense of social difference that even the most "advanced" of them have seldom been "democrats" in the American sense.

On the continent, where revolution has swept away much more history than in Great Britain, social change has been both easier and less assured. Of the greater countries, France went furthest towards both political and social democracy. Yet even in nineteenth century Germany, people commented on the relative ease of communication and association between different social grades, as compared with England. But it was only in the New World that the full sweep of equality could obtain. Even there, there were stubborn little strongholds of resistance, slowly being worn away, with another class system growing up, one that might in time exhibit, under other forms, rigidities similar to the old.

Among the English social reformers – the term comes easily into use in the second half of the century – John Ruskin was eminent. He had spent his life up to about the age of forty as art critic (*Stones of Venice, Seven Lamps of Architecture*, and others) and had achieved a certain reputation. Then about 1860, he seems to have had a semi-religious experience which led to very different kinds of books. His *Unto This Last*, 1860, was a full dress assault on the economic thought of the day. From Adam Smith, through Malthus, Ricardo and then Mill, there stretched the line of thought that enthroned as the highest wisdom the idea of *laissez-faire,* the idea that men may do as they like with their own, that the state's full duty was done when it kept order, that in everything else men should be left to stand on their own feet (with some exception made for John Stuart Mill). It was a doctrine that fitted admirably into Darwin's idea of "the survival of the fittest," but it had little to do with the conceptions of the good society which had flitted through men's minds over the centuries. Was there no room in life for justice, goodness, beauty, compassion? Such words might be idle to many a man of business, the "hustlers," "boomsters," "developers," in modern parlance, but they were words of power. Ruskin originally would have placed *beauty* first among them; he was an ancestor of our modern *conservation* movements. With the writing of *Unto This Last,* the other words took the lead. In a letter of 1862, he burst out in heresy against the accepted creed:

> The Science of Political Economy is a Lie – wholly and to the very root (as hitherto taught). It is also the Damnedest – that is to say, the most utterly and to the lowest pit condemned of God and his Angels – that the Devil, or Betrayer of Man, has yet invented . . . To this 'science' and to this alone (the professed organized pursuit of Money) is owing All the evil of modern days . . .[6]

Other books of similar portent followed *Unto This Last,* such as *The Crown of Wild Olive* and *Munera Pulveris.* Gradually they reached a wide public, and, permeating English opinion, were major factors in deflecting the current of the times from the mere "dog-eat-dog" view of life – to the co-operative humaneness of the present. For example, in 1906 a journalist put to the new Labour Members of Parliament the question, "What work has influenced you most?" *Unto This Last* was the work.[7] In the war against gross materialism, Ruskin has never lost his influence. Part of his audience was "working class," and he never lost his personal contact with men of that type.

Ruskin's books were written in half-poetical prose and they did not condescend to the semi-literate. Evidently his shots reached their mark. He seriously wounded the beast of unrestrained greedy capitalism (though he certainly did not kill it), and it has never been quite the same since. Few people today, even in the United States, would preach the old doctrines of completely free competition, which in essence are simply the claims of the strong to the right to do as they wish. Yet it is never wise to ascribe too much influence to one man in discussing great social changes, for society is an infinitely complicated organism and one man by himself cannot move mountains. Ruskin was fortunate in the time at which he made his statement. Society was already beginning to move in the direction in which he thought it should go. But he accelerated its rate of movement.

Since those days, a new world has come into being wherein much that was then reprobated has come to be taken for granted. One of Ruskin's doctrines was that of St. Paul – "we are all members one of another." By many avenues, the world is closer to active acceptance of that doctrine than it was in the nineteenth century.

Ruskin and his like were the vocal "prophets." They spoke in cultured accents. But down at the bottom, under leadership drawn mostly from the people, the wide social movement cast up by the Industrial Revolution, was steadily preparing. Men cannot be gathered together in factories without ideas about their work emerging and from ideas to action is a natural and prompt progression. The law and the powers that were could hold up combination, but eventually, it had to come and the world found itself with the trade union on its hands. The story is a large one, for with this emergence of a third social class, the ancient order of society received a major blow. The advance was irregular, both by country and by year. It was in 1848 that Karl Marx managed to get his "Communist Manifesto" proclaimed. That represented doctrinaire thinking, but it held its own and in the 1860s Marx followed it up with his *Das Kapital* which not only analyzed the world as it was and had been but also laid down what it would be in the long future. Marxism had come to stay, so to speak, and with various ups and downs, it went on to its "one divine event to which (its) whole creation moved," that is to say, the Russian Revolution of 1917, when it got the chance of taking over a great state. The apocalyptic tone in the Tennysonian quotation just used is thus not inappropriate. As the socialist way of thinking gained strength, this tone became louder. In the end socialism, especially in its Communist expression would take on many of the traits of a religion.[8]

During the nineteenth century, there were almost as many separate kinds of socialism as there were socialists, which is normal to new movements. Towards the end of the century the tendency was for groups to coalesce and to build up into national organizations of trade unions and particularly national political parties, such as the British Labour party. Leadership rapidly came forward. In Great Britain, men like Kier Hardie appeared, but there was a similar evolution elsewhere. In unfree countries such as Russia, "agitators" being harshly treated "went underground" and took their agitations with them; these surfaced again when Lenin and Trotsky got back to Russia in 1917. Where national parties were formed, they steered for power. In the twentieth century, the British Labour party first won power in 1924, since when Britain has oscillated from one side of the political camp to the other. In most modern countries the prospect of a Labour, or socialist, government no longer looks like the ultimate catastrophe, but there is still a long way to go before the vast series of adjustments is made that stand between the present and the kind of society that would be found acceptable to the majority. In other words, the imbalance and ferment occasioned by the injection into the social order of a new, powerful and uneducated class will long continue, and society, as a result, will constantly be in a more or less revolutionary state. It is to be hoped that the progress of adjustment will not again light fires to burn heretics.

In 1941 a distinguished scholar at Columbia, C.J.H. Hayes, published a book which he entitled *A Generation of Materialism, 1871-1900*.[9] What we see in life depends upon the angle from which we view it, so Professor Hayes probably felt his title warranted. Yet that very generation provided so many examples of the non-material! Ruskin has just been mentioned. His elder, Thomas Carlyle, of whom he was in a sense a disciple, could equally well be discussed, though Carlyle had little of the accurate aim of his disciple. There were many others, and they were not merely voices crying in the night. There was General Booth, for example, and his Salvation Army: there was the vast missionary effort at home and abroad, the impressive statistics of which, for 1900, Hayes himself presents.[10] There was the very large movement called "the Social Gospel," "the New Social Order" and by various other names. There were the Catholic Socialist movements of Europe. There were a thousand enterprises, a thousand efforts made, which it seems stretching the meaning of words to dub "materialistic." Were Andrew Carnegie's vast benefactions for building libraries "materialistic"? Is a hospital an evidence of materialism, or a university? Such institutions consist of material objects, but what about the spirit behind them?

Is everything that makes for man's well-being "materialistic"? If so, a tenuous area is left for the "spiritual." Perhaps that is not unfortunate. Towards the end of the nineteenth century and increasingly as time wore on, the "purely religious aspects of life" (and the phrase may well be almost meaningless) were apparently laid aside (by the mass of intelligent people and many of the unintelligent too), in favour of what it seems absurd to call "the purely materialistic." As the old conceptions of religion weakened, life, life here and now, its intrinsic "holiness," its worth, its improvement, came to get more and more attention. "I am come that ye may have life and that ye may have it more abundantly." Not an unworthy sentiment, surely. And since it will forever be impossible for finite minds to solve the riddle of infinity, (The farthest out galaxy (1975), reported to be eight *billion* light years distant) perhaps there is common sense in resigning ourselves to our fate, taking ourselves as we appear to be, animals along with other animals, and devoting ourselves to making the best of it.

That by no means is mere hedonism – the "let us eat, drink and be merry" philosophy. The scientists tell us that the species *man* may well have a million years ahead of it. The long-range plans for a million years should surely be enough to engage the loftiest imagination. Of course that naked ape in us may still make fools of us all, and arrange for us to commit suicide by our own cleverness and destroy our earth, too. But the effort to prevent that fate might make life worth while.

Whatever our philosophical point of view, the trend of the last part of the nineteenth century is surely not to be disputed. Unregulated competition begins to be regulated, Labour appears as a political force and steadily grows in strength, in nearly all countries the conditions of life are constantly ameliorated. A very different atmosphere marks the end of the century from its beginning, a more humane atmosphere, much more concerned with general human welfare. The change in the human climate, already far advanced by the end of the century was to go to still greater lengths in the new century.

If a person writing in 1820 had been able to live again and write in 1900 he probably would have agreed that the race had reached the highest point of its progress. To him, the golden age might well have seemed to have come. But if you stand at the top, there is only one way to go – down! And there has hardly been an observer yet in whatever age he has lived, who has not felt that that is the way in which the road leads – down! Observers of their times are invariably pessimists "O tempora O mores!" The biological development has been immense, but with some exceptions, it has not gone so far as to injure life rather than improve it. Mr. Gandhi, unsparingly critical of Western civilization as he was, was compelled to seek the attention of a European surgeon when he developed appendicitis. Praise and blame are equally easy. Are there convincing reasons for the observer of about 1900 to have believed that the West had reached the top and that thenceforward, the path must lead downward? Prophets of doom abound in every age, and most of them may be disregarded. Were there those who should not have been?

The "end of century" observer – and the century should be taken as ending in 1914, rather than in 1900 – could have looked in practically every direction and complimented himself and his fellows on the magnificence of their attainments. Power, national and imperial, good order, prospects for peace rather than for the perpetual state of war of past ages, and a very good degree of liberalism in all the leading countries. Even Russia was given a constitution and in a stumbling way it seemed as if it were beginning to work. No limit to industrial and commercial growth. New countries, new cities. Excellent municipal facilities. There was no question of the unceasing triumphs of science, both abstract and applied. The last generation or so had been the great age of "records"; the largest ship, the fastest train, the tallest building (the Eiffel Tower, 984 feet, 1889) the biggest city – the list was endless.

In the non-mechanical world, the situation was perhaps not so assured, but optimism from one area of life communicated itself to another, so that in the non-mechanical area a similar confidence prevailed. In England, the Victorian giants in the fields of the novel and poetry had not been replaced, though there were many of still excellent calibre, but the stream of first-class French novelists seemed in no danger of drying up. Germany, great land of knowledge, whose professors had extended men's horizons in so many directions, may have been diverting its mental energies to the more practical fields but presumably this was but momentary. In backward Russia, the novel and music despite "backwardness" had risen to splendid heights and Leo Tolstoi (1828-1910) was still writing.

The English-speaking world had seemed to find fresh breath even in the sphere of religion. The old suavities of High Church Anglicanism had attractions only for the few, that might be true, but the crudities of the "hell and damnation" sects also seemed to be moderating, replaced by sober middle class conceptions of common sense, a religion more and more interested in loving neighbours than in speculations about eternal life. Even the Roman Catholic church seemed to be turning in this direction for had not Pope Leo XIII in 1891 officially expressed the church's concern for the well-being of the labouring man and issued his encyclical *Rerum novarum*, which has been called "the charter of Catholic Socialism."[11] It is interesting to note how extremes may meet; the spirit of the age – the *zeitgeist* – was bringing the Catholic church and socialists out to the same point – the welfare of man. And what liberal would have dissented?

The latter part of the century was an age of great brilliance in every branch of science. It is only necessary to name a few specific points: the nature of the minute areas of life was being laid bare, carrying exploration so far that it seemed impossible to determine whether a given organism was plant or animal and beyond that, far into its cellular structure. In reverse direction, more powerful telescopes were steadily expanding the visible size of the universe: it had long been necessary for astronomers to talk of distances in terms of light years, and now the number of light years[12] to which the telescope extended the human eye constantly increased. In short it would have been possible to make a roll-call of the sciences and get from every name called much the same answer: the unlimited possibilities of the extension of knowledge including the grandest possibility of all, that man himself might one day learn the secret of life itself and be able to make life at will.

By the end of the nineteenth century, well could the words of the old Greek philosopher be echoed, "Man is the measure of all things."

Notes

1.   By Rev. A. Rogge, in Robertson, *Readings, op. cit.*, II, pp. 594ff. gives the Official Account.

2.   Arthur de Gobineau, *The Inequality of Human Races*, Trans. Adrian

Collins, Intro. by Dr. Oscar Levy, Ed. of *Authorized English Version of Nietzsche's Works* (Heinemann, London, 1915), p. 87. See also p. 91.

3. See *inter alia,* Captain James Abbott, *Narrative of a Journey from Heraut to Khiva, Moscow and St. Petersburgh during the late Russian Invasion of Khiva* (2 Vols., 3rd Ed., London, 1884). This book was written about 1840. It marks an early Anglo-Indian reaction to the Russian advance in Central Asia. A similar book, dealing with some other phases of this mid-Asiastic contact is Gerald Morgan, *Ney Elias: Explorer and Envoy Extraordinary in High Asia, 1844-1897* (Allen and Unwin, London, 1971). Elias was the man who persuaded the Afghans to annex the strip of territory which still separates India from Russia.

4. See G. V. Lantzeff and R. A. Pierce, *Eastward to Empire: Exploration and Conquest in Russian Open Frontier to 1750* (McGill, Queen's University Press, Montreal, 1973).

5. See Farley Mowat, *Siberia* (McClelland and Stewart Limited, Toronto, 1970, 1973).

6. R. H. Murray, *Studies in the English Social and Political Thinkers of the Nineteenth Century* (2 Vols., W. Heffer and Sons, Cambridge, England, 1928), Vol. II, p. 117.

7. *Ibid.,* p. 120.

8. See in this, Chapter 17 p. 254.

9. Hayes, *A Generation of Materialism, 1871-1900 op. cit.*

10. *Ibid.,* p. 150.

11. See also p. 312

12. See also p. 296.

CHAPTER TWENTY

Making God in Man's Image

I

The Cultural Demise of
The Nineteenth Century

By the end of the century, the scientific attitude was being commonly reflected in literature and the arts. The cool intellectual approach was taking the place of the displays of passion and zeal which had marked an earlier generation. The second phase of another of the great revolutions in the *zeitgeist* was well under way. Feeling was yielding to knowing. Illustrations of this abound. The "problem plays" of Henrik Ibsen (1828-1906) were posing intellectual questions about human relationships. The novels of Emile Zola (1840-1902) were shriekingly "realistic" in their examinations of life situations. In Britain, the novels of Thomas Hardy (1840-1928) were "painting life as it was" (or as it seemed to him!), with no sentimental nonsense about them. Like a bright meteor, George Bernard Shaw was shooting across the stage, burning up old rubbish, being brutally frank about old reticences, making people everywhere stand and look at themselves in full-length mirrors (possibly convex). If an exact illustration of the shift from feeling to intellect is required it surely is provided by Shaw (1856-1950), who was approaching the height of his powers as the century ended. Shaw's characters are opinions walking about the stage. His women – are they women? One of Dickens's characters (Pecksniff, was it not, in *Martin Chuzzlewit*), Dickens represents as sedulously avoiding "anything that would bring the blush of shame to a young girl's cheek.'' Shaw has no hesitation in introducing topics that would bring the blush of shame, but he puts them into abstractions that safely sterilize them. It is to be suspected that his own Victorian Puritanism prevented him from carrying his discussions further than "the life force" and similar abstractions. Despite the "bloody" of Eliza Dolittle, which rude word was first heard from a public stage in 1912, the age of vulgarity had not arrived.

In religion, Shaw needed no vulgarity to be the complete iconoclast. In one of his *Prefaces,* he tells how, talking to a Jesuit on the topic, he pulled out his watch and dared God to strike him dead in the next five minutes. The Jesuit could not endure the horror of that spectacle. But God did not strike Shaw dead.

In the other arts, the same movement towards the ratiocinative side is evident. In painting, the thundering gallantries of Napoleonic battlefields were no longer depicted, nor were the sentimentalities of English life (an extreme example: "Can't you talk, Jack" – little girl to "friend of man"). In architecture, the revived Gothic of the preceding generation had disappeared before the simplified styles of the end of the century. The last great public buildings to be in a Gothic style were the Parliament Buildings at Ottawa, Canada (1864-1867). But Gothic floridity was accorded one final outbreak of decoration, flamboyance, grotesqueness, ornateness and the ridiculous – in an appropriate place, an outpost of empire – the railway station of Bombay! Such buildings have to be seen to be believed. Soon afterwards, the road was being opened to the experimental starknesses of the next century.

In music, most impenetrable of arts to the non-professional, it is hard to walk with certain step. But music is composed for audiences and audiences make their judgements upon it, and certain aspects of it reveal themselves plainly enough. It is easy to follow the transition from the classical work of the eighteenth century to the "romantic" of the nineteenth, but getting beyond 1850 is harder. Is Richard Wagner (1813-1883) a "Romantic" composer? To disregard the musical technicalities of classification it would appear that his operas, characters, plots and music, are Romantic in the sense that Heinrich Heine's *Beide Grenadiere* (already commented upon) is Romantic. Both, indeed, seem the quintessence of Romanticism. Wagner sets up a new pantheon which is his version of the ancient pantheon of the old Germanic gods. He may or may not have thought of his material in anything but a musical sense. If he did, if he endowed his heroes and heroines with actuality and in some way believed in them, then he was founding a new quasi-religion. That would bring him to Nietzsche and the two of them then lead on through racialism and "supermanism" to the far-out theorists of the twentieth century and eventually to Hitlerian atrocities. It has been remarked that there is more than a mere collocation in time between musicians and men of ideas:

German music – surely as telling an expression of the German character as the crimes committed by the Nazis, and one, as Thomas Mann has argued at length that is not at all unrelated to the Germans' political ineptitude.[1]

The joy of Franz Schubert and the serenity of Beethoven are not in Wagner. And with Johannes Brahms (1833-1897), we look into dark and stormy seas, the soul of a German foreboding trouble for the German soul.

But after Brahms, what? Nothing. At least nothing of importance. A sudden wrench had been given to the times.

Italian music gives the same impression. Generations of the most delightful floods of melody and harmony, and in the nineteenth century all the raptures, the sheer power of creation rendered into sound which gave Italy its second Renaissance. Name after name: it is idle to put them down. As late as 1900 it seemed as if that well of life would never dry up. Giacomo Puccini's *La Boheme* had been staged in 1897. In 1904 came his *Madame Butterfly*. Of it, the *New York Times* musical critic, Richard Alden, wrote: "The delicacy, the shifting pictorial beauty, the completely penetrating atmosphere . . ." Such phrases could never be used to describe music written since those days. Puccini died in 1910. After Puccini? Nothing, or nothing very much.

That glamorous old pre-war world, if only a memory, is a happy memory. One evening in Vienna, the old Strauss theatre, whose name gives it its character, was mounting an operetta by Franz Lehar (1870-1948), author of the well-known *Merry Widow*. The operetta, a mere bon-bon for Vienna, was *Friedericke*. Friedericke was that daughter of the pastor of Sesenheim who was the first and most idyllic of Goethe's loves. The opera had all the verve and sentiment and delightful music that had been ringing through that old theatre for a century. The audience clamoured enthusiastically for Lehar, for it was Lehar himself who was conducting. He appeared upon the stage and was rapturously applauded. It was a sunset scene. The light was fading from the sky for the old Empire and well the audience knew it. But how they loved their music and their city!

And in place of all the beauty? The horrible groanings, the ear-splitting raucousness, the vulgar belly-achings, the inanities, that are thrust upon us by the "media" and welcomed by the debased taste of the rest of us. Gone the nineteenth century.

Were there then no warning signs of such sterility to come, no "speed limits" so to speak, on the splendid highway? Yes, there were, for the few who might be interested in them.

II
The Failure of Faith:
The Triumph of Knowledge

The discoveries of the scientists could be disconcerting. So could the speculations of the philosophers and the findings of the scholars. All these went to the roots of the old question: "what's it all about?" But that question throughout the ages has only fleetingly troubled the multitude.

Throughout the century the so-called "higher critics" had been burrowing deeper and deeper into the nature of the Bible. They were mostly Germanic, frequently Lutheran clergyman, and their sincerity, honesty, and competence could not be gainsaid. Nevertheless their work went far in the direction of disintegrating what had hitherto been the foundation of the Christian religion. "Historical" records turned into mythological or legendary accounts, miracles disappeared, "inspiration" disappeared, the authorship of important books of the New Testament became uncertain, passages within them were shown to have been late interpolations. The very figure of Jesus himself became shadowy and doubt was cast on his actual existence. "Higher Criticism" made many of the dogmas of the church impossible of acceptance by intelligent people. What had once been solid as a rock became shifting sand.

It was because of the work of the Biblical critics, plus that of the scientists that Matthew Arnold wrote his profoundly pessimistic poem *Dover Beach*, with those haunting words:

. . . The sea of faith
Was once, too, at the full, and round earth's shore
Lay like the folds of a bright girdle furled,
But now I only hear
Its melancholy, long-withdrawing roar,
Retreating to the breath
Of the night-wind, down the vast edges drear
And naked shingle of the world.

The splendid lines echo the sound and action of the water on the shingle beach at Dover, as anyone who has stood on that beach can bear witness. More than that, in graphic words they put the plight of those who no longer can find basis for their faith. Faith withdraws, like the tide going out from the stony beach, carrying with it into the mysterious depths so much of life, leaving behind "the naked shingle of the world."

Tennyson had earlier handled the same themes.[2] Many others had faced the same loss of faith, and struggled on, like Arnold himself, in an old-fashioned Stoicism. But through Biblical criticism, had not the axe been laid to the root of the tree? How simple those old days when God was still in his heaven and all was still right with the world!

If the Christian faith was being worn away, was there any other faith waiting, ready to rush into the vacuum? By the end of the century that query, which would have seemed foolish to most people, was beginning to press for an answer.

Then there were the German philosophers. All during the century, they had been propounding their puzzling opinions, as often as not cancelling each other out in heavy verbal blows. The world could have ignored the German philosophers, but the Biblical critics were another matter. And had not the philosophers taken some peculiar directions? Especially after Darwin's books appeared, for men rushed to apply the idea of the survival of the fittest to every conceivable situation in life. Most of Darwin's English disciples used the idea with a certain discretion. Huxley, for example, recognized that the doctrine cannot be applied in unmodified form to man, especially civilized man. There must be some distinction made between right and wrong. For man, there must be a region of values.

This the most prominent of the German post-Darwinian philosophers does not seem to have recognized. Friedrich Nietzsche (1844-1900) in poetic but often obscure prose worked out his application of Darwin's ideas to the human situation. His way of putting things was penetrating and disconcerting. When, for instance, you fall out with a woman, there is one certain way of "bringing her round." "Become pregnant," you must say to her, and then – act! Her feminine whimsies will disappear in the performance of nature's deepest functions.

The name of "Social Darwinism" has been used by a later writer for such doctrines.[3] Nietzsche's Darwinism, reflected in the titles of his books, naturally produced "the will to power," the "transvaluation of all values" and the notion of *Superman (Der Übermensch), that* biological descendant of our present miserable species who would inherit all the excellence of beings from whom "the survival of the fittest" had weeded out the weak, the diseased, the poorly endowed, the incompetent, yes, the humane. No pity would dwell in the eyes of the Nietzschean Superman: he would be as a god, having left far behind him that crawling, servile morality which had long before enabled Christian slaves to ensnare their Roman masters.

The "Great Blond Beast," that is, physically idealized Germanism, was evidently destined for this wave of the future. Not surprisingly, applied Nietzscheism, taught in the universities, approved by many an intellectual, had much to do, later on, with the rise of Hitlerism and the actual attempt to secure the appearance of the Superman by massacring the unfit, those who could not protect themselves, those who by their very origins, must be the unfit, that is, the Jews.

The whole Hitlerian aberration – much too mild a word – shows how easily a great theory can miscarry when too rashly applied to so complex a laboratory specimen as man. "The fittest survive" had lent itself only too readily to the whole idea of ruthless competition in the business world and it was to have substantially the same effect in that world of power symbolized by the state. Darwin himself had to some extent been the victim of his own hypotheses, for it is on record that he had opposed the idea of birth control, believing it would be best for humanity to breed up, by Malthusian rule, to the limits of subsistence, then die off at a rate to allow the tough to survive.[4]

That is nature's way, of course. Let plants in the garden fight it out. But men have long known that the weeds would probably crowd out the flowers were it not for the gardener. Parenthetically, it may be asked "what gardener?" Much of the race's effort to struggle upward has been devoted to protecting the "flowers" as against the "weeds." That man who proclaimed that "the meek shall inherit the earth" was probably a better social theorist than Nietzsche and the Darwinians, for he saw how difficult it is to secure the future for the apparently desirable type. Man has had perhaps a million years, more or less, to produce by unrestricted competition, "the fittest," the "superman." He has come a long way, but can we expect to do in a twinkling what has taken these immense un-selfconscious processes of time? Hitler and his lot tried to be God-like gardeners. History has ruled against them and it is probable that no agreement will ever be reached on what is meant by "the fittest." If it ever comes to a war of survival between man and the insects, it may be the insects that will survive. Would they then be "the fittest"? Evolution, conceivably can go "down" as well as "up." Must man forget his notions of what is "up"?

German ruminations about survival led easily into the doctrines of race. The idea of selected or chosen people is as old as history. Joseph de Gobineau,[5] sharpened it up and indicated the direction in which the finger of God was pointing. It was, of course, towards the descendants of those northerners who had long before flocked into and appropriated the Roman empire, "scourges of God," he might have called them. De Gobineau's book, *The Inequality of Human Races,* at least tells us how far men had to go even in mid-nineteenth century, before they learned much about the way the world had been put together. He soon found favour in the southern United States, where his ideas supported negro slavery. In Germany his and similar ideas were utilized to form the new "science" of *Rassenwissenschaft* ("Race Knowledge," or "Racial Science").

Writings such as de Gobineau's once more suggested how easy it is for legitimate lines of inquiry to go astray. Evidently, it was only "superior races" that should survive. But how decide what were the superiors? And how manage their survival? "Superiors" are usually outbred by "inferiors." As a nineteenth century poet puts it: in his lines on the country maid "Maud Muller"

She married a man unlearned and poor
And many children played round her door.

Or, to be more formal, as the Scripture also puts it, "deposuit magnifices de sedibus et exaltavit humiles": "He hath put down the mighty from their seats and hath exalted them of low degree," which is one of the most profound observations on the socio-historical process ever given to men: "the meek shall inherit the earth."

There can be little question of the place which the player *Germany* took during the nineteenth century in the European orchestra. Her role was that traditionally ascribed to the poets: that of "mover and shaker." At first her moving was in the area of the intellect and later on she "shook" in the area of action. Germans may take legitimate pride in the achievements of their countrymen in every phase of nineteenth century intellectual life. One thinks of historians like von Ranke, of legal philosophers like Friedrich Savigny, of the long succession of the philosophers, of the Biblical students such as David Strauss (1808-1874)[6] or F. C. Baur (1792-1860), of the philologists like Max Müller (1823-1900) and of many, many others. There is no doubt that in this sense of intellectual preoccupation and accomplishment, Germany was indeed ruling the clouds. Add to the scholars, the musicians, that flow of genius that ceased only with the coming of night to the new Germany.

Then after 1870, the new empire quickly transformed itself into an industrial giant and in relentless logic into a colonial and naval power, "seeking a place in the sun." After the Franco-Prussian war, no European statesman could sleep quietly in his bed, for there was a giant in the house, stirring restlessly. As German power mounted, so did German ambition. At last, more or less openly expressed, it came to the aim of "world power of downfall." It seemed as if Germany were deliberately offering a challenge to her neighbours, the other great powers, for after 1895, nearly every year saw some provocative word or gesture delivered in their faces. At last the tension in the power circles became too strong to be contained. Rivalries and challenges mounted up until in August of 1914, the great war to the death broke out. World power or downfall? It was to be downfall. Samson had pulled down the pillars of the temple upon himself. And upon others too. A world had crashed.

III
The Remarkable Century:
And a Failure?

What a remarkable hundred years lay between 1815 and 1914. Three generations of men – many a man was alive in 1914 whose father had remembered Waterloo – and a world transformed, a world of giants, industrial giants, artistic giants, a world of giant cities, of giant ships, giant

states, giant problems. A world of blinding brilliance. A world conse-
crated to the religion of submerging the accomplishments of yesterday in
the greater accomplishments of tomorrow, a world that had few doubts of
its ability to do just that, a world hopeful of infinite achievement. Jules
Verne (1828-1905) had written *Around the World in Eight Days, Twenty
Thousand Leagues Under the Sea* and similar early "science fiction." H.
G. Wells (1866-1946) was to surpass such accomplishments with stories of
"The First Men in the Moon," "The War of the Worlds" and others of
the sort. By our day, the first men had got to the moon!

But was all this to be a Daedelian feat, with the wings of accomplishment dropping off as the flyer got too close to the sun? Only the extreme
pessimists would have dared talk like that. Had not scientific knowledge
increased the very span of life itself, nearly wiped out some of the ancient
curses of disease – think of the work of Louis Pasteur (1822-1895) and his
like – vastly increased the numbers of the species and yet provided far
more food than ever before for it to live on? Had it not subdued great
stretches of the earth's surface not only to raise that food but give good
homes to happy people? Was not the scientist daily laying bare more and
more of nature's deepest mysteries, such as the Roentgen rays, and
placing them at the disposal of man for his daily use? It was hard to believe
that there was or would be "a top."

Those who lived before 1914 – especially those of the Western world –
can be forgiven for what seems today their excessive optimism. Yet there
were not lacking among them those who could ask the fundamental
question: with all its prowess, could science bring in "the golden age"?
Could its gold be real gold? Could it find answers to those deep, disturbing
questions that from the beginning have troubled man even as much as the
task of finding his daily bread, questions revolving around the meaning of
life, and the nature of the universe and the place and conduct of man in it?

Here were the nagging questions that lay at the base of the world's
religions and all their varied historical manifestations. It was the essence
of man's history, that same ceaseless inquiry – "what's it all about?"
Prophets had tried to find answers, religious seers of the most varied
settings had tried to find answers, philosophers had tried over and over
again. The world's great poets had addressed themselves to it – "a tale
told by an idiot"? "No, no," man always cried, "it must be more than
that." When the astronomers began to work out their mathematical
universe, to many men the problem seemed resolved and the informed
areas of eighteenth century society had accepted the solution. The universe had become mathematical, mechanical, God respectable and remote. And, said the Romantics, uninteresting and boring. So feeling
within themselves, many of them, daemonic energies that mocked
mechanics, they had made another universe out of their imaginations and
out of the ruins of the older world that had preceded the Enlightenment.

The world the Romantics made served well enough for much of the nineteenth century, it gave that century a powerful aesthetic impulse and an equally powerful revival of traditional religion. It supplied the weapons with which neo-orthodoxy, the new Puritanism, could fight the heavy battles of the mid-century.

But now, as the century wore on, down below the surface, things did not seem certain. When the *Origin of Species* had appeared in 1859, it was harshly assailed. When the *Descent of Man* followed it in 1871, the assault was still of great vigour but gradually its strength began to fail. By the end of the century, most informed people were accepting the Darwinian doctrines, though perhaps without knowing too much about them. Evolution, however, was as it were, in the air. While the educated world had not got back to an eighteenth century rationalism, it had made more than a beginning in that accommodation of the traditional with the scientific which is so marked in modern times. It had greatly expanded the scope of the compartmentalized mind. Or had it merely found refuge in hypocrisy?

The sophisticated world is not the whole world and it can be brushed aside rather easily, as our own day has demonstrated. There has always been a thick layer of human society unconcerned with what goes on above its head. This layer looks suspiciously like the Marxist "proletariat." It can become a mere weapon in clever hands. It is "the rabblement (which) clapped their chopped hands, and threw up their sweaty nightcaps and uttered such a deal of stinking breath because Caesar refused the crown that it had almost choked Caesar . . ."[7] It has many sub-layers. It is a major source of the world's fanaticisms and probably of most of its new religions. From it, religions with all their credulities and aspirations constantly arise (as for example, Mormonism or the Jehovah's Witnesses or Naziism), to be as constantly reshaped and reduced to doctrines and practices more or less acceptable to the descendants of the founders.[8]

In our own day, Naziism and its horrors would appear to have fitted quite well into this conception of religious origins. Luckily it has been rooted out. But the same material out of which it grew, we may be sure is still in existence and it might be shaped up again if leadership appeared. Hence the informed portion of society never scores a total victory: relapse is always possible and the battle between "religion" (the quotation marks are important) and science, the enormous concern of mid-nineteenth century, cannot be considered over. Science could still "take a beating."

That possibility aside, science – knowledge – can always be wounded in the house of its friend, for thinking is the most divisive exercise man can indulge in. Conservative or radical social forces can bring a degree of emotional reinforcement to their aid not possible for the purely intellectual. The strength of ignorance, its assuredness and self-confidence, its own convictions of its rightness and righteousness, are never to be underestimated. It fits in nicely with that which gives men one of their deepest satisfactions, a good bout of destruction – every school boy loves to hear the sound of breaking glass. And most men, too, in secret. Mind, disembodied mind, so to speak, is chilly. The wonder is that the intellectual has put up such a good fight.

IV
Knowledge and Destruction

And knowledge has had its own stones to throw. How delightful the sound of breaking windows in the ears of the Tyndalls and the Huxleys of the last century: it is good fun "shocking the bourgeois." Every social advance involves some destruction and in no area are men so sensitive to destruction as in that of religion. Change in it opens daunting gulfs of uncertainty. The result is stubborn fighting at every inch of the way: for example, take the struggle of the Russian "Old Believers," in the seventeenth century, against the innovation of making the sign of the Cross with two fingers instead of three. Or was it the other way round? To us it is not a matter of importance. To those brought up to the three-fingered sign it became a matter of salvation or damnation. So religions go down fighting hard and their death struggles are not short.

If knowledge had its own New Jerusalem to present, the transition might be easier to make. But knowledge has no New Jerusalem to present, or at least its New Jerusalem is not of the *right* kind. Knowledge – and let us try to do without the confusing and false distinction between *knowledge* and *science* – can give man a Heavenly City with only silver streets, not golden. And it cannot command the services of bands of trumpeters and harpers. There is no royal road to knowledge (though the modern "educator" seems to think he has found one) and the climb up Parnassus is arduous.

But it will be asked, are not all these extraordinary appurtenances to modern life – trains, cars, airplanes, coloured television, space ships, heart and kidney transplants and all the rest of them *knowledge?* No, they are not: they are the result of the climb up after *knowledge*. The human brain has step by step produced these extraordinary things and showered them upon humanity at large, but humanity in accepting them has not necessarily made itself wiser or happier. It has not brought itself closer to an answer to its everlasting perplexity – what is it all about? What it has done, this extraordinarily developed, perhaps overdeveloped, perhaps pathologically overdeveloped, brain of ours, is to have presented us with a never-ending set of mechanical toys with which we can play to our heart's content and which will more or less divert attention from the eternal question but will never answer it.

That is the nemesis of materialism. We open up this gulf for ourselves, get out all our mechanical devices and then find that we can see no farther across it with their aid than without it. That, it is to be assumed, is what the poets have seen in their distrust of materialism, what the religious seers have found so horribly wrong with the mechanical view of the universe. *Knowledge* has turned its scientific by-products into "opium for the people." It has also destroyed that structure of "cloud-capped towers and gorgeous palaces" which seemed to previous generations so soul-sustaining, and blandly assures us, with Prospero, that these all, yes, the great globe itself, like the airy fabric of a vision faded, shall dissolve and leave not a wrack behind.

A rather chilly way of looking at life, so no wonder that plain people put it aside, stick to the gadgets and go on thinking as they have usually thought, or what is even more comfortable, not thinking at all.

In the light of what has happened since 1914, does it all represent the failure of the intellectual assault on Parnassus, and perhaps retreat – retreat to the imaginative self-indulgences of the Romantics or worse, the miseries of a perhaps juvenile, perhaps brutal "sub-culture"?

V
The Ultimate Pessimism

To return the discussion to historical terms, does it mean that the Century of Hope was ending in pessimism? Matthew Arnold's sad lines *(Dover Beach)*,[9] had they and others such, been the poets' vision in which man, this paragon of animals, had got up so far, only to face a future of mere existence, of mere animal existence? By the end of the century, it was possible to go farther than that, not a distant future of mere existence but one of extinction, nothingness.

Man . . . is no longer the Heaven descended heir of all the ages. His very existence is an accident, his story a brief and transitory episode in the life of one of the meanest of the planets. Of the combination of causes which first converted a dead organic compound into the living progenitors of humanity, science indeed as yet knows nothing. It is enough that from such beginnings, famine, disease and mutual slaughter, fit nurses of the future lords of creation, have gradually evolved, after infinite travail, a race with conscience enough to see that it is vile, and intelligence enough to know that it is insignificant. We survey the past, and see that its history is of blood and tears . . . We sound the future and learn that after a period . . . the energies of our system will decay, the glory of the sun will be dimmed, and the earth . . . will no longer tolerate the race which for a moment has disturbed its solitude. Man will go down into the pit, and all his thoughts will perish. The uneasy consciousness, which in this obscure corner, has for a brief space broken the contented silence of the universe, will be at rest. Matter will know itself no longer. 'Imperishable monuments' and 'immortal deeds', death itself, and love stronger than death, will be as though they had never been. Nor will anything that *is* be better or be worse for all that the labour, genius, devotion and suffering of man have striven through countless ages to effect . . .[10]

These are dreadful words. Few of us could face their implication without flinching. Words that completely deprive us humans of hope. They put us in the same condition as those workmen pinioned years ago under the wreckage of the great fallen bridge across the St. Lawrence near the city of Quebec: the tide relentlessly rising upon them, inch by inch, until at last they drowned. Few of us can face that, perhaps not so much the suffering as the utter helplessness of the victims. So we try to quit thinking about them, turn our faces in other directions.

By the end of the century, life had not yet presented itself to many people in this light. It probably has not to this day, for if it had, it would almost surely have paralyzed action. Its logic is suicide – the logic of the "population growth, zero" group, of the child-haters. The gloomy picture did not deter its author from leading a normal life, for he went on after painting it to become prime minister of Great Britain. It is to be hoped that the view of the future which he presented, a view shared by many another good mind, never will come home to men in the mass. "Ye shall know the truth and the truth shall make you free." Free of what? it may be asked.[11]

Again, do we come back to the point reached by many after the light in the Age of Light began to dim? Has knowledge presented us with more light than we can live with? That happened before. Will it happen again? Is the intellectual approach again to be a failure?

VI
Rearguard Actions
Socialism: The Class War
Protestantism: The Social Gospel

Towards the close of the century, there were some signs of that. New rigidities were returning to Roman Catholicism, largely the consequences of the previous generation of *Syllabi of Errors*. French army officers were necessarily affected by the links of the military life with order and authority. Many of them had been educated in the Jesuit preparatory schools, based by the very nature of the Jesuit Order, on authoritarianism. After 1870, officers of that type were remoulding the army on its ancient lines, obedience, aristocracy and even monarchy. It was the Dreyfus affair which prevented those tendencies being pushed to some logical limit such as a military *coup* to re-establish the ancient royal house.

On the other hand, the missionaries of the left wing became more and more vigorous. They could claim good minds, such as Jean Jaurès (1895-1914, Professor of Philosophy, *Deputé* and murdered).

They could launch such books as Georges Sorel's *Reflections on Violence*[12] with its stirring collection of hortatory half-truths ("The workers have no money but they have at their disposal an even more efficacious weapon: they can inspire fear . . . The workers and their leaders know that they must profit by middle class cowardice, to impose their will"). Sorel was the proclaimer of the general strike as the ultimate weapon in the class war. The class war and its deductions constituted a new religion. Sorel proclaimed them with a lack of restraint, a strength of conviction that would have done credit to an early Christian apostle. The progress of science, as Sorel in effect declared, could wait until the battle was over and the victory of the proletariat had ushered in the millennium. Sorel, among others, moved socialism one long step closer to a religion.

In those last years of the old century, the currents were running in every direction. In 1891 Pope Leo XIII in his famous encyclical *Rerum novarum* sought to introduce Christian principles into the relations of capital and labour: labour, the pope preached, must not be regarded as a mere commodity, for behind strong arms, there lay Christian souls. Leo's humane attitude was to have considerable effect in once more emphasizing the intrinsic nature of traditional Christianity. It was a more hopeful attack on the age that had been the head-on charge of his predecessor Pio Nono in his *Syllabus of Errors*. That document, however, remained the breastwork from behind which Catholicism could shoot, for the successor of Leo XIII (Pius X) when faced with the Catholic movement of reform known as *Modernism*, about 1906, displayed against it just the same attitudes as had Pius IX.[13]

The historical significance of these various indications of concern with the human condition lies in the concept they all have of betterment, whether spiritual, as Catholicism would have interpreted it, or material, as the socialist left wing. Here possibly was the foundation of a new religious era, one wherein Catholicism despite the *Syllabus of Errors* that could have been so easily compiled against it, was being edged forward into a more nominal concern for men's souls and a more actual concern for their material welfare. Constantly at war with it, though in many respects not far removed from it, was the concern of the socialists, allegedly for men's material circumstance, but in many instances, more for the power that would be given by control of large masses of "factory fodder." Although the struggle for power has a large place in every social movement, no matter how idealistic, this concern with well-being in this world, from whichever wing of thought it came, was in high contrast with that disdainful contempt for things terrestrial, that veneration of poverty, which had so strongly marked certain aspects of the Middle Ages.

One area of the world it is not easy to bring into line with European continental movements, material or spiritual – that of the English-speaking peoples. Someone has remarked on the "complete opacity of the English mind to abstract ideas." That may have held good while the English working classes were still unorganized and unchampioned. When they found leadership, however, as they did increasing from the 1880s, whether they were opaque to abstract ideas or not, they proved just as ready to follow their leaders as continental social groups, and those leaders were often under the influence of the same body of abstract ideas. That has been the situation down to today: the English Labour party may not have as well-co-ordinated a body of doctrine as have Communists, but it has within it many men who are quite conversant with abstract ideas and the doctrines of Marxian Communism. It does not take much observation of English life to see how the "behind-the-scenes" operations are carried out.

By the 1880s, a new breath of life was also coming into Victorian Protestantism, giving to it a noteworthy change of direction and a wider appeal. The spirit and the source of the spirit had always been there, as the review offered in previous pages of such topics as Methodism and Evangelicalism indicated, but overmuch concern for "the spirit" had decreased effectiveness. Left-wing Protestantism had to cast out a good deal of its merely evangelical fervour before it could increase its weight in the world. The new Evangelicalism which enabled it to do this has been given various names, of which "the Social Gospel" is probably the best. "The Social Gospel" represented the attempt to take the scriptures, more especially the New Testament gospels, and apply their ethical teaching to society. The gospels were to be the touchstone used to test the merits of every public question. "Christ came not to save individual souls," exclaimed the Welsh Methodist clergyman, Hugh Price Hughes, "but to organize a Christian Church that would work to reconstruct human society . . . and to recover for all men their divine birthright of a noble life."[14] Such thinking, which was widespread, necessarily changed the nature of the impact of the West upon the outer world. It put missionary endeavour into practical terms, laid increasing stress on *well-being*. It was a leading factor in promoting the idea of *stewardship* in empire, an idea that eventually would have a large place in ending empire.

This combination of Bible Christianity with a direct practical attitude towards the urgent social tasks of the world, while it may not be completely unique, has been more prominent in the English-speaking Protestant part of the Christian world than elsewhere.

The *Social Gospel* movement is said to have received major impetus from "the world-wide evangelical movement of the times" (the end of the nineteenth century).[15] If "world-wide," the preceding statements might have to be modified. But only to a small degree. In the late nineteenth century, the energies of the English-speaking world were at their height. A new country was being built in the American west. A new country was being built in the Canadian west. New countries were being built in Australia and in New Zealand. Those who have not shared in the tremendous and idealistic task of building a new country can only dimly understand what magnificent vistas are opened, how common it becomes for men to be dominated by idealistic ends. It is impossible for thinking men not to ask themselves "a new country – for what"? Granted, there will always be present the usual quotas of human ill-will, perversity, selfishness and corruption. Granted also that one section of the English-speaking people had long before embraced the defence of one of the least defensible of human institutions, slavery and still clung to many of the attitudes arising out of its past. Granted these short-comings and many more of the sort, but granted also the amplitude of the space and resources at men's disposal and granted an idealism in the northern states quite as strong as the attachment to slavery and its heritages had been in the south, granted in short, the whole genius of the institutions that had radiated out from the British Isles, and it is not hard to see where the so-called "Social Gospel" came from.

An important correlation is to be noted between religion and labour (as organized class) during the nineteenth century. Methodism had arisen largely as a working or lower middle class denomination and Methodists all during the century continued to be prominent in matters affecting the condition of those classes. When labour became Labour, an organized political force, Methodists and other non-conformists retained their prominence in the movement. It was only slowly that the British Labour party came to be purely secular. The idea of human brotherhood carrying with it the logic of humane conditions in industry and constant improvement in them gives much common ground between Christianity and labour, as indeed the Papal Encyclical of 1891 had clearly recognized. On the continent, common ground did not seem to produce conspicuous common action. In Great Britain, there was little of the anti-clericalism manifested by the French or Italian working man, hence the two strands of social action could go along together. It was not until the twentieth century that the non-conformist influence in labour weakened. Although the times have become increasingly secular, in some respects, it is still strong.

At the end of the century the currents were running in every direction, quite true, but insofar as the validity of the philosophies dominating the Western world went and despite the roseate tinge supplied to the English-speaking portion of it by an all-embracing optimism, perhaps this end-of-century flare of traditionalism, the "Social Gospel" – it could be called "practical traditionalism" – was deceptive. The basic question could not fail to be raised: could societies that had always considered themselves as standing on certain well-understood religious foundations, shift off those foundations and yet go on functioning healthily? All along the routes of history, there had been no end of assertion that the society was doomed which would turn against the church, or the clergy, or which followed "godless" leaders, or suffered atheists, or heretics, or what not. But by the end of the century, it had begun to look to intelligent, well-informed people and that, like it or not, that was the kind of society the Western world was probably going to have. The English-speaking part of it responded with its normal illogic and emphasized the "Social Gospel." "Do something about it!" Other parts tried to dig in behind the ancient authority of the church, still others were building up their own versions of "Social Gospels" without the Gospel. What would the future bring?

VII
The Gulf of Nothingness

Did "Social Gospels" and other such concepts, including Marxism, hang to life merely by the thread of human goodwill? Had science won the field? Was knowledge not only power, but all powerful? Was the disembodied intellect enough? Could "values" be dispensed with? Had the ancient faith suffered a mortal wound? If so, had the course of history made an abrupt turn? Without the guidance that religion had always supplied, could man, divorced from whatever gods might be, go on and order his society? Could mortal eyes stand gazing upon the gulf of nothingness?

What would the future bring?

Notes

1.   Hans Eichner, reviewing Eric Kahler, *The Germans* in *Queen's Quarterly*, 81-4, Winter, 1974, p. 626.
2.   See Chapter 18, pp. 270-272.
3.   Richard Hofstadter, *Social Darwinism in American Thought* (Braziller, New York, 1959). An older book, a classic in its way, is W. G. Sumner, *Folkways* (Boston, 1904). Much of Herbert Spencer's thought lies in the same direction.
4.   J. M. Robertson, *A History of Free Thought* (Dawson, New York, 1969), p. 336ff. citing Mrs. Annie Besant, *Autobiographical Sketches*, 1885, p. 136, *et alia*.
5.   See Chapter 19, p. 283.
6.   His *Leben Jesu, Life of Jesus*, of 1835 was a revolutionary book at the time.
7.   *Julius Caesar*, I, 2, II. 234ff.

8. *Christian Science,* mainly upper middle class in origin and membership seems an exception. Roman Catholicism has its own way of dealing with these impulses from below.

9. See p. 303.

10. Arthur Balfour, *Foundations of Belief* (1895), quoted in J. H. Randall, *The Making of the Modern Mind* (Cambridge, Massachusetts, 1940), p. 581.

11. Nearly fifty years later, Balfour's picture was presented in hard scientific terms by the astronomer George Gamow in his *Biography of the Earth, op cit.*

12. George Sorel, *Reflections on Violence,* (Tr. T. E. Hulme, New York, 1908 and 1912).

13. See Paul Sabatier, *Modernism* (The Jowett Lectures, 1908), Tr. C. A. Miles (London, T. Fisher Unwin, 1908). This book contains, as appendices, translations of the papal bombardments directed against "Modernism," which stopped the growth of that particular expression of revisionism. These were *Lamentabile Sane Exitu* (July 3, 1907 – "With truly lamentable results" . . . "and *Pascendi Gregis* . . ." ("of feeding the flock . . ." September 8, 1907. They are each many pages long.

14. Quotation from Richard Allen, "Children of Prophecy" in *Red River Valley Historical Society* (Winnipeg, Canada), Summer, 1974, p. 15.

15. *Ibid.*

CHAPTER TWENTY-ONE

From Past to Present

In the summer of 1914, a series of events, which while serious, did not seem of primary importance, rapidly mounted up like the banks of clouds that presage a thunder storm and when the storm burst in war its violence convulsed mankind. Before it passed, one world had been destroyed and another was not yet born.

The First World War has been the subject of infinite studies. Before sufficient time had elapsed for its deeper meaning to sink in, another storm of equal violence had arisen – the Second World War. That war ended in 1945 but the disturbances the two colossal conflicts had touched off were limitless and they continue. Muddy water stirred up gradually clarifies if left still. In some such way, so also does time clarify the course of history. Probably not enough time has yet gone by to allow man's troubled affairs in this twentieth century to clarify. It is easy to set down a sequence of events and not much more difficult to give specific explanations for most of them, but there have been myriads of events, multitudes of historical sequences, hundreds of prominent actors on the world's stage and thousands upon local stages of scarcely inferior dimensions. The two generations since the tempest broke can be summed up but probably not yet placed accurately in the long procession of the centuries.

It is difficult for the living to disentangle themselves from their own times past, for the age in which past and present conjoin is that in which "cold" memories are replaced by the "warm" memories of days that have been lived through. A rapid sketch of the course of things within the present century may help in making the crossing from times past to times present.

I
The First War and its Aftermath

There is never a moment when the sea of history is at rest, and the period of the late nineteenth century had its share of turmoil. The rapid rise of the German empire to tremendous power may be singled out. "The trident of Neptune must be in our hands" cried emperor William II in one of his indiscreet speeches, "Our future is on the sea." The naval rivalry between the old dog and the young dog was never absent from the mind of statesmen and large numbers of the public after the years in which such speeches were made, from 1895 on. Then there was the growing uneasiness of the new Balkan states, and the fears aroused in the "polyglot empire," Austria-Hungary, many of whose inhabitants were Slavs. The immense potential of Russia, where Slavic sentiment together with strategic considerations, forced intensive interest in the other Slavic peoples, was a third factor in the situation. In the years before 1914 such causes of tension had become so prominent that fear of an approaching storm had been in the air long before the storm burst. At last burst it did and no natural cyclone ever did a fraction of the damage that the hurricane of war inflicted on the world.

When the storm was half over the old Europe lay in ruins. Austria-Hungary, the proud heir of the ancient "Holy Roman empire," with eleven centuries behind it, had ceased to exist. The Turkish empire had shrunk to the national state of Turkey. The new German empire of 1870, so strong, so buoyant, so self-confident, so arrogant, had descended into a shaky republic. The Czar of All the Russias had been obscurely murdered in distant Siberia and a new and revolutionary régime with strange new doctrines stood in his stead. The Western nations, Great Britain, France, Italy, had lost millions of their sons, and they all were enormously weakened economically. Their victory had been dearly bought and it might not have been bought at any price if it had not been that the world beyond the oceans had joined in, with its men, its munitions, its ships its food and its moneys, all apparently in almost limitless supply. Parts of that world had gone to war as to a glad crusade – Australia, Canada, New Zealand, parts of South Africa – the other part, the United States, more reluctantly, for the United States saw descend upon it, owing to the war, the unwelcome responsibility of putting behind it its attempts at isolation and becoming a great world power. Another world power, too, though one not of the weight of the United States, had emerged before the war had ended, Japan.

The power structure of the post-war world was thus completely different from that previous to 1914. In place of the nineteenth century's six "Great Powers," there were the three European powers, the United States , Japan, and dubiously, Russia. Quite evidently, Russia was capable of taking care of itself and powerful beyond words within the 8,000,000 square miles of its own vast territory. The United States, as some one put it after 1919, "retired to its own private world beyond the Atlantic," but events were soon to show that the Atlantic was not as wide as it once had been and that even the vast Pacific was not much wider. One of the major political situations that built up in the post-war years, more especially after 1930, was the tension between Japan and the United States, which was the immediate occasion of the entry of the United States into the Second World War.

In the 1920s, international events were confused and troublesome but not menacing. No further major conflicts broke out. In the leading states, domestic affairs were, in some countries, prosperous, in others, if not flourishing, at least endurable. One ugly infected sore did develop: the relations between France and Germany, which were shaped mainly by the internal condition of Germany. The chief points in that situation were the impossible financial provisions of the Treaty of Versailles, which had closed the war; the inexperience of those who erected the government of post-war Germany which had become a republic (after an incomplete revolution), the so-called Weimar Republic, and their betrayal from within by the "die-hard" elements of the former German armed forces; the occupation of the Ruhr, 1923 (Germany's rich district of coal and iron), by the French in an effort to force Germany to fulfil the peace terms imposed on her; the inflation in Germany of the middle 1920s; and generally, the humiliation of a proud people and their inability to understand what had happened to them.

Since those days, Western countries, having undergone, up to a point, a similar inflationary experience, are in a better position to understand what inflation means than they were in the 1920s. The German inflation was "total": that is, paper money was issued until it ceased to have any value. In the year 1929, the writer was presented, as a souvenir, with notes for several *billion marks*. What inflation of that type meant can be understood if it be recalled that anyone who had any kind of fixed income or resources, lost everything he had. A large insurance policy, for example, could fall due and be paid off at the current equivalent of, shall we say, a cake of soap. The internal war debt of the German empire was by this means completely got rid of. It is no wonder that Germans lost confidence in their institutions and in the 1930s were to plunge wildly for what seemed stability.

It is easy to build up a large account against the Western governments, but it must be remembered that peace came at the end of the most abominable war in modern history. Napoleon's wars had been bad enough, but his campaigns *moved,* so that the injuries done here this year were done somewhere else next. The Second World War lasted six years and no one will regard its horrors as minor. But they were hardly compar-

able with those of the First World War. They did not involve the years of
mud, icy water, filth, lice, rotting corpses, which the men of the First War
had to endure. Comparisons are odious, so perhaps they should not be
made. Both wars were ghastly: let it rest at that. Their deep subterranean
effects will keep coming to the top for many a year yet.

II
The Inter-War Years

The inter-war period is conveniently divided into two. The first decade of
relative well-being and the second decade marked by the great depression
of the 1930s, the rise of Hitlerism and the slide down into the abyss of war
again in 1939.

Could anything more irrational be found than the depression? There
was the violent New York stock crash of October, 1929, but it destroyed
only paper values, the values printed on bonds or stock exchange apprais-
als of value. There were, it is true, several droughts and crop failures in
succession which worked great hardships in North America and actually
destroyed good farm land, but apart from these there was no natural
calamity sufficient in itself to account for the unparalleled stagnation that
marked the life of most of the world during the 1930s. The land was there,
forests, mines, fisheries, were there as before. Yet everything stopped.
Coming through London early in a morning of those depression summers,
a traveller, passing along the central parks, could see the grass covered
with men finishing their night's sleep. They lay there on old newspapers –
in their hundreds, the only place they had to lie. That at the centre of the
civilized world. Similar scenes were widespread. To use a hackneyed
phrase, men were starving in the midst of plenty – though, in reality,
thanks to emergency organizations, few people did, literally starve.[1]

No doubt despairing men had a good deal to do with the political
upheavals that brought Hitler to the top. At any rate, he came to the top,
and when he got there (1933) it quickly became clear that he was trying not
only for the restoration of prosperity to Germany but for such a measure
of aggrandizement as to lead to war. Each year he occasioned some crisis
whose settlement called for a surrender on the part of the British and
French and each surrender provided the making of another. Britain and
France, in the midst of their economic difficulties, also had the misfortune
to be saddled with a succession of weak governments. "The worst foreign
minister we have had since Ethelred the Unready," said an Englishman in
reference to Sir John Simon. It was the age of Stanley Baldwin and Neville
Chamberlain, whose humiliation at Munich has become a classical passage in history, giving the world a powerful word, *Appeasement*. At last,
after some years of alarm once more the world was plunged in war.

The Second World War was also a world revolution. Militarily, humanity conducted itself heroically on the battlefield, but the heroism of the battlefield was equalled by the grit with which the noncombatants endured the endless bombing that turned every quiet town into a battlefield. At last, after six long years, it was over, Hitler was dead and his "Thousand Year empire" had crumbled after twelve. Germany was divided, Russia had recovered all her old lands and more, France was relatively intact and Britain was exhausted. Across the Atlantic, a great new world power had made itself evident. Its language was English and it had drawn around itself the hopes, the aspirations, the outlooks, of nearly all the peoples throughout the world who spoke the English tongue.

III
After the Second War

The war over, efforts had to be made to rebuild the world. A new international organization was created, the *United Nations,* which everyone hoped would be more effective than its predecessor, the *League of Nations,* but to which no nation so hoping would surrender the one thing needful, its own sovereignty. There were the usual optimistic and empty platitudes enunciated by public men, but underneath them, it was easy to see lurking the old problem of power. The war left two states so great that they stood in a class by themselves, the "super-powers," the United States and Russia. Russia had been badly mauled by the Germans, but there were still those 8,000,000 square miles of land under its control and its 200,000,000 people. Its capacity at that moment for offence might not be great, its capacity for defence, thanks to the collapse of Germany, greater than ever. The United States had not been impaired. Said an American journalist "This country is in the war only up to its knees." Hardly up to its knees indeed: it had given a demonstration of almost boundless strength, and extremely well-co-ordinated strength, too. Moreover, it had taken over from the British their work on the horrible secret that had decisively ended the war – the atomic bomb. The "bomb" itself was a revolution, not only as a scientific "breakthrough" but also as putting within human hands a capacity for destruction hitherto unimaginable. The atom bomb robbed science of its claim to be beneficent. It made science quite as much threat as promise.

After the war, down to the present, the nature of the world's affairs divides clearly into two. Internationally, the dominant theme has been the rivalry between the two worlds of which the United States and Russia form the poles. While there are few areas in which this – "the Cold War" as it was called – has not been apparent, the most prominent has been the Middle East, the country of the Euphrates River valley and Arabia. The astonishing lakes of oil that lie underneath this region – obviously put there by Allah himself, for the benefit of his faithful – are dominant in the world supply. Since the countries sitting on top of the oil are able to turn off the tap at will, they are in the strongest of positions. The strength of their position depends on the virtual certainty that armed Western intervention would bring in Russia on their side. They are thus in a situation to hold to ransom those countries dependent on their oil.

The position on the eastern coast of Asia has been rather different. The United States has feared that left to themselves, the appendant peninsulas of that continent, Korea, Malaya and Indo-China being the chief, would be overcome by Chinese Communism, and thus some strategic points lost. This consideration might be extended to the Philippines and Japan. Since after much civil war, the Chinese Communists had triumphed, the conclusion was drawn that such aggrandizement would greatly strengthen the potential enemy. Persons who saw further did not think that two great world powers as close neighbours, Russia and China, would be too likely to see eye to eye. This was what happened. In the 1950s, Stalin was asked, so it is said, "Which do you fear most the United States or China?" "At the moment," he replied, "the United States; in ten years, China." That is exactly how it turned out. The consequence has been that since China emerged as another super-power, though mostly in defensive terms, the world has rested, as it were on a three-legged stool, tilting uneasily from two legs to two legs as the exigencies of the day have demanded. This uneasy balance would enter still another phase by the consolidation of Western Europe into something like a state. The power such a state would have would give the fourth leg to the stool.

The situations which arose in the Near East and the Far East were closely associated with what might be called the Colonial Revolution. After the Second War several factors united in Great Britain's leading the way in a relaxation of the bonds that held her colonies attached to her. The white colonies had long been self-governing and most of them by 1945 were attached to the erstwhile mother country only by the common language, common traditions, sentiments and institutions. As Edmund Burke had long ago said of the old American colonies before the Revolution, "these are bands that, light as air are strong as iron chains." So it had proved in both World Wars. There was nothing revolutionary in Canada, Australia, New Zealand and South Africa moving into the status of independent nations, bound only by a loose common allegiance to the crown. It was the almost precipitate way in which self-government was extended to the innumerable "possessions" that constituted the Colonial Revolution. India had long been moving towards self-government and by 1945 it would have been impossible much longer to have retained her in a dependent status. Mr. Clement Attlee's action in completely withdrawing from India was therefore a wise one, and it resulted in closer relations rather than looser. In similar fashion other British colonies were left to make their own way in the world.

Following British example and probably also hastened by American public opinion which, for a power possessing its own colonies, was singularly hostile to the possession of colonies by others, the other chief colonial powers, France and Holland, also divested themselves of most of their overseas possessions. Only Portugal hung stubbornly on, until in 1975, she too followed suit. Today, there are only scattered bits of the world retained under European rule. Since many of the former colonial territories were admitted to the United Nations, the result has been to create a third block of states which fluctuates between the Eastern constellation around Russia and the Western, around the United States. These states are so numerous that they can, by majority vote, shape the decisions of the United Nations. Their principal bond of union lies in their hostile memories of the old days of white overlordship. The colour and racial problem of the world is thus posed in much sharper terms than ever before. Meanwhile the "West" (the "West" of course includes South America, product of the sixteenth century wave of European expansion) is back to the ground it held in the middle eighteenth century, over 200 years ago, before the second great wave of expansion had begun.

Internally, the world's affairs since 1945 have divided into two phases: the first, that of adjustment and prosperity down to the 1960s; the second the uneasy years of the late 1960s and 1970s when every manner of confusion, foolishness and division seemed to be boiling up within even the most stable communities. By the middle 1970s most of it seemed to have disappeared as mysteriously as it had emerged and once more something more familiar was taking its place, a conventional commercial depression, along with a threat of disaster through inflation. This too might pass, for mankind will no more be crucified on a cross of paper money than on "Bill" Bryan's *Cross of Gold*. What comes immediately after is anyone's guess. If the line of interpretation followed in this book has any validity, the remaining quarter of the century will be a period of deepening confusion, perhaps coming close to anarchy, after which, sometime later the light may once more break. But it will be a light quite unlike the light that has been theretofore visible, the light of another new age.

IV
Looking Into the Dark

As these words are written, 1978, the historian, with his fellows, stands peering into the dark.

Notes

1. For a vivid personal account laid in an area not usually associated with want, the Canadian west, see James Gray, *The Winter Years*, (Macmillan, Toronto, 1966). For international affairs, huge libraries full of books have been written and no sooner does one appear than something occurs which has not been included in it. There seems little point in including a list of books as of 1978 which would be out of date, by, say 1979. Let the reader seek the nearest public library!

CHAPTER TWENTY-TWO

A World Adrift

It is relatively easy to sketch outlines of the relationships between states or the day-to-day development within them, but how is that unsubstantial ghost to be described that we dub "the spirit of the times." Age differs from age, not only on a local scale, but over areas almost world-wide. Nothing illustrates that more graphically than today. A new world is taking shape before our eyes. We are present at the first days of creation, we see the figure emerging from the stone under the skilful strokes of . . .? There we must stop, for we never see that which makes the strokes and it is only in uncertain light that we see the strokes. But they are made and a figure takes shape, or, to keep to the more conventional language, one age passes into another.

Man and his world in this present year 1978 is about as different from man and his world in the year 1900 as well could be in such a short space of time. How can the difference be readily put into simple words? Rough road signs of change can easily be read: everyone knows there were no aeroplanes in 1900, or any of a thousand things that now are common. But can we get beyond such matters into the deeper levels of change? These pages have been efforts to dig down to those levels: their very number indicates how much digging is necessary. Is there one great diamond buried deep down in the clay, that may be uncovered? Probably not, or if so, buried too deeply to be found. But there are many smaller diamonds, and if well cleaned, they will shine. They will help us to understand how we got from there to here.

I
Equality as the Key Word
to the Period

One such diamond is suggested by a word, the word *equality*. The idea of equality was long ago dissected and satirized by W. S. Gilbert in the opera *The Gondoliers:* the quaintness of the satire indicates how far society in the interval has moved in the direction of the condition satirized, equality. These words are written facing a house inhabited by students. As they go in and out, men and women, they look exactly alike, whichever their sex. Their clothes are identical, all of them of dingy hue. Their demeanour is identical. They live and sleep in a house that knows no distinction of status and probably little of sex. (How different from the North American "fraternities" and "sororities" whose purpose was precisely that of emphasizing social gradations!) Such students form a typical sector of their community. Their instructors, up to a senior level, are in appearance like the students. Neither instructors or students differ appreciably from the general community in appearance, status or way of life. Apparently equality has been achieved. What has happened in the small sector of the student world has happened over large areas of society as a whole. Everybody owns a car, every house has its due range of electrical appliances, every woman gets the same "hair-do." A cat may not only look at a queen, it may look like a queen.

II
Equality as Illustrated
in the Field of Communications

Equality of this mechanical sort clearly comes out of the unlimited inventiveness of the species, which in our day, manifests itself in geometric progression. Necessarily it must invade every nook and cranny of life.

Effects of this penetration of sheer technical capacity can easily be traced in all the devices associated with that most distinctive of human accomplishments, communication. Much of the historic effort in the development of communication has been devoted to reducing it to order, to reducing indiscriminate shouting and babbling to some logical presentation of thought. But the enormous development of devices for communication has gone some distance to reducing it from order once more to shouting and babbling. Instances abound. Take music, for example. Electronic devices, more especially the radio, made possible such a wide distribution of "product" that "product" was necessarily reduced to the lowest common denomination of audience. A quick result was the substitution of mere noise for an ordered sound. The popular and semi-popular music of previous generations was not continued. Instead the mournful, sentimental slave dirges of the American south began to flood in. An unhappy people, the Americans, far too rich for happiness, adopted as their own an unhappy music. By mid-century, save for resurrected and emaciated scraps of folk music, most of the northern world had ceased to sing. It had transferred making music to the juke box. The cults of "blues" singers, "torch" singers and other makers of animal noises had swept away almost all but the high islands of symphony and opera reserved for a diminishing élite and for conscripted school children. The mid-twentieth century was becoming a musical wasteland, an offence to the ears, a cacophony such as the Western world had never before had to endure. The place of the technical device in all this is surely evident.

But it was all "popular" and "democratic."

A similar development was conspicuous with the printed word. Year by year, the amount of printed material placed before the public advanced astronomically. It is true, only the barest fraction of it lasted more than a few moments: people bought endless numbers of those blowsy old whores the newspapers, only to throw them away. The newspapers themselves grew larger and larger, filled mainly with advertisements but also with such cultural achievements as "the funnies" (which had long ceased to be "funny") with sentimental answers to the woes of the lovelorn, with infinite attention to gladiatorial combats, with large quantities of carelessly arranged "news," as often as not misleading, with endless "stories" of a "back-fence" gossip sort, constant reiteration of reports about crime and scandal (public and private) and with editorials read only by the few. The daily newspaper presented an impressive reflection of *equality*.

An actual instance of the height to which newspaper overproduction had risen, even as long ago as the 1920s is provided by an eyewitness. This person took the bus from New York to Boston a day or two after Christmas, 1925. As the passengers entered, nearly every one of them bought a copy of the *New York Times,* that excellent "paper." It had been snowing and the snow was tracked into the bus. As people turned over the innumerable sheets of *The Times* (very few of them gave more than a passing glance at them), most of them dropped them in the aisle. Others tramped over these, and they were soon reduced to pulp. Every now and then the bus driver would "make a pass" at clearing up the mess, dropping it outside. By the time the bus got to Boston, the aisle was full of sodden newspaper. It is probable that few copies of the *New York Times,* however much excellent material they contained, met different fates. Clearly an overproduction of communication.

By the second half of the century, this overproduction was having its necessary effect and just as necessarily, it was the better class of production that suffered soonest: magazines and periodicals. Even the redoubtable *Saturday Evening Post* had to stop publishing. In Great Britain, the long-established *Twentieth Century* (which had begun as *The Nineteenth*

Century), a journal for the well-informed, had shrunk to a shadow. With some brilliant, traditional or snobbish exceptions, such as *The New Statesman and Nation,* or *The Illustrated London News,* most others of the sort had gone the same way.

From the beginning newspapers have been classifiable both as sources of amusement and as public "gazettes." In each capacity they are mainly new forms of gossip and "chit-chat." Gossip and chit-chat may often rise up to the dignity of "public opinion." In this latter role, vehicles for public opinion, the newspaper is indispensable and it would be hard to imagine the huge democracies of our day enduring long without it. It is both curse and blessing, but as plain a mark of the present age as the automobile: both are for everyone.

The newspaper has three centuries of historical experience behind it. Not so those other forms of entertainment that project themselves in pictures. The "moving picture" will no doubt always serve as a fairly important historical source, especially in bringing back the detail of an event or a period. Its chief use, however, has not been to aid the historian but to entertain the masses. As such, it has to cater to the mind of the masses, said by experts to represent the mental level of a child of twelve years of age. Before it appeared, there was relatively little opportunity for public depiction of the aspects of life that make the widest and most primitive appeal; sentimentality, violence, lust and pornography. With the "movie," though the average film was merely vapid, these could always find an outlet. A small number of talented people tried to make a new art form out of the film: some succeeded and an acting genius appeared in Charlie Chaplin (after 1975 , Sir Charles, d. 1977).

The major contributions of the "movie" were (1) to provide "opium for the people" on a scale not previously attainable (2) to provide the basis for a new art form and (3) in all but the largest North American cities by indirect pressure and deliberate policy on the part of the large corporations that quickly secured control, to kill off the "legitimate theatre." In Europe, where the film encountered an older and more deeply rooted culture, the "legitimate" theatre made a better fight for it, but it was nevertheless deeply affected. The day of the flesh and blood actor appearing upon a real stage seemed to be drawing to a close. The day of the electronic shadow was upon the world.

Outside, in the streets, as the "movie" theatres emptied, the most elaborate electrical advertising displays could be witnessed, "paradises" it was remarked at the time, "for those who cannot read."

The "silent movies" had been succeeded about 1925 by the "talkies," by which the dialogue was synchronized with the acting. This development obviated the need for the minimum literacy required to read the explanations of the story. It also proved capable of penetrating any language barrier, for it was possible to have a story originally made, say, in Swedish, presented to an audience whose language might be Chinese. Any "talkie" of sufficient attractiveness could obtain virtually world-wide showing.

When the "movie's" successor, television, came along just after the Second World War, still another layer was added to the already gaudily iced cake of electronic communications. It is generally agreed that television has been the most powerful of all the media, not excluding the printed word, in its penetrative strength. It knows no boundary of nation, race or creed and it sits at the fireside, the dinner table, the bedside of rich and poor alike. Like all these other technical contrivances, it is a good servant but a bad master. From the first many wonderful things could be seen on television, of immense novelty, well-presented, instructive, amusing, easily grasped. These attributes of excellence constituted its severest condemnation, for they were the very qualities that people in the mass did not want. Television at first was used with some discretion, but how could discretion continue when there was presented to the average man – and child – a succession of spectacles as powerfully attractive as an automobile accident just outside the front door? In the nature of things, television had to be perverted. Its nature made it into a device for atomizing the mind, drawing it on from sensation to sensation, at the expense of coherence. In its more noxious aspects, it nudged the mass of men towards the ancient norms of primitive behaviour, towards vapidity, violence, lust. This new form of mass torpidity was reminiscent of those eighteenth century gin drinking aids to unconsciousness satirized by William Hogarth: "Drunk for a penny, dead drunk for two pence."

The effects of this new form of narcotic, television, cannot yet be determined, but men being what they are, it seems likely to work towards the enfeeblement of thought and the destruction of the arts, both of which results would be warmly welcomed by the great majority of people, to whom the myriad gadgets and conveniences provided by technology must far outweigh any attention to the subtleties of their effects. No doubt there will always be a saving remnant that will succeed in fencing off some space for itself and quite possibly lead the way to building some new kind of civilization to replace that old magnificence that perished with the nineteenth century.

Technology, that is, man's inventiveness, once it had power tools placed at its disposal, necessarily led to all aspects of equality. The mass man, who had been tucked away by the status-creating devices of previous ages, once more emerged, bawling raucously. Under the weight of numbers and animal vigour, how could anything but a rough state of equality result?[1]

III
Other Routes to Equality

The same end could be reached by other routes, though these probably all may be given some environmental explanation. It is to be remembered that the discovery and occupation of the New World meant for the vast majority of people who came to it voluntarily one major thing – opportunity! Opportunity in every direction, but men being men, mainly opportunity to get what they wanted – gold, land, women, slaves, power, position, even idyllic societies. To the efforts of those who saw life in terms of idyllic societies – the phrase will cover order and justice as well as social utopias, we owe the erection in the New World of that shaky building called civilization. To the average new-comer, however, the New World represented the more or less crude aspects of opportunity. Opportunity took many forms in the many lands acquired by Europeans, and that story forms the history of European expansion. In that part of it with which this book is the most closely associated, the English-speaking countries, to the natural drive of opportunity was added the fuel of free institutions. Free institutions and opportunity made the modern English-speaking world, with all its shortcomings and all its excellence. In the choicest and richest area grasped by that world, now the United States of America, free institutions meant, among many other things, generations of indoctrination with the idea that a man could have what he wanted and do as he liked. It is a natural consequence that out of such notions should flow those doctrines, if doctrines they can be called, known as "permissiveness." The "permissive society" is that society in which people may have what they want and do as they like. A few lines must necessarily be drawn: one must not drive up the wrong side of the road, at least on a crowded highway. But if you don't like the wife you have, or the husband, there is no reason why you should not get rid of her, or him, and have another. "Permissiveness" clearly is destructive of established society, that is, of the civilization the few have so painfully managed to build.

IV
Equality and Permissiveness

A set of values is built up only after long, slow, effort: effort that in the biggest matters, extends over centuries. To understand this is to understand history. It took centuries to gain acceptance of the values commonly called "Christian." It took centuries to gain acceptance for the concept of a free society and to build the institutions such as Parliament and the courts, which protect it and in some measure establish it. A strong society cannot be built on "permissiveness," which is something that North

Americans are, in this last quarter of the twentieth century, just beginning to discover, or to rediscover. Older societies still have something of their old codes to guide them and some older societies, such as Russia, have adopted entirely new codes, whose severities take little note of freedom but provide the power that comes from discipline.

An easily identified aspect of the transition from the nineteenth century to the twentieth lies in the replacement of creativeness by inventiveness. Emotion, that is, gives place to intellect. Putting things together gives place to taking things apart, analyzing them. The twentieth century is the age of analysis. Analysis cannot make for unity of attitude, for a sense of solidarity, for a scale of values. It leads us by another route back to permissiveness. A good illustration lies in the artistic conceptions and perceptions of Pablo Picasso (1881-1973) and his disciples. In many of the paintings of this modern school, man himself disappears: he is replaced by a scattering of separate parts. Picasso's paintings must have been influential in moulding the attitudes of many gifted people. They seem to stand for determinism at its bleakest. The individual disappears, to be replaced by cells, chromosomes, genes and other components of heredity. "When the coster's finished jumping on his mother," while no doubt "he loves to lie a baskin' in the sun," he cannot be held responsible for his act of jumping: that is just in the genes of which what is called "an individual" is an accidental assemblage. No blame can be placed on him: there is no "him." This seems to be the point we, in the West today, have reached over large areas of life. You cannot really blame anyone for anything. Things are just as they are: responsibility has disappeared. Note the words "over large areas." All is not lost, not by any means, but the disorder mounting up to chaos of modern times, is real, not imaginary, and it may well increase.

Notes

1. A Nobel Peace Prize winner, Hon. L. B. Pearson, gave it as his opinion that about 2 per cent of the population is sophisticated (*Memoirs,* Vol. III, (University of Toronto Press, Toronto, 1975) p. 211.

CHAPTER TWENTY-THREE

Prelude to Chaos?

"Today!" This book has arrived at "today." But as these words are written, "today" becomes "yesterday." In the metaphor often used in these pages, how difficult it is to place "now" in the chart of time.

Yet anyone writing in the 1970s will probably think of the period as one of rapid change, change so rapid that it may fairly be called revolutionary. There are few aspects of life to which the term could not be applied. A depiction in detail of "now," the contemporary scene, would take up a book by itself – and it would only be one man's depiction. Yet, as an attempt to bring the long story of Western civilization down as far as possible and to look a little way into the future, some of the major components of this revolutionary age may be set down.

I
This Revolutionay Age
and Some of Its Components

"War is the forcing house of social change." The twentieth century has had its deep experience of war and can testify to the truth of the quotation. It has seen revolutions in Russia and China which have virtually transformed these countries. It has seen changes almost as deep in Germany, Italy and Japan. It has vastly altered the scale of weights of every major state, making heavier some, especially the United States and Russia and lighter others, especially Great Britain and France. It has witnessed men rise from nothing to astounding heights only to fall as suddenly. Such were

Mussolini and Hitler. It has heard great men speak in the names of their countries and of humanity. Such were Churchill and Roosevelt, whose voices were heard not by a few but by everyone. It has seen vast territorial changes. Nearly all maps have had to be torn up and new ones drawn. Not new maps such as are called for in looking at the long generations of Europe, involving a few square miles here, or a city there, but maps showing the changes in sovereignty over huge tracts of the earth's surface, and the emergence of states that were undreamed of when the century began. In particular and emphatically, the tremendous phenomenon of European expansion into the outer world, after having been almost continuous for 500 years has suddenly within a matter of a few years ceased, and a reverse movement has set in, which in some instances has brought large numbers of the former colonized or enslaved peoples into the homelands of the colonizers, there to give rise to the problems stirred up by their migrations.[1]

"Decolonization" was not only a huge political and historical phenomenon, it also marked and accentuated the still deeper social and anthropological problems of colour. Europe had grown up in its own local white world and until a couple of centuries ago, the Europeans who had even seen human beings differing from themselves in this respect were few.

Colonial expansion had brought some knowledge of what nearly all Europeans would have been quite ready to call "lesser breeds," but "lesser breeds" they had remained (with the possible exception of the Japanese after about 1870.) Yet the white world had taken one conclusive step which was to prevent this attitude of patronizing superiority continuing indefinitely and that lay in its own ingenuity in the techniques of communication and transportation. The Western steamship and the airplane brought the East to the West, the South to the North, and the confrontation was not often a pleasant one. It is true that in the colonial outliers of Europe, white had been impinging on black – or various non-white shadings of black – over several centuries, but invariably in this relationship of superior to inferior. In two important sections of the outer world, America and South Africa, the relationship had taken on its ultimate logical form of slavery, in America, both North and South, a condition that the white had himself deliberately created. Now from the middle of the twentieth century, the consequences, not only of slavery but of white superiority generally, had to be faced. And one important component in their facing was white idealism itself. Would the old two worlds become one world? There indeed was a problem for the future.

It may be contended that most of the vast changes of "the present," particularly those almost suddenly exploding after the Second World War, arose from the pretentious development of technique, technique much of which sprang from the accumulating findings of science. These it is surely not necessary to list in detail. We have only to think of the miraculous growth of ''electronics,'' the innumerable applications of electric power to implements great and small, from the jet airplane – or indeed the space ship – to the microscopic listening device or the humble pocket electric shaver. Possibly it is the restless mind of man, limitless in its ingenuity, expressing itself in mechanical extensions of itself, which has always – though ''always'' is a large term – upset things as they are. The bow and arrow must once have been a magical and alarming novelty. At any rate, invention, descending like rain upon us, has doubled, trebled, quadrupled in this present period and the end is not yet. One explanation of revolution and the restlessness that precedes it, surely lies in technical invention. The word normally used for that has been ''progress,'' but our own day has shown us that there is another side to ''progress'' – pollution of air and water is one example of that – so that the feeble current of thought and action which hitherto has had the temerity to question this version of ''progress'' may well in the future increase in strength and volume.

Whether behind the more visible connotations attached to the word, there lies a deeper more philosophical content to ''the idea of progress'' would form the subject of a large debate that would carry us at last into investigation of the very meaning of life itself. Far into such a great debate it is not possible, in this last concluding chapter, to go, but some major aspects of it must here briefly be reviewed. They could almost be set down in two columns of ''plus's and minus's'' in some attempt to answer man's perpetual question ''Is the world getting better or worse?'' but the columns would not add up and they would leave the question unanswered. It could, however, safely be said that each item in them would have some bearing on the restlessness of our times.

The leading item on the ''plus'' side would be *public well-being*. The origin of the concept, if a complete examination were being made, would have to be traced to those dim beginnings in which the physical safety and preservation of the group was the first consideration – *salus populi – safety of the state, suprema lex* – the safety (or well-being) of the people is the supreme law. The concept broadens and deepens as the centuries roll. The idea of humane concern for others comes in and gradually swells to huge proportions. It forms a major story in itself for it goes from the praiseworthy efforts at charity of the mediaeval monastery to the rise of the modern hospital, from the rude schools of the ''Dark Ages'' to that vast and ever expanding modern preoccupation, education, from the reluctant efforts of the state to give a modicum of attention to ''the poor'' and the old to the ''welfare state'' of today. The public well-being in the eighteenth century extended only a short distance beyond protection against the invader, the punishment of the criminal, the preservation of what was still a rather elementary public order, the security of property through the law and the courts. Today there is hardly a nook or cranny of life into which those responsible for "the public well-being" do not have authority to look – examples lie about on every hand. No one may keep a dog without a licence. (No licensing for cats yet.) No one may build a minor shed in his back-yard (the exaggeration is not grotesque) without permission of a public body. All this leads to an orderly highly regulated, highly efficient mode of life. Throughout the West it is accepted by nine people out of ten and for those who do not accept it, there are commodious, uncomfortable jails provided, in which are made strenuous, usually vain, attempts to reform the inmates.

The idea of the perfect society has been carried so far, especially in the English-speaking world, and it has had such powerful assistance from the affluence flowing in from the natural treasures of the world (take oil as an example) that it has seemed to many as if the Heavenly City were once more in sight. Many could believe that the day would come when practically all physical disability would be conquered, when *want* would disappear, when war would be no more and all men be brothers. The prodigious strides made during the nineteenth and twentieth centuries seemed to justify the optimism and not even the fiery furnaces of the two World Wars were sufficient to dissipate it. The late twentieth century is still, for the most part, optimistic, but its optimism is tempered by a realism that might have seemed strange to the late nineteenth. The late twentieth century has caught a glimpse of something quite other than the New Jerusalem – a glimpse of want, the age old spectre of mankind, once more descending. Oil may run out. Soil can be destroyed. The prolific race of man can once more, as in much simpler conditions, breed up in numbers that instead of blessings, have become curses. The very inventiveness of man can be turned against himself, as indeed it has always been. But never so suicidally as through the development of the atom bomb and other destructive agencies which are lying in wait for humanity. And in the rise and terror of Naziism, the world caught rather more than a glimpse of something that seemed to make a mock of that pleasant picture of man painted by such eighteenth century dreamers as Jean-Jacques Rousseau – man as naturally good, given a chance. In Naziism with its grim holocaust among the Jews, evil, not good, seemed to stalk the earth, evil that the victories of those who did not have this ultimate evil in their hearts, may only have covered up. Naziism revealed man to himself again and in lurid colours – that horrible, ravening wild beast was there inside him, ready to leap out of its cage unless constantly restrained.

But were the restraints strong enough? Could they ever be strong enough? Time would tell. *Nil desperandum* – "one must never despair" – hope remained, take the goods the gods provide you; they have never been more munificent.

Public well-being, our goal and our endeavour, has been advanced by many agencies. Many people would at once pick out the medical profession as among the chief. This profession has had a long history with many ups and downs. Apart from original self-help, it probably began with the medicine man, shaman and witch doctor. It rose to considerable heights on the stimulus of the Greek mind, only to fall practically to the witch doctor level during the darkest of "the Dark Ages." The Renaissance brought science to its enhancement and produced illustrious names, such as Vesalius, the great anatomist and Harvey, the discoverer of how the blood circulates. From those days on medicine has been more and more closely linked with scientific achievement. The doctor, however, is not primarily a scientist but an applied scientist and until he had some great scientific achievements to apply, that is, until about the middle of the nineteenth century, he may well have killed as many people as he cured. When, however, men like Jenner, Pasteur and Lister came along, the situation changed. The medical profession not only began to save lives, but to fight epidemics and to work the wonders of surgery upon the human body. Such things were perhaps major factors in the prodigious increase in the human species.[2] It nevertheless remains probable that, asked what one thing has most increased the sum of human lives, the average person would answer "the advance of medical science."[3] This popular view has raised the status of the profession to a great height, of which its members have taken full monetary advantage, though it can be argued that underneath the science there still lies the old faith in the medicine man, the first individual to be called when trouble comes, so that perhaps the doctor's chief asset today is still not so much his knowledge as "a good bedside manner."

More important than that is what medical and surgical skill is actually doing to the race, for to every accomplishment there is a counter account. Today the "typical" person wears glasses, has no tonsils or appendix; he may well have had other surgery. As he advances in life, he takes to a hearing aid, has ulcers or heart trouble, yet he may well never have suffered an infectious disease. He lives a long life and may be lucky to die suddenly of his heart trouble.[4]

Is not this to the good? The average man would surely say yes. Is it producing a breed that is, as it were, cobbled together, things of shreds and patches? Medical science preserves the unfit whom nature would discard. It preserves the weak in mind, the weak in body and has nothing to say as to their responsibilities to the next generation. The medical profession has as its goal – necessarily – the saving and prolongation of life, it is not its to reason why. Why, it may be asked, under certain circumstances, save life? That is, how much value has life? Again, we come to an ultimate problem. Certainly no culture has been as careful and parsimonious of life as our own, perhaps because we no longer produce it abundantly. The problem is probably not yet of first importance, for in the advanced countries at least, most people are healthy and probably could also be made fit if occasion required. Nevertheless it is worth pondering. Does our solicitude and success in such matters rob us of those sparks of Nature's fire that may have given us our great men? Is our well-being tending to reduce us all to well-fed, well-watered domestic cattle?

A closely related problem is that of the aging of the population, which today includes a steadily increasing proportion of people over the customary age of retirement, sixty-five. The scriptures "three score years and ten," which when it was formulated probably pointed to the extreme life-span to be expected, has crept up into the late seventies and today for a person to have reached the upper eighties occasions little surprise. Many people live into their nineties. Much could be said about extreme old age, but except in the rarest of cases can it carry energy along with it? An aging population must be, it would be thought, slower in decision and action than one having a high share of young people. Conceivably that might make it more peaceful, but not necessarily, for it would continue to depend on youth to do its fighting for it. It might make it more judicious, wiser, less demanding. On the other hand, old people necessarily leave most of life to younger people. They thus represent a load to be carried along. Primitive societies have simply disposed of them – more or less humanely, usually less. The problem of the old people in an "advanced," affluent society is not yet solved.[5]

There are of course many aspects of modern life that breed a soft race. In American cities, the sidewalks slowly fall to pieces because nobody walks any more – people ride perpetually in cars. They are overweight, they eat silly foods – the list is endless. In the United States, the fat boy, a youngster of say eleven, weighing many pounds more than he should and stuffing potato chips and ice cream into him is fairly common. In Canada, the beer-bellied young man in his twenties has become a frequent sight.

In battle with a hard, disciplined people like the Russians, the Westerners (especially English and North Americans) would fare badly. But providing the acid test is not war, physical unfitness may not be of first importance. In war, all rules would be changed. Still, physical unfitness, with its accompanying grossnesses and laxities does seem a rather pitiable outcome for a century that once thought it saw the gates of Paradise just over the horizon.

II
Education, Public Well-Being, Numbers, Values

One of the vehicles carrying man to the promised land has always been held to be the school. The school in one shape or another goes back deep into the classical world and probably farther than that. Informally if not formally, it has probably always existed, for initiating the young into the habits and practices of the tribe is older than man. Education rose to great heights in Greece and Rome but sank low in the abyss between Rome and the high Middle Ages. Recovery came and the advance and elaboration of the school from its low point has scarcely ever halted. Today education in its innumerable forms and institutions is surely among the most prominent aspects of society. In the West everyone reads and writes (after a fashion!), and can do simple arithmetical problems. As the complexities of learning increase with the successive steps up the ladder, the numbers of learners unavoidably decrease, but even at the giddiest heights of the university, students are many: they far outnumber their predecessors of even the previous generation, to say nothing of those of the previous century. They do so both in actual numbers and in the proportions they form of the total population. They are housed in good, often splendid, buildings and have stores of libraries and laboratories that would have made the Victorians gasp. The well-ordered, efficient society must have its efficient "social engineers" and these the modern educational system quite efficiently supplies.

There are many absurdities in modern education, for so large and respected a profession as that of the teacher (at whatever level) must give much opportunity for the crank and the faddist to find shelter in it. Sometimes the antics of such people are simply ludicrous, sometimes they are dangerous, as when they merely confuse children and young people instead of doing what is imperative in our complex world, systematizing knowledge and ordering thought. Such people seem to find ready refuge in Departments of Education (not the classroom, which is too tough for them). They fit well into the logic of the saying attributed to George Bernard Shaw and since improved on: Those who can, do. Those who cannot, teach. Those who cannot teach, teach how to teach. Those who cannot teach how to teach, administer. While they are dangerous, they cannot be dominant, for the main work of school and university will always be done in the classroom by the humble foot-slogging infantry of the profession, the actual teachers. And teachers being of necessity what they have always been in the main, persons who strive after excellence will continue their search, ranking, classifying and qualifying, putting upon those under their instruction the labels of good, indifferent and poor which they have always used and thus mightily determining the future.

In both health and education, there is one enemy who is hard to conquer, and his name is *legion,* that is, mass numbers. There are many instances of this throughout the world, the most conspicuous probably being India, where millions of new people are added to the population every year and food supplies increase but slowly. But even in Western Europe, the horrible destruction of life during the two World Wars did not arrest the growth in total numbers and all the devices for birth control have not arrested it. In extremely overcrowded countries like Holland, Belgium and England, the total slowly goes higher. Efforts to deal with sheer numbers are made in every direction, as anyone familiar with the transportation maze of London will readily testify. Transportation nevertheless presents the simpler side of this problem of numbers. It is in the subtler, more intricate and complex aspects of life that the greatest difficulties occur – health and well-being and all the various implications to be found in such words as *education, citizenship* and *human relations.* Think of the number of new universities opened since the end of the Second War. Building them has been relatively easy. Staffing them is another matter. A scholar or a scientist cannot be conjured out of space.

Mankind constantly outnumbers and outflanks all those who make the effort to drag it an inch or two further forward, or what they consider *forward* for *forward* is another question – begging word. To shift, then, let us say, the monster Juggernaut of humanity in the mass one step in any given direction. That is the aim of the educationalist – and it is necessary, surely, for him to seek the mark he is aiming at. And that brings up the vast subject of *values.*

This struggle with numbers finds good illustration not only in education but in the field of the arts. Take music as an example. Today (1978) there probably are several times as many symphony orchestras in the Western world as there were a few years ago, and many times as many as in the great nineteenth century age of music. There are corresponding numbers of professional musicians and persons learning to be professional musicians. Conservatories of Music, Faculties of Music have multiplied to match. The radio and television daily dispense the music of the great masters. Opera can be heard, though perhaps not seen, by almost anyone. Yet it is to be doubted whether all this greatly affects the public taste in music or increases the level of musical appreciation. It of course does so in absolute numbers, but the point here is its effect on relative numbers.

It is quite possible, of course, that the present vigorous level of appreciation of "classical" music may rise up sooner or later into a new golden age of music as magical as that of the nineteenth century. That is not yet in sight. After listening to various concerts of contemporary music (including a major work by an almost contemporary, Bartok, as presented by the Boston Symphony Orchestra, February 16, 1978, the present writer hazards his untutored personal opinion that no forecast of greatness is as yet possible. Modern "good" music lacks vitality. Modern composers seem to spurn their audiences. They write for themselves. It may be that they are groping for that which at present is beyond their reach. They may be fore-runners. Or they may be winding up the musical vitality of their predecessors. Music is universally among the most powerful of social forces, summing up a society and shaping it. What kind of society is modern music shaping? It is intellectual music that does not touch the depths, certainly not the hearts. It may be that out of the modern cacophony of jazz, rock, hard rock, and the rest, some future master or masters will distil a new music, strange to the present, that will use the vitality in our modern confusions which will capture the depth and spiritual intensity of what has gone before. That, however, is for the future, when the world may have recaptured something of that stability and confidence out of which great art probably proceeds.

Much the same could be said about the other arts. There is far more opportunity to see good paintings, either actually or in good reproduction, but relatively our artistic appreciation may not greatly have altered. And so with literature: libraries are numerous; book borrowers numerous. Is the range and effect of good literature much increased as compared with an older day? Everyone interested in the future must hope so, no one can be sure, for despite the powerful agencies at work, there still seem to be just about as large a percentage of people outside their range, or only barely within their range as say, a century ago. It takes more than the means to secure the end. It is incredibly difficult to move mankind along.

The vast increase in *means* would give some reason for believing that the West was on the edge of a new Renaissance that might carry the human spirit to fresh heights of attainment. No one would belittle the magnitude of the tasks accomplished and it might be that we shall go on in an upward sloping line into an indefinite future. Providing man can refrain from destroying himself, something of the sort is possible. This concluding chapter is not an argument for pessimism, nor is this book as a whole. The point is simply that history moves from age to age, that one age is very different from another and that the period of transition is usually stormy. If this is a revolutionary period as it seems to be, what are the storm signals, the portents of trouble, the negative signs to be placed before so much of the positive?

Some of these are clearly visible in one of the areas alluded to just above – public health. It may not be a gain to have built a population fraying at the edges and growing steadily older in average age. It may not be a gain merely to prolong life, to stretch out by various devices the mere life of a person suffering from an incurable or painful disease. Through such a channel we may have to re-examine our whole attitude towards this mystery called life. That does not mean that the Nazi death camps are upon us. It may mean a re-evaluation of the weight we attach to mere life. The slogan that was popular for a time was "Safety First." It was a necessary slogan but not a very gallant one. We may have to revise such mottoes. There are plenty of places in the world where human life is still held pretty cheap. Our own societies have swung to the opposite extreme – at all costs life must be saved. This trend is relatively recent. It derives more immediately from the increase in humanitarian attitudes and presumably, in ultimate terms from Christian conviction: every individual is held by Christians to have an immortal soul and to be a child of God. What right, then, have we, organized society, to interfere with immortal souls and their lot? There was also the commandment "Thou shall not kill." Christian societies brushed this position aside easily enough but in the nineteenth century they were called on to be their brothers' keepers. This came home to enough people to affect thought and conduct. Add to that the mere squeamishness produced by life quite remote from the final realities (how many good people who enjoy roast beef have ever seen beef cattle killed?). Such considerations help to explain the twentieth century solicitude for life. It may be that as traditional religious teaching weakens, the solicitude for life will weaken too. Until quite recently Christianity has taught that one's own life is not to be valued too highly, for death to the true Christian has simply meant some kind of reunion with his Maker. There not having been any great amount of solicitude for life in days before our own, it may be that civilization reached its peak in the twentieth century.

But again, the First World War, that bloodiest of all modern wars, with its insensate slaughter, upsets surmise and shows what a work is man and what a complexity his "civilization."

Similar points also come out with respect to another topic discussed above, education. It is almost impossible in casting an eye over the whole field of modern education with its plethora of schools, colleges, "institutes," universities, societies, libraries, to avoid painting a picture "couleur de rose." Yet nearly everyone inside the system is severe, often scathing, over what he sees going on. Not only the wasted time, though adolescence through the schools, is often prolonged into manhood, but the poor response of the privileged "inside the walls" to the privileges offered them, their failure to develop, their narrowness, the way in which they persistently turn the road of learning into the road to riches. And the barrenness of much that is presented to them and the futility of the way in which it is presented. Here again we confront the problem of mass. A class of fifteen or a class of fifty – which? Enough books for a few or a few books for everyone? And so on. In other days a handful of people received thorough training, the masses were neglected. Today we make things "go round" everyone gets a little. Or so we like to think, for formerly the reality was very different and those who were not able to teach themselves got very little teaching. No doubt standards have been raised, even for the masses, even if the result is what has been alleged of the people of the United States – that they are "the best half-educated people in the world."

There is no limit to the amount that may be written about modern education; and however much is written it seldom gets us very far. The school boy goes his way "creeping like snail, unwillingly to school," and possibly he is the same school boy, yesterday, today and tomorrow.

Nevertheless it is clear that if self-government and democratic institutions are to work reasonably well, they require a reasonable degree of education for all citizens and a great deal for a good many. The question is whether the educative process of our day is filling that need. Intentions evidently are of the best. Is fulfilment more or less abreast of intention? In this modern shouting world, a thousand voices are raised, each urging us to go this way or that. Except on very large and nebulous points (e.g. "the democratic way of life") there is little sense of direction. Once more, then, we come to the problem of *values*.

No doubt every common school and every common school teacher stand formally for a very ancient set of values. Teachers in many respects have stepped into the shoes of the parson or the priest. It is their duty to instruct their charges in every copy book virtue from cleanliness to honesty and fair play. They are to prepare their charges for entry into the life of the tribe, and the tribe no longer demands heroes who can take a scalp or worst their foe in combat, in single combat, at any rate, for the virtues of collective combat are still set high. The maxims of perfectionism in character still have the primary place. In the higher ranges of education, however, while they no doubt are taken for granted, they are not stressed. Many a university discipline, especially the strategic social sciences, seeks to rid itself of *values*. It seeks to be objective, value-free. The duties of instructor and instructed are confined to the intellectual, scientific approach, the collection and examination of evidence with not too much emphasis on the conclusions to be drawn from it. This shift in approach and motivation cuts deep. It puts everything forward as proper subject for discussion and analysis. It removes, when carried to extremes, the bed-rock of things agreed upon, destroys what former ages cherished as "the sacred" and leaves every individual with no chart or compass save that which he may have constructed from the knowledge he has amassed and his thinking upon it. It is the spectre which haunted Pio Nono when he promulgated his Syllabus of Errors and which has haunted every good mind since the old bed-rock began to give way, every good mind which does not rejoice in anarchy and understands that men must have some fixed points to guide them through life. If modern education is leading us in this way, it is indeed a "Prelude to Chaos."

The number of attempts to supply fixed points is endless. The situation is reminiscent of the ancient days when the old classical gods were tumbling down and many efforts being made to fill their places – the Oriental mystery religions like Mithraism that made so strong a bid for the succession, or the numerous Greek "philosophers" who went about the empire each preaching his own particular gospel for the explanation of life and the regulation of conduct. In our own day both Naziism and Fascism could have been regarded as substitute gods set up to lure the multitudes. The doctrines of Karl Marx, his powerful analysis of history and society that goes by the name of socialism was a much more reputable god – true or false, whichever you deem it – and there have been dozens of others, such as imperialism or nationalism. There have also been countless "godlets" – the nineteenth century "Single Tax" doctrine of Henry George, or Christian Science or British Israelitism, or Mormonism or Seventh-Day Adventism. Dozens of gods and godlets, but as yet none filling the vacuum left by the collapse of the ancient deity provided by the Christian religion. No universal god and hence plenty of room left for each to struggle for adherents.[6] These are discussed below.

It might be possible for each of these "one and seventy warring sects"[7] to be grouped in some sense as constructive and therefore idealistic social forces, though it is hard to see Naziism in that light, and they are therefore to be distinguished from that dark force, so shapeless that it is hard to give it a name, the force, of the indeterminate many that shouts at us every day through all the many media by which it finds expression. Even to write about it is to incur the hostility of those who delight in it. It is the voice of the many, the mob, the "lumpen proletariat" of Karl Marx, the voice of those who when a crown was proposed for Caesar, in Shakespeare's words, "clapped their chapped hands and emitted such a deal of stinking breath that it almost choked Caesar." The many cannot easily be described. Applicable words are not exactly synonyms of each other: mob, crowd, rabble, philistines, obscurantists, "cultural illiterates," and others such all have different shades of meaning.

Victorian writers could inveigh against this element in society because there was still ready acceptance in Victorian England – and to some degree, in the United States, especially, of course, the South – of a society of ranks and classes and to talk of "the poor" or "the labouring classes" raised few hackles. To use class labels today to describe any large group of people would be misleading, for at every level of rank and status, whether of family, fortune or profession, there is to be found an inter-mixture of what writers such as Matthew Arnold described as barbarians or philistines. This of course has always been so. To be a rich "peer of the realm" has never prevented you from passing your days "as drunk as a lord." Today it is probably not possible to be more exact than to divide people into two indeterminate groups, those who take a constructive and more or less idealistic attitude towards society and those who think and act in short-range selfish and self-indulgent terms; or, to put it in other words, those who are concerned with "the human situation" and those who are not. And few people are totally committed to one attitude or the other they easily pass from one to the other. A few illustrations, put tersely, may help to make the distinction clearer – are you against pollution? Do you read? Do you give some of your time and money to serving the public? Where do you stand on pornography? Do you favour public town planning? Would you join a Civil Liberties organization? The reader can go on framing such questions to his heart's content. They will help define the two groups. Earlier writers, practically all Europeans, not North Americans, have boldly proclaimed civilization invariably to be the work of the few, the devoted few – the doctrine is too undemocratic for North America, and probably for most of Europe nowadays. But let anyone look around a community he knows well, and soon in any group working constructively for that community's advancement in the amenities he will come to recognize many of the same people. It is much the same for the larger community called the state; the few are active, the many, inert or devoted only to their own interests. When the few are concerned with the human situation, things go more or less well. When they are not, things go badly.

The other kind of people simply want to do as they like, to live in pursuit of their own interests. They are "the many." They may be those who look on public office mainly as a route to private profit and they may be among the myriads who go to cheer "their team" at a football game or a hockey match. They are certainly those who fight for the removal of all inhibitions, alcohol, drugs, sex or sky-scrapers. Every advanced society has had a battle with the grosser aspects of "the right to do as you like," that is, it has had in some way to find the reasonable limits of liberty and finding them gives it most of its conception of right and wrong, decency and its reverse. For our Western society, they are first laid down in the old Jewish scriptures, whence they were caught up by the church and made central as "the Commandments." Roman lawyers hammered out a roughly parallel code: *fas aut nefas*. The criminal law as it develops and expands, becomes the mirror of the society's thinking about its moral code. We come again to the question of *values*.

III
Inanity, Vulgarity:
Women and The Sexual Revolution

Our modern societies are overwhelmingly urban: urbanism creates and demands quite different values from ruralism – the crowded city and the quiet countryside are in perpetual contrast and collision. The victory invariably goes to the city, for numbers count – numbers in whatever way they may be expressed, whether markets, demands, votes or control of "the media." Since numbers win, it will be the highest common factor among numbers that will win, which means that city numbers will respond to things on a low plane: the highest common factor will be some element of pleasure; as such phrases as "the bright lights" clearly indicate. Much city life and energy go to providing pleasure high or low, good or bad, common or uncommon, and here again, "numbers count." The result is that a large share of our modern life comes down to sheer inanity. If any proof is needed, turn on your radio or television. And men and women, being men and women and by no means angels, inanity readily turns into vulgarity as the note inserted at this point illustrates.[8] Here is an example of "high grade" vulgarity. It is taken from the columns of an important newspaper that makes its pitch to the upper half of the social structure, which devotes one section of its week-end issue to what it apparently considers "culture," such as film, book and concert reviews. These are not aimed at the "man in the street." "The film bedevils the audience with one question: Will Brando's pants finally drop? And damn it they do!"[9]

Our Western civilization is certainly the most remarkable that man has built, the most remarkable, by far the most affluent. Also the noisiest, the most vulgar – and the most inane!

Inanity and vulgarity most commonly seek expression in matters relating to sex, and they have had their expression, as a rule subterranean, since "the Year One." What is normal human behaviour, especially male behaviour, no doubt does not differ much from age to age. The point about them (inanity and vulgarity) in this period of revolution whose nature an attempt is here being made to describe, is the wide range of devices they have for their diffusion and the explosive way in which they have been brought out into the open. The "snippets" given in note number 8 were taken from the daily newspaper in a small city, a newspaper that goes into the average home. Such wide diffusion of such material would not have been possible in any previous age. It is as if all the sewer gas were suddenly being allowed to escape into the streets.

The snippets could be added to *ad infinitum*. They are not put into the book as contributions to the ancient and dishonourable art of pornography, but as illustrations of a quite exceptional turn in history's path with respect to public expression. The Romans had their Ovid and the early Renaissance its Boccaccio, whose *Decameron's* popularity is quickly understandable to anyone who looks into it. There was also much vulgarity in the Carolinian playwrights (such as Shirley). Remarkably little, really, in Shakespeare and again a good deal in the eighteenth century. But after that until about the inter-war period there was very little, at the height of Victorianism, practically none.

Then the dam broke, and the world has been flooded with it. No comment need be made as to the morals involved for, as just said, human sexuality may not differ a great deal from age to age. It is the public expression which is the phenomenon. If this unparallelled shift in allowable public expression does not mark a revolutionary historical turn, what could? No more decided turnabout could well be imagined than the rapid transition from the ultra-propriety of yesterday to the ultra-"realism" of today.

Surely there is a counter-account, some reader will protest. Of course there is a counter-account. No age was ever all of one piece. Offsets to inanity and vulgarity are easily found. But this section is concerned with the "many," rather than with the "few," and the offsets to vulgarity and inanity must be sought among the "few" rather than the "many."

This wide dispersion of inanity and vulgarity which marks the age takes many forms, in pornography, for example, which in the years around 1970 was making a fight for unrestricted public expression.[10] Its more sophisticated exponents talked about the right of free speech, thereby bringing up an interesting and important aspect of the progression emphasized in these pages – the progression from the emotional attitude through the intellectual and from it, through reason and discussion, to conceptions of freedom that ultimately become anarchic. Society has always imposed limits on liberty when liberty has threatened to become anarchic, and "the right of free speech" in pornography gives a good illustration of what usually occurs. Wide limits of expression are often tolerated but sooner or later public opinion frowns on those that overstep the mark, and the tide turns. The erotically stimulating movie advertisements mentioned above in the notes to this chapter and the films they advertised eventually turned the more responsible public against them and caused them to be very much toned down. In most countries and times official action has been taken but the strong emphasis on freedom in most of the modern Western world which brings opposition at once to anything savouring of *censorship,* has often as not, resulted in the matter being left to "public opinion," which has its own way of applying censorship. North Americans, in particular, still have in their subconscious memories, the old, all too repressive "Thou shalt not's" of their ancestors, readily to accept much censorship.

It is a topic that would lead us far afield but one that should at least be glanced at in this effort to assess the nature of the present period of history, the place and responsibility of "the media" in the dispersion not only of inanity and vulgarity but of futility. Every invention from the use of fire onward has had the old saying applied to it – "A good servant but a bad master." Contrivances of every sort proceed from the mind of man and the mind of man should be able to control them. This, however, is much too simple; there are minds and minds, some strong, some weak. Devices, therefore, from fire to television take on a kind of life of their own, practically independent of man's control. The "media" in all their variety fit exactly into this position. They come to have "lives of their own." Of all of them, one is outstandingly conspicuous, namely, television, especially television. Few people can resist its hypnotic spell. When it speaks other voices are silent. Through it, a public man can address millions of his fellows. Through it nearly every aspect of the arts can be brought into the humblest home. There is hardly a phase of life that it does not touch. All this is obvious of the obvious. Where does the all-powerful medium stand in the never-ending struggle of the few and the many? It stands just where the public that looks at it stands and in its portrayal of what interests that public probably little more is to be said about it than about, say, the newspaper.

The approach to assessment must take another line. It is not the program, which may be good, bad or indifferent, but the technical apparatus for the program that must be examined. Across the television screen a never-ending succession of images flows, images accompanied by sounds coherent or incoherent. People gaze at the screen. They gaze at it hour after hour – especially old people, for whom it becomes a useful soporific, and children, who should be out at their games. In all cases, the television fills minds with far too many images, mostly disjointed, with far too many scraps of information, mostly scrambled. It forces on the weak-willed who cannot avoid looking at it (how many people can?) a jumble of odds and ends, a thicket, a jungle, of scenes, sayings, views, impressions, opinions, a colossal rag-bag. It suspends talk and thought. It is the true opiate of the people, far more powerful than Lenin's "religion" as opiate, and every dictator should value it beyond rubies.

What its long range effects are to be, who is to say. The empty-headed will be empty-headed still, but will those to whom nature has given minds find their mentality, fragmented, disordered, disrupted?

The analysis could go on indefinitely. Threat or promise – or both? If the world can escape destruction through the very abundance of the gifts that come tumbling out of science's cornucopia, television among them, it will indeed be doing well. Another apt illustration is afforded by "the pill." Unlimited child-bearing was woman's curse and she is well rid of it. But is it good to see "the pill" rendering so many couples childless? In North America, "the pill" is effectively killing off the "WASPs." Good or bad? Good, the non-WASPs no doubt think. As for the WASPs, they seem little concerned.

Knowledge, science, technical accomplishment. These words are atom bombs. Each one carries revolution within it. Each may keep humanity in some kind of perpetual revolution. Each is speeding up the machinery of our lives to the point which makes us wonder whether it will go on turning or fly to pieces.

Small wonder that all that which is denominated "values" is responding along with everything else to the centrifugal stress. One small object alone tumbling out of the cornucopia has gone far to work vast changes in behaviour – the "pill." The "pill," lifting from woman the fear of the consequences of the sexual act, has apparently basically altered her attitude towards it. Until the middle of this, twentieth century, much of the morality of the West that did not have to do with property was built on the notion of womanly virtue and fidelity. Should the word rather be "idealism?" It would be hard to say. Was womanly virtue simply a reflection of male possessiveness, something forced on woman and not having too much to do with her own nature? Every male is sexually possessive, jealous of rivals. That is one of the deep laws of life, as Darwin pointed out, and it goes far beyond the human species into the very depths of creation. But man has refined the original possessive urge and built on it most of his poetry, his music and his art. His most beautiful dreams, his greatest accomplishments, his bitterest struggles have directly or indirectly been "all for the love of a lady." "Tis love that makes the world go round."

Not many people seem to take in the magnitude of the sex revolution. For centuries woman's pre-marital virginity and marital chastity have been the bed-rock of Western idealism. It does not matter how often the bed-rock has given way, for no matter how many times the code has been violated, it still has remained the code. It does not matter that it is a code that may well have been built up by men in a silly misconception of the nature of women, or in a mere reflection of their own egotism and jealousies, it has remained the code. It is a code that has been the base for every Western literature, inspired the greatest and most moving of our poems, our novels and our plays: it has given us Dante's Beatrice, Shakespeare's Desdemona, Goethe's Margaret, Beethoven's Fidelio and many, many others. Abolish the ideal of womanly virtue and you change the nature of our literary past and of much of our idealism; you destroy a world of the deepest passions, the tenderest affections, the most poignant emotions, the highest conceptions of love, devotion and self-sacrifice. It is impossible, short of poetic heights, to depict the overwhelming place that the conception of woman has had in Western life. Surely no one needs to be told that. Mary, the Mother, stands there as the testimony.

The question is, is this concept of woman being lost? If it is, it is largely woman's own doing, for in gaining a new dimension of freedom – perhaps illusory – she is exchanging her position on that pedestal which Western man has lifted her for – a pill! For the right to be, if she likes, the subject of man's passions.

It is not inappropriate at this point to reflect on the lines of one of the world's great poets, Goethe, in whose drama, *Faust,* the topic occupies a central place. Gretchen (Margaret) has been seduced by Faust, by Faust with the aid of the evil spirit Mephistopheles. Her brother Valentine, trying to drive away Faust from his sister, has been slain by him, backed by Mephistopheles. In dying, Valentine says to Margaret:

My Gretchen, see: thou still art young
And not yet with much experience,
Thou managest thy affairs badly . . .

Then he adds the bitter words:

I tell thee, betwixt the two of us,
Thou art already – a whore!

He has more to say: he predicts her future and that, of other girls like her:

> Thou secretly began with one,
> Soon more to thee will come
> And when a dozen have thee had,
> So has the whole town also.[11]

There may be put alongside the story of Margaret, and of similar stories, snippets like the following, of which the modern press has been full. In a letter to "The Women's Page" a young woman writes:

Dear Editor:

> Don't you realize that you are behind the times to hold on to the moral code of twenty or more years ago (1950s)? Don't you know that the 'teenager' is just not one of the crowd if she doesn't have a boy-friend and she doesn't go all the way with him? What is sex for anyway?

Is some such view as this becoming general and approved? There is much evidence in that direction. "My daughter's been on the pill since she was sixteen," said one mother. "My sister's living with her boyfriend" says a man in his thirties, as if it were a matter of course. Perhaps it is. "About as ordinary as shaking hands" was one man's way of putting it, referring to promiscuous fornication.

It may be the great-grandchildren's way of "getting their own back" on the falsities and hypocrisies of their ancestors. At any rate, the erotic impulse seems to be going full speed ahead. Youth is having its fling. What is more, it is being paid the dividends without subscribing to much of the stock. And it is unlikely that its great-grandchildren will curse it for its conduct, for there will be no great-grandchildren.

IV
Should Every Dog Have Its Day? Why Not?

At the present point in history, it is the "values" (or better, perhaps, the desires) of the many that seem to have the upper hand. This is fairly recent. It coincides with the expansion of democracy. While there have been minor instances of democracy scattered through history, the condition, in contrast with the idea, arose mainly in North America: it was the English constitutional ideas brought to America by the colonists plus the wide freedom afforded by a rich, almost empty new world plus the teachings of the more radical wing of the American revolutionaries, especially Thomas Jefferson, that brought forth *democracy* in America. Similar conditions without much attention to formal political doctrines, and with practically no philosophical expositions have produced like results in the other English-speaking New World lands. And similar teaching has produced more or less similar results in many other countries, notably France. Today, some approach to "democracy" extends far beyond its original homeland.

Jefferson started off the Declaration of Independence with a resounding bang: all men are created equal and equally entitled to life, liberty and the pursuit of happiness; the American people ever since have been groping after this idealistic state. Naturally they have not attained to it, but it has been a goal, and it has deeply influenced many other peoples also. This idea of equality, so forcefully introduced to mankind, has worked away like a slow consuming fire and today it is perhaps the dominant notion of the age. It is not new, by any means, in political and social thinking. Instance the well-known jingle popular in England during the Peasants' Revolt of 1383:

When Adam delved and Eve span
Who was then the gentleman?

But it has a much older ancestry than that and a highly respectable one for it is implicit in various New Testament assertions, "He that is the greatest among you, let him be the servant of all." "In Christ, there is neither Jew nor Greek, neither bond nor free." The idea has slowly fermented through the centuries receiving little attention in practice until increasing productivity increased the assertive power of those on the bottom or near it, and always greatly buttressed by the actual conditions obtaining in the outer world, for those with white skins, it might be said somewhat cynically, no group on top has ever willingly given up its seats of power and the world has by no means yet attained Bobbie Burns' vision of Paradise (when "man to man, the wide world o'er shall brothers be and a 'that'.")

Yet who can deny the penetration today of this idea of equality? It has always been the ideal of the underdog, of course.[12] And one of the major trends of the present point in history is towards giving every dog his day. In fact, in the years during which these pages are written, one of the major public crimes, it would seem, is "élitism," the view that it is allowable that anyone should be richer, wiser, better informed, better educated, than anyone else. There is not overly much objection (as yet) to somebody being of better character than somebody else, perhaps because the rewards of mere *goodness* are not conspicuous. So it does not go quite as far as demanding that no one shall be *better* (morally) than anyone else. Anti-élitism would reduce society to one level plane. Anti-élitism would permit no mountains to exist, just flat planes. Anti-élitism, equalitarianism, is hardly a formal political philosophy, for it runs too sharply against the nature of things (for example, it would have difficulty finding intellectual justification for leadership), but it responds to widespread deeply-held currents of emotion and it greatly increases the dif-

ficulties of securing a stable society. Anti-élitism was a powerful ingre-
dient in the student disturbances of the late 1960s, with its talk of an
"unstructured" society and "unstructured" curricula. It may be receding
in importance, as have the bubbles and more than bubbles – which were
interspersed with it for while there will always in a free society, be deep
appeal in egalitarian concepts, the impossibility of carrying them to their
logical conclusions soon becomes clear. One local campus advocate of
the "unstructured society" in the 1960s contended for the medical
student's freedom in deciding how he would shape his medical studies,
what he would study and how. It was pointed out to him that he would
hardly get into the college football team on that basis. It is interesting to
observe that that country which fought the most tremendous civil war of
modern times, to keep itself together, the United States, was also the
country to have produced three of our most divisive doctrines,
equalitarianism, and the pursuit of happiness (because where all "pursue," few can catch) and Woodrow Wilson's right of self-determination,
which may yet wreck great states. The above points would properly lead
to a discussion of *class* in modern society, but that is a topic too big to be
more than alluded to at this point. Suffice it to say that in any society
people quickly sort themselves out into ranks and classes, find what
seems to them the proper "pecking order" and that if this is upset in some
way, as it was so radically in the Russian Revolution, it soon comes to be
reconstituted under some other form, such as power, wealth, education or
native ability.

One important way already indicated in which undue emphasis on
equality affects society is the unwillingness to accept informed leadership. This is, paradoxically, accompanied by great faith in the expert. In
this, as in most other matters, men's minds are in a jumble and may afford
an opportunity for the demagogue. The present age does not appear to
differ from most others in that respect and is probably neither more or less
successful in finding leadership. The vast size of modern communities
greatly increases that problem. Leadership has always been and always
will be one of man's major problems. But it is well to remember that a wise
man, Aristotle, once equated "democracy" with mob rule and condemned the latter as the worst form of government. The presence of
equality in the Western world, commendable in itself and if kept under
control, can lead into dangerous places. An extensive study of "equality"
would embrace almost the entire range of political philosophy, from
Greek and Hebrew, to our own day. It would include not only formal or
literary expositions but descriptions of society over the centuries.

A discussion of *equality* immediately raises the general topic of *values:*
what is the sanction for acting in this way or that? To be concrete, what is
the answer to be given when someone asks "Why shouldn't I?" The
natural state of the animal is natural freedom. Man in society gives up

much of his freedom and the more complex his society becomes, the more of his natural freedom he has to give up.

Only very slowly have the semi-anarchic results of natural freedom come under the control of civilization, of "law and order." In another great country of the Western world in addition to the United States to have had an almost unlimited experience of freedom in space and resources, Brazil, the process of controlling those who feel that they are entitled to do as they like and have what they want still has far to go:

> The good old days, their simple plan
> That those shall take who have the might
> And those shall keep who can.

The values of a society are established by long usage and very likely a plentiful supply of hard knocks. They change with the times, but always the factor of acceptance, more or less general, is present. And for the "advanced" societies, the sources of the sanctions are ascertainable. As said above, in the discussion of equality, for the West, these sources are mostly classical and Biblical, plus local conditions. Most men, even the primitives, even very simple men, have some notion of the fundamentals. "What is mine and what is not mine" is elementary and goes right down to the depths of animal life. Ideas of "fair play," honesty, honour, get formalized, they mount up into grand discussions of *justice,* such as in Plato's *Republic*.

The quandary in all this is the matter of sanctions. Why should I do this and not do that? Most cultures rest the sanction ultimately on some notion or other of the will of gods. Greeks and Romans quickly got further than that. The profundities in Aristotle's *Politics* are witness to that. *Fas aut nefas:* asked the Roman, right or wrong? His answer rather inadequately was the law, *lex*. Or *mos,* custom, or *jus,* use, that which has always been done. This is the root idea of the world *justitia,* justice. It was Christianity that carried the sanction back to "the gods," or rather to *God*. The *will of God* became the supreme sanction, as found in his *Word,* his "revealed" word (plus such additions and amendments as church and in some respects, state put upon it.)

The Christian sanction for our whole ethical system has lasted with little fundamental change throughout the entire course of the Christian religion and it has been carried far beyond the Western world. For the ordinary believer, the simple unsophisticated man, prince or peasant, "thou shalt not" has been enough. The original "thou shalt's" and "thou shalt not" have widened out to cover practically every aspect of life. It is unnecessary surely to observe that they have as often been honoured in the breach as in the observance ("Thou shalt not steal!).

But the point is that they have been honoured, honoured not only in the declaration from ten thousand pulpits, but by many and rigorous codes of law. The notification of these codes has been complex, and no doubt one of its chief components has been the protection of a valuable piece of property, a wife, Even so, they have resulted in what might be frivolously called "the married woman's trade union," perhaps the strongest union ever to emerge (and today under serious infiltration by "the scab worker"). The sanction behind every code (perhaps obscurely, but there) has been "The revealed Will of God."

The point in all this, and probably the principal point in this concluding chapter, is that in our day and age, this revolutionary age, the sanction, after about two centuries of erosion and disintegration, has broken down. Broken down almost completely. It remains in a kind of fossilized state in communities and groups still lucky enough to remain simple, but for the Western world as a whole, it has broken down. Few law makers indeed, there must be who, on their knees, seek the will of God in arriving at their decisions. No doubt there have been many peculiar interpretations of *"the Will of God"* as when in the 1860s the American south interpreted the Will of God as commanding slavery and the north as commanding its abolition, the leaders of both sides frequently on their knees, and Napoleon's cynicism may not have been far wrong ("God is on the side of the heaviest battalions"). Nevertheless the sanction was always there, earnestly if confusedly accepted by nearly everyone.

And now, in those old terms the sanction has gone. Neither in law or conduct does "the will of God" longer have much to do with matters What is to replace it and what will be its binding power?

"Permissiveness," say some. Let everybody do as his heart desires, and all will come right in the end. This is the modern version of having what you want and doing as you like. It has had a great vogue in the society of the late twentieth century. It is a fine code for bank robbers. It illustrates very nicely what happens when the old sanctions break down. "Why shouldn't I?" "Permissiveness" is, of course, a loose term.

Elucidation of "permissiveness" would get us into still another interminable discussion of one of the great abstractions. In view of the patent inadequacy of "permissiveness," we no doubt rely on that foundation which, in all probability, has always underlain "the will of God" – custom (*mos*) and expediency ("what seems best"). Freedom is one of the most inspiring of human concepts and almost as many great poems have been written in its praise as for the love of women. "We must be free, or die who speak the tongue that Shakespeare spake . . ." cried Wordsworth. Beethoven's magic symphony, the Ninth, still more his opera, Fidelio, both are majestic hymns to freedom. And there can be no line drawn between "permissiveness" and freedom. It is entirely a matter of degree. Society oscillates between extremes of freedom and of constraint. The one extreme means anarchy, the other, tyranny. It is the singular good fortune of the English-speaking world to have stumbled long ago on the public institutions which have given it the best of the two worlds and enabled it for the most part to avoid the worst.

Freedom versus order is an old theme yet one never exhausted. It is one of the principal components of this study, which has tried to trace the historical oscillations, under various forms, of the two obstractions. The question now is, where do we stand, during this last quarter of the twentieth century, in the swing between the two? This chapter is built up on the assumption that the present age is (socially and culturally) revolutionary. At what point in the revolution do we stand?

Many items could be listed to illustrate this revolutionary process, some great, some small. Revolutions involve the idea of freedom. They "strike off chains" (if only later to rivet them on again). Possibly one of the greatest effects of the two World Wars consisted in the shattering of many of the old concepts of order and the opening of the gates to new conceptions of freedom. In accordance with this "law" of oscillation some of the new concepts of freedom have gone so far as to become anarchic. The result is the turbulent modern world. There are already some signs on the horizon that excesses of freedom are meeting with opposition, possibly working their own cure. In this way the "swing" will no doubt be completed and once more an age of order be upon us. How far that will go is for the future to reveal.

Some of the items to be entered under the heading of "increase of freedom" follow. None of them can be explored within the limits of a chapter. They are merely stated, not arranged in any logical scheme.

(1) The holding of the Vatican Councils of the 1960s, their declarations, the results of these, their effects on Roman Catholicism and indirectly on the rest of the West. "The Catholic Church has gone Protestant," someone said at the time. This may be extreme but there is no question as to the great shift in Catholic attitudes resulting from the Councils. No more Pio Nonos! The Catholic Church has moved into the stream of modern intellectual life and it will be difficult for it to preserve intact its beautifully symmetrical structure of authority, dogma and tradition.

(2) The upsurge of political localism. Every age sees peoples "struggling to be free," so perhaps not too much should be made of this as marking the modern revolution. But it is related to basic principles. Historically it goes back directly to Woodrow Wilson's enunciation of the doctrine of "self-determination" which itself came directly out of the American south and its attempt in 1861-1865 to get out of the Union (Wilson came from Virginia and Georgia). It got into the idealism that lay under the League of Nations and the United Nations and the innumerable small states which are members of the latter are its recognition. It provided the dynamic for de-colonization, and the

equality of peoples regardless of skin colour and strengthens the latest manifestations, in Scotland and Wales, Brittany and Quebec, among the Basques and the Cattalonians. There are even rumbles heard from within the Soviet Union. It might some day decentralize, federalize or disintegrate some of the great historic nations.

(3) "The Women's Movement," The words are indefinite, so is what they signify. It is clear, however, that the place of woman in Western society has greatly changed in the last hundred years. Women's legal rights have been enlarged in most countries and today in the most "advanced," there would appear to be not many shackles left to strike off. Nevertheless the movement to strike them off goes on with perhaps increasing vigour. It has already secured woman her place as a citizen in full equality with man, as also in most respects her property rights. Necessarily it is in the area of sex relationships that the fiercest fight goes on. In this area it has lessened the stability of the family, through the new attitudes towards separation, divorce and bastardy. This has had considerable social effect in permitting the emergence of an almost new class of persons – children of divorced or separated parents. In that they may well proceed from the upper rather than the lower economic areas of society, they are to be distinguished from the familiar "waifs and strays" whom society has always had on its hands. Modern attitudes towards marriage may cause a great "jumble" in family relationships. One lady claimed she was the product of the third marriage of her father and the fourth of her mother.

Most revolutions strike at once for loosening the marriage relationship – it is one of the "chains" to be cast off. Later on, it gets tightened up again. In most societies it is possible that the real nature of the relationship does not change a great deal. Surely over the long sweep of history, and of pre-history, practically every variety of this matter of men and women living together will have been tried, discarded, accepted, again and again. Presumably men and women will continue to beget children – some will anyway – and men will always want to have some assurance that the children of their wife are their children and not someone else's. A very material consideration but not unrelated to the far finer idea of fidelity and loyalty which, too, no doubt has enough vitality to survive.

At the moment, then, perhaps all that can be said about "the Women's movement" is that it is working great changes in society and is likely to work more, the effects of which still have to be evaluated.

(4) Linguistic change. This has been discussed in connection with previous changes in "the nature of the times." At present it seems to be proceeding at a very rapid rate. New words come and go with the

speed of light. "Scenario," for example, with a new meaning made its appearance about 1973. In a year or two it was everywhere and now, 1978, seems to be receding. Some changes in construction make themselves acceptable, such as "it's up to . . ." meaning "it's your duty to do such and such." The English language continues to surmount all barriers and pour itself in more or less distorted form into nearly all others. There is a cheap German song that goes: "Minnie, zieh' die hot pants an" – "Minnie, pull on the hot pants," – the latter another passing expression for a sexually exciting article of female clothing. In Italy, English has displaced French in speaking to foreigners. It is close to becoming "the world language" and the wonder is that it has not broken down into a dozen different local languages. This it would have done if it had not been for the printed word. As it is, those to whom meaning, clarity, beauty and the other classic qualities of language mean anything, run from the barbarism that rises from the depths – run as offended and horror stricken as any noble Roman ever ran from the barbarian gobble-de-gook he heard murdering his sonorous Latin.

(5) Music and the other Arts. In all the arts including literature, by the inter-war period, the intellectual element had displaced the emotional. Eloquence is no more, simply "public speeches." Modern formal music (as apart from popular) appeals to the intellect, not to the heart. Painting goes to abstractions. "In that picture," said an observer, "beauty raises its ugly head," speaking of a rather pleasant landscape scene. This shift in approach is highly diagnostic for fixing the point of our evolution, as previous analyses of other ages have emphasized. After the intellectual, artistic experience becomes freer and freer, possibly looser and looser, going on to the point where meaning may be lost, that is to artistic anarchy. In some areas, especially sculpture, we seem already to have reached this point, possibly also in some reaches of modern poetry. Prose, however, holds together, though rapidly changing. What is to be looked forward to? More "heart," less "head"? Popular music is one long tale of horror ever since the old natural "popular" songs gave way early in the century to the animal noises that at present are heard. The origins of these can be traced. They fit admirably into the folklore of a generation that has no focus or collective meaning and delights mainly in mere noise.

(6) Changes in behaviour. During the 1960s students in many countries and in America coloured people, got into a state of semi-rebellion. Property was destroyed, riots involving loss of life occurred. The Kent State University shooting in Ohio, May 1970, became notorious. American cities were burned. Queer cults arose, such as the Manson murder cult in California. The rich began to "soak the rich"

and the rich young rebels like Pattie Hearst caused a great deal of trouble to the authorities. In the United States, and elsewhere, no woman dared be out alone after dark. All this was an offshoot of the loosening up occasioned by the Vietnam war (plus too much money), a seeking after some kind of new society. It looked for a few years as if "chaos were come again." But the intense phase of social rearrangement quickly passed and the evolution to whatever it is we are evolving to, proceeded without so much commotion.

(7) Minor matters. The sudden outbreak of beards in the 1960s, followed by long masculine hair, was spectacular rather than important. Bearded and beardless ages succceed each other through history and their inner significance may only be matter for speculation. Is a bearded generation more masculine than a beardless? No interpretation could be more ridiculous. The accompanying changes in clothing should also be noted. They have been more rapid than in generations of previous usage. That symbolic garment, the skirt, is close to being discarded. Men's clothing until about 1950 or 1960 was among the most stable of all social artifacts. Since then it has changed radically. It has burst out into colours that would have horrified an older generation. But again, this is minor. The deep change in the age has to do with the fundamentals, belief, sex, technical accomplishment.

To those listed above and classified as in one way or another widening freedom, two more should be added, for brief discussion.

Our present age has seen the idea of humanitarianism rise to great heights, perhaps to a peak. Charitable attitudes are an old story, they have been organized from age to age in many forms and the feeling that man is his brother's keeper, though often at a low ebb, has never been wholly lost. Not in the West, anyway. This feeling has been objectified in many forms (hospitals, schools, poor laws, etc.). It spreads out into missionary movements abroad and "organized charity" at home. It finds close relationship with the various forms of socialism. Today, in the English-speaking world at any rate, organized charity has almost superseded the simpler charitable impulses of individuals. As such it is closely linked to conceptions of public well-being.

Organized charity has also taken on large international dimensions. These are quite recent in origin, though, like other forms of human conduct, their motivation is necessarily mixed. International "good works" might be said to have begun with such measures as Roosevelt's "Lend-lease" arrangements and the later Marshall plans. They have widened out into the large-scale governmental grants to "undeveloped countries." Much of this naturally has a considerable element of self-interest in it, but it also contains a good deal of the view that man is his brother's keeper. It could fairly be classed under the heading "humanitarianism." Its fairly close dependence on the original New Testament should be obvious. (The oil-rich Arab countries help their poorer Arab neighbours, but as far as known, they do not share up with those outside the Moslem faith.)

Against modern humanitarianism should be set modern materialism. Materialism is the older story of the two, for the natural world is entirely materialistic. "Survive and use any means whatever to enable you to survive." Materialism is necessarily always with us. Its particular modern facet lies in the emphasis on material goods often to the hurt of what might be called "higher values." The "high standard of living" becomes a synonym merely for an abundance of material things. In the affluent societies of the West, it takes such forms as newspapers an inch thick, so many cars that they clog every road, so many radio stations that their clatter drowns each other out and a kind of hoggish attitude to food.

Some cynics might contend that our humanitarianism comes from the same source – abundant productivity – and might not last long without it. But it also pays high cultural dividends.

*   *   *

Any revolutionary age will turn its back on the past. A new world is to be created. Why bother about the old one? Our present age displays this characteristic to a considerable degree. The phase is "present-mindedness." And that is a mindless phrase. "Don't you understand," cried an *avant-garde* young man, "that this is *now:*" Logically it can easily be shown that there is no *now:* as these words are written *now* changes into *then.* There is time past and there will be time to come: the partition between them is an infinitesimal moment. It is the Euclidean *point* – that which has position but no magnitude. For practical purposes the average person works in a practical dimension of *now. Now* is a space of a few easily remembered years. For the historian *now* can be given indefinite extension.

A revolutionary age runs its course and its conception of *now* gradually sinks back into the traditional, work-a-day attitude. The attempt of the French revolutionists to change the calendar eventually failed. The Russians still stick to "A.D." (whatever meaning they may attach to the letters). "Present-mindedness," however prominent an aspect of a revolutionary period it may be, is a passing phenomenon. Its passing indicates the reaching out of society for order, after a period of rapid change. The entire period since the discovery of America might be considered illustrative of this. Enormous bustling and hustling, much confusion, disorder, in both continents while their settlement was going on, a more sedate and (possibly) more thoughtful attitudes now that they have filled up.

With that, we come up against the idea of "now" as it pertains to this study of history. The study has arrived at "now." Save by way of surmise, it can go no further.

"The moving finger writes, and having writ, moves on . . ." What will it write?[13]

Where, then, has the ship of history arrived at this point in its unending voyage? The "weather forecast" is not of the best. Our present age has destroyed that long hope that sustained men over the centuries. It has destroyed the faith that sustained that hope. It has damaged, if not totally destroyed, mankind's ideal of womanhood. It may have injured men's conceptions of loyalty and allegiance. It has made itself into a hard age, an age of realism, an age without illusions and therefore perhaps without dreams, except the disturbed nightmares of its own begetting. No dreams, no ideals. Our age is one in which realism plays havoc with ideals. Knowledge plays havoc with ideals. Our age is the age of knowledge.

Yet man cannot live long without faith and ideals, which are hope. We shall find a faith of some sort. It could, but not forever, be an evil faith, as was Naziism. More likely in the age to follow ours, we shall catch glimpses of what seems to man his eternal verity, and put it back, in some measure in its seat. Western man (and many men elsewhere too) has been climbing up the steep hill of history for a long time now. He has climbed, slipped back, climbed again. He may or may not be coming closer and closer to a summit. He has often thought so, and the hope that it might be so has given him strength for the next advance. And so the pulsations of the ages have gone, and no doubt will go. Hope will provide the fuse for the shell; the propellant will be the intrinsic dynamic energy of man; the flight in part guided by the great words that have come echoing down the ages. "Nothing in excess," said the Greeks. "Let justice be done though the heavens fall," added the Romans. "Love mercy and do justice," cried the Hebrew prophet. "Do unto others . . ." echoed the Christian. Duty, "stern daughter of the voice of God," cried Wordsworth. These are great words. They all mean substantially the same thing. They are lodestones. They will always draw men. They will never pass into nothingness.

Notes

1.   For example, people from India and the Caribbean into Great Britain, American negroes into northern cities, southern Europeans and northern Africans into northern Italy, France, and Germany.

2.   Whether they actually were major factors is debatable, for there were so many others to be considered, such as steam power, new lands, more food, and so on.
3.   Yet a short tour of any large hospital soon shows how long is still the road ahead.
4.   The attempts of the surgical virtuosos to transplant hearts have not yet been very successful.
5.   The late Dean Inge of London "the gloomy Dean" used to think so and wrote several books arguing his view.
6.   One of the latest aspects of this confused search for values lies in the appearance of what are smartly called "counter cultures."
7.   This quotation is from FitzGerald's *Omar Khayyam* and refers to the sectarianism of Mohammedanism. Mohammedanism nevertheless retains a fair degree of uniformity, probably more than the modern versions of Christianity.
8.   These "snippets" may interest posterity and should be preserved as illustrative of "now": "Stars discuss their sexual initiation: She, too, felt guilty about sleeping with a man, but only for a month or so. 'Terrific, wonderful, how great! I'm not a virgin anymore and I've never regretted it.' " Kingston (Ontario) *Whig Standard,* September 30, 1975, from Reuters, New York.

From movie advertisements, Kingston *Whig Standard,* during 1975:

"Torrid Eroticism"

"Naked and Free: The New Life Style"

"Scenes and Bizarre Practices Too Intense for the
Emotionally Immature"

"Girls of Passion: Six Erotic Sizzlers"

From the United Church (of Canada) *Observer,* September, 1976, p. 49:

Even the 1975 New York Film Festival programmed hard-core pornography. The film was *Exhibition,* which on the promise of a documentary became an excuse for an actress to demonstrate, among other things, masturbation – in the most visually explicit way possible. Recently it was showing in a respectable multi-movie theatre in Montreal, side by side with family entertainment.

The above reflect a considerable sickness of the age. It cannot be assumed that they reflect new sexual practices, for in its long history, mankind must have long ago discovered all the tricks that can be played. It is the prurience of expression which is the phenomenon. It was this sad, recurrent openness which led a disgusted old man to comment grumpily on such items and what they represent: "Sex sniggery, such stuff could be called, not honest animal appetite. It is diseased. The dirty little boys of today are chalking up their four-letter words on stinking outhouses. Except that they put them into print or film and are adults making the air reek with sex, sex, sex, – nasty old, overfed, constipated, lecherous men probably tired old dogs sniffing about the bitch in heat and quite unable to copulate."

9.   Toronto, *Globe and Mail,* June 9, 1973, p. 29.

10.   See extract from United Church *Observer* given in note 8.

11.   Goethe, *Faust,* II, 3726-3739.

12.   *Deposuit magnifices de sedibus et exaltavit humilis,* sang Mary, the Mother in her *Magnificat.* "He has put down the mighty from their seats and exalted them of low degree."

13.   An interesting idea in any attempt to impose some kind of pattern on history is the possibility always present, of there being a quite unforeseen obstacle in the ship of history's course, an "iceberg" as it were, which may wreck the *Titanic.* "The Black Death" (fourteenth century) is a good example: no forewarning, no means of averting it, nothing that could be done, a colossal "accident." There may be icebergs up ahead.

Index

Index